Over Becher's Brook

An A to Z of The Grand National

by
Reg Green

This edition first published in 1997
by
Sport In Word Limited
Specialist Sports Publishers

ISBN 1 874645 507

Sport In Word Limited
Chorley, England

Printed in Great Britain by
Antony Rowe Ltd, Chippenham, Wiltshire

● Over and clear – Corbiere takes second Becher's in 1983.

When time stands still...

THERE'S a moment, no more than a few seconds, when the packed course holds its breath. Even the starlings out in the country settle from their wheeling flight. The only things that move are a few horses and their anxious jockeys . . . urging, kicking, scrambling for position in the cavalry charge to come.

All eyes are on the starter...

The outside world is a long way away. Time stands still.

And then, suddenly, the roar goes up.

THEY'RE OFF!

Nothing in the world of horse racing; nothing in the world of sporting endeavour can match the moment as the greatest race in the world, the Grand National, charges away from the flying tape and heads out to face one of the most daunting challenges faced by man and beast.

Ahead of the 40 or so runners lie 30 towering fences and nearly four and a half miles of history in the making.

Queen Victoria had been on the throne for a matter of months when the first National was held at Aintree. This year the course stages its 150th running of a race that has become not only a national institution but an event famous throughout the world.

Through the medium of television it is watched by millions in every corner of the globe. But nothing can match the atmosphere, the colour and the excitement of actually being there; a part of a wondrous spectacle that never fails to thrill and leave lasting memories of courage, danger, skill and fighting spirit.

No other race, probably no other sporting occasion, has thrown up more stories of dreams and nightmares; desperation and determination. It is the supreme test of horse and rider. And while some of the fences may not be as forbidding as yesteryear they are still a challenge that can't be found anywhere else.

The Grand National is a story of blood, sweat and tears. For just a few, a lucky few, it is a story of wild elation; of success against all the odds; the supreme moment of sporting achievement.

This book is the detailed history of that race, compiled by the undoubted expert - Reg Green, who lives just a few miles from the course and whose book "A Race Apart", written ten years ago, is the definitive history of the race.

Now, he has gathered together archive material which he has been collecting since first falling in love with the race as a young boy and woven it into the first ever A to Z account of the heroes - and heroines - who have made the Grand National probably the most famous sporting event in the world.

ARTHUR
1840 . . . Finished 2nd of 12. (Mr Barry) Mr.A.McDonough. 8/1. Remounted*.

AUGEAN, THE
1840 . . . Fell. Owner unknown. R.Christian. n/q

ANONYMOUS
1842 . . . Failed to finish. (Mr Moore) Mr.Moore. n/q

AVOCA
1847 . . . Failed to finish. (Capt.Gambier.) Capt.Broadley. 15/1.

ASHBERRY LASS
1848 . . . Failed to finish. (Mr J.W.Haworth) 6.11-3. Collis. n/q

ARISTIDES
1848 . . . Failed to Finish. (Mr Brettle) - 11-1. Rowlands. n/q

ALFRED
1849 . . . Finished 4th of 24. (Mr Buchanan) 5.10-6. D.Wynne. 12/1.

ARAB ROBBER
1849 . . . Failed to finish. (Mr Russell) 6.11-2. Phillips. n/q

ABD-EL-KADER
bay gelding by Ismael - English Lass. Bred by Mr D.Osborne in County Meath.
1850 . . . WON. (Mr J. Osborne) 8. 9-12. 32 Ran. C.Green. n/q.
1851 . . . WON. (Mr J. Osborne) 9.10-4. 21 Ran. T.Abbot. 7/1.
1852 . . . Pulled-up. (Mr J. Osborne) 10.11-4. D. Wynne. 9/1.
1853 . . . Finished 5th of 21. (Mr J. Osborne) 11.10-10. T.Abbot. 20/1.
1858 . . . Fell. (Mr Briscoe) 16.10-5. C. Green. 25/1.

AGIS
1852 . . . Refused. (Capt. J.L.Little) - 10-10. T.Olliver. n/q.

ALBATROSS
1857 . . . Failed to finish. (Mr J.Dennis) - 9-6. D.Meaney. n/q.

ANATIS
bay mare by King Dan - Johnstown Lass. Bred by Mr.Langan.
1859 . . . Finished 5th of 20. (Mr C. Capel) 9.9-4. Mr.Thomas. 25/1.
1860 . . . WON. (Mr C.Capel) 10.9-10. Mr.Thomas. 7/2 Fav.*
1861 . . . Fell. (Mr C.Capel) 11.10-4. Mr.Thomas. 4/1 Fav.*
1862 . . . Pulled-up. (Sir E.Hutchinson) 12.10-12. Mr.Thomas. 9/1.

ACE OF HEARTS
1859 . . . Fell. (Lord Waterford) - 9-12. J. Ryan. 25/1.

ARBURY
1863 . . . Finished 2nd of 16. (Mr J.Astley) - 11-2. Mr.A.Goodman.25/1.
1864 . . . Finished 2nd of 25. (Mr J.Astley) -11-12. B.Land, jnr. 40/1.
1865 . . . Fell. (Count A.de Dampoerre) - 11-8. C.Boyce. 100/8.

AVALANCHE
1863 . . . Finished 5th of 16. (Baron de Mesnil) 6.10-0. Palmer. 33/1.

ALCIBIADE
chestnut horse by The Cossack - Aunt Phillis. Bred in France.
1865 . . . WON. (Mr B.J.Angell) 5.11-4. 23 Ran. Capt.H.Coventry. 100/7.
1866 . . . Fell. (Mr B J.Angell) 6.12-2. B. Land, jnr. 9/1.
1868 . . . Finished 3rd of 21. (Mr B.J.Angell) 8.11-10. Col.G.W.Knox. 16/1.
1869 . . . Finished 4th of 22. (Mr B.J.Angell) 9.11-2. Col.G.W.Knox.20/1.
1870 . . . Finished 8th of 23. (Mr B.J.Angell) 10.10-12. Capt.Harford. 33/1.
1871 . . . Failed to finish. (Mr B.J.Angell) 11.10-4. Walling. 100/1.

ACROBAT
1865 . . . Refused. (Captain J.Machell) - 11-9. W.Mumford. 50/1.

ACE OF HEARTS.
1866 . . . Fell. (Lord Poulett) 6.10-2. Mr. Edwards. 50/1.

ASTROLABE
chestnut mare by Allez-y-gaiment - Aganisia. Bred in France.
1867 . . . Knocked-over. (Baron Finot) - 12-7. Cassidy. 20/1.
1868 . . . Finished 5th of 21. (Msr M.E.Bouruet) - 12-0. A.French. 30/1.

ACTON
brown horse by Lacydes - Rupert's dam.
1872 . . . Fell. (Mr Finchley) 6.10-7. J.Rudd. 40/1.
1873 . . . Failed to finish. (Mr Jones) 7.11-1. R.I'Anson. 30/1.

ALICE LEE
bay mare by The Ranger - Rosalba.
1873 . . . Finished 5th of 28. (Mr Studd) 7.10-3. G.Waddington. 14/1.

AUSTERLITZ
chestnut horse by Rataplan - Lufra. Bred by Lord Scarborough.
1877 . . . WON. (Mr. F.G.Hobson) 5.10-8. 16 Ran. Mr.F.G.Hobson.15/1.

ARBITRATOR
brown horse by Umpire - Sappho.
1877 . . . Fell. (Sir C.F.Rushout) 6.10-6. Mr.Crawshaw. 100/7.

ABBOT OF ST MARY'S
bay horse by Blinkhoolie - Miss Hawthorn
1881 . . . Finished 6th of 13. (Sir G.Chetwynd) 5.10-9. J.Adams. 8/1.

ATHLACCA
bay gelding by Lord Gough - Anxiety.
1883 . . . Pulled-up. (Mr T.McDougal) 8.11-4. J.Adams. 9/1.

ALBERT CECIL
chestnut horse by Albert Victor - Emotion.
1884 . . . Failed to finish. (Mr R.Sheriffe) 6.11-2. Mr.R.Sheriffe. 50/1.
1885 . . . Finished 6th of 19. (Mr R.Sheriffe) 7.10-9. J.Childs. 20/1.

AXMINSTER
chestnut gelding by Kidderminster - Marion.
1885 . . . Finished 5th of 19. (Mr J.Rutherford) 8.10-7. W.Sayers. 25/1.

AMICIA
bay mare by Hollywood - Madeline.
1886 . . . Failed to finish. (Mr H.Wood) 5.10-0. Mr F.Cotton. 25/1.

ALADDIN
bay gelding by Sir Bevys - Ocyroe.
1888 . . . Finished 5th of 20. (Mr L.de Rothschild) 6.11-0. Mr.C.W.Waller. 33/1.

ADELAIDE
bay mare by Ben Battle - Countess Adelaide.
1891 . . . Pulled-up. (Mr E.H.Wolton) 7.10-0. Mr. A.H.Ripley. 200/1.

ARDCARN
black gelding by The King, or Buckshot - Valerie.
1892 . . . Finished 4th of 25. (Major Kirkwood) 5.10-10. T.Kavanagh. 10/1.
1894 . . . Pulled-up. (Mr G.Grant) 7.10-12. Capt.Bewicke. 11/2.
1895 . . . Fell. (Mr Egerton Clarke) 8.10-10. R.Woodland. 50/1.
1896 . . . Fell. (Mr Egerton Clarke) 9.11-1. G.Williamson. 8/1.

AESOP
bay gelding by Chippendale - Fable.
1893 . . . Finished 2nd of 15. (Capt. M.Hughes) 7.10-4. A.H.Barker. 100/12.
1894 . . . Finished 5th of 14. (Capt. M.Hughes) 8.10-12. G.Mawson. 6/1.
1895 . . . Fell. (Capt. M.Hughes) 9.10-8. A.Nightingall. 5/1Fav.*

11

ALPHEUS
black gelding by Esterling - Arethusa.
1896 . . . Bolted. (Mr R.C.Vyner) 5.10-10. Mr.A.Gordon. 20/1.
1900 . . . Fell. (Mr R.C.Vyner) 9.10-10. A.Waddington. 40/1.

ARGONAUT
grey gelding by Nautilus - Beatrice Grey.
1897 . . . Finished 10th of 28. (Mr J.A.Miller) 7.10-12. R.Woodland. 33/1.

ATHELFRITH
brown gelding by Atheling - Wynberg's dam.
1898 . . . Fell. (Mr A.Coats) 8.10-4. W.Hoysted. 100/1.

AMBUSH II
brown gelding by Ben Battle - Miss plant.
1899 . . . Finished 7th of 19.(H.R.H.The Prince of Wales) 5.10-2. A.Anthony. 100/12.
1900 . . . WON. (H.R.H.The Prince of Wales) 6.11-3. 16 Ran. A.Anthony. 4/1.
1903 . . . Fell. (H.R.H.The Prince of Wales) 9.12-7. A.Anthony. 100/6.
1904 . . . Fell. (His Majesty The King) 10.12-6. A.Anthony.7/2Fav.*

ARNOLD
bay horse by Galway - dam's pedigree unknown.
1902 . . . Brought down. (Mr J.A.Scorror) 8.10-1. T.Bissill. 33/1.

AUNT MAY
chestnut mare by Ascetic - Mayo.
1902 . . . Failed to finish. (Mr B.W.Parr) 6.10-0. M.Walsh. 20/1.
1903 . . . Fell. (Mr B.W.Parr) 7.10-0. D.Read. 10/1.
1905 . . . Fell. (Mr B.W.Parr) 9.10-9. E.Sullivan.100/8.
1906 . . . Finished 3rd of 23. (Mr B.W.Parr) 10.11-2. Mr.H.S.Persse. 25/1.

ACTUARY, THE
black horse by Insurance - dam by Cadet.
1905 . . . Pulled-up. (Mr Leslie Rome) 7.10-9. E.Matthews. 66/1.

ASCETIC'S SILVER
chestnut horse by Ascetic - Silver Lady. Bred by Mr P.J.Dunne.
1905 . . . Fell. (Mr P.J.Dunne) 8.10-5. T.H.Dunn. 20/1.
1906 . . . WON. (Prince Hatzfeldt) 9.10-9. 23 Ran. Mr.A.Hastings 20/1.
1907 . . . Finished 6th of 23. (Prince Hatzfeldt) 10.12-7. Mr.A.Hastings. 7/1 jnt/Fav.*
1909 . . . Failed to finish. (Prince Hatzfeldt) 12.12-7. Mr.A.Hastings. 20/1.

ALERT III
chestnut mare by Skedaddle - Merry Lass.
1908 . . . Fell. (Mr T.G.Paget) 8. 9-11. L.Harland. 66/1.

ALBUERA
brown gelding by Wellington - Kardomah.
1910 . . . Fell. (Sir P.Walker) 10.10-12. F.Lyall. 100/7.

AXLE PIN
brown gelding by Quidnunc - Hairpin.
1912 . . . Finished 3rd of 24. (Lord Derby) 8.10-4. I.Anthony. 20/1.
1913 . . . Fell. (Lord Derby) 9.11-4. Mr.P.Whitaker. 100/8.

ALL GOLD II
chestnut gelding by Soleil d'Or - dam's pedigree unknown.
1914 . . . Fell. (Sir J.D.Tichborne) aged.10-7. Capt.Stokes. n/q.

ANOTHER DELIGHT
brown gelding by General Symons - Annie's Delight.
1914 . . . Fell. (Capt. E.H.Wyndham) 10.11-7. G.Brown. 33/1.

● **Ascetic's Silver won the Grand National in 1906 by ten lengths.**

ALLY SLOPER
bay or brown gelding by Travelling Lad - Sally In Our Alley. Bred by Mr.C.J.Hill.
1915 . . . WON. (Lady Nelson) 6.10-6. 20 Ran. Mr.J.R.Anthony. 100/8.
1916 . . . Completed course.(Lady Nelson) 7.11-13. Mr J.R.Anthony. 9/2 Fav.
*1917 . . . Finished 3rd of 19.(Lady Nelson) 8.11-10. I.Anthony. 20/1.
1918 . . . Fell. (Lady Nelson) 9.11-9. J.Walsh. 5/1 co/Fav.
1919 . . . Failed to finish. (Lady Nelson) 10.11-3. I.Anthony. 100/6.

ALFRED NOBLE
bay gelding by Garry Herrmann - Ethel Pace. Bred in U.S.A.
1915 . . . Finished 4th of 20. (Mr T.Barnard) 10.10-12. T.Hulme. 25/1.

AWBEG
chestnut gelding by Galgreina - Little Margery.
*1918 . . . Completed course. (Mr Horatio Bottomley) 7.10-0. L. Jones. 100/1.
1922 . . . Fell. (Mr M. S. Thompson) 11.10-9. Mr A. Knowles. n/q/

ALL WHITE
brown gelding by White Eagle - Colonia.
1919 . . . Finished 5th of 22. (Col.Hall Walker) 5.9-10. T.Williams. 66//1.
1920 . . . Fell. (Lord Wavertree) 6. 9-13. R.Chadwick. 33/1.
1921 . . . Finished 3rd of 35. (Lord Wavertree) 7.10-13. R.Chadwick. 33/1. Remounted*
1922 . . . Fell. (Lord Wavertree) 8.11-0. R.Chadwick. 100/7.
1924 . . . Refused. (Lord Wavertree) 10.10-11. M.Tighe. 40/1.
1925 . . . Fell. (Lord Wavertree) 11.10-0. J.Mason. 66/1.
1927 . . . Pulled-up. (Lord Wavertree) 13.10-5. J.Mason. 100/1.

ABOU BEN ADHEM
grey gelding by Roi Herode - Debris.
1919 . . . Fell. (Mr J.Buchanan) 8.12-0. A.Stubbs. 100/1.

ARDONAGH
chestnut gelding by Ardoon - Turkish Delight 11.
1920 . . . Fell. (Capt.C.B.Hanbury) 7.10-6. Mr P.Whitaker. n/q.

ANY TIME
brown gelding - pedigree unknown.
1921 . . . Fell. (Mr G.W.Hands) 10.10-6. F.Wooton. 50/1.
1922 . . . Fell. (Mr G.W.Hands) 11.10-5. G.Wall. n/q.

A DOUBLE ESCAPE
chestnut gelding by Swynford - Duma.
1922 . . . Finished 5th of 32. (Mr H.Adams) 8.10-3. Capt. G.H.Bennet. 40/1. Remounted*
1924 . . . Fell. (Mr H.Adams) 10.10-3. G. Smith. n/q.

ARRAVALE
bay horse by Ardoon - Lady Ina.
1922 . . . Fell. (Mr C.R.Baron) 7.10-11. Mr. P.Whitaker. 100/7.
1923 . . . Fell. (Mr C.R.Baron) 8.11-2. Mr. P.Whitaker. 10/1.
1924 . . . Fell. (Mr C.R.Baron) 9.11-3. Mr. P.Whitaker. 33/1.
1925 . . . Pulled-up. (Mr C.R.Baron) 10.11-0. J.Meaney. 66/1.

ARABIAN KNIGHT
bay horse by Poor Boy - Shaft.
1922 . . . Fell. (Mr J.P.Westlake) 6.10-2. R.Spares. n/q.

AMMONAL
chestnut horse by Oppressor - Tippytoes.
1923 . . . Fell. (Mrs F.M.Lloyd) 6.10-7. I.Morgan. 40/1.
1925 . . . Pulled-up. (Mr J.W.Wood) 8.10-10. R.Trudgill. 66/1.

AUCHINROSSIE
brown mare by Huon II - Campsie.
1924 . . . Pulled-up. (Mr W.G.P.Kincaid Lennox) 8.10-2. E.Foster. 25/1.

ALCAZAR
bay horse by Yerres - Good Gracious.
1925 . . . Fell. (Mr R.McAlpine) 9.12-3. Squadron Leader C.A.Ridley. 50/1.

ARDEEN
brown gelding by Evicted - Penryn.
1925 . . . Fell. (Sir Keith Fraser) 8.11-2. A.L.Lefebve. 28/1.
1926 . . . Fell. (Sir Keith Fraser) 9.11-9. R.Trudgill. 33/1.
1928 . . . Failed to finish.(Sir Keith Fraser) 11.11-2. J.Hamey. 40/1.
1929 . . . Fell. (Sir Keith Fraser) 12.11-2. R.Lyall. 25/1.

AMBERWAVE
bay gelding by Wavelet's pride - Ambergris.
1927 . . . Baulked. (Lady Helen McCalmont) 9.12-0. Mr.J.E.O'Brien. 20/1.
1928 . . . Fell. (Lady Helen McCalmont) 10.11-13. Mr.J.E.O'Brien. 10/1.

ACE II, THE
bay or brown gelding by Hollister - Foreshore.
1928 . . . Refused. (Mr R.B.Strassburger) 6.11-6. T.Morgan. 50/1.
1929 . . . Fell. (Mr R.B.Strassburger) 7.11-3. Mr.G.H.Evans. 66/1.
1932 . . . Pulled-up.(Marquis de San Miguel) 10.10-7. F. Maxwell. 100/1.
1934 . . . Fell. (Lady Mary Dunn) 12.10-11. Capt.A.Head. 66/1.

ARDOON'S PRIDE
bay gelding by Ardoon - Nancy.
1929 . . . Fell. (Mrs W.Mure) 9.10-10. P.Thrale. 200/1.

ALIKE
brown mare by Southannan - The Very Same.
1930 . . . Fell. (Lady Helen McCalmont) 7.11-0. Mr.M.Barry. 28/1.
1931 . . . Fell. (Mr R.K.Mellon) 8.10-10. Mr.F.R.Sclater. 28/1.
1932 . . . Fell. (Mr R.K.Mellon) 9.10-11. G.Turner. 50/1.

AGDEN
bay gelding by Cyclops Too - Thelema.
1930 . . . Pulled-up. (Mr O.G.Moseley) 13.10-9. Mr.D.P.G.Mosely. 50/1.

ANNANDALE
brown gelding by Southannan - Lady Noggs.
1930 . . . Fell. (Lady Glenapp) 8.10-0. F.Gurney. 100/1.
1931 . . . Finished 3rd of 43.(Lady Glenapp) 9.10-7. T.Morgan. 100/1.
1932 . . . Finished 7th of 36.(Lady Glenapp) 10.10-10. W.Stott. 100/7. Remounted*
1933 . . . Fell. (Lord Inchcape) 11.10-10. D.Morgan. 20/1.
1934 . . . Fell. (Lord Inchcape) 12.10-9. Mr P.Payne-Gallwey. 66/1.

APOSTASY
brown mare by Cecilian - Faithless.
1931 . . . Fell. (Lady Lindsay) 10.10-12. F. Brookes. 40/1.
1932 . . . Fell. (Lady Lindsay) 11.11-0. W. Parvin. 66/1.
1933 . . . Brought down. (Lady Lindsay) 12.10-9. R.Lyall. 100/1.
1934 . . . Finished 6th of 30.(Lady Lindsay) 13.10-7. E.Brown. 66/1.

ASPIRANT
chestnut gelding by Birk Gill - Mount Grace.
1931 . . . Fell. (Mr C.S.Green) 8.10-10. W.Parvin. 66/1.
1932 . . . Finished 5th of 36.(Sir P.Grant Lawson) 9.10-10. Sir P.Grant Lawson. 66/1.

ARUNTIUS
bay gelding by Call O' The Wild - Wine Gal.
1932 . . . Refused. (Mr M.D.Blair) 11.10-7. F.Mason. 100/1.

ALPINE HUT
chestnut gelding by Mountaineer - Little Haven.
1933 . . . Finished 5th of 34.(Sir Alfred Butt) 8.11-6. Mr.R.Harding. 50/1.
1934 . . . Fell. (Sir Alfred Butt) 9.11-6. Mr.R.Harding. 20/1.

ALEXENA
bay mare by Meleager - Alexa.
1935 . . . Refused. (Mr J.A.Redman) 9.10-7. Mr.P.Payne-Gallwey. 28/1.

AVENGER
bay gelding by Black Gauntlet - Vendramina.
1936 . . . Fell. (Mrs Violet Mundy) 7.11-8. T.F.Rimell. 100/30Fav.*

AIRGEAD SIOS
chestnut gelding by Werwolf - Orna.
1938 . . . Fell. (Sir Francis Towle) 8.12-0. T.McNeill. 25/1.

ASTROMETER
brown gelding by Vesington Star - Golden Meter.
1946 . . . Fell. (Miss D.Paget) 8.10-3. M.Gordon. 50/1.

ALACRITY
bay gelding by Marcus Friar - Cladagh Belle.
1946 . . . Unseated rider. (Mr J.Bowden) 13.10-0. G.Bowden. 100/1.

ARDNACASSA
brown gelding by Wilson - Lena's Fancy.
1949 . . . Brought down. (Mr S.H.Martin) 11.10-5. M.Connors. 66/1.
1950 . . . Fell. (Mr S.H.Martin) 12.10-5. Mr T.Brookshaw. 100/1.

ASTRA
bay gelding by Edgehill - Heart's Delight.
1949 . . . Brought down. (Mr J.W.Ellis) 8.10-4. A.P. hompson. 50/1.

ARRANBEG
brown gelding by Arran Chief - Cross Lady.
1949 . . . Fell. (Mrs V.H.Parr) 12.10-2. R.McCarthy. 66/1.

15

ACTHON MAJOR
chestnut gelding by Achtenan - Foiled.
1949 . . . Fell. (Mrs J.S.Gorman) 9.10-11. R.J.O'Ryan. 50/1.
1950 . . . Finished 3rd of 49.(Mrs J.S.Gorman) 10.11-2. R.J.O'Ryan. 33/1.

ANGEL HILL
bay mare by Tonton - Haputale.
1950 . . . Fell. (Capt. T.R.Colville) 10.10-3. T.Shone. 33/1.

ARMOURED KNIGHT
bay gelding by Steel Point - Kerry Dancer.
1951 . . . Brought down. (Mr G.H.Dowty) 7.10-8. T.Cusack. 66/1.
1953 . . . Fell. (Mr G.H.Dowty) 9.10-1. T.Mabbutt. 66/1.

ARCTIC GOLD
chestnut gelding by Iceberg II - Honeyweed.
1951 . . . Fell. (Mr J H.Whitney) 6.10-13. T.Molony. 8/1 Fav.*

ANOTHER DELIGHT
bay gelding by Glen of Kilcash - Ratilio.
1952 . . . Fell. (Lord Lewes) 9.10-10. G.Kelly. 25/1.

ALBERONI
chestnut gelding by His Reverence - Lady Pamela.
1954 . . . Fell. (Mr J.Crowe) 11.10-12. Mr E.Cousins. 66/1.

ANOTHER RAKE
bay gelding by Clearcash, dam by Wildfellow.
1955 . . . Fell. (Mr F.H.Gilman) 10.10-1. D.Leslie. 45/1.

ATHENIAN
brown gelding by The Phoenix - Felorbia.
1956 . . . Fell. (Col. W.H.Whitbread) 7.10-3. R.J.Hamey. 66/1.
1957 . . . Fell. (Col. W.H.Whitbread) 8.10-7. D.Ancil. 66/1.
1958 . . . Fell. (Col. W.H.Whitbread) 9.10-11. D.Ancil. 22/1.

ARMORIAL III
bay gelding by Souverain - Skiperia.
1956 . . . Fell. (Mme. K.Hennessy) 7.10-10. J.Dowdeswell. 20/1.
1957 . . . Fell. (Mme. K.Hennessy) 8.11-1. J.A.Bullock. 50/1.

ACE OF TRUMPS
bay gelding by King Of Trumps II - Persian Carpet.
1958 . . . Pulled-up. (Mr C.Nicholson) 10.10-12. P.A.Farrell. 40/1.

ALIFORM
bay gelding by Saint's Fly - Ilona.
1960 . . . Fell. (Mr A.Summers) 8.10-0. T.W.Biddlecombe. 45/1.

APRIL QUEEN
bay mare by Aprolon - Tolgus Queen.
1961 . . . Fell. (Mr M.P.Fear) 10.10-2. A.Biddlecombe. 100/1.

ARLES
bay gelding by Mieuxce - Mela.
1960 . . . Finished 7th of 26. (Mr H.K.Jones) 8.10-4. Mr.A.Moule.45/1.

AVENUE NEUILLY
bay gelding by My Babu - Eudemis.
1963 . . . Fell. (Major D.Hague) 8.10-4. D.Nicholson. 66/1.

AYALA
chestnut gelding by Supertello - Admiral's Bliss.
1963 . . . WON. (Mr P.B.Raymond) 9.10-0. P.Buckley. 66/1.
1964 . . . Fell. (Mr P.B.Raymond) 10.10-7. D.Nicholson. 33/1.
1965 . . . Fell. (Mr P.B.Raymond) 11.10-13. S.Mellor. 50/1.

APRIL ROSE
chestnut gelding by Raincheck - Roses Sweet.
1964 . . . Finished 7th of 33. (Mrs M.Cowley) 9.10-0. E. P. Harty. 22/1.
1965 . . . Finished 11th of 47.(Maj P.Bengough) 10.10-13. Maj P. Bengough. 100/1.
1966 . . . Pulled-up. (Maj P.Bengough) 11.10-7.Maj P. Bengough. 100/1.
1967 . . . Fell. (Maj P. Bengough) 12.10-8. Maj. P. Bengough. 66/1.

ANGLO
chestnut gelding by Greek Star - Miss Alligator. (Formerly named Flag Of Convenience) .
Bred by Mr W. Kennedy.
1966 . . . WON. (Mr S.Levy) 8.10-0. 47 Ran. T.Norman. 50/1.
1967 . . . Pulled-up. (Mr J.R.Gaines) 9.11-1. H.R.Beasley. 100/8.

AUSSIE
bay gelding by Ossian 11 - Happy Flower.
1967 . . . Finished 7th of 44. (Mrs R.H.Preston) 10.10-0. F. Shortt. 50/1.

AERIAL III
chestnut gelding by Aeolian, dam by Sandyman.
1967 . . . Fell. (Mr T.Durant) 11.10-9. Mr.T.Durant. 100/1.

ARCTURUS
bay gelding by Arctic Slave - Snow Goose.
1969 . . . Finished 6th of 30. (Lady Hay) 8.11-4. P.Buckley. 100/6.

ASSAD
chestnut gelding by Preciptic - Princess Badoura.
1970 . . . Finished 7th of 28. (Mrs E.A.Clarke) 10.10-1. J.Gifford.28/1.

ALL GLORY
grey gelding by Harwin - Glory's Lass.
1970 . . . Fell. (Mr A.S.Robinson) 9.10-0. A.L.T.Moore. 50/1.

ALASKA FORT
bay horse by Fortina - Beauty Contest.
1972 . . . Brought down.(Mrs G.Mulholland) 7.10-13. H.R.Beasley. 33/1.

ASHVILLE
bay gelding by Little Buskins - Edenagrena.
1973 . . . Fell. (Mr R.R.Guest) 8.10-4. J.King. 14/1.

ARGENT
chestnut gelding by Even Money - Some Toi.
1974 . . . Brought down. (Mr J.J.Byrne) 10.11-10. R.Coonan. 50/1.

ANDY PANDY
bay gelding by Garland Knight - Blue Sprite.
1977 . . . Fell. (Mrs S.D.Mulligan) 8.10-7. J.Burke. 15/2 Fav.*

APRIL SEVENTH
bay gelding by Menelek - Loughlahan.
1975 . . . Brought down. (Mrs B. Meehan) 12.10-11. A. Turnell. 28/1.

ARTISTIC PRINCE
chestnut gelding by Indigenous - Artiste Gaye.
1979 . . . Fell. (Mr Rbt.Stigwood) 8.10-0. P.Blacker. 25/1.
1982 . . . Fell. (Mr Rbt.Stigwood) 11.10-0. C.Brown. 50/1.
1983 . . . Refused. (Mr Rbt.Stigwood) 12.10-0. C.Brown. 66/1.

ALPENSTOCK
bay gelding by Vulgan - Clan Alpine.
1979 . . . Brought down. (Mr H.Thomson) 12.10-0. Mr.D.Gray. 100/1.

ALVERTON
chestnut gelding by Midsummer Night ll - Alvertona.
1979 . . . Fell. (Snailwell Stud Co.) 9.10-13. J.J.O'Neill. 13/2 Fav.*

17

ANOTHER DOLLY
brown gelding by Mon Capitaine - Little Bomb.
1980 . . . Fell. (Mr I.Urquhart) 10.10-0. J.J.O'Neill. 12/1.

ALDANITI
chestnut gelding by Derek H - Renardeau.
1981 . . . WON. (Mr S.N.J.Embiricos) 11.10-13. 39 Ran. R.Champion. 10/1.
1982 . . . Fell. (Mr S.N.J.Embiricos) 12.11-8. R.Champion. 12/1.

ANOTHER CAPTAIN
bay gelding by Mon Capitaine - Little Bomb.
1981 . . . Fell. (Mr A.Scott) 9.10-0. C.Hawkins. 40/1.
1984 . . . Finished 19th of 40.(Mr A.Scott) 12.10-1. A.Stringer. 66/1.

ANOTHER PROSPECT
bay gelding by New Brig - Broadside.
1981 . . . Fell. (Mr H.M.Thursfield & Mr P.J.Corbett) 9.10-3. Mr A.J.Wilson. 40/1.

AGAIN THE SAME
bay gelding by Mon Capitaine - Kali Maere.
1982 . . . Pulled-up. (Mr D.McLaughlin) 9.11-8. J.J.O'Neill. 16/1.

ARRIGLE BOY
chestnut gelding by Arrigle Valley - Beehive.
1983 . . . Refused. (Mr D.Eddy) 11.10-0. C.Pimlott. 100/1.

ASHLEY HOUSE
bay gelding by Fidel - Vicker's Pride.
1984 . . . Fell. (Mr J.McLoughlin) 10.11-13. G.Bradley. 20/1.

ANOTHER DUKE
bay gelding by Arizona Duke - Golden Age.
1986 . . . Fell. (Mr Desmond Lynam) 13.10-0. P.Nicholls. 200/1.

ACARINE
bay gelding by Le Prince - Cloonadoon.
1986 . . . Brought down. (Mrs P.W.Harris) 10.10-13. R.Stronge. 33/1.

ATTITUDE ADJUSTER
chestnut gelding by Deep Run - Careless Biddy.
1987 . . . Finished 8th of 40.(Mrs J.Magnier) 7.10-6. N.Madden. 25/1.
1988 . . . Finished 5th of 40.(Mrs J.Magnier) 8.10-6. N.Madden. 33/1.
1989 . . . Finished 12th of 40.(Mrs J.Magnier) 9.10-6. N.Madden. 25/1.

AGAINST THE GRAIN
bay gelding by Oats - Bench Game.
1990 . . . Pulled-up. (Mr J.F.Mawle) 9.10-0. J.Osborne. 25/1.

ABBA LAD
chestnut gelding by Le Bavard - Rosina Royale.
1991 . . . Pulled-up. (Mrs A.Taylor & Miss L.H.Taylor) 9.10-0. D.Gallagher. 250/1.

AUNTIE DOT
bay mare by Hallodri - Dream Isle.
1991 . . . Finished 3rd of 40.(Mrs R.Wilson) 10.10-4. M.Dwyer. 50/1.
1992 . . . Finished 16th of 40.(Mrs R.Wilson & Mr D. Wade-Jones) 11.10-7. M.Dwyer. 12/1.

ANTONIN
chestnut gelding by Italic - Pin 'Hup. Bred in France.
1996 . . . Finished 8th of 27. (G.R.Bailey Ltd.) 8.10-0. J.Burke. 28/1.

BARKSTON
1839 . . . Fell. (Mr T.Ferguson) Byrne.

BANATHLATH
1842 .. Fell. (Mr T.Ferguson) Colgan. 20/1.

BANGALORE
1842 . . . Failed to finish. (Mr Ramsey) Captain Peel. 20/1.

BUCEPHALUS
1843 . . . Finished 6th of 16. (Mr R.Hunter) - 11-5. Whitworth. n/q.

BRENDA
1845 . . . Ran Out. (Mr Perkins & Capt.France) -11-7. J.Abbot.6/1.
1846 . . . Fell. (Mr Hammond) - 11-4. Mr.Powell. 100/6.

BOXKEEPER
1845 . . . Failed to finish. (Mr Barnett) - 11-4. Bradley. n/q.

BOURTON
bay gelding by Drayton - dam unknown. Not in the General Stud Book. Formerly named UPTON.
1852 . . . Fell. (Mr Martin) - 10-10. S.Darling. n/q.
1853 . . . Fell. (Mr Higginson) - 11-2. S.Darling. 7/1.
1854 . . . WON. (Mr W.Moseley) - 11-12. 20 Ran. J.Tasker. 4/1Fav.*

BRILLIANT
1845 . . . Failed to finish. (Mr Wesley) - 10-4. Noble. 10/1.

BRUNETTE
1847 . . . Finished 6th of 26. (Mr Preston) 13.12-6. Mr.A.McDonough. n/q.

BALLYBAR
1847 . . . Failed to finish. (Mr Robertson) - 11-12. Turner. n/q.
1849 . . . Fell. (Mr Wesley) - 9-12. H.Bradley. n/q.

BARMAID
1847 . . . Failed to finish. (Mr Lockwood) - 10-8. Mr.Lockwood. n/q.

BRITISH YEOMAN
1848 . . . Finished 3rd of 29. (Mr Elmore) - 11-4. Mr.Bevill. n/q.
1849 . . . Finished 6th of 24. (Mr Elmore) - 11-4. Mr.Bevill. 12/1.
1850 . . . Failed to finish. (Mr Elmore) - 11-10. Philpot. n/q.
1856 . . . Brought down. (Mr T.F.Mason) - 9-4. Mr.A.Goodman.40/1.

BLUE PILL
1848 . . . Fell. (Mr E.Cary) aged 10-3. Allensby. n/q.

BEDFORD
1852 . . . Fell. (Mr Chance) - 9-12. A.Taylor. 12/1.

BEDFORD
1852 . . . Fell. (Mr Barling) - 10-10. Ablett. 12/1.
1854 . . . Broke leg. (Mr Barling) - 10-4. Eatwell. n/q.

BETSY PRIG
1853 . . . Fell. (Captain D.Lane) - 10-0. Meaney. n/q.

BURNT SIENNA
1854 . . . Finished 7th of 20. (Mr Slater) - 8-12. T.Burrows. 25/1.
1855 . . . Failed to finish. (Mr Jenkins) - 9-0. T.Burrows. 50/1.

BASTION
1855 . . . Failed to finish. (Mr Roberts) - 10-4. T.Olliver. 15/1.

BOUNDAWAY
1855 . . . Failed to finish. (Mr Magee) 6.10-0. J.Byrne. 50/1.

BANSTEAD
1856 . . . Fell. (Mr Dixon) 6. 9-4. Mr.W.Bevill. 50/1.

20

BLACK BESS
1858 . . . Fell. (Mr T.Bay) - 9-6. D.Wynne. 20/1.

BREWER, THE
1859 . . . Fell. (Mr T.Hughes) - 9-10. W.White. 100/30Fav.*

BORDER CHIEF
1859 . . . Failed to finish. (Mr H.E.Johnstone) - 9-10. Watling. n/q.

BRIDEGROOM
1860 . . . Finished 6th of 19. (Sir George Wombwell) - 10-6. Mr.Ekard. n/q.
1861 . . . Finished 4th of 24. (Mr B.J.Angell) - 10-7. Mr.FitzAdam. 25/1.
1862 . . . Finished 2nd of 13.(Mr B.J.Angell) - 10-13. B.Land,jnr.10/1.

BRUNETTE
1860 . . . Finished 7th of 19. (Mr Barrett) - 12-0. J.Kendall. 100/6.
1861 . . . Pulled-up. (Mr F.Rowlands) - 11-0. Mr.F.Rowlands.33/1.

BROTHER TO LADY'S MAID
1861 . . . Failed to finish. (Mr J.Stokes) - 10-3. Harris. n/q.

BUCEPHALUS
1862 . . . Finished 5th of 13. (Mr R.Rowan) - 10-9. McGrillon.100/7.

BIRDBOLT
1863 . . . Pulled-up. (Mr Spence) - 9-11. Mr.Spence. n/q.

BANTAM
1864 . . . Pulle-up. (Mr Aspinall) - 11-8. G.Holman. 5/1.

BELL'S LIFE
1864 . . . Fell. (Major Wombwell) - 10-12. Griffiths. 30/1.

BRIAN BORHOIME
1864 . . . Pulled-up. (Mr Lawrence) - 10-4. Poinons. n/q.

BALLYCASEY
1865 . . . Fell. (Mr J.A.Reed) - 11-0. T.Barton. n/q.

BANKER
bay gelding - pedigree unknown.
1867 . . . Failed to Finish. (Mr J.Dally) - 11-10. T.Ablett. n/q.

BUSZKE
chestnut gelding by Conyngham - Eveline. Bred in Hungary.
1868 . . . Pulled-up. (Count Karolyi) aged 12-0. Count Szapary. 40/1.

BARBARIAN
chestnut gelding by Glenmasson - dam unknown.
1869 . . . Pulled-up. (Mr S.J.Welfitt) 6.10-10. G.Waddington. 40/1.

BISHOPTON
brown gelding by Windhound - Miss Birch.
1869 . . . Knocked over. (Mr F.G.Hobson) 7.10-4. Potter. n/q.

BOGUE HOMA
brown horse by Newminster - Zoe Mou. Bred in France.
1871 . . . Failed to finish. (Lord Anglesey) 6.10-4. Tomlinson. 40/1.

BROADLEA
grey horse by Master Bagot - Violante.
1873 . . . Fell. (Lord Poulett) 6.10-5. Mr.Thomas. 12/1.

BRETBY
chestnut horse by Buccaneer - Zelle.
1874 . . . Refused. (Mr B.J.Angell) 8.10-0. W.Daniels. n/q.

BAR ONE
bay gelding - Pedigree unknown.
1875 . . . Fell. (Mr L.Nicholson) 8.11-4. Mr.L.Nicholson. n/q.

21

BOYNE WATER
bay horse by Solon - Lyra.
1878 . . . Finished 7th of 12. (Mr J.Jessop) 6.10-12. J.Adams. 5/1.

BEAR, THE
bay horse by Pace or Vaucresson - Berthe. Bred in France.
1878 . . . Knocked-over. (Duke of Hamilton) 5.10-4. R.Marsh. 10/1.
1879 . . . Refused. (Duke of Hamilton) 6.10-7. R.Marsh. 10/1.

BOB RIDLEY
grey gelding by Master Bagot - dam by West Australian.
1879 . . . Finished 5th of 18. (Mr T.D'Arcy Hoey) 8.10-9. Mr.E.P.Wilson. 33/1.

BRIGAND
bay gelding by Buccaneer - Crafton Lass.
1879 . . . Finished 10th of 18. (Count Festetic,jnr.) aged. 10-10. Count Metternich. 50/1.

BACCHUS
chestnut horse by Uncas - dam unknown.
1879 . . . Fell. (Mr Dunlop) 5.11-1. J.Cannon. 10/1.

BELLRINGER
chestnut horse by Rataplan - Bonny Bell.
1879 . . . Fell. (Mr Vyner) 7.10-7. Mr.A.Coventry. 100/7.

BURIDAN
bay gelding by Le Sarrazin - La Bastille. Bred in France.
1881 . . . Refused. (Mr A.Yates) 7.10-0. J.Childs. 50/1.

BLACK PRINCE
black gelding by The Warden of Galwey - Empress.
1882 . . . Fell. (Mr P.George) 7.10-0. F.Wynne. n/q.
1883 . . . Finished 2nd of 10.(Mr P.George) 8.10-4. D.Canavan. 33/1.
1884 . . . Finished 6th of 15. (Mr P.George) 9.10-11. Mr.T.Widger. 50/1.
1885 . . . Finished 3rd of 19.(Capt.J.Machell) 10.10-5. T.Skelton.33/1.
1886 . . . Brought down. (Capt.J.Machell) 11.10-12. W.Nightingall. 50/1.

BELMONT
bay horse by Cambuslang - Geraldine.
1885 . . . Pulled-up. (Mr James Daly) 8.10-11. W.Canavan. 100/6.
1886 . . . Fell. (Mr James Daly) 9.10-10. Westlake. 33/1.

BEN MORE
brown gelding by Ben Battle - dam by Outcast.
1885 . . . Fell. (Mr H.T.Barclay) 5.10-7. Mr.W.H.Moore. 100/8.

BADGER, THE
bay gelding by New Oswestry - Dodona.
1886 . . . Finished 5th of 23. (Baron C.de Tuyll) 9.10-3. A.Nightingall. 25/1.
1888 . . . Finished 9th of 20.(Baron C.de Tuyll) 11.11-1.A.Nightingall. 10/1.

BILLET DOUX
brown gelding by Billet - Eppie L. Bred in the U.S.A.
1886 . . . Pulled-up. (Count Zborowski) 6.10-11. J.Behan. 100/1.

BELLONA
brown mare by Lord Gough - Metz.
1887 . . . Fell. (Mr George Lambton) 5.10-10.Mr.G.Lambton.100/8.
1888 . . . Fell. (Mr T.B.Miller) 6.11-12. Mr.C.J.Cunningham.18/1.
1889 . . . Finished 4th of 20. (Mr Abington) 7.11-2. Mr.C.W.Waller. 20/1.
1890 . . . Fell. (Mr Abington) 8.11-9. A.H.Barker. 11/2.

BALLOT BOX
brown gelding by Candidat - Susan.
1887 . . . Fell. (Mr P.Nickalls) 8.10-5. Capt.E.R.Owen. 40/1.
1888 . . . Finished 3rd of 20. (Mr P.Nickalls) 9.12-4.W.Nightingall.25/1.
1889 . . . Fell. (Mr P.Nickalls) 10.12-7. W.Nightingall. 20/1.

BATTLE ROYAL
chestnut gelding by Ben Battle - dam unknown.
1889 . . . Finished 9th of 20. (Mr W.Fulton) 5.10-8. Mr.H.Beasley.25/1.
1890 . . . Fell. (Mr W.Fulton) 6.11-13. Mr.H.Beasley. 100/8.

BRUNSWICK
brown horse by Brunswicker - dam unknown.
1890 . . . Finished 4th of 16. (Mr Lancashire) 6.10-4.G.Mawson.100/1.
1891 . . . Fell. (Mr H.W.Lancashire) 7.10-4. G.Mawson. 40/1.
1892 . . . Fell. (Mr H.W.Lancashire) 8.10-2. Mr.Levison. 100/1.

BRACEBOROUGH
bay gelding by Onslow - Evelyn.
1890 . . . Fell. (Mr F.E.Lawrence) 7.10-13. Mr.F.E.Lawrence.100/1.

BACCY
bay gelding by Old Tom - Manilla.
1890 . . . Fell. (Mr E.Woodland) 7.10-8. Mr.W.Woodland. 100/1.

BAGMAN
bay gelding by Traveller - Skipaway.
1892 . . . Finished 11th of 25. (Capt.R.W.Ethelstone) aged.10-7. Mr.F.Hassall. n/q.

BILLEE TAYLOR
brown gelding Ben Battle - Mary Walker.
1892 . . . Bolted. (Major Keearsley) aged.10-3. Mr.H.Beasley. 25/1.

BISCUIT
bay mare by Burnaby - Reversion.
1896 . . . Finished 3rd of 28. (Mr W.C.Keeping) 8.10-0.E.Matthews. 25/1.

BARCALWHEY
black gelding by Barcaldine - Junket.
1896 . . . Finished 4th of 28. (Capt.A.E.Whitaker) 6. 9-8. C.Hogan. 1000/30.
1897 . . . Fell. (Capt.A.E.Whitaker) 7.10-1. C.Hogan. 25/1.
1898 . . . Fell. (Capt.A.E.Whitaker) 8.10-6. R.Chaloner. 100/7.
1900 . . . Fell. (Capt.A.E.Whitaker) 10.10-0. T.Lane. 20/1.

BALLYOHARA
bay or roan mare by Ben Battle - dam unknown.
1897 . . . Pulled-up. (Lord Shrewsbury) 8.10-3. W.G.Denby. 100/1.

BARSAC
chestnut horse by Barcaldine - Stillwater.
1898 . . . Finished 8th of 25. (Mr C.A.Brown) 6.9-12. Mr.M.B.Bletsoe. 25/1.
1899 . . . Finished 5th of 19. (Mr C.A.Brown) 7.9-12. Mr.H.M.Ripley. 25/1.
1900 . . . Finished 2nd of 16. (Mr C.A.Brown) 8.9-12. W.Halsey. 25/1.
1901 . . . Finished 9th of 24. (Mr C.A.Brown) 9.9-13. Mr.H.M.Ripley. 100/14.
1902 . . . Finished 8th of 21. (Mr C.A.Brown) 10.9-12. F.Mason. 7/1.

BREEMOUNT'S PRIDE
bay mare by Kendal - Mavourneen.
1900 . . . Finished 4th of 16. (Mr G.Edwardes) 7.11-7. Mr.G.S.Davies. 20/1.

BUFFALO BILL
chestnut gelding by Master Bill - Etna.
1901 . . . Finished 3rd of 24. (Mr J.E.Rogerson) 7.9-7. H.Taylor. 33/1.

BENVENIR
black mare by Bennitthorpe - Souvenir.
1903 . . . Finished 5th of 23. (Mr J.Meleady) 7.9-12. Mr.Hayes. 100/1.
1904 . . . Brought down. (Mr W.N.W.Gape) 8.9-10. P.Woodland. 20/1.

BAND OF HOPE.
bay gelding by Enthusiast - Infula.
1904 . . . Finished 6th of 26. (Capt.M.Hughes) 8.10-0. P.Cowley. 40/1.
1905 . . . Finished 6th of 27. (Mr W.M.G.Singer) 9.9-11. W.Donnelly. 100/1.

BIOLOGY
brown gelding by St Hilaire - Myrrh.
1904 . . . Fell. (Mr Horatio Bottomley) 7.10-1. D.Read. 33/1.
1905 . . . Fell. (Mr Horatio Bottomley) 8.10-2. H.Woodland.40/1.

BUCKAWAY II
black gelding by Bennitthorpe - Souvenir.
1905 . . . Finished 3rd of 27. (Mr P.E.Speakman) 7.9-11. A.Newey. 100/1.
1906 . . . Fell. (Mr P.E.Speakman) 8.10-4. A.Newey. 20/1.
1907 . . . Finished 7th of 23.(Mr P.E.Speakman) 9.10-4.H.Aylin. 40/1. Remounted*
1909 . . . Fell. (Mr F.S.Gilbert) 11.9-13. R.Wall. 100/1.

BUCHERON
bay gelding by Calet - Bannerol.
1905 . . . Fell. (Count de Songeon) 10.10-6. U.David. 100/1.

BARABBAS II
brown horse by Batt - Siberia. Bred in South America.
1907 . . . Finished 5th of 23. (Mr S.J.Unzue) 6.10-7. R.Morgan. 20/1.

BOUCHAL OGUE
bay gelding by Kentford - Spraight-In-Chint.
1907 . . . Fell. (Mr J.Meynall-Knight) 11.10-7. C.Graham. 50/1.

BLACK IVORY
black gelding by Ivor - Miss Jameson.
1909 . . . Pulled-up. (Mr A.Scott) 9.10-12. Mr.A.Scott. 100/1.

BRINEOGE
bay gelding by Enthusiast - Wild Honey.
1909 . . . Failed to finish. (Mr C.F.K.Mainwaring) 10.10-7. H.Smyth. 100/1.
1910 . . . Refused. (Mr C.F.K.Mainwaring) 11.10-4. Mr.F.A.Brown. 100/1.

BLOODSTONE
bay gelding by Cherry Stone - Royal Bride.
1910 . . . Fell. (Mr C.Bower Ismay) 8.11-8.S.Walkington.100/7.
1912 . . . Finished 2nd of 24. (Mr C.Bower Ismay) 10.11-6. F.Lyall. 40/1.
1913 . . . Fell. (Mr C.Bower Ismay) 11.12-7. F.Lyall. 100/6.
1914 . . . Fell. (Mr C.Bower Ismay) 12.11-7. F.Lyall. 100/6.

BUSHIDO
bay horse by Bona Vista - Reve d'Amour. Bred in Hungary.
1910 . . . Knocked-over. (Mr J.A. de Rothschild) 5. 9-7. J.Hetherington.66/1.

BRIDGE IV
brown gelding by Baddiley - Bridget.
1911 . . . Fell. (Mr F.S.Francis) 7. 9-9. Mr.P.Roberts. 100/1.
1912 . . . Failed to Finish.(Mr F.S.Francis) 8.10-8.Mr.G.C.Poole. 25/1.

BALLYHACKLE
bay gelding by Hackle - Ballymacarney.
1912 . . . Failed to finish. (Mr K.F.Malcolmson) 9.10-7. I.Morgan. 20/1.
1913 . . . Fell. (Mr K.F.Malcolmson) 10.11-11.Mr.Ussher.5/1Fav.*
1914 . . . Fell. (Mr K.F.Malcolmson) 11.12-0. Mr.H.Ussher. 100/7.
1915 . . . Broke-down. (Mr K.F.Malcolmson) 12.11-9. S.Avila. n/q.

BLACK PLUM
bay gelding by Persimmon - Princess Athenais.
1913 . . . Failed to finish. (Mr F.S.Watts) 9.11-5. R.Morgan. 66/1.

BLOW PIPE
bay gelding by Bird Of Paradise - Ballista.
1913 . . . Fell. (Mr M.M.Henderson) 8.11-4. W.J.Smith. 25/1.
1914 . . . Fell. (Mr A.Shepherd) 9.10-3. H.B.Bletsoe. 25/1.
1915 . . . Failed to Finish.(Mr A.Shepherd) 10.10-4. W.Smith. n/q.
*1917 . . . Completed course. (Mr G.H.Jones) 12.10-0. E.Lancaster. n/q.

BAHADUR
chestnut gelding by Nunthorpe - Azeeza.
1914 . . . Fell. (Mr G.Lambarde) 11. 9-12. Mr.R.H.Hall. 33/1.
1915 . . . Fell. (Mr G.Lambarde) 12. 9-7. Mr.P.Roberts. n/q.

BALSCADDEN
chestnut horse by Pilot - dam by Wellington.
1915 . . . Finished 5th of 20. (Mr C.Bower Ismay) 8.11-8. F.Lyall. 10/1. Remounted*

BULLAWARRA
bay gelding by Sir Simon - Nacrite. Bred In Australia.
1915 . . . Fell. (Mr J.M.Niall) 10.11-12. C.Hawkins. 100/7.

BABE, THE
brown gelding by Karma - Cute.
1915 . . . Pulled-up. (Mr F.Bibby) 7.10-0. R.Chadwick. n/q.

BACHELOR'S FLIGHT
bay gelding by Flying Hackle - Lady Dern.
1915 . . . Fell. (Mr F.Barbour) 8. 9-8. H.Harty. 100/9.

BALLYNEETY
brown gelding by Kilteel - Thomond's Pride.
*1916 . . . Completed course. (Mr H.F.Malcolmson) 7.9-7. W.J.Smith. 50/1.

BLIGH
bay gelding by Golden Crown or Darnley - Miliolite.
*1916 . . . Pulled-up. (Mr J.R.Heaton) 10. 9-7. B.Roberts. n/q.

BALLYMACAD
bay gelding by Laveno - Ballymacarney.
* 1917 . . . WON. (Sir George Bullough) 10.9-12. 19 Ran. E.Driscoll. 100/9.
* 1918 . . . Finished 3rd of 17. (Sir George Bullough) 11.11-3. I.Anthony. 7/1.

BERNERAY
bay gelding by Torpoint - Miss Bobs. Formerly named ME.
*1918 . . . Finished 4th of 17. (Mr Barclay Walker) 7.10-4. S.Avila. 100/7.

BALLYBOGGAN
chestnut gelding by Frustrum - Gentle Annie.
1919 . . . Finished 2nd of 22. (Mr E.W.Hope-Johnstone) 8.11-10. W.Head. 9/1.
1920 . . . Fell. (Mr E.W.Hope-Johnstone) 9.11-3. Mr.C.Brabazon. 100/7.

BALLINCARROONA
bay gelding by Uncle Mac or Santoi - Lizzie Kendal.
1919 . . . Fell. (Capt.Ian Straker) 11.10-4. Capt.I.Straker. 20/1.

BORE, THE
bay gelding by Ormondale - Bettie Bramble.
1920 . . . Finished 3rd of 24. (Mr H.A.Brown) 9.10-1. Mr.H.A.Brown. 28/1.
1921 . . . Finished 2nd of 35.(Mr H.A.Brown) 10.11-8. Mr.H.A.Brown. 9/1Fav.* Remounted*

BONNIE CHARLIE
chestnut gelding by Stoccado - Prevoyance.
1920 . . . Fell. (Capt.Willoughby Norrie) 12. 9-11. Mr.M.D.Blair. n/q.
1921 . . . Fell. (Mr M.D.Blair) 13.10-4. Mr.M.D.Blair. n/q.

BOBBYDAZZLER
bay horse by Marcovil - Vain Chick.
1921 . . . Fell. (Sir F.Price) 7.11-1. A.Stubbs. n/q.

BALLYSAX
bay gelding by Saxham - Silver Vixen.
1921 . . . Fell. (Mrs J.Putnam) 7.10-5. G.Goswell. n/q.

BLAZERS
bay gelding by Flying Hackle - Lady Blazes.
1921 . . . Fell. (Major W.T.M.Buller) 7.10-4. W.Watkinson. 30/1.

BALLINODE
chestnut mare by Machakos - Celia.
1924 . . . Finished 8th of 30. (Mr C.J.Bentley) 8.10-4.G.Fitzgibbon.25/1.
1925 . . . Fell. (Mr C.J.Bentley) 9.11-6. G.Fitzgibbon. 10/1.

BEN CRUCHAN
chestnut gelding by Ben Alder - Scotch Flower.
1925 . . . Fell. (Mr W.H.Whitbread) 11.11-3. Mr.W.H.Whitbread. 40/1.
1926 . . . Finished 13th of 30. (Mr W.H.Whitbread) 12.11-2. Mr.W.H.Whitbread. 66/1. Remounted*

BALLYMACRORY
bay gelding by Wavelet's Pride - dam by Perth Medley.
1925 . . . Fell. (Mr R.C.Ross) 8.10-3. J.Moylan. 33/1.

BRIGHT'S BOY
chestnut gelding by Soulouque - Divine Flower.
1926 . . . Finished 3rd of 30. (Mr S.Sanford) 7.11-8. E.Doyle. 25/1.
1927 . . . Finished 3rd of 37. (Mr S.Sanford) 8.12-7. J.R.Anthony. 100/7.
1928 . . . Fell. (Mr S.Sanford) 8.12-7. M.Rayson. 20/1.
1929 . . . Fell. (Mr S.Sanford) 9.12-4. E.Foster. 25/1.

BOVRIL III
chestnut gelding by Simonson - Bovril.
1927 . . . Finished 2nd of 37. (Mr G.W.Pennington) 9.10-12. Mr.G.W.Pennington. 100/1.

BALLYSTOCKART
bay glding by Zria - Isle Of The Blessed.
1927 . . . Finished 7th of 37. (Capt.R.E.Sassoon) 8.11-1. Capt.R.E.Sassoon.100/1.
1928 . . . Failed to finish. (Capt.R.E.Sassoon) 9.11-2. Capt.R.E.Sassoon. 40/1.
1929 . . . Failed to finish. (Capt.R.E.Sassoon) 10.11-0. Capt.R.E.Sassoon.66/1.

BLAENOR
chestnut gelding by Courtisan 11 - Queen Of The Rye.
1927 . . . Fell. (Lord Marchamley) 10.10-7. E.Doyle. 33/1.

BILLY BARTON
brown gelding by Huon - Mary Le Bus. Bred in U.S.A.
1928 . . . Finished 2nd of 42. (Mr Howard Bruce) 10.10-11. T.B.Cullinan. 33/1. Remounted*
1929 . . . Fell. (Mr Howard Bruce) 11.11-7. T.B.Cullinan. 20/1.

BURGORIGHT
brown gelding by Borgomaster - Ruby Right.
1928 . . . Failed to finish. (Mr B.L.Behr) 13.10-7. Mr.F.A.Bonsal.200/1.

BEECH-MARTIN
bay gelding by Marten - Land Toll.
1929 . . . Failed to finish. (Mr D.Faber) 8.10-8. L.B.Rees. 50/1.

BALLYHANWOOD
chestnut gelding by Cookhill - Crissy.
1929 . . . Refused. (Mr M.D.Blair) 8.10-2. J.Goswell. 100/1.
1930 . . . Finished 5th of 41. (Mr M.D.Blair) 9.10-4. E.Foster. 33/1.
1931 . . . Finished 5th of 43. (Mr M.D.Blair) 10.10-7. T.Isaac. 40/1.
1933 . . . Fell. (Mr M.D.Blair) 12.10-7. J.Goswell. 50/1.

BIG WONDER
bay gelding by Sunningdale - Miss Broomfield.
1929 . . . Failed to finish. (Mr G.S.L.Whitelaw) 9.10-2. J.Bisgood.50/1.
1930 . . . Fell. (Mr G.S.L.Whitelaw) 10.10-11. Capt.H.N.Weber. 50/1.

BEST HOME
brown gelding by Dunholm - Best Birthday.
1929 . . . Fell. (Mr G.Elliott) 8.10-0. Mr.G.Elliott. 200/1.

BLENNERHASSET
bay gelding by Ednam - Lady Liverton.
1930 . . . Fell. (Mr T.L.Parke) 11.10-2. Mr.W.P.Dutton. 66/1.

BALLASPORT
bay gelding by Drinmore - dam by Druce.
1931 . . . Fell. (Sir Harold A.Wernher) 7.11-0. D.Williams. 100/6.

BIG BLACK BOY
brown gelding by Lorenzo - Miss Soliman.
1931 . . . Fell. (Major C.H.Stevens) 9.10-12. W.Payne. 66/1.

BALLYBRACK
bay gelding by Marchmond - Hermit 11.
1933 . . . Completed the course. (Lt.Col.R.W.Tweedie) 9.11-0. Mr.G.Elliott. 50/1. Remounted*
1935 . . . Fell. (Lt.Col.R.W.Tweedie) 11.10-8. Mr.R.R.Tweedie. 50/1.

BLUE PETER III
brown gelding by Rockaway - Jealousy.
1934 . . . Finished 8th of 30. (Commander A.V.Courage) 11.10-7. Mr.F.Cundell. 66/1.

BLUE PRINCE
chestnut gelding by Prince Galahad - Boyne Blue.
1935 . . . Finished 2nd of 27. (Lady Lindsay) 7.10-7. W.Parvin. 40/1.
1936 . . . Unseated rider. (Lady Lindsay) 8.11-0. W.Parvin. 20/1.
1938 . . . Fell. (Lady LIndsay) 10.10-5. W.Parvin. 50/1.

BACHELOR PRINCE
bay gelding by Hopeful Bachelor - Culleen's Princess.
1935 . . . Finished 6th of 27. (Miss M.Lark) 8.10-10. W.O'Grady.25/1.
1936 . . . Finished 3rd of 35. (Mr J.V.Rank) 9.10-9. J.Fawcus. 66/1.
1938 . . . Finished 10th of 36.(Mr J.V.Rank) 11.10-6. D.Morgan. 25/1.
1939 . . . Finished 10th of 37.(Mr J.V.Rank) 12.10-2. T.Isaac. 66/1.
1940 . . . Fell. (Mr R.Loewenstein) 13.10-9. Mr.R.Loewenstein. 100/1.

BRIENZ
brown gelding by Blink - Blue Lake.
1935 . . . Fell. (Mr G.Beeby) 9.11-0. W.Kidney. 22/1.
1936 . . . Fell. (Mr G.Beeby) 10.11-0. J.Hamey. 40/1.

BRAVE CRY
bay gelding by Brave Chap - Squeal.
1935 . . . Fell. (Mr J.C.W.Lewis) 13.10-7. Mr.J.C.W.Lewis. 100/1.

● **Battleship (centre) comes to challenge Royal Danieli at the last in 1938**

27

BUCKTHORN
bay gelding by Drinmore, dam by Goldcourt.
1936 . . . Fell. (Mr C.M.L.Clements) 8.10-9. Capt.R.Harding.40/1.
1937 . . . Fell. (Capt.C.M.L.Clements) 9.10-9. K.Piggott. 40/1.

BOY IN BLUE, THE
chestnut gelding by Bucks Hussar - Rawfolds.
1936 . . . Fell. (Mr N.Dixon) 7.10-8. Mr.P.Vaux. 100/1.

BLAZE
chestnut gelding by Salvo - Bedazzle.
1936 . . . Fell. (Sir Ernest Wills) 7.10-7. K.Piggott. 100/1.
1937 . . . Fell. (Sir Ernest Wills) 8.10-0. W.Parvin. 50/1.

BATTLESHIP
chestnut horse by Man O' War - Quarantaine. Bred in U.S.A.
1938 . . . WON. (Mrs Marion Scott) 11.11-6. 36 Ran. B.Hobbs.40/1.

BLUE SHIRT
brown gelding by Apron - Fairy Ford.
1938 . . . Finished 7th of 36. (Mr A.Sainsbury) 7.10-3. R.Smyth. 8/1Fav.*
1939 . . . Fell. (Mr A.Sainsbury) 8.10-4. R.Smyth. 10/1.

BRIGHTER COTTAGE
brown gelding by Cottage - Shining Hope.
1938 . . . Fell. (Capt.D.W.Daly) 8.10-2. W.O'Grady. 40/1.

BIRTHGIFT
brown gelding by Birthright - Royal Missie.
1939 . . . Refused. (Mr N.E.Dixon) 8.10-0. T.McNeill. 100/1.

BRENDAN'S COTTAGE
bay gelding by Cottage - Brendan's Glory.
1939 . . . Fell. (Mrs A.Smith-Bingham) 9.11-2. G.R.Owen. 25/1.

BLACK HAWK
bay gelding by Eaglehawk - Black Lamb.
1939 . . . Fell. (Mrs C.Jones) 8.10-8. J.Moloney. 40/1.
1940 . . . Fell. (Mrs C.Jones) 9.11-0. T.F.Rimell. 100/6.

BOYO
brown gelding by Le Brige - Wise Girsha.
1940 . . . Fell. (Lord Sefton) 9.10-4. R.Morgan. 66/1.

BOGSKAR
brown gelding by Werwolf - Irish Spring.
1940 . . . WON. (Lord Stalbridge) 7.10-4. 30 Ran. M.A.Jones. 25/1.
1946 . . . Fell. (Lord Stalbridge) 13.10-9. R.Matthews. 66/1.
1947 . . . Fell. (Lord Stalbridge) 14.10-4. R.Burford. 100/1.

BRICETT
brown gelding by Baytown - Beauty Spot.
1946 . . . Fell. (Mr H.Linsley) 9.10-2. J.Brogan. 28/1.
1947 . . . Fell. (Mr H.Linsley) 10.11-1. M.C.Prendergast. 22/1.
1948 . . . Fell. (Mr H.Linsley) 11.11-3. T.Molony. 100/1.
1949 . . . Finished 9th of 43. (Mr H.Linsley) 12.10-9.T.Molony. 20/1.

BLACK JENNIFER
brown gelding by Black Watch - Winsome Jennifer.
1947 . . . Fell. (Mr M.Uglow) 7.10-0. J.Sheehan. 50/1.

BOMBER COMMAND
chestnut gelding by Lucca - Greenogue Princess.
1947 . . . Fell. (Mr A.B.Askew) 8.10-0. A.Jarvis. 100/1.

BRIGHTER SANDY

bay gelding by Sandyman - Brighter Pinion.
1947 . . . Finished 17th of 57. (Mr M.Barker) 9.10-7. Capt.J.Eustace-Smith. 66/1.
1949 . . . Brought down. (Mr T.M.Barker) 10.11-2. R.Turnell. 40/1.

BORDER BOB

chestnut gelding by Jehangir, dam's pedigree unknown.
1947 . . . Fell. (Mr J.R.Bower) 9.10-0. J.Neely. 100/1.

BRICK BAT

bay gelding by Rolling Rock - Flying Rose.
1947 . . . Finished 11th of 57. (Mr J.V.Rank) 8.10-0. E.Newman. 66/1.

BULLINGTON

chestnut gelding by Gallini - Norton Rose.
1947 . . . Fell. (Major W.W.Higgins) 11.10-6. J.P.Bissill.66/1.

BORA'S COTTAGE

bay gelding by Cottage - Bora.
1948 . . . Fell. (Mr F.L.Vickerman) 10-10-0. E.Vinall. 100/1.
1949 . . . Fell. (Mr F.L.Vickerman) 11.10-3. E.Kennedy. 50/1.

BARN DANCE

bay gelding by Royal Dancer - Cottage Lass.
1949 . . . Fell. (Mrs E.G.Williams) 10.10-0. E.Newman. 50/1.

BARNEY VI

bay or brown gelding by Baydrop, dam by Stripes.
1950 . . . Fell. (Mr W.Quirke) 12.10-2. T.P.Burns. 100/1.

BATTLING PEDULAS

bay gelding by Irish Battle - Duchess Of Pedulas.
1950 . . . Fell. (Mr J.Lipton) 11.10-11. D.Marzani. 50/1.

BINGHAMSTOWN

brown gelding by Caddle Combe - Glenamaddy.
1950 . . . Refused. (Mr L.Furman) 11.10-7. Mr.L.Furman.100/1.
1951 . . . Fell. (Mr L.Furman) 12.10-0. Mr.L.Furman.100/1.

BROOMFIELD

bay gelding by Flamenco - Juliana.
1951 . . . Fell. (Mr W.P.Westhead) 10.10-4. R..Emery. 33/.

BROWN JACK III

brown gelding by Jm Newcombe - Atlanta II.
1952 . . . Fell. (Duque de Alburquerque) 8.10-10. Duque de Alburquerque.40/1.

BRONZE ARROW

bay mare by Sanspear - Silverseal.
1952 . . . Fell. (Mr J.Straker) 10.10-2. Mr.J.Straker. 100/1.

BORDER LUCK

chestnut gelding by Squadron Castle or Port Of Call - Luck.
1952 . . . Unseated rider. (Mr J.R.Bower) 7.10-12. T.Shone. 20.1.
1954 . . . Fell. (Mr J.R.Bower) 9.10-0. T.Shone. 66/1.
1956 . . . Refused. (Mr J.R.Bower) 11.10-0. M.O'Dwyer.66/1.

BAIRE

bay horse by Amador - Double Call 11. Foaled in France.
1953 . . . Fell. (Mr M.L.Marsh) 7.10-0. J.Foster. 40/1.
1954 . . . Fell. (Mr M.L.Marsh) 8.10-0. J.Foster. 66/1.

BROOKLING

bay gelding by Brooksby - Emily Square.
1958 . . . Fell. (Mr C.Rooney) 9.10-3. T.Taaffe. 28/1.

BELSIZE II
brown gelding by Open Bridle, dam by Oojah.
1959 . . . Fell. (Mr W.G.Boomer) 10.10-0. Mr.G.Rooney. 28/1.
1960 . . . Fell. (Mr W.G.Boomer) 11.10-0. P.Shortt. 66/1.

BADANLOCH
bay gelding by Bakhtawar - Mischievous.
1960 . . . Finished 2nd of 26. (Lord Leverhulme) 9.10-9. S.Mellor. 100/7.
1961 . . . Finished 8th of 35. (Lord Leverhulme) 10.10-11. S.Mellor. 20/1.

BRIAN OGE
bay gelding by Fortina - Senria.
1961 . . . Fell. (Mr F.R.Pullen) 10.10-10. J.Guest. 100/1.

BANTRY BAY
brown gelding by April The Fifth - Stalbridge Weston.
1961 . . . Fell. (Mr H.W.Dufosee) 10.10-7. Sir Wm.Pigott-Brown. 40/1.

BLONDE WARRIOR
bay gelding by War Star - Blonde Venus.
1962 . . . Finished 11th of 32. (Mr A.H.East) 10.10-6. T.W.Biddlecombe.66/1.
1963 . . . Finished 16th of 47. (Mr M.Naylor-Leyland) 11.10-9. B.Lawrence. 66/1.
1965 . . . Fell. (Mrs K.B.Nicoll) 13.10-13. Mr.D.Crossley-Cooke. 100/1.

BAXIER
brown gelding by Contest II - Album.
1964 . . . Finished 8th of 35. (Lord Fermoy) 8.10-0. Mr.W.McLernon. 40/1.

BORDER FLIGHT
chestnut gelding by Airborne - Over The Border.
1964 . . . Fell. (Mr E.Courage) 9.10-3. P.A.Farrell. 100/6.

BALLYGOWAN
bay gelding by Overthrow - Elton Village.
1965 . . . Refused. (Mrs W.L.Pilkington) 11.10-13. A.Redmond. 66/1.

BLACK SPOT
bay gelding by Black Tarquin - Yorkshire Rose.
1965 . . . Fell. (Mrs V.M.McGregor) 8.10-13. J.Gamble. 100/1.
1966 . . . Fell. (Mrs O.M.Lusty) 9.10-0. J.Speid-Soote. 100/1.

BOLD BIRI
bay gelding by Birikan - Bonniebriar.
1965 . . . Fell. (Mr J.E.Bigg) 9.10-13. M.Scudamore. 100/1.
1966 . . . Pulled-up. (Mr J.E.Bigg) 10.10-0. J.Lehane. 100/1.

BROWN DIAMOND
brown gelding by Vulgan - Little Blue Star.
1965 . . . Finished 10th of 47. (Mrs P.M.Lamb) 10.10-13. Mr.W.A.McLernon. 50/1.
1966 . . . Fell. (Mrs P.M.Lamb) 11.10-0. F.Shortt. 100/1.

BARLEYCROFT
bay gelding by Wilwyn - Lady Barle.
1965 . . . Brought down. (Mr A.J.Moore) 10.10-13. P.Harvey. 100/1.

BIG GEORGE
brown gelding by Gay Presto - Miss Muffet V.
1966 . . . Finished 11th of 47. (Mrs R.J.McAlpine) 11.10-0. J.Morrissey. 33/1.

BORDER FURY
bay gelding by Border Chief - Pre Fleuri.
1967 . . . Fell. (Mr D.Crossley-Cooke) 8.10-2. Mr.D.Crossley-Cooke.100/1.

BOB A JOB
chestnut gelding by Drybob - Brown Curls.
1967 . . . Finished 12th of 44. (Mr T.D.Hudson) 13.10-0. C.Young. 100/1.

BARBERYN
chestnut gelding by Bewildered - Mary Stuart.
1967 . . . Refused. (Mr P.Milner) 12.10-1. N.Mullins. 100/1.

BASSNET
brown gelding by Manet - Bassenden.
1967 . . . Fell. (Mr W.A.Silvester) 8.10-11. D.Nicholson. 10/1.
1968 . . . Brought down. (Mr W.A.Silvester) 9.10-12. D.Nicholson. 18/1.
1968 . . . Finished 5th of 30.(Mr W.A.Silvester) 10.10-12. J.Gifford. 100/8.

BEECHAM
bay gelding by Honeyway - Chamosura.
1968 . . . Fell. (Mr P.S.Williams) 9.10-0. B.R.Davies. 100/1.

BALLINABOINTRA
brown gelding by Artist's Son - Guapa.
1969 . . . Fell. (Mr L.Sachs) 10-10-1. P.Kelleway. 100/1.

BEECHES, THE
grey gelding by Mossborough - Foliage.
1969 . . . Finished 4th of 30. (Mr Paul Mellon) 9.10-1. W.Rees. 100/6.
1970 . . . Fell. (Mrs R.Lomer) 10.10-0. S.Mellor. 22/1.

BATTLEDORE
bay gelding by Combat - Samanda.
1970 . . . Brought down. (Mr W.E.Morton) 9.10-5. T.S.Murphy. 25/1.
1971 . . . Refused. (Mr W.E.Morton) 10.10-6. J.Enright. 40/1.

BOWGEENO
chestnut gelding by Bowsprit - Avageeno.
1970 . . . Fell. (Mr H.J.Joel) 10.10-13. J.Haine. 22/1.
1971 . . . Finished 4th of 38.(Mr V.T.Holt) 11.10-5. G.Thorner. 66/1.

BRIAN'S BEST
brown gelding by Richard Louis - Dromara V.
1971 . . . Brought down. (Lord Leverhulme) 11.10-11. R.Evans. 33/1.

BEAU BOB
chestnut gelding by Beau Prince - Bob Run.
1971 . . . Unseated rider. (Mr W.H.Whitbread) 8.10-3.R.Dennard.40/1.
1974 . . . Fell. (Mr W.H.Whitbread) 11.10-0. J.Glover. 100/1.
1975 . . . Fell. (Mr W.H.Whitbread) 12.10-1. J.Glover. 100/1.

BLACK SECRET
bay gelding by Black Tarquin - Secret Pact.
1971 . . . Finished 2nd of 38. (Mrs J.Watney) 7.11-5. Mr.J.Dreaper. 20/1.
1972 . . . Dead-heated 3rd of 42.(Mrs J.Watney) 8.11-2. S.Barker. 14/1.
1973 . . . Finished 10th of 38.(Mrs J.Watney) 9.11-2. S.Barker.22/1.

BULLOCK'S HORN
bay gelding by Rockavon - Let It Be Me.
1972 . . . Refused. (Mrs E.P.Barker) 9.10-0. Mr.R.Smith. 28/1.

BRIGHT WILLOW
chestnut gelding by Brightworthy - Willowbrook.
1972 . . . Finished 7th of 42. (Mr A.Cure) 11.10-1. W.Smith. 28/1.

BEAU PARC
bay gelding by Beau Sabreur - Hall It In.
1972 . . . Fell. (Mrs C.Gordon-Creed) 9.11-2. Mr.A.Nicholson. 50/1.
1973 . . . Pulled-up. (Mr D.Ancil) 10.10-1. A.Turnell. 100/1.

BEGGAR'S WAY
brown gelding by Royal Highway - Beggar Princess.
1973 . . . Fell. (Mr D.W.Samuel) 9.10-1. T.Kinane. 33/1.
1974 . . . Refused. (Mr H.Jackson) 10.10-2. V.Soane. 66/1.

BALLYATH
chestnut gelding by Pandofell - Leova.
1975 . . . Pulled-up. (Mr N.H.Le Mare) 9.10-0. J.Bourke. 100/1.

BALLYRICHARD AGAIN
brown gelding by Menelek - Newhaven Again.
1975 . . . Unseated rider. (Mr J.Webber) 10.10-1. A.Webber. 40/1.

BARONA
bay gelding by Neron - Barita.
1975 . . . Fell. (Mr W.H.Whitbread) 9.10-8. P.Kelleway. 40/1.
1976 . . . Finished 4th of 32.(Mr W.H.Whitbread) 10.10-6. P.Kelleway. 7/1Fav.*

BOOM DOCKER
chestnut gelding by Reverse Charge - Gigginstown.
1976 . . . Brought down. (Mr R.G.Pilkington) 9.10-0. J.Williams. 50/1.
1977 . . . Refused. (Mr R.G.Pilkington) 10.10-0. J.Williams. 66/1.

BALLYBRIGHT
black gelding by Sunny Way - Kilballyshea.
1976 . . . Fell. (Mrs B.A.Waller) 9.10-0. Mr.S.Morshead. 80/1.

BLACK TUDOR
chestnut gelding by Ace Of Clubs -Tudor Lace.
1976 . . . Finished 10th of 32. (Mr F.D.Chapman) 8.10-0. G.Thorner. 50/1.

BARONY FORT
chestnut gelding by Fortina - Sunset Slave.
1977 . . . Refused. (Mrs R.Brew) 12.10-1. Miss C.Brew. 200/1.

BURRATOR
bay gelding by Hot Brandy - Miss Bartok.
1977 . . . Fell. (Mrs B.Ward) 8.10-0. Mr.J.Docker. 50/1.
1978 . . . Fell. (Mrs M.A.Berry) 9.10-0. J.Suthern. 66/1.

BROWN ADMIRAL
brown gelding by Bargello - Dream Of Durrow.
1977 . . . Fell. (Mr H.R.K.Zeisel) 8.10-1. S.Morshead. 28/1.
1978 . . . Finished 10th of 37. (Mr H.R.K.Zeisel) 9.10-0. J.Burke. 33/1.
1979 . . . Unseated rider. (Mr T.A.Rathbone) 10.10-0. S.Morshead. 100/1.

BEN NEVIS
chestnut gelding by Cashiri - Ben Trumiss.
1979 . . . Brought down. (Mr R.C.Stewart,jnr) 11.11-2. Mr.C.Fenwick. 14/1.
1980 . . . WON. (Mr R.C.Stewart,jnr) 12.10-12. 30 Ran. Mr.C.Fenwick. 40/1.

BARNEY MACLYVIE
chestnut gelding by Cantab - Topping News.
1981 . . . Fell. (Mr M.Malone) 10.10-8. M.Lynch. 33/1.

BRYAN BORU
chestnut gelding by Armagnac Monarch - Pattara.
1981 . . . Refused. (Mr J.Carden) 10.10-0. Mr.J.Carden) 100/1.

BEACON TIME
brown gelding by Babu - The Combe.
1983 . . . Pulled-up. (Mr F.S.Markland) 9.10-6. J.J.O'Neill. 25/1.

BONUM OMEN
chestnut gelding by Spartan General - Bonded.
1983 . . . Refused. (Mr L.B.Thwaites) 9.10-9. K.Mooney. 15/1.

BEECH KING
bay gelding by Majetta - Beg Annagh.
1983 . . . Fell. (Mrs J.J.Jones) 9.10-3. Mr.P.Duggan. 60/1.
1984 . . . Finished 14th of 40. (Mrs J.J.Jones) 10.10-0. P.Kiely. 66/1.

BURNT OAK
bay gelding by Pitpan - Plebs Choice.
1984 . . . Pulled-up. (Brigadier C.B.Harvey) 8.10-7. P.Scudamore.25/1.

BUSH GUIDE
bay gelding by Flatbush - Guide Post.
1984 . . . Fell. (Miss Valerie Alder) 8.10-5. Miss V.Alder. 25/1.

BROOMY BANK
brown gelding by Ginger Boy - Straight Jet.
1984 . . . Finished 8th of 40. (Viscountess Boyne & Capt.J.M.G.Lumsden) 9.10-12. Mr.A.Wilson. 12/1.
1985 . . . Refused. (Viscountess Boyne & Capt.Lumsden) 10.10-7. Mr.A.Wilson. 33/1.
1986 . . . Finished 6th of 40.(Viscountess Boyne & Capt.Lumsden) 11.10-3. P.Scudamore. 20/1.

BLACKRATH PRINCE
bay gelding by Moulton- Moss-Ralia.
1985 . . . Finished 10th of 40. (Mr R.Dowsett) 9.10-0. B.Reilly. 66/1.

BALLYMILAN
bay gelding by Milan - Ballyfin.
1986 . . . Fell. (Mr F.Sheridan) 9.10-0. C.Hawkins. 50/1.

BALLINACURRA LAD
bay gelding by Chinatown - Lu-day.
1986 . . . Fell. (Mrs A.Moynihan) 11.10-8. G.Bradley. 22/1.

BEWLEY'S HILL
bay gelding by Mystic 11 - Miss Milt. Bred in U.S.A.
1987 . . . Brought down. (Mr W.B.Dixon Stroud,jnr) 10.12-0. Mr.W.B.Dixon Stroud,jnr. 100/1.

BROWN TRIX
bay gelding by Laurence O - Russian Fun.
1987 . . . Unseated rider. (Mr D.F.Pitcher) 9.10-8. Mr.D.F.Pitcher. 100/1.
1988 . . . Fell. (Mr D.F.Pitcher) 10.10-5. Mr.D.F.Pitcher.300/1.

BRIGHT DREAM
chestnut gelding by Lucifer - Dream Of Escart.
1987 . . . Finished 18th of 40. (Mr J.F.Holmes) 11.10-2. R.Rowe. 50/1.
1988 . . . Brought down. (Mr J.F.Holmes) 12.10-2. R.Rowe. 66/1.

BIG BROWN BEAR
bay gelding by Menelek - Lady Laurel.
1987 . . . Finished 13th of 40. (Mr G.B.Barlow) 10.10-2. R.Stronge. 200/1.
1988 . . . Refused. (Mr.G.B.Barlow) 11.10-2. R.Stronge. 66/1.

BROWN VEIL
brown mare by Don't Look - Miss Ormond.
1987 . . . Pulled-up. (Mrs A.G.Lawe) 12.10-1. Mr.M.Armytage. 200/1.

BRIT
bay mare by Pardigras - Brighty.
1987 . . . Finished 21st of 40. (Mr T.Jarvis) 8.10-1. A.Jones. 500/1.

BUCKO
bay gelding by Royal Buck - Tame Cindy.
1988 . . . Pulled-up. (Mr J.P.McManus) 11.10-5. M.Dwyer. 16/1.

BORDER BURG
bay gelding by Perhapsburg - Border Knife.
1988 . . . Pulled-up. (Mr J.S.Delahooke) 11.10-7. S.Sherwood. 16/1.

BRASS CHANGE
grey gelding by Town Crier - Brass Finisher.
1988 . . . Fell. (Mr N.J.Goodliff & Mr J.N.L.Banister) 10-10-0. M.Kinane. 100/1.

BONANZA BOY
bay gelding by Sir Lark - Vulmid.
1989 . . . Finished 8th of 40. (Mr S.Dunster) 8.11-1. P.Scudamore. 10/1.
1990 . . . Finished 16th of 38.(Mr S.Dunster) 9.11-9. P.Scudamore. 16/1.
1991 . . . Finished 5th of 40. (Mr S.Dunster) 10.11-7. P.Scudamore. 13/2Fav*
1992 . . . Unseated rider.(News International) 11.10-11. S.Smith Eccles. 25/1.

BEAMWAM
brown gelding by Bing II - Canute Lady.
1989 . . . Pulled-up. (Mr D.Naylor-Leyland & Mr Mel Morris) 11.10-6. Mr.D.Naylor-Leyland.100/1.

BOB TISDALL
chestnut gelding by Deep Run - Amphibian.
1989 . . . Refused. (K.Al-Said) 10.10-7. J.White. 25/1.
1990 . . . Finished 20th of 38. (Mr R.Ogden) 11.10-5.K.Mooney.66/1.

BARTRES
chestnut gelding by Le Bavard - Gail Borden.
1989 . . . Pulled-up. (Mrs D.Buik) 10.10-3. G.Bradley. 33/1.
1990 . . . Finished 8th of 38. (Mrs D.Buik) 11.10-0. M.Bowlby. 66/1.

BROWN WINDSOR
bay gelding by Kinglet - Cauldron.
1990 . . . Finished 4th of 38. (Mr W.Shand Kydd & Mr M.Buckley) 8.10-10. J.White. 7/1Fav*
1992 . . . Fell. (Mr W.Shand Kydd & Mr M.Buckley) 10.10-8. R.Dunwoody. 8/1.

BIGSUN
bay gelding by Sunyboy - Stella Roma.
1990 . . . Finished 6th of 38. (Mr J.F.Horn) 9.10-2. R.Dunwoody. 15/2.
1991 . . . Pulled-up. (Mr J.F.Horn) 10.10-4. R.Dunwoody. 9/1.

BALLYHANE
chestnut gelding by Crash Course - Golden Approach.
1991 . . . Finished 11th 40. (Mr H.J.Joel) 10.10-3. D.Murphy.22/1.

BUMBLES FOLLY
chestnut gelding by Sea Anchor - Casurina. Bred in New Zealand.
1991 . . . Pulled-up. (Mr C.Lewis) 10.10-5. J.Frost. 150/1.

BLUE DART
chestnut gelding by Cantab - Maisie Owen.
1991 . . . Unseated rider. (Mr H.K & Mrs D.Padfield) 11.10-2. H.Davies. 80/1.

BLACK HUMOUR
bay gelding by Buckskin - Artiste Gaye.
1994 . . . Fell. (Sir Andrew & Lady Lloyd Webber) 10.10-12. G.Bradley. 33/1.

BISHOPS HALL
brown geldin by Pimpernels Tune - Mariner's Dash.
1995 . . . Fell. (Mr J.Carroll) 9.10-0. C.Maude. 66/1.
1996 . . . Unseated rider. (Mr J.Carroll & Mr H.de Bromhead) 10.10-1. Mr.M.Armytage. 22/1.

BAVARD DIEU
chestnut gelding by Le Bavard - Graham Dieu.
1996 . . . Unseated rider. (Saguaro Stables) 8.10-1. J.F.Titley. 50/1.

BRACKENFIELD
chestnut gelding by Le Moss - Stable Lass.
1996 . . . Unseated rider. (Messrs T & J.A.Curry) 10.10-0. G.Lewis. 100/1.

CONRAD
1839 . . . Fell. (Captain Childe) Captain M.Becher.

CRAMP
1839 . . . Fell. (Mr Robertson) Wilmot.

CANNON BALL
1839 . . . Fell. (Mr Newcombe) Mr.Newcombe.

CHARITY
bay mare by Woodman, dam unknown.
1839 . . . Refused. (Mr Vevers) Hardy.
1841 . . . WON. (Lord Craven) Mr.A.Powell. 14/1.
1844 . . . Fell. (Mr Vevers) Powell. 13/1.

COLUMBINE
1840 . . . Fell. (Marquis of Waterford) Mr.Won.
1842 . . . Finished 5th of 15. (Lord Waterford) L.Byrne.

CIGAR
1841 . . . Finished 2nd of 11. (Mr Anderson) Mr.A.McDonough.4/1.

CONSUL
1842 . . . Fell. (Baron Rothschild) Oldaker. 10/1.
1843 . . . Refused. (Baron Rothschild) Oldaker. n/q.

CLAUDE DUVAL
1843 . . . Finished 4th of 16. (Colonel Hanson) Tomblin. n/q.

CROXBY
1843 . . . Pulled-up. (Honourable F.Craven) - 11-6. Mr.W.McDonough. n/q.

CAESAR
1844 . . . Finished 4th of 15. (Lord Maidstone) - 11-10. Barker. n/q.

CURE-ALL
brown gelding by Physician - dam unknown.
1845 . . . WON. (Mr W.Sterling Crawford) - 11-5. 15 Ran. Mr.W.J.Loft. n/q.
1846 . . . Pulled-up. (Mr W.J.Loft) -12-4. Mr.W.J.Loft. 16/1.

CLANSMAN
1845 . . . Fell. (Mr J.Kelly) - 11-6. Mr.J.Kelly. n/q.

CEREMONY
1845 . . . Failed to finish. (Mr Atkinson) - 11-0. T.Abbot. n/q.

CURATE, THE
1848 . . . Finished 2nd of 29. (Mr Brettle) -11-12. T.Olliver. 6/1.Fav*
1849 . . . Fell. (Mr Brettle) -11-11. Power. 6/1.

CULVERTHORPE
1846 . . . Finished 2nd of 22. (Mr Payne) - 11-4. Rackley. 12/1.
1847 . . . Finished 5th of 26. (Mr D'Arcy) - 11-6. H.N.Powell. 10/1 jnt/Fav.*

CARLOW
1846 . . . Fell. (Mr G.Lambden) - 11-4. T.Olliver. n/q.

CAVENDISH
1847 . . . Failed to finish. (Mr Walter) - 10-10. Scott. n/q.

CLINKER
1847 . . . Fell. (Mr Kirkpatrick) - 10-7. J.Mason. n/q.

CUMBERLAND LASSIE
1847 . . . Ran-out. (Mr Smith) - 10-4. Meddock. n/q.

CHANDLER
brown gelding by Doctor Faustus, dam unknown.
1848 . . . WON. (Capt.J.L.Little) 12.11-12. 29 Ran. Capt.J.L.Little. 12/1.
1849 . . . Finished 5th of 24. (Capt.J.L.Little) 13.12-2. Capt.J.L.Little. n/q.
1850 . . . Failed to finish. (Capt.J.L.Little) 14.11-3.Capt.J.L.Little.16/1.

CHEROOT
1848 . . . Failed to finsh. (Mr Davies) - 11-2. McGee. n/q.

COUNSELLOR
1848 . . . Fell. (Mr W.Coutts) - 10-12. Frisby. 25/1.

CORIANDER
1849 . . . Fell. (Mr E.W.Rudyard) - 10-6. Bally. n/q.

CHATHAM
1849 . . . Fell. (Lord Strathmore) - 10-6. Frisby. 20/1.

COLUMBINE
1850 . . . Failed to finish. (Mr Pocket) - 10-4. T.Olliver. 20/1.

CURRIG
1851 . . . Failed to finish. (Mr Barry) - 9-12. J.Debean. 25/1.
1852 . . . Pulled-up. (Mr J.Bourke) - 10-4. J.Debean. n/q.
1853 . . . Finished 7th of 21. (Mr J.Bourke) - 10-5. D.Wynne. 15/1.

CHIEFTAIN
1851 . . . Finished 4th of 24. (Mr Atkinson) - 10-12. Harrison. 10/1.

COGIA
1852 . . . Fell. (Mr J.Bird) - 9-9. J.Tasker. n/q.

CHATTERBOX
1853 . . . Pulled-up. (Mr Bretherton) - 9-8. Mr.McGaman. n/q.

CRABBS
1853 . . . Pulled-up. (Mr J.R.Henderson) - 9-2. W.Fowler. n/q.
1854 . . . Finished 2nd of 20. (Mr J.R.Henderson) - 9-2. D.Wynne. 10/1.

COCKCROW
1854 . . . Failed to finish. (Lord Waterford) 6.9-8. Maher. 25/1.

CUTAWAY
1855 . . . Failed to finish. (Mr A.Sait) - 9-10. C.Boyce. 50/1.

CASSE CON
1857 . . . Failed to finish. (Baron Monuecove) - 10-2. Johnson. n/q.

CONRAD
1858 . . . Finished 5th of 16. (Mr Tempest) - 8-4. E.Jones. 14/1. Remounted*

CLAUDIUS
1858 . . . Fell. (Mr J.C.Manby) - 10-7. Poole. n/q.
1859 . . . Failed to finish. (Mr J.C.Manby) - 10-0. T.Olliver. n/q.

CURATE, THE
1860 . . . Fell. (Mr Burling) - 9-4. G.Eatwell. n/q.

CONGREVE
1860 . . . Refused. (Capt.Clifton) - 9-0. Gammeridge. n/q.

CONDUCTOR, THE
1861 . . . Fell. (Mr G.Hodgman) - 8-12. J.Nightingall. 40/1.

COCKATOO
1861 . . . Fell. (Mr S.Gooderham) - 8-8. C.Green. 7/1.

CHESTER
1864 . . . Finished 3rd of 25. (Mr Dalton) - 10-0. W.White. 40/1.

CZAR, THE
1865 . . . Fell. (Mr Goodliffe) - 10-0. Mr.A.Goodman. 20/1.

CORTOLVIN
brown gelding by Chicken or Cheerful Horn. Not in the General Stud Book.
1866 . . . Finished 2nd of 30. (Lord Poulett) 7.11-6. J.Page. 8/1.
1867 . . . WON. (Duke of Hamilton) 8.11-13. 23 Ran. J.Page. 16/1.

CREOLE
1866 . . . Finished 3rd of 30. (Mr Welfitt) -10-10.G.Waddington. 15/1.

CUTLER
1866 . . . Failed to finish. (Mr Barber) - 10-0. Thorpe. 50/1.

COLUMBIA
1866 . . . Failed to finish. (Mr R.Herbert) - 10-10. Mr.Herbert. 100/15.

CAPTAIN CROSSTREE
1868 . . . Finished 4th of 21. (Mr R.Herbert) - 10-5. W.Reeves. 33/1.

CHIMNEY SWEEP
1868 . . . Broke leg. (Lord Coventry) 6.12-0. J.Adams. 7/1Fav.*

CHARMING WOMAN
1868 . . . Failed to finish. (Mr J.Milling) - 10-0. Terratta,jnr. 66/1.

COLONEL, THE
brown horse by Knight Of Kars - Boadicea. Not in the General Stud Book. Bred by Mr J.Weyman.
1869 . . . WON. (Mr J.Weyman) 6.10-7. 22 Ran. G.Stevens.100/7.
1870 . . . WON. (mr J.Weyman) 7.11-12. 23 Ran. G.Stevens. 7/2Fav.*
1871 . . . Finished 6th of 25. (Baron Oppenheim) 8.12-8.G.Stevens. 8/1.

CINNA
1870 . . . Failed to finish. (Baron Finot) - 10-7. Count. 33/1.

CRISTAL
1870 . . . Pulled-up. (Lord Poulett) 5.10-6. Mr.Crawshaw. 100/6.

CASSE TETE
chestnut mare by Trumpeter - Constance. Bred by the Duke of Newcastle.
1870 . . . Failed to finish. (Mr E.Brayley) 5.10-0.J.Rudd. 100/1.
1871 . . . Failed to finish. (Mr E.Brayley) 6.10-10.J.Rudd. 66/1.
1872 . . . WON. (Mr E.Brayley) 7.10-0. 25 Ran. J.Page. 20/1.
1873 . . . Knocked-over. (Mr E.Brayley) 8.11-3. J.Page. 10/1.
1874 . . . Fell. (Mr E.Brayley) 9.11-0. H.Day. 100/15.

CECIL
1871 . . . Fell. (Mr Etches) 6.10-6. R.I'Anson. 10/1.
1873 . . . Fell. (Mr Etches) 8.10-9. R.Wyatt. 10/1.

CINDERELLA
1872 . . . Fell. (Lord Anglesey) 5. 10-7. J.Adams. 100/15.
1873 . . . Pulled-up. (Lord Anglesey) 6. 10-13. J.Adams. 100/12.

COLUMBINE
brown mare by Merryman, dam unknown.
1873 . . . Finished 3rd of 28. (Mr W.H.P.Jenkins) - 10-9.Harding. n/q.
1874 . . . Finished 7th of 22. (Mr W.H.P.Jenkins) - 10-6.Harding. 12/1.

CURRAGH RANGER
bay gelding by The Ranger - Antelope.
1873 . . . Failed to Finish. (Capt.J.F.Montgomery) 7.11-3. Ryan. 25/1.

CRAWLER
bay gelding by Loiterer - Curatrix.
1873 . . . Fell. (Mr Lynton) 6.10-10. Mr.A.Yates. 50/1.

CONGRESS
brown gelding by Compromise - Countess.
1873 . . . Failed to finish. (Mr H.Wilson) 7.10-10. Mr.E.P.Wilson.40/1.
1874 . . . Fell. (Mr H.Wilson) 8.11-4. Mr.E.P.Wilson. 16/1.
1875 . . . Finished 8th of 19. (Mr Gomm) 9.12-4. Mr.E.P.Wilson. 7/1.
1876 . . . Finished 2nd of 19. (Mr Gomm) 10.11-8. Mr.E.P.Wilson. 25/1.
1877 . . . Finished 2nd of 16. (Lord Lonsdale) 11.12-7. J.Cannon. 20/1.

CHARLIE
bay gelding by Van Galen - Eccola.
1873 . . . Fell. (Mr T.Horwood) - 10-9. Gregory. n/q.

CHIMNEY SWEEP
brown gelding by Planet, dam unknown.
1874 . . . Finished 2nd of 22. (Lord Marcus Beresford) 7.10-2. J.Jones. 25/1.
1876 . . . Finished 4th of 19. (Lord Marcus Beresford) 9.10-8. J.Jones. 25/1.
1877 . . . Finished 4th of 16. (Lord Marcus Beresford) 10.10-13. J.Jones. 7/1.

CLONAVE
bay or brown horse by Mainstay - Crystal.
1875 . . . Fell. (Sir W.Nugent) 7.12-1. Gavin. 9/1.
1876 . . . Refused. (Sir W.Nugent) 8.11-5. Gavin. 25/1.

CHANDOS
chestnut horse by Oxford, dam unknown.
1876 . . . Fell. (Capt.J.Machell) 6.11-7. Jewitt. 3/1.Fav.*

CITIZEN
chestnut gelding by Citadel - Beauty.
1877 . . . Finished 7th of 16. (Sir J.L.Kaye) 6.10-5. W.Reeves. 100/8.

CURATOR
bay horse by Lecturer - Curative.
1878 . . . Finished 6th of 12. (Lord Lonsdale) 5.10-5. Mr.E.P.Wilson. 20/1.

CONCHA
brown horse by Asteroid - Arapeile.
1879 . . . Pulled-up. (Sir T.Hesketh) 6.10-2. Mr.W.B.Morris. 50/1.

CROSS QUESTION
bay gelding by The Lawyer - Waver.
1881 . . . Finished 7th of 13. (Mr R.Carington) 6.10-0. J.Jones.100/15.

CYRUS
bay gelding by Xenophon, dam by Newton-le-Willows.
1882 . . . Finished 2nd of 12. (Mr J.Gubbins) 5.10-9.Mr.T.beasley. 9/2.
1884 . . . Finished 4th of 15. (Mr J.B.Leigh) 7.12-2. J.Jewitt. 9/1.

CORTOLVIN
bay gelding by Gunboat - Spitfire.
1883 . . . Fell. (Lord Rossmore) 6.10-5. Barker. 33/1.
1884 . . . Fell. (Lord Rossmore) 7.10-0. Capt.Smith. 100/12.
1886 . . . Finished 7th of 23. (Mr Abington) 9.11-7. W.Dollery. 50/1.

CANDAHAR
bay horse by Scottish Chief - Fenella.
1885 . . . Refused. (Mr H.B.Craig) 6.10-12. W.Hunt. 25/1.

CORONET
bay gelding by Blood Royal - Mavourneen.
1886 . . . Finished 6th of 23. (Mr J.G.Muir) 5.10-7.Capt.Lee Barber. 3/1 Fav.*

CONSCRIPT
bay gelding by Austerlitz - L'Orpheline.
1886 . . . Fell. (Captain Childe) 5.10-0. H.Escott. n/q.

CHANCELLOR
bay gelding by Exchequer, dam unknown.
1887 . . . Finished 6th of 16. (Capt.Foster) 7.10-12. Mr.W.H.Moore. 20/1.
1888 . . . Failed to finish. (Mr Wardour) 8.11-5. Mr.W.H.Moore. 15/2 jnt/Fav.*

CHANCERY
bay gelding by Howth or Rob Roy - Fair Play.
1887 . . . Finished 5th of 16. (Mr A.L.Popham) 9.11-6. W.Dollery. 100/1.

CORK
bay gelding by Speculation - Virginia.
1888 . . . Fell. (Doctor Adrian) 7.10-6. Mr.Woodland. 100/1.

COME AWAY
bay gelding by Umpire or Cambuslang - Larkaway.
1891 . . . WON. (Mr W.G.Jameson) 7.11-12. 21 Ran. Mr.H.Beasley. 4/1.Fav*

CLOISTER
bay gelding by Ascetic - Grace 11. Bred by Lord Fingall.
1891 . . . Finished 2nd of 21. (Lord Dudley) 7.11-7. Capt.E.R.Owen. 20/1.
1892 . . . Finshed 2nd of 25. (Mr C.G.Duff) 8.12-3. Mr.J.C.Dormer. 11/2.Fav*
1893 . . . WON. (Mr C.G.Duff) 9.12-7. 15 Ran.W.Dollery. 9/2Fav.*

CRUISER
chestnut gelding by Gunboat, dam unknown.
1891 . . . Finished 5th of 21. (Major Bunbury) 6.10-8. Mr.T.Beasley. 7/1.
1892 . . . Finished 7th of 25. (Capt.J.Byrom) 7.11-7. Mr.W.P.Cullen. 25/1.

CHOUFLEUR
chestnut gelding by Macaroon - Blanchefleur.
1891 . . . Fell. (Lord Zetland) 5.11-3. T.Kavanagh. 25/1.
1893 . . . Pulled-up. (M.T.Toynbee) 7.10-13. T.Kavanagh. 100/1.

CARROLLSTOWN
brown horse by Hollywood, dam unknown.
1894 . . . Finished 7th of 14. (Lord Shaftesbury) 7.10-13. G.Williamson. 50/1.

CALCRAFT
pedigree unknown -
1894 . . . Fell. (Mr J.C.Leslie) 7. 9-10. Mr.A.H.Ripley. 100/1.

CATHAL
bay gelding by Cassock or Hominy - Daffodil.
1895 . . . Finshed 2nd of 19. (Mr F.B.Atkinson) 6.10-9. H.Escott. 100/8.
1896 . . . Finshed 8th of 28. (Mr R.Ward) 7.11-13. Mr.R.Ward. 100/9.
1897 . . . Fell. (Mr R.Ward) 8.11-10. Mr.R.Ward. 7/1.
1898 . . . Finished 2nd of 25.(Mr R.Ward) 9.11-5. Mr.R.Ward. 7/1.

COCK OF THE HEATH
bay gelding by Ascetic - Caper 111.
1895 . . . Bolted . (Mr H.M.Dyas) 7.10-2. W.Hoysted. 100/6.

CAUSTIC
bay horse by George Mansfield - Capability.
1895 . . . Fell. (Mr B.Benison) 6.10-1. Mr.A.Gordon. 100/1.
1896 . . . Fell. (Mr B.Benison) 7. 9-7. H.Mason. 100/7.

CLAWSON
bay gelding by Wizard - Clove.
1896 . . . Fell. (Mr A.Jolland) 6.10-4. Mr.W.H.Bissill. 66/1.
1897 . . . Pulled-up. (Mr A.Jolland) 7.10-10. Mr.W.H.Bissill. 33/1.

CONTINENTAL, THE
bay gelding by Boulevard - Fair Haven.
1897 . . . Fell. (Mr A.H.Hudson) 6.10-2. H.Brown. 100/1.

● **Cloister won the National in 1893 carrying 12st 7lbs.**

CHEVY CHASE
chestnut gelding by Ballinafad - Lady Jane.
1897 . . . Pulled-up. (Mr F.F.MacCabe) 8. 9-13. A.Anthony. 28/1.

CRUISKEEN
bay mare by Bacchus - The Sap.
1898 . . . Pulled-up. (Mrs Sadleir-Jackson) 6.10-0. T.Kavanagh.100/1.

CUSHALEE MAVOURNEEN
bay mare by Torpedo, dam unknown.
1898 . . . Pulled-up. (Mr G.R.Powell) 7. 9-11. H.Smith. 100/1.

CORNER
brown gelding by Falcon - Little Duchess.
1899 . . . Finished 11th of 19. (Mr W.Harris) 8. 9-7. D.Read. 200/1.

COVERT HACK
bay or brown gelding by Hackler- Cinnamon.
1900 . . . Fell. (Capt.Eustace Loder) 6.11-0. F.Mason. 100/6.
1901 . . . Finished 7th of 24. (Major Eustace Loder) 7.11-4. A.Anthony. 10/1.

CORAGH HILL
bay gelding by Gallinule - Jenny.
1901 . . . Finished 6th of 24. (Mr J.Lonsdale) aged 9-9. C.Hogan. 25/1.

CUSHENDUN
chestnut gelding by Timothy - Craftiness.
1901 . . . Failed to finish. (Capt.H.A.Johnstone) 6.11-2. Mr.G.S.Davies. 20/1.
1903 . . . Fell. (Mr Horatio Bottomley) 8.10-10. F.E.Cole. 100/1.
1904 . . . Fell. (Mr Horatio Bottomley) 9.10-7. D.Morris. n/q.

COOLGARDIE
brown gelding by St Serf - Trentonia.
1901 . . . Failed to finish. (Mr R.Davy) 7.10-6. A.Waddington. 40/1.

CHIT CHAT
chestnut gelding by May Boy - Small Talk.
1901 . . . Failed to finish. (Capt.J.Machell) 8.10-2. C.Clack. 25/1.

COMFIT
bay gelding by Butterscotch, dam by Clanronald.
1904 . . . Fell. (Mr F.Bibby) 6.10-5. F.Hartigan. 25/1.
1906 . . . Fell. (Mr F.Bibby) 8. 11-0. F.Mason. 10/1.

COTTENSHOPE
chestnut gelding by Enthusiast - Maidstone.
1905 . . . Finished 7th of 27. (Mr C.Levy) 9. 9-11. D.Morris. 66/1.

CRAUTACAUN
brown gelding by Hackler - Fair Saxon.
1906 . . . Finshed 4th of 23. (Mr J.Wynford Philipps) 8.10-6. I.Anthony. 100/6.

CANTER HOME
bay gelding by Retreat - Canterbury.
1906 . . . Fell. (Lord Sefton) 11. 9-13. A.Aylin. 66/1.

CENTRE BOARD
bay gelding by Speed - Ballast.
1907 . . . Refused. (Lord Howard de Walden) 7.10-11. J.Cain. 20/1.

CHORUS
chestnut mare by Chorister - Helena.
1908 . . . Finished 8th of 24. (Mr Foxhall Keene) aged.10-5. R.Chadwick. 66/1.

CAUBEEN
bay horse by Chad - Revenue Cutter.
1909 . . . Finished 3rd of 32. (Mr F.Bibby) 8.11-7. F.Mason. 20/1.
1910 . . . Knocked-over. (Mr F.Bibby) 9.11-8. F.Mason. 8/1.
1911 . . . Fell. (Mr F.Bibby) 10.11-5. A.Newey. 8/1.
1912 . . . Failed to finish. (Mr F.Bibby) 11.11-5. A.Newey. 100/9.

CARSEY
bay gelding by Kersey - Fiction.
1909 . . . Finished 9th of 32. (Mr J.M.Kerne) 6.10-8. Mr.J.M.Kerne. 100/1.
1910 . . . Finished 4th of 25. (Prince Hatzfeldt) 7.10-7. E.R.Morgan. 100/8.
1911 . . . Fell. (Mr C.H.Wildenburg) 8.10-6. P.Cowley. 100/9.
1912 . . . Finished 4th of 24.(Mr C.H.Wildenburg) 9.10-13. Mr.H.W.Tyrwhitt-Drake.100/8.
1913 . . . Finished 3rd of 22.(Mr C.H.Wildenburg) 10.12-0. Mr.H.W.Tyrwhitt-Drake.100/9. Remounted*

COUNT RUFUS
chestnut gelding by Wise Count - dam by Araby.
1909 . . . Finished 16th of 32. (Mr W.Charters) aged.10-0. W.Payne. 50/1.

CAPTAIN FARRELL
bay gelding by Laveno - Mast Head.
1910 . . . Refused. (Sir J.Smiley) 6. 9-10. G.Brown. n/q.

CIRCASSIAN'S PRIDE
bay or brown mare by Circassian - Nyanza.
1911 . . . Knocked-over. (Lady Torrington) 7. 9-13. I.Morgan. 25/1.

CARDER
bay horse by Hackler - Cinnamon.
1911 . . . Fell. (Mr C.Luttrell) 8. 9-7. B.Roberts. 50/1.

COVERTCOAT
bay gelding by Hackler - Cinnamon. Bred Mr.J.J.Maher.
1912 . . . Failed to finish. (Sir C.Assheton-Smith) 6.10-5. J.Walsh,jnr. 33/1.
1913 . . . WON. (Sir C.Assheton-Smith) 7.11-6. 22 Ran. P.Woodland. 100/9.
1914 . . . Failed to finish. (Sir C.Assheton-Smith) 8.12-7. P.Woodland. 7/1.Fav.*

42

COUVREFEU II
bay or brown gelding by Curfew - Regime.
1914 . . . Failed to finish. (Sir W.Nelson) 10.11-7. Mr.J.R.Anthony. 20/1.
* 1916 . . . Completed course. (Sir W.Nelson) 12.12-7. F.Dainty. 40/1.

CHANG
chestnut gelding by Cupid - Threnody.
* 1917 . . . Finished 2nd of 19. (Mr H.Trimmer) 7. 9-9. W.Smith. 11/2.
* 1918 . . . Completed course. (Mr F.S.Watts) 8.10-2. Mr.O.J.Casebourne. 100/8.
1919 . . . Failed to finish. (Mr F.S.Watts) 9. 9-8. J.Reardon. 50/1.

CARRIG PARK
bay gelding by Succoth or Bushey Park - Ardcarrig.
* 1917 . . . Fell. (Mr Douglas Stuart) 7.11-6. C.Hawkins. 7/2.Fav.*

CHARLBURY
bay gelding by Succoth - May Hack.
* 1917 . . . Pulled-up. (Mr H.Trimmer) 9.10-6. J.Dillon. n/q.
* 1918 . . . Completed course. (Mr H.Trimmer) 10. 9-10. J.Dillon. 33/1.
1919 . . . Pulled-up. (Mr H.Trimmer) 11. 9-7. P.Woodland. 7/1.
1921 . . . Fell. (Mr H.Trimmer) 13. 9-7. B.Ellis. n/q.

CAPTAIN DREYFUS
bay or brown gelding by Santoi - Madame Dreyfus.
* 1918 . . . Finiished 2nd of 17. (Mr F.R.Hunt) 10.12-7. J.Reardon.20/1.

CLEAR MONEY
bay gelding by Matchmaker - Mollusc.
* 1918 . . . Completed course. (Col.H.P.Burnyeat) 5.11-2. Mr.Pepper. 100/1.

CLONREE
bay gelding by Atlas - Miss Eager. formerly named Kruiscik.
1920 . . . Fell. (Mr O'Toole) 6.10-10. E.R.Morgan. 25/1.
1921 . . . Fell. (Mrs A.Blain) 7.12-0. T.Hulme. 33/1.
1922 . . . Fell. (Mrs A.Blain) 8.11-6. J.Mahoney. 33/1.

CUPID'S DART
chestnut gelding by Target - Heart's Desire.
1921 . . . Fell. (Mr James Daly) 7.10-0. J.Hogan,jnr. n/q.

CLASHING ARMS
brown gelding by St Martin - Glen Inch.
1922 . . . Fell. (Colonel W.S.Anthony) 7.11-3. J.R.Anthony. 9/1.

CONFESSOR
chestnut gelding by Magic - Reverend Mother.
1922 . . . Fell. (Mr T.Galletly) 8.10-0. R.Trudgill. n/q.

CONJUROR II
bay gelding by Garb Or - dam by Juggler.
1923 . . . Finished 3rd of 28. (Major C.Dewʰurst) 11.11-0. Mr.C.P.Dewhurst. 100/6.
1924 . . . Knocked-over. (Major C.Dewhurst) 12.11-0. Mr.H.A.Brown. 5/2.Fav.*

CINDERS II
grey gelding - pedigree unknown -
1923 . . . Finished 7th of 28. (Mr J.H.Betts) 11.10-2. W.Williams. n/q.

CANNY KNIGHT
bay gelding by The White Knight - Ceannacroc.
1923 . . . Fell. (Mr Adam Scott) 9.10-0. A.Vause. n/q.

CINZANO
brown gelding by Dalmellington - Yvonne de Feyrolles.
1923 . . . Refused. (Mr J.Kemp) 6.10-0. F.Brown. n/q.

CHIN CHIN
bay horse by Santoi - Focus.
1924 . . . Fell. (Sir F.Price) 8.11-7. A.Stubbs. 25/1.

CLONSHEEVER
bay gelding by Avidity - Wise Gull.
1924 . . . Fell. (Mr J.E.Tyrrell) 9.11-2. F.Brookes. 66/1.

CASH BOX
bay gelding by Just Cause - Mary Hughes.
1926 . . . Fell. (Mr R.Havelock-Allen) 9.10-0.Mr.R.Read. 66/1.
1927 . . . Fell. (Mr R.Havelock-Allen) 10.10-12. G.Green. 100/1.

CORAZON
chestnut gelding by Charles O'Malley - Noramac.
Fell . . . Fell. (Major F.W.Barrett) 9.10-8. T.Morgan. 100/1.

COYOTE, THE
bay gelding by Sea Sick - Francisca.
1928 . . . Failed to finish. (Mr V.Emanuel) 8.11-12. J.Hogan,jnr. 40/1.

CARFAX
brown gelding by Drinmore - Zena.
1928 . . . Failed to finish. (Mr B.W.Ancil) 12.10-10. Mr.B.W.Ancil. 25/1.
1929 . . . Fell. (Mr B.W.Ancil) 13.11-1. Mr.B.W.Ancil.40/1.

COMMONSIDE
bay gelding by Very Wise - Silda.
1928 . . . Failed to finish. (Lt.Col.G.S.Brooke) 9.10-5. Mr.C.B.Harvey. 200/1.

CAMPERDOWN
bay gelding by Apprentice - dam unknown.
1929 . . . Finished 10th of 66.(Mrs E.Hutchinson) 10.10-9. Mr.K.Goode. 200/1. Remounted*

CLORINGO
chestnut gelding by Jingo - Sweet Clorane.
1929 . . . Fell. (Mr J.C.Paterson) 8.10-0. A.Wall. 200/1.

CRYPTICAL
bay gelding by St Gris - The Crypt.
1930 . . . Pulled-up. (Mr F.H.Bowcher) 15.10-6. J.Bisgood. 100/1.

CURTAIN RAISER
chestnut gelding by Scene Lifter - Longestline.
1930 . . . Pulled-up. (Mrs E.W.B.Leake) 7.10-0. P.Powell. 100/1.

COUP DE CHAPEAU
bay gelding by Chardonneret - Mistinguette.
1932 . . . Fell. (Mr J.Drake) aged. 11-10. G.Wilson. 28/1.
1933 . . . Fell. (Mr J.Drake) aged. 12-2. G.Wilson. 28/1.

COLLIERY BAND
chestnut gelding by Polyphonic - What Fettle.
1933 . . . Completed the course. (Mrs H.M.Collins) 9.11-9. G.Hardy. 40/1.

CHADD'S FORD
chestnut gelding by Essexford - Edina.
1933 . . . Completed the course. (Mrs F.Ambrose Clark) aged. 10-7. Mr.E.Williams. 50/1.

CANTILLIUS II
brown gelding by Kircubbin - Cestus.
1934 . . . Fell. (Mr V.H.Smith) 8.10-7. J.Mason. 22/1.

CASTLE IRWELL
bay gelding by Brave Chap - Miss Gaunt.
1935 . . . Feil. (Mr G.H.Bostwick) 7.10-10. Mr.G.H.Bostwick. 100/7.
1936 . . . Finished 7th of 35. (Mr G.H.Bostwick) 8.11-3. Mr.G.H.Bostwick. 8/1.

CROWN PRINCE
bay gelding by The Winter King - dam unknown.
1936 . . . Finished 4th of 35. (Mr R.Strutt) 11.10-7. Mr.R.Strutt. 66/1.
1937 . . . Finished 5th of 33. (Mr R.Strutt) 12.10-6.Mr.R.Strutt. 50/1.

COOLEEN
chestnut mare by Loch Lomond - Trim And Tidy.
1937 . . . Finished 2nd of 33. (Mr J.V.Rank) 9.11-4. J.Fawcus. 33/1.
1938 . . . Finished 4th of 36. (Mr J.V.Rank) 10.11-8. J.Fawcus. 8/1 jnt/Fav.*
1939 . . . Finished 4th of 37.(Mr J.V.Rank) 11.11-8. J.Fawcus. 22/1

COMEDIAN
chestnut gelding by Burslem - Dodo.
1936 . . . Finished 10th of 35. (Mr R.E.Morel) 8.10-7. G.Turner.100/1. Remounted*

CASTLE VIEW
bay gelding by Cottage - Llwyn-yr-Eos.
1936 . . . Fell. (Mr H.Dyke Dennis) 9.10-7. G.R.Owen. 100/1.

CABIN FIRE
bay gelding by Cottage - Shining Hope.
1938 . . . Fell. (Mrs P.Kiely) 7.10-4. T.Hyde. 33/1.

CORN LAW
bay gelding by Foxlaw - Corusca.
1940 . . . Fell. (Mr W.Hutchinson) 8.10-3. T.McNeill. 100/1.

CLOSURE
bay or brown gelding by Obliterate - Apres Vous.
1946 . . . Fell. (Mr J.D.Norris) 9.10-0. Mr H.Applin. 100/1.

CAUGHOO
brown gelding by Within The Law - Silverdale. Bred by Mr.P.Power.
1947 . . . WON. (Mr J.J.McDowell) 8.10-0. 57 Ran. E.Dempsey. 100/1.
1948 . . . Pulled-up. (Mr J.J.McDowell) 9.11-1. E.Dempsey. 28/1.
1949 . . . Ran-out. (Mr J.J.McDowell) 10.11-0. D.McCann. 66/1.

CLYDUFFE
bay gelding by Knight Of Kilcash - Countess Rowland.
1947 . . . Completed the course. (Mr N.P.Donaldson) 12.10-0. M.Hogan. 50/1.
1949 . . . Finished 10th of 43. (Mr A.A.Stuart Black) 14.10-0. J.Power. 66/1.

CLONABOY
brown gelding by Piper's Son - Clonkea.
1948 . . . Fell. (Mr A.H.Wood) 10.10-10. E.Hannigan.66/1.

CLONCARRIG
brown gelding Bidar - Miss Dulcie.
1948 . . . Fell. (Sir Allan Gordon-Smith) 8.10-13. Mr.J.Hislop. 22/1.
1949 . . . Fell. (Sir Allan Gordon-Smith) 9.11-7. K.Gilsenan. 18/1.
1950 . . . Fell. (Sir Allan Gordon-Smith) 10.11-9. R.Turnell. 25/1.
1951 . . . Fell. (Mr J.Olding) 11.12-0. R.Turnell. 10/1.
1952 . . . Fell. (Mr W.Dugdale) 12.11-13. Mr.W.Dugdale. 50/1.
1953 . . . Fell. (Mr W.Dugdale) 13.11-5. Mr.R.McCreery. 66/1.

CROMWELL
bay gelding by Landscape Hill - Fort Defiance.
1948 . . . Finished 3rd of 43. (Lord Mildmay) 7.10-11. Lord Mildmay. 33/1.
1949 . . . Finished 4th of 43. (Lord Mildmay) 8.11-3. Lord Mildmay. 6/1.Fav.*
1950 . . . Fell (Lord Mildmay) 9.11-4. Lord Mildmay. 18/1.

CADDIE II
brown gelding by Link Boy - Brown Jill.
1948 . . . Fell. (Mr Paul Mellon) 10.11-7. J.Maguire. 50/1.
1949 . . . Fell. (Mr Paul Mellon) 11.10-10. J.Maguire. 66/1.

CAVALIERO
bay gelding by Steel Point - dam by Baytown.
1949 . . . Fell. (Mr W.R.Porter) 8.11-1. J.Brogan. 100/8.
1950 . . . Fell. (Mr W.R.Porter) 9.11-6. J.A.Bullock. 66/1.

CELTIC CROSS
bay gelding by Cameronian - Bona Dea.
1949 . . . Fell. (Mr T.Southern) 11.10-0. J.Parkin. 66/1.

COMERAGH
bay gelding by Brownie - Careless Crag.
1950 . . . Fell. (Major Noel Furlong) 9.11-0. P.J.Kelly. 50/1.

CONFUCIUS
bay gelding by Sun Yat-sen - Coiner.
1950 . . . Pulled-up. (Mr J.P.Frost) 9.10-0. C.O'Connor. 40/1.
1951 . . . Fell. (Mr J.Mayson) 10.10-0. M.O'Dwyer. 100/1.

COTTAGE WELCOME
bay gelding by Cottage - Altavon.
1950 . . . Fell. (Mr E.Dobson) 11.10-3. C.Hook. 100/1.

COLUMN
bay gelding by Columcille - French Marten.
1950 . . . Brought down. (Mr A.Sainsbury) 10.10-2. A.Mullins. 100/1.
1951 . . . Fell. (Sir Arthur Pilkington) 11.10-1. Mr.A.Corbett. 100/1.
1952 . . . Finished 8th of 47.(Sir A.Pilkington) 12.10-0. P.Pickford. 100/1.

CASTLEDERMOT
bay gelding by Foroughi - Layola.
1950 . . . Fell. (Mrs M.H.Keogh) 8.10-9. T.Molony. 20/1.

CADAMSTOWN
bay gelding by Walinson - Greek Fairy.
1950 . . . Fell. (Mr R.McIlhagga) 10.10-8. E.Dempsey. 66/1.
1951 . . . Fell. (Mr A.E.Bullen) 11.10-4. J.Dowdeswell. 50/1.

CAESAR'S WIFE
grey mare by Tiberius - Borrow.
1951 . . . Fell. (Mr G.B.Rogers) 9.10-8. Mr.G.B.Rogers. 100/1.
1952 . . . Unseated rider. (Mr G.B.Rogers) 10.10-6. Mr.G.B.Rogers. 50/1

COURT PAINTER
bay gelding by Rose Princess - Sixtime.
1952 . . . Refused. (Lt.Col.E.Harris-St John) 12.10-0. F.Carroll. 100/1.

CREAM OF THE BORDER
chestnut gelding by Trigo - Devonshire Cream.
1952 . . . Refused. (Mr G.Mackie) 7.10-0, A.Kelly. 50/1.
1953 . . . Brought down.(Mr G.Mackie) 8.10-0. B.Wilkinson. 66/1.

CARDINAL ERROR
bay gelding by His Reverence - Etna May.
1952 . . . Brought-down. (Lady Joicey) 8.11-8. J.Power. 33/1.
1953 . . . Fell. (Lady Joicey) 9.11-5. R.Curran. 100/7.

CONEYBURROW
bay gelding by Foroughi - Glenamaddy.
1954 . . . Fell. (Mr I.E.Levy) 8.10-11. P.Taaffe. 8/1.

CHURCHTOWN
bay gelding by Abian - Honey Lomond.
1954 . . . Finished 4th of 29. (Mrs M.V.O'Brien) 9.10-3. T.Taaffe.10/1.

COPP
Bay gelding by Pinxit - Crested Plover.
1955 . . . Fell. (Mr C.C.Allan) 11.10-8. T.Molony. 7/1Fav*

CLEARING
bay gelding by Labrador - Celimene VI.
1955 . . . Finished 7th of 30. (Mr M.Kinglsey) 8.10-2. R.J.Hamey.50/1.
1956 . . . Finished 8th of 29. (Mr M.Kingsley) 9.10-1.J.A.Bullock.66/1.
1957 . . . Fell. (Mr M.Kingsley) 10.10-1. R.Curson. 45/1.

CAREY'S COTTAGE
bay gelding by Uncle Willie - Halo.
1955 . . . Finished 3rd of 30. (Mr D.J.Coughlan) 8.10-11. T.Taaffe. 20/1.
1956 . . . Finished 7th of 29. (Colonel W.H.Whitbread) 9.10-11. R.Turnell. 10/1.
1957 . . . Refused. (Colonel W.H.Whitbread) 10.10-6. T.Shone.50/1.

CROFTER, THE
brown gelding by Tartan - Dawn Cottage.
1957 . . . Finished 5th of 35. (Lt.Col.D.M.Baird) 9.10-0. J.Power. 66/1.
1958 . . . Fell. (Lt.Col.D.M.Baird) 10.10-0. J.Power. 40/1.
1959 . . . Fell. (L.t.Col.D.M.Baird) 11.10-0. S.Mellor. 100/1.

CHERRY ABBOT
chestnut gelding by Cherry Lad 11 - Anetta.
1957 . . . Fell. (Mr C.Ferrie) 12.10-0. G.Underwood. 66/1.

CHINA CLIPPER II
bay gelding by Long Walk - dam by Gartoi.
1957 . . . Fell. (Major W.D.Gibson) 10.10-3. Maj.W.D.Gibson. 66/1.

COLLEDGE MASTER
bay gelding by Grandmaster - Collence.
1958 . . . Pulled-up. (Mr L.R.Morgan) 8.11-2. W.Rees. 25/1.
1962 . . . Finished 14th of 32. (Mr L.R.Morgan) 12.10-13. Mr L.R.Morgan. 33/1.

COMEDIAN'S FOLLY
bay gelding by Jubilee Day - Swift Eagle.
1958 . . . Refused. (Mr L.G.Scott) 10.10-0. Mr.D.Scott. 66/1.

CANNOBIE LEE
brown gelding by Soldado - Droptown.
1959 . . . Fell. (Miss D.Paget) 8.10-10. D.Nicholson. 45/1.
1960 . . . Refused. (The late Miss D.Paget) 9.10-7. D.Nicholson. 100/9.
1962 . . . Finished 8th of 32.(Mrs A.M.Bancroft) 11.10-1. E.P.Harty. 40/1.

CLANYON
bay gelding by Canyonero - Miss Clare.
1960 . . . Fell. (Mr W.N.Johns-Powell) 12.10-8. R.E.Jenkins. 50/1.

CLOVER BUD
brown mare by Phebus - The Hayseed.
1960 . . . Pulled-up. (Mr G.G.Llewellin) 10.10-1. T.Taaffe. 20/1.
1961 . . . Brought down.(Mr G.G.Llewellin) 11.10-10. D.Mould. 50/1.
1962 . . . Finished 10th of 32.(Mr G.G.Llewellin) 12.10-4. D.Nicholson. 100/1.

CLEAR PROFIT
chestnut gelding by High Profit - Rent Free.
1960 . . . Finished 3rd of 26. (Mr B.Sunley) 10.10-1. B.Wilkinson.20/1.
1962 . . . Finished 17th of 32.(Mr B.Sunley) 12.10-0. T.J.Ryan. 66/1.

CARRASCO
bay gelding by Loliondo - Chaudiere.
1961 . . . Fell. (Mr D.J.W.Jackson) 9.10-3. P.Pickford. 40/1.

CLIPADOR
roan gelding by Cacador - The Clip.
1962 . . . Pulled-up. (Mr F.L.Vickerman) 11.10-4. P.A.Farrell. 66/1.

CHAVARA
chestnut gelding by Royal Tara - Cherubim.
1962 . . . Pulled-up. (Mrs I.Evans) 9.10-7. M.Scudamore. 50/1.
1963 . . . Finished 12th of 47. (Mrs.I.Evans) 10.10-2. R.Edwards. 40/1.

CARRAROE
brown mare by Sweeping Jack - Minerstown Lass.
1962 . . . Fell. (Mrs Miles Valentine) 10.10-0. Mr.W.McLernon. 66/1.
1963 . . . Finished 13th of 47.(Mrs Miles Valentine) 11.10-1. Mr.W.McLernon. 33/1.

COLLEGE DON
chestnut gelding by Donatello - School Days.
1963 . . . Pulled-up. (Mrs I.Watts) 11.10-0. B.Wilkinson. 66/1.

CONNIE II
bay mare by Cacador - a hunter mare.
1963 . . . Fell. (Mr P.W.Hicks) 11.10-0. J.Guest. 50/1.

CAPRICORN
grey gelding by Mytholm - Dutch Princess.
1963 . . . Pulled-up. (Mr R.A.Phelps) 10.10-0. A.Major. 66/1.

CARRICKBEG
brown gelding by Control - Florida.
1963 . . . Finished 2nd of 47. (Mr G.Kindersley) 7.10-3. Mr.J.Lawrence. 20/1.

CLAYMORE
brown gelding by Cameron - Clemency.
1964 . . . Finished 13th of 33. (Mr C.Davies) 11.10-0. Mr.C.Davies.50/1.

CROBEG
chestnut gelding by Iceberg 11 - Astrography.
1964 . . . Finished 9th of 33. (Mr M.J.Richardson) 11.10-4. Mr.J.Lawrence. 50/1.
1965 . . . Brought down. (Mr M.J.Richardson) 12.10-13. Mr.M.C.Gifford. l00/1.

CENTRE CIRCLE
chestnut gelding by Hyacinthus - Royal Circle.
1964 . . . Fell. (Mr W.L.Pilkington) 9.10-0. J.Haine. 40/1.

COLEEN STAR
brown gelding by Nearcolein - May Star.
1965 . . . Refused. (Mr P.Milner) 11.10-13. J.Leech. 100/1.

CULLEENHOUSE
chestnut gelding by Hyacinthus - Culleen's Coup.
1965 . . . Finished 12th of 47. (Mrs L.Carver) 11.10-13. T. W. Biddlecombe. 25/1.

CUTLETTE
bay mare by Woodcut - Counselette
1965 . . . Pulled-up (Mr B.Parker) 8.10-13 M. Roberts 50/1.

CASTLE FALLS
bay gelding by Fortina - Lady Rill.
1967 . . . Finished 14th of 44. (Mr C.Nicholson) 10.10-3. S.Hayhurst. 50/1.
1969 . . . Finished 13th of 30. (Mr C.Nicholson) 12.10-0. S.Hayhurst. 66/1.

CHU-TEH
bay gelding by Big Time - In Doubt.
1968 . . . Brought down. (Mrs M.McMeekin) 9.10-0. Mr.N.Gaselee. 33/1.

CHAMORETTA
bay mare by Chamossaire - Tiberetta.
1968 . . . Brought down. (Major A.W.C.Pearn) 8.10-1. D.Elsworth. 100/1.

CHAMPION PRINCE
brown gelding by Prince Richard - Ballinveney 11.
1968 . . . Brought down. (Mr R.W.Wates) 9.10-12. Mr.A.Wates. 66/1.

COMMON ENTRANCE
chestnut gelding by Vulgan - April The Second.
1971 . . . Finished 13th of 38. (Mr A.J.Maxwell) 10.10-0. Mr.M.Morris.100/1. Remounted*

COUNTRY WEDDING
chestnut mare by Question - Clover Bunny.
1971 . . . Brought down. (Mr H.Billington) 9.10-0. R.Champion.50/1.
1972 . . . Fell. (Mr H.Billington) 10.10-4. R.Champion.50/1.

CRAIGBROCK
chestnut gelding by Vulgan - Goldenstown.
1971 . . . Fell. (Sir A.Edmonstone) 12.10-0. P.Ennis. 80/1.

CHARTER FLIGHT
by gelding by Even Money - Flying.
1971 . . . Pulled-up. (Mrs J.Rogerson) 9.11-8. W.Rees. 25/1.

COPPERLESS
chestnut gelding by Doubtless 11 - Spinning Coin.
1971 . . . Fell. (Mr A.S.Neaves) 10.10-1. M.Gibson.100/1.

CNOC DUBH
bay gelding by Autumn Gold - Lady Artist.
1971 . . . Fell. (Mr R.R.Guest) 8.10-11. T.Carberry. 20/1.

CLOUDSMERE
brown gelding by Little Cloud - Cashmere Image.
1972 . . . Fell. (Mr W.H.Whitbread) 8.10-4. D.Mould. 18/1.
1974 . . . Carried-out. (Mr W.H.Whitbread) 10.10-4. P.Kelleway. 100/1.

CARDINAL ERROR
bay gelding by High Hat - Past Folly.
1972 . . . Fell. (Mrs J.M.Ceballos) 8.10-4. J.Francome. 12/1.

CRISP
bay gelding by Rose Argent - Wheat Germ. Bred in Australia.
1973 . . . Finished 2nd of 38. (Sir Chester Manifold) 10.12-0. R.Pitman. 9/1.jnt/Fav. *

CANHARIS
brown gelding by Haris II - Canny's Last.
1973 . . . Brought down. (Lord Zetland) 8.10-1. P.Buckley. 16/1.

CHARLEY WINKING
bay gelding by Vulgan - Weston Girl.
1973 . . . Fell. (Mr L.G.Scott) 8.10-0. Mr.D.Scott. 100/1.

CULLA HILL
chestnut gelding by Star Signal - Devil's Darling.
1973 . . . Fell. (Mr B.J.Brookes) 9.10-7. Mr.N.Brookes. 100/1.
1974 . . . Fell. (Mr B.J. & N.H.Brookes) 10.10-8.Mr.N.Brookes. 100/1.

CHARLES DICKENS
chestnut gelding by Pampered King - Red Tape.
1974 . . . Finished 3rd of 42. (Lt.Col.P.Bengough) 10.10-0. A.Turnell. 50/1.

CLEAR CUT
chestnut gelding by Articulate - Grey Rose.
1975 . . . Fell. (Mr J.Hemingway) 11.11-1. T.Stack. 20/1.

CASTLERUDDERY
bay gelding by Vulgan - Scottish Spider.
1975 . . . Refused. (Mrs K.Harper) 9.10-4. Mr.T.Walsh. 33/1.
1977 . . . Fell. (Mrs K.Harper) 11.10-0. L.O'Donnell. 40/1.

COLONDINE
brown gelding by Colonist 11 - Diaphragm.
1976 . . . Finished 15th of 32. (Mrs E.K.Dudgeon) 9.10-0.B.Forsey. 60/1.

CEOL NA MARA
chestnut gelding by Appolonius - Doreanna.
1976 . . . Finished 5th of 32. (Mrs M.Seddon-Brown & Mrs D.Warnes) 7.10-6. J.Glover. 22/1.

CHURCHTOWN BOY
bay gelding by Arctic Slave - Churchtown Maid.
1976 . . . Finished 11th of 32. (Mr J.Lovell) 9.10-6. M.Salaman. 33/1.
1977 . . . Finished 2nd of 42. (Mr B.Arnold & Mr J.Watkins) 10.10-0. M.Blackshaw. 20/1.
1978 . . . Fell. (Mr B.Arnold) 11.10-0. M.Blackshaw. 14/1.
1979 . . . Brought down. (Mr B.Arnold) 12.10-0. M.Salaman. 25/1.
1980 . . . Brought down. (Mr B.Arnold) 13.10-0. A.Turnell. 50/1.

CARROLL STREET
bay gelding by Combat - Just So.
1977 . . . Finished 8th of 42. (Mr B.H.McGrath) 10.10-0. R.Linley. 50/1.

COLLINGWOOD
bay gelding by Escart 111 - Hall It In.
1977 . . . Finished 9th of 42. (Mrs J.D.Tombs & Mr R.L.Chapman) 11.10-1. C.Hawkins. 50/1.

CORNISH PRINCESS
brown mare by True Code - dam by Command Performance.
1978 . . . Fell. (Mr W.G.Turner) 10.10-1. R.Hoare. 66/1.

COOLISHALL
bay gelding by Kabale - Mona's Deal.
1978 . . . Finished 4th of 37. (Mr & Mrs P.W.Harris) 9.10-0. M.O'Halloran. 16/1.
1979 . . . Fell. (Mr & Mrs P.W.Harris) 10.10-2. A.Webber. 12/1.
1980 . . . Unseated rider. (Mr B.Munro-Wilson) 11.10-10. Mr.B.Munro-Wilson. 40/1.
1981 . . . Finished 8th of 39.(Mr B.Munro-Wilson) 12.10-3.W.Smith. 25/1.
1982 . . . Fell. (Mr B.Munro-Wilson) 13.10-3. R.Barry. 25/1.

CARTWRIGHT
bay gelding by Ribotlight - May Wyne. Bred in New Zealand.
1979 . . . Brought down. (Mr R.F.Fisher) 10.10-0. A.Phillips. 200/1.

CHAMP, THE
bay gelding by Dies - Rose Eclat.
1979 . . . Brought down. (Miss Leila Smith) 11.10-12. W.Smith. 25/1.

CASAMAYOR
bay gelding by Cullanhall - Que Reina.
1980 . . . Fell. (Mr R.R.Guest) 10.10-12. J.King. 50/1.
1981 . . . Refused. (Mr R.R.Guest) 11.10-6. Mr.P.Webber. 100/1.

CHEERS
bay gelding by Be Friendly - No Court.
1981 . . . Finished 12th of 39. (Mr J.W. & Mr M.R.Evans) 9.10-0. P.Scudamore. 20/1.
1982 . . . Finished 8th of 39. (Mr C.Mackenzie) 10.10-0. Mrs.Geraldine Rees. 66/1.

CHORAL FESTIVAL
bay gelding by Choral Society - Belle Of New York.
1981 . . . Fell. (Mr M.J.Low) 10.10-2. Mr.M.J.Low. 66/1.
1982 . . . Unseated rider. (Mr.M.J.Low) 11.10-4.Mr.M.J.Low. 100/1.

CHUMSON
brown gelding by Sobig - Gay Amber.
1981 . . . Fell. (Mr J.E.Beirne) 10.11-7. Mr.A.O'Connell. 50/1.

CARROW BOY
chestnut gelding by Beau Tudor - Festive Queen.
1981 . . . Fell. (Mr W.Durkan) 9.11-6. G.Newman. 33/1.
1982 . . . Fell. (Mr W.Durkan) 10.11-7. G.Newman. 40/1.
1983 . . . Fell. (Mr W.Durkan) 11.10-12. G.Newman. 33/1.

COLD SPELL
bay gelding by Arctic Slave - May Foliage.
1982 . . . Brought down. (Lord Leverhulme) 10.10-0. S.Jobar. 40/1.

CURRENT GOLD
chestnut gelding by Current Coin - Souvergold.
1982 . . . Finished 5th of 39. (Mr A.Picke) 11.10-8. N.Doughty. 25/1.

CORBIERE
chestnut gelding by Harwell - Ballycashin. Bred Mr.M.Parkhill.
1983 . . . WON. (Mr B.R.H.Burrough) 8.11-4. 41 Ran. B.De Haan. 13/l.
1984 . . . Finished 3rd of 40. (Mr B.R.H.Burrough) 9.12-0. B.De Haan. 16/1.
1985 . . . Finished 3rd of 40. (Mr B.R.H.Burrough) 10.11-10. P.Scudamore. 9/1.
1986 . . . Fell. (Mr B.R.H.Burrough) 11.11-7. B.De Haan. 14/1.
1987 . . . Finished 12th of 40. (Mr B.R.H.Burrough) 12.10-10. B.De Haan. 12/1.

COLONEL CHRISTY
bay gelding by Mon Capitaine - Christy's Bow.
1983 . . . Finished 9th of 41. (Mrs H.R.McLaughlin) 8.10-0. P.Hobbs. 66/1.
1987 . . . Finished 15th of 40.(Mr R.A.Keen & Mr R.H.Hardy. 12.10-0. S.Moore.300/1.

CANFORD GINGER
chestnut gelding by Twiberry - Stella's Courage.
1983 . . . Pulled-up. (Mr A.W.H.Sykes) 8.10-0. J.H.Davies. 33/1.
1984 . . . Finished 23rd of 40.(Mr A.W.H.Sykes) 9.10-1. C.Brown.100/1.

CLONTHTURTIN
chestnut gelding by Harwell - Clonroche Hawk.
1984 . . . Fell. (Mr F.Conroy) 10.10-0. T.J.Taaffe. 100/1.
1985 . . . Pulled-up. (Mrs F.P.Rawnsley & Mr D.C.Rawnsley) 11.10-5. Mr.T.Thomson Jones. 50/1.

CARL'S WAGER
chestnut gelding by Carlburg - Queen's Wager.
1984 . . . Unseated rider. (Leisure Racing Ltd.) 9.10-2. Mr.R.J.Beggan.28/1.

CLASSIFIED
bay gelding by So Blessed - Crag Bay.
1985 . . . Finished 5th of 40. (Mr G.A.Rogers) 9.10-7. J.White. 20/1.
1986 . . . Finished 3rd of 40. (Cheveley Park Stud) 10.10-3. S.Smith Eccles. 22/1.
1987 . . . Unseated rider. (Cheveley Park Stud) 11.10-3. S.Smith Eccles. 9/1.

CAPTAIN PARKHILL
chestnut gelding by Free Boy - dam by Vivi Tarquin.
1985 . . . Finished 11th of 40. (Mr B.McLean) 12.10-0. C.Grant. 100/1.

CROSA
brown mare by Crozier - Bois de Rose.
1985 . . . Fell. (Mr S.C.Jones) 10.10-0. S.Moore. 100/1.

CRANLOME
bay gelding by Menelek - Austrian Maid.
1987 . . . Finished 14th of 40. (Mrs P.F.N.Fanning) 9.10-0. M. Richards. 500/ 1.
1989 . . . Fell (Mrs P.F.N.Fanning) 11.10-0. K.F. O'Brien. 66/1.

COURSE HUNTER
bay gelding by Crash Course - Miss Hunter.
1988 . . . Finished 8th of 40. (Mr D.Buik) 10.10-1. P. Croucher. 20/1.
1990 . . . Finished 15th of 38. (Mr D.Buik) 12.10-4. G.Bradley. 66/1.

CERIMAU
bay gelding by Beau Chapeau - Prospective Lady.
1989 . . . Fell.(Mrs E.Eliis) 11.10-0. P.Hobbs. 80/1.

CALL COLLECT
chestnut gelding by Ballymore - Regal Bell.
1990 . . . Finished 7th of 38. (Mr J.Clements) 9.10-5. Mr.R.Martin. 14/l.

CHARTER HARDWARE
bay gelding by Hardboy - Unsinkable Sarah.
1990 . . . Finished 12th of 38. (Charter Racing Ltd) 8.10-0. N.Williamson. 66/1.

CONCLUSIVE
chestnut gelding by Crash Course - French Cherry.
1990 . . . Fell. (Mr & Mrs R.Shaw) 11.10-4. S.Smith Eccles. 28/1.

CRAMMER
bay gelding by Crash Course - Miss Hunter.
1991 .. Unseated rider. (Mr W.Matthews) 11.10-2. Mr.J. Durkan.28/1.

COOL GROUND
chestnut gelding by Over The River - Merry Spring.
1992 . . . Finished 10th of 40. (Whitcombe Manor Racing Stables) 10.11-1. M.Lynch. 10/l.
1995 . . . Finished 11th of 35. (Whitcombe Manor Racing Stables) 13.10-0. P.Holley. 50/1.

CLONEY GRANGE
brown gelding by Bargello - Pampas Wind.
1992 . . . Fell. (Mr E. O'Dwyer) 13.10-0. D.O'Connor. 100/1

CAPTAIN BRANDY
chestnut gelding by Step Together - Manhattan Brandy.
1994 . . . Unseated rider. (Mr M.A.Cooney) 9.10-0. K.O'Brien. 50/1.

CHANNELS GATE
bay gelding by Fine Blue - Collies Pet.
1994 . . . Refused. (Cabalva Racing Partnership) 10.10-0. T.Jenks. 100/1 .

CHATAM
bay gelding by Big Spruce - Cristalina.
1995 . . . Fell. (Dr.B & Mr A.F.Nolan) 11.10-6. A.P.McCoy.25/1.
1996 . . . Pulled-up. (Dr.B & Mr A.F.Nolan) 12.10-3. J. Lower. 40/1.

CAMELOT KNIGHT
brown gelding by King's Ride - Jeanette Marie
1995 . . . Fell. (Mr M.Gates) 9.10-2. Mr.M.Rimell. 66/1.

CRYSTAL SPIRIT
bay gelding by Kris - Crown Treasure.
1995 . . . Finished 14th of 35. (Mr Paul Mellon) 8.10-4. J.Osborne. 12/1.

COUNTRY MEMBER
chestnut gelding by New Member - Botnany Serenade.
1995 . . . Fell. (Mrs C.C.Williams) 10.10-0. L.Harvey. 11/1.

CAPTAIN DIBBLE
bay gelding by Crash Course - Sailor's Will.
1996 . . . Finished 11th of 27. (Mrs R.Vaughan) 11.10-0. T.Jenks. 40/1.

DICTATOR
1839 . . . Fell. (Mr J. S. Oswell) Carlin. n/q.

DAXON
1839 . . . Fell. (Mr T.Ferguson) Mr.T.Ferguson. n/q.

DRAGSMAN
1843 . . . Finished 3rd of 16. (Mr Holman) Ml.Crickmere. 10/1.

DISCOUNT
chestnut horse by Sir Hercules - Minikin. Bred by Mr.Fowler. Formerly named Magnum Bonum.
1844 . . . WON.(Mr Quartermaine) 6.10-12. 15 Ran. Mr.Crickmere. 5/1 jnt/Fav *

DOLLY'S BRUE
1852 . . . Failed to finish. (Mr Maugan) aged 10-0. McGee. n/q.

DUC AU BHURRAS
1853 Failed to finish. (Lord Waterford) aged 10-10. J.Ryan. 6/1.

DWARF, THE.
1853 . . . Fell. (Mr Morris) aged 9-0. H. Lamplugh. n/q.

DANGEROUS
1855 . . . Finisded 5th of 20. (Mr J.R.Henderson) aged 9-0. Fowler. 6/1
1857 . . . Finished 5th of 28. (Mr A.Rice) aged 9-8. F. Page. 50/1.

DAN O'CONNELL
1856 .. Failed to finish. (Mr J.Tayleure) aged 9-4. W.Archer. n/q.

DANE, THE
1861 . . . Fnished 2nd of 24. (Capt.Christie) 5.10-0. W.White. 33/1
1863 . . . Pulled-up. (Capt.Christie) 7.11-6. W.White. 10/1.

DIAMANT
1861 . . . Refused. (Mr J.L. Manby) aged 10-4 Enoch. n/q

DR. LEETE
1861 . . . Failed to finish. (Marquess of Hartington) 8-8. W. Mason. n/q.

DWARF, THE
1865 . . . Pulled-up. (Mr Studd) aged 10-0. Igoe. 25/1.

DOCTOR, THE
brown gelding by The Cure - Margaret Of Anjou.
1866 . . . Failed to finish. (Mr Mytton) 5.10-0. G.Stevens. 20/1.
1870 . . . Finished 2nd of 23.(Mr V. St. John) 9.110-7. G.Holman. 5/1.
1871 . . . Refused. (Duke of Hamilton) 10.11-13. Mr.Crawshaw. 12/1.

DAISY
brown gelding by hercules - dam unknown.
1868 . . . Pulled-up. (Mr W.R.H.Powell) aged 11-7. Mr.Thomas 11/1.

DESPATCH
brown gelding by Dough - dam by Sir Hercules.
1869 . . . Finished 6th of 22. (Mr Studd) aged 10-8. Mr.Edwards. 5/1.
1871 . . . Finished 2nd of 25.(Mr Studd) aged 10-0. G.Waddington. 10/1.
1872 . . . Finished 3rd of 25.(Mr Studd) aged 10-4. G.Waddington. 100/30.Fav*

DICK TURPIN
bay gelding by Bucolic - Miss Hatch.
1869 . . . Fell. (Mr Foulkes) aged 10-0. J.Knott. 40/1.

DOG FOX
bay gelding by Vedette - Vixen.
1871 . . . Broke-down. (Mr Mannington) aged 10-0. J.Potter. 33/1.

DERBY DAY
brown gelding by Claret - Princess.
1872 . . . Fell. (Lord Conyngham) aged 10-0. Marsh. 25/1.

DISTURBANCE
bay horse by Commotion - Polly Peacham. Bred by Mr.Barber.
1873 . . . WON. (Captain J.Machell) 6.11-11. 28 Ran. Mr.J.M.Richardson. 20/1.
1874 . . . Finished 6th of 22. (Capt.J.Machell) 7.12-9. J. Cannon. 25/1.

DEFENCE
bay gelding by Defender - dam by Augur.
1874 . . . Finished 4th of 22. (Capt.J.Machell) 8.11-13. Mr.Rolly. 33/1.
1876 . . . Pulled-up. (Mr H.Baltazzi) l0.11-11. Mr. Thomas. 100/8.

DERVICHE
bay horse by Fitz-Gladiator - Deer Aquila. Bred in France.
1874 . . . Failed to finish (Lord Marcus Beresford) 7.10-12. R.I'Anson. 33/1.

DAYBREAK
bay gelding by Zouave - Twilight.
1874 . . . Failed to finish. (Mr H.Houldsworth) 8.10-11. Holt. n/q.

DAINTY
brown mare byLoyola - Tit-bit.
1874 . . . Fell. (Mr S.Davis) 8.10-7. Mr.Hathaway. 66/1.
1875 . . . Finished 2nd of 19.(Mr S.Davis) 9.11-0. Mr. Hathaway. 25/1.
1877 . . . Finished 5th of 16.(Mr S.Davis) 11.10-4. Mr.J. Goodwin.20/1.
1880 . . . Finished 10th of 14.(Mr S.Davis) 14.10-2. S.Darling. 66/1.

DUC DE BEAUFORT
chestnut horse by Ventre St Gris - Dame d'Honneur. Bred in France.
1875 . . . Failed to Finish. (Mr Vyner) 6.11-13. Capt.Smith. 100/8.

DOWNPATRICK
grey horse by Master Bagot - Lady Wilde.
1880 . . . Finished 3rd of 14. (Colonel Lloyd) 6.10-7. P. Gavin.100/15.
1883 . . . Finished 4th of 10. (Colonel Lloyd) 9.10-7. Mr.T.Widger.100/7.
1885 . . . Fell. (Colonel Lloyd) 11.10-0. Capt.W.B. Morris. 20/1.

DOG FOX
brown gelding hy Xenophon - Brown Vixen.
1885 . . . Finished 7th of 19. (Mr C.Archer) 6.10-3.Capt.Lee Barber. 25/1.

DOMINION
bay gelding by Robert The Devil - Ottawa.
1891 . . . Pulled-up (Mr W.H.Russell) 6.10-13. W. Thornton. 66/1.

DAWN
chestnut gelding by Silver Crown - Old Fashion.
1894 . . . Pulled-up. (Mr E..Storey) 6.9-7. G.Morris. 25/1.

DALKEITH
brown gelding by Keith - Maid Of Lorne.
1895 . . . Finished 9th of 19. (Mr W.Murray-Threipland) aged 9-12. J.Knox. 33/1.

DOLLAR II
black gelding by Doubloon - Roseid.
1896 . . . Fell. (Mr J.A.Miller) 6.10-11. W.Halsey. 50/1.

DAIMIO
bay or brown gelding by Swiveller - Butterfly 11. Bred in Australia.
1897 . . . Pulled-up. (Mr O.Gibson) aged 12-6. H.Escott. 40/1.

DROGHEDA
bay gelding by Cherry Ripe - Eglantine. Not in the General Stud Book. Bred in Ireland
1898 . . . WON. (Mr C.G.M.Adams) 6.10-12. 25 Ran. J.Gourley. 25/1.

DEAD LEVEL
bay horse by Isobar - Paragon.
1898 . . . Finished 5th of 25. (Mr. G.Hamilton) 6.10-7. A. Anthony.25/1.
1899 . . . Finished 4th of 19. (Mr J. C. Dormer) 7.10-6. F. Mason. 33/1.

DRUMCREE
bay gelding by Ascetic - Witching Hour. Bred by Mr. C.Hope.
1901 . . . Finished 2nd of 24. (Mr O. J. Williams) 7.9-12. Mr.H.Nugent. 10/1.
1902 . . . Finished 7th of 21. (Mr J. S. Morrison) 8.10-10.Mr.H.Nugent. 10/1.
1903 . . . WON. (Mr J.S.Morrison) 9.11-3. 23 Ran. P. Woodland. 13/2.Fav*
1906 . . . Finished 8th of 23. (Mr J. S.Morrison) 12.12-0.Mr. W.Bulteel.33/1.
1907 . . . Fell. (Mr J. S. Morrison) 13.11-9. Mr. W. Bulteel. 25/1.

DETAIL
bay gelding by Curley - Rosara.
1902 . . . Finished 4th of 21. (Mr White-Heather) 6.9-9. A. Nightingall. 25/1.
1903 . . . Finished 2nd of 23 (Mr White-Heather) 7 9-13.A.Nightingall. 100/14.
1904 . . . Knocked-over. (Mr White-Heather) 8.10-7.A.Nightingall. 100/14.
1905 . . . Fell. (Mr White-Heather) 9.10-8. P. Cowley. 100/7.
1907 . . . Fell (Mr White-Heather) 11.10-0. W. Payne. 40-1

DRUMREE
bay gelding by Royal Meath - Connie.
1902 . . . Knocked-over. (Duke of Westminster) 6.11-4. A. Anthony. 6/1 jnt/Fav. *
1903 . . . Fell. (Duke of Westminster) 7.11-4. J. Phillips. 25/1.

DIRKHAMPTON
bay gelding by Dirk Hatteraick - Woodhampton.
1902 . . . Fell. (Col.W.A.W.Lawson) 8.10-0. Mr. J. Sharpe. 50/1.

DEARSLAYER
chetsnut gelding by Hawkeye - Wallflower.
1903 . . . Fell. (Mr J.G.Bulteel) 7.10-1l. E. Piggott. 25/1.
1904 . . . Fell. (Prince Hatzfeldt) 8.10-10. J. Phillips. 25/1.
1905 . . . Fell. (Prince Hatzfeldt) 9.10-8. Mr. A. Hastings.100/6.
1906 . . . Pulled-up.(Prince Hatzfeldt) 10.10-4. Mr. P. Whitaker. 50/1.

DATHI
chestnut gelding by Entusiast - Freshet.
1906 . . . Fell. (Mr T.Clyde) 9.10-4. A. Birch. 25/1.
1908 . . . Pulled-up.(Mr J.Wynford Philipps) 11.10-2. I. Anthony. 66/1.

DOMINO
chestnut gelding by Jeddah - Rondino.
1909 . . . Fell. (Mr H. M. Hartigan) 7.11-1. P .Cowley. 100/8.

DAVY JONES
bay gelding by Britannic - Wardrobe.
1909 . . . Fell. (Lord St Davids) 6 10-2. I. Anthony. 100/6.

DYSART
chestnut gelding by Bealderg dam by Gay Reveller.
1913 . . . Fell. (Capt. H. C. Higgins) 8.12-4.Capt.O'Brien Butler. 50/1.

DUTCH PENNANT
chestnut mare by Count Schomberg Topsail Yard.
1914 . . . Fell. (Capt.Crawshay) 8.10-5. A. Parnham. n/q.

DIPLOMATIST II
chestnut gelding by First Consul - Alice.
1914 . . . Ran-out. (Mr N. B. Davis) 9.9-7. Mr.N.B.Davis. n/q

DISTAFF
bay mare by Hackler - Circe.
1915 . . . Pulled-up. (Sir George Bullough) 7.10-10. E.Piggott. 25/1.

DENIS AUBURN
bay gelding by General Peace or Denis Richard - Auburn's Pride.
1915 . . . Fell. (Sir George Bullough) 8.9-7. J.Reardon. 33/1.
* 1916 . . . Completed course.(Sir G.Bullough) 9.10-7.E.Driscoll. 8/1.
* 1917 . . . Pulled-up. (Sir George Bullough) 10.10-4. R.Burford.n/q.

DRUMLANE
bay gelding by Pilot - Onyx.
* 1916 . . . Pulled-up.(Sir W. W. Williams) 8.9-10. J.Kelly. n/q.

DUNADRY
chestnut gelding by Captivation - Glenavy.
1920 . . . Fell. (Mrs A.Blain) 7.9-8. S.Walkington. n/q.
1922 . . . Fell. (Mrs A.Blain) 9.10-7. J.Higan,jnr. 66/1.

DAYDAWN
bay horse by Bungebah - Princess Olga.
1921 . . . Fell. (Baron F. de Tuyll) 8.10-13. J. R. Anthony. 100/7

DRIFTER.
brown gelding by The Raft - Katie Darling.
1922 . . . Finished 2nd of 32. (Mr J. Widger) 8.10-0. W.Watkinson. l8/1.
1923 . . . Finished 5th of 28. (Mr J. Widger) 9.10-10.W.Watkinson. 20/1.
1924 . . . Finished 4th of 30.(Mr S. Sanford) 10.10-5. G. Calder. 40/1.
1925 . . . Finished 9th of 33.(Mr S. Sanford) 11.10-3. W.Watkinson. 20/1.

DUNSTANBURGH
chestnut gelding by Sir Harry - Honey.
1922 . . . Fell. (Mr J. W. Burnett) 10.10-0. H.Watkin. n/q.

DUETTISTE
bay gelding by Ethelbert - Dulcibella.
1923 . . . Pulled-up. (Mr J.E.Widener) 10.11-7. A.Escott. 40/1.

DOUBLE CHANCE
chestnut gelding by Roi Herode or Day Comet - Kelibia. Bred by Mr. L de Rothschild.
1925 . . . WON. (Mr D. Goold) 9.10-9. 33 Ran. Major J. P. Wilson. 100/9.

DWARF OF THE FOREST
bay gelding by The Giant - Blackbird.
1925 . . . Finished 6th of 33. (Mr H. Kennard) 8.10-10.Mr.H.Kennard. 66/1.
1926 . . . Finished 9th of 30. (Mr H. Kennard) 9.10-10.Mr.H.Kennard. 28/1.
1927 . . . Fell. (Mr H. Kennard) 10.11-4. Mr.H.Kennard. 33/1.
1929 . . . Fell. (Mr H. Kennard) 12.10-10. Mr.H.Kennard. 200/1.

DARRACQ
brown gelding by Littleton - Sea Pink.
1926 . . . Finished 5th of 30. (Major R. F. Samson) 11,10-11. F.Gurney. 40/1.
1928 . . . Failed to finish. (Mr A.C.Schwartz) 13.11-2. J.Moloney. 20/1
1929 . . . Fell. (Mr A.C.Schwartz) 14.11-0. Mr. G. S. Poole. 40/1.

DRINMOND
bay gelding by Drinmore - Miss Desmond.
1927 . . . Finished 4th of 37. (Mr G. Balding) 10.11-2. Mr. J. B. Balding. 66/1.
1928 . . . Refused. (Mr J.B.Balding) 11.10-13. Mr. J.B.Balding. 33/1.
1929 . . . Fell. (Mr J.B.Balding) l2.10-10. Mr. J. B. Balding. 50/1.

DE COMBAT
brown gelding by Atlas - Hors de Combat.
1928 . . . Failed to finish. (Mr C.Mulholland) 11.10-0.F. Croney.100/1.

D. D. B.
chestnut gelding by Wax Bullet dam by Wavelet's Pride.
1929 . . . Finished 7th of 66. (Major A. W.Huntington) 9.10-11. Mr. R. Gubbins. 66/1

DELARUE
bay gelding by St Dunstan - Rose Amber.
1929 . . . Finished 8th of 66. (Mr J. B. Snow) 7.10-3. G.Wilson. 200/1.
1930 . . . Knocked-over. (Mr J. B. Snow) 8.10-6. G.Wilson. 100/1.
1932 . . . Refused. (Mr J. B. Snow) 10.10-7. W. Kidney.100/1.

DENBURGH
chestnut gelding by Denis Richard - Poppy.
1929 . . . Fell. (Mr F.Usher) 10.10-3. G. Hardy. 200/1.

DUKE OF FLORENCE
bay gelding by Duke Of Brandon - Florence.
1929 . . . Failed to finish. (Mr. A. D. McAlpine) 8.10-2. G.Turner. 50/1.

DONZELON
bay gelding by Chaucer - Tortor.
1930 . . . Fell. (Colonel G.Foljambe) 9.11-7. R. Lyall. 66/1

DONEGAL
bay gelding by General Gough - The Jewess.
1930 . . . Fell. (Mr. A. Bendon) 13.11-2. W.Speck. 25/1.

DERBY DAY II
chestnut gelding by Irawaddy dam by Travelling Lad.
1930 . . . Fell. (Mr C.Nicholson) 8.10-0. Mr.E. V. Stephenson.100/1.

DRINTYRE
brown gelding by Drinmore - Lady Longwood.
1931 . . . Refused. (Capt. C. N. Brownhill) 8.11-7. Capt. C. N. Brownhill. 20/1.

DRIN
black or brown gelding by Drinmore dam by Balsamo.
1931 . . . Fell. (Mr A. Bendon) 7.11-2. W. Speck. 20/1

DUSTY FOOT
bay or brown gelding by Martin Lightfoot - Omaha.
1932 . . . Refused.(Mr J.H.Whitney) 8.10-7. W. Speck. 25/1.
1933 . . . Fell (Mr J. H. Whitney-) 9 10-7. Mr. G. Bostwick. 50/1.

DELANEIGE
brown gelding by Santair - Kylestrome. Formerly named Sanstrome.
1933 . . . Finished 4th of 34. (Mr J. B. Snow) 8.11-3. J. Moloney. 100/1.
1934 . . . Finished 2nd of 30.(Mr J. B. Snow) 9.11-6. J.Moloney.100/7.
1936 . . . Fell. (Mr J. B. Snow) 11.11-2. H. Nicholson. 25/1.
1937 . . . Fell. (Mr J. B. Snow) 12.11-2. J.Hamey. 2011.

DESTINY BAY
bay mare by Foresight - Dancing Water.
1934 . . . Fell. (Mr. H. Lloyd Thomas) aged 11-2. Mr.H.Lloyd Thomas. 40/1.

DOUBLE CROSSED
brown gelding by Martin Lightfoot - Lady May.
1936 . . . Finished 8th of 35. (Mr J. H. Whitney) 8.11-4. D.Morgan. 20/1.

DAVY JONES
chestnut horse by Pharos - Panic.
1936 Ran-out. (Lord Mildmay) 7.10-7. Mr.A.Mildmay. 100/1.

D'EYNCOURT
bay gelding by Sicyon - Wild Marjorie.
1936 . . . Fell. (Mr F. W. Dennis) 8.10-7. P. Carey. 50/1

DON BRADMAN
chestnut gelding by Irawaddy - Carminetta.
1937 . . . Finished 7th of 33 (Mr S. Wilkinson) 11.10-8. Mr. A. Marsh. Remounted 100/8.

DAWMAR
brown mare by Jackdaw - Gold Market.
1937 ...Fell. (Mr W. S. Murphy) 7.10-13. J. Richardson. 40/1.
1938 . . . Pulled-up. (Mr W. S. Murphy) 8.10-7. R.Burford. 100/1.

DIDORIC
brown gelding by Zambo - Apres L'Ondee.
1937 . . . Fell (Mr R. Lehman) 8.10-10. H.Nicholson. 100/8
1938 . . . Fell. (Mr R.Lehman) 9.10-2. D.Butchers. 50/l.

DELACHANCE
chestnut gelding by Prince Thello - Druce.
1937 . . . Fell. (Mr J. B. Snow) 8.10-9. T. F. Rimell. 100/6.
1938 . . . Finished 5th of 36.(Mr J. B. Snow) 9.10-9. J. Moloney. 100/9.

DRYBURGH
bay gelding by Buchan - Mother Superior.
1937 . . . Fell. (Mr R.B.Vick) 8.10-0 B. Carter. 28/1.

DRIM
brown gelding by Drinmore - Standard Bearer.
1937 . . . Fell. (Mr B. K. Tighe) 10.10-9. Mr.B. K. Tighe. 100/1.
1938 . . . Finished 13th of 36 (Mr B. K. Tighe) 11.11-3 Mr. B. K. Tighe. 100/1.
1939 . . . Fell. (Mr J. Morris) 12.10-6. Mr. J. Morris. 100/1.

DUNHILL CASTLE
black gelding by Cottage - Martenette.
1938 . . . Fell. (Sir Warden Chilcott) 8.10-12 H.Nicholson. 20/1.
1939 . . . Fell. (Sir Warden Chilcott) 9.11-9. F. Walwyn. 28/1.
1940 . . . Fell. (Sir Warden Chilcott) 10.11-5. G. Wilson. 50/1.

DOMINICK'S CROSS
chestnut gelding by La Brige or Catalin - Star of Kildare.
1938 . . . Fell (Mr. A. Donn) 7.11-0. R. Everett. 22/1
1939 . . . Finished 6th of 37 (Mr A.Donn) 8.11-1. R.Everett. 33/1
1940 . . . Finished 10th of 30 (Mr A.Donn) 9.11-1. C.Mitchell. 40/1.

DESLYS
bay mare by Golden Myth - Mousme.
1939 . . . Fell. (Mrs Ackernley) 10.10-0. Mr.A.Marsh. 100/1.

DOWNRIGHT
bay gelding by Right Arm - Blinky Dhow.
1940 . . . Finished 14th of 30. (Capt.J.Seely) 11.10-6. Capt.J.Seely. 100/1.

DOUBLE FLUSH
chestnut gelding by Double - Flush Of Dawn.
1946 . . . Fell. (Mr L.Michaelson) 10.10-0. E.Newman. 100/1.

DUNSHAUGHLIN
brown gelding by Werwolf - Oak Lawn.
1946 . . . Fell. (Miss D.Paget) 8.10-0. R. O'Ryan. 100/8.

DOUBLE SAM
bay gelding by Apple Sanlmy - Samarinda.
1947 . . . Fell. (Mr S.D.Clark) 12.10-0. H.J.Haley. 100/1.

DAY DREAMS
brown gelding by Cottage - Elegant Girl.
1947 . . . Pullled-up. (Mr L.Michaelson) 8.10-0. M.Browne. 100/1.

DOMINO
bay gelding by Noble Star - Bow Bell. Formerly named Stardom.
1947 . . . Pulled-up. (Maj. W. H. McKenzie) 7.10-0. D. Morgan 28/1.

DYNOVI
brown gelding by Blue Doctor - Southern Bell.
1950 . . . Brought down. (Mr G. Coxon) 9.10-0. A.Jack. 100/1.

DERRINSTOWN
bay gelding by J'Accours - Inherit.
1951 . . . Finished 3rd of 36. (Mr P. Digney) 11.10-0. A.Power. 66/1. Remounted*
1952 . . . Pulled-up. (Mr P.Digney) 12.10-0. A.Power. 100/1.

DOG WATCH
brown gelding by Black Watch - Claimed.
1951 . . . Fell. (Mr A. Lloyd) 10.10-2. T.Brookshaw. 33/1.

DOMINICK'S BAR
bay or brown gelding by Embargo - Dominic's Bell.
1952 . . . Fell. (Mrs P Kiely) 8.10-13. A. Prendegast. 66/1
1954 . . . Fell. (Mrs P.Kiely) 10.10-7. T. Molony. 33/1.

DESIRE
bay gelding by Columbo - Isolda
1953 . . . Pulled-up. (Mr C. C. Cameron) 12.10-0. T. Cullen. 66/1.

DARK STRANGER
brown gelding by Mazarin - Impromptu.
1955 .. Fell. (Mr L. A. Coville) 10.10-5. Mr.J.Bosley. 40/1.

DUNBOY II
dun gelding by Pinxit - Gaiety IV.
1956 . . . Fell. (Mrs M.Bruce) 12.11-0. Mr.R.Brewis. 66/1.

DOMATA
bay gelding by Domaha - Sunita.
1956 . . . Fell. (Mr E.Stanning) 10.10-4. D.Ancil. 66/1.

DEVON LOCH
brown gelding by Devonian - Coolaleen.
1956 . . . Fell near post. (H.M.Queen Elizabeth, The Queen Mother) 10.11-4. R.Francis. 100/7.

DONE UP
bay gelding by Donatello 11 - Fasten.
1959 . . . Brought down. (Mr J. U. Baillie) 9.11-3. F.T.Winter. 100/7.

DONDROSA
grey gelding by Donino - Pampas Rose.
1959 . . . Refused. (Mr C. B. Taylor) 7.10-11. Mr.C.B.Taylor. 66/1.

DANDY SCOT
bay gelding by Pearl Orient - Heroic China.
1960 . . . Fell. (Mr S. C. Banks) 10.11-7. F. T.Winter. 10/1.

DOUBLE CREST
bay gelding by King Elal - Corbeg.
1961 . . . Refused. (Mrs R.M.Byers) 9.10-7. A.Irvine. 50/1.

DUPLICATOR
brown gelding by Control - Copycat.
1962 . . . Fell. (Miss A.H.Robertson) 9.10-2. G.Milburn. 28/1

DARK VENETIAN
bay mare by Black Tarquin - Malcontenta.
1962 . . . Finished 6th of 32. (Mrs T. M. Stuck) 7.10-0. P.Cowley. 100/1.
1963 . . . Finished 9th of 47. (Mrs T. M. Stuck) 8.10-2. D. Bassett. 33/1.
1965 . . . Fell. (Mr F. Vincent) 10.10-13. J. Renfree. 100/1.

DANDY TIM
brown gelding by Last Of The Dandies - Carbury's Hall.
1962 . . . Fell. (Mr C. J. Baines) 9.10-0 R.Carter. 50/1.
1963 . . . Finished 22nd of 47. (Mr C. J. Baines) 10.10-0. L. Major. 50/1.

DAGMAR GITTELL
bay gelding by His Slipper - Dagmar.
1963 . . . Pulled-up. (Mrs L. Brotherton) 8.10-5. H.J.East. 100/7

DANCING RAIN
chestnut gelding by Souverain - Dancing Sunbeam.
1964 . . . Refused. (Capt.P. T.Fenwick) 9.10-0. O McNally. 66/1.

DORIMONT
bay gelding by Domaha - Monacrasia.
1966 . . . Unseated rider. (Mr W.Shand-Kydd) 12.10-0. Mr.W.Shand-Kydd. 50/1.
1967 . . . Fell. (Mr W.Shand-Kydd) 13.10-0. R.Pitman. 100/1.

DIFFERENT CLASS
bay gelding by Beau Sabreur - Wiolette
1967 . . . Brought down. (Mr Gregory Peck) 7.11-2. D.Mould.100/8.
1968 . . . Finished 3rd of 45.(Mr Gregory Peck) 8.11-5. D.Mould. 17/2.Fav. *

DUN WIDDY
dun gelding by Weensland - Dapple Dun.
1967 . . . Pulled-up. (Mr J.A.C.Edwards) 11.10-10. Mr.J.Edwards. 100/1.
1968 . . . Finished 16th of 45. (Mr A.P.Moore) 12.10-2. Mr.A.P.Moore. 100/1.

DOZO
bay gelding by Prince's Game - Queen Of The Dandies.
1970 . . . Finished 4th of 28. (Mrs E.W.Wetherill) 9.10-4. E.P.Harty. 100/8.

DEBLIN'S GREEN
bay gelding by Pinacola - Pandy's Folly.
1972 . . . Pulled-up. (Mr G. H. Yardley) 9.10-0. D.Cartwright.. 33/1.
1974 . . . Brought down. (Mr G. H. Yardley) 11.10-0. N.Wakley. 25/1.

DUNNO
bay horse by Dionisio - Hot Curry.
1974 . . . Finished 13th of 42. (Mrs E.Mitchell) 10.10-1. Mr.N.Mitchell.100/1.

DIKLER, THE
bay gelding by Vulgan - Coronationa Day.
1975 . . . Finished 5th of 31 (Mrs D. August) 12.11-13. R.Barry. 20/1.
1976 . . . Finished 6th of 32. (Mrs M. A. Boddington) 13.11-7. R.Barry. 25/1.

DAVY LAD
bay gelding by David Jack - Chateau.
1977 . . . Fell. (Mrs J. B. McGowan) 7.10-13. D.T.Hughes. 10/1.

DUFFLE COAT
bay gelding by Sea Moss - Stainton Cotes.
1977 . . . Fell. (Mr G.A.Hubbard) 9.10-4. B.R.Davies. 100/1.

DOUBLE BRIDAL
bay gelding by Dual - Mam'zelle.
1978 . . . Fell. (Major General Sir James d'Avigdor-Goldsmid) 7.10-l. W.Smith. 50/1.

DRUMROAN
brown gelding by Chou Chin Chou - Eineen.
1978 . . . Finished 3rd of 37. (Mrs G.St John Nolan) 10.10-0.G. Newman. 25/1.
1979 . . . Fell. (Mrs G. St John Nolan) 11.10-4. (G.Newman. 20/1
1980 . . . Fell. (Mrs G.St John Nolan) 12.10-5. T.McGivern. 22/1.
1981 . . . Fell. (Mrs G.St John Nolan) 13.10-0.Mr. M. Graffe. 50/1.

DOUBLE NEGATIVE
chestnut gelding by Double-U-Jay - Ulverno
1978 . . . Fell. (Mrs M.Wood Power) 8.10-0. C.Tinkler. 33/1.
1979 . . . Fell. (Mrs M.Wood Power) 9.10-1. Mr.E.Woods. 66/1.

DROMORE
bay gelding by No Argument - Slip On.
1979 . . . Pulled-up. (Mr P.Duggan) 11.10-0. Mr. P.Duggan. 50/1.
1980 . . . Pulled-up. (Mr P.Duggan) 12.10-0. Mr.P.Duggan. 100/1.
1981 . . . Refused. (Mr P.Duggan) 13.10-0. Mr.P.Duggan. 100/1.

DELMOSS
bay gelding by Dalesa - Turfmould.
1980 . . . Fell. (Mrs F.Vessels) 10.10-2. G.Newman. 25/1.
1981 . . . Fell. (Mrs F.Vessels) 11.10-1. L.O'Donnell. 50/1.
1982 . . . Finished 4th of 39. (Mr J.Goodman) 12.10-3. W.Smith. 50/1.
1983 . . . Finished 10th of 41.(Mr R.Q.Sutherland) 13.10-0. W.Smith. 50/1.

DEIOPEA
chestnut mare by Spartan General - Woodland Wedding.
1981 . . . Refused. (Mr W. R. Sheedy) 10.10-0. Mrs.L.Sheedy. 100/1.

DEEP GALE
bay gelding by Deep Run - Cathy Gale.
1982 . . . Fell. (Mr J. McManus) 9.11-2. T.J.Ryan. 20/1.

DEER MOUNT
brown mare by Boreen - Golden Deer
1982 . . . Fell. (Mrs M. Babbage) 8.10-0. J.P.Byrne. 100/1

DUNCREGGAN
bay gelding by Cantab - Persian Helen.
1983 . . . Fell. (Mr B.Desmond jnr.) 10.10-0. G.McGlinchey. 75/1.

DOORSTEP
chestnut gelding by Cantab - Kelly's Door.
1984 . . . Fell. (Mr J.Horgan) 8.10-2. Mr. J. Queally. 100/1

DOUBLE U AGAIN
bay gelding by Double-U-Jay - Halfsixagain.
1984 . . . Finished 13th of 40 (Mr P. J. McBennett) 10.10-5. T.Morgan. 100/1
1986 . . . Brought down. (Mr B. Clark & Mr C. Holmes) 12.10-0. C.Mann. 500/1.

DRUNKEN DUCK, THE
bay gelding by Pony Express - Polly Buckle.
1984 . . . Pulled-up. (Mr B.Munro-Wilson) 11.10-3. A.Brown. 100/1.

DRUMLARGAN
bay gelding by Twilight Alley - Avro Jet.
1985 . . . Pulled-up. (Mrs G.Webb Bronfman) 11.11 -8. J.Francome. 8/1.
1986 . . . Fell. (Mrs G.Webb Bronfnlan) 12 11-6. T. J. Ryan. 40/1.
1987 . . . Pulled-up. (Mr G.J.D.Wragg) 13.11-2. Mr. G.Wragg. 66/1.

DUDIE
bay gelding by Karabas - En Clair.
1985 . . . Fell. (Mr.M.B.Moore) 7.10-0. A.Mullins. 50/1.
1986 . . . Unseated rider. (Mr J.Halewood) 8 10-0. K.Doolan. 100/1.

DOOR LATCH
chestnut gelding by Cantab - Kelly's Door.
1986 . . . Fell. (Mr H.J.Joel) 8.11-0. R.Rowe. 9/1.

DARK IVY
grey gelding by My Swanee - Cloudy Dawn.
1987 . . . Fell. (Mrs S.Catheswood) 11.10-2. P.Tuck. 11/2.

DALTMORE
brown gelding by Pauper - Zaleg.
1987 . . . Pulled-up. (Mr N. Coburn) 9.10-0. A.Mullins. 100/1

DURHAM EDITION
chestnut gelding by Politico - Level Stakes.
1988 . . . Finished 2nd of 40. (Mr R.Oxley) 10.10-9. C.Grant. 20/1.
1989 . . . Finished 5th of 40. (Mr R.Oxley) 11.10-11. C.Grant. 15/2.
1990 . . . Finished 2nd of 38. (Mr R.Oxle.y) 12.10-9. C.Grant. 9/1.
1991 . . . Finished 6th of 40. (Mr R.Oxley) 13.10-13 C.Grant. 25/1.

DIXTON HOUSE
bay gelding by Cantab - Bird Of Honour.
1989 . . . Fell. (Mr P.S.Hill) 10.10-3. T.Morgan. 7/1/Fav.*

DOCKLANDS EXPRESS
bay gelding by Roscoe Blake - Southern Moss.
1991 . . . Fell. (Mr R.H.Baines) 9.10-3. A.Tory. 20/1.
1992 . . . Finished 4th of 40. (Mr R.H.Baines) 10.11-2. P.Scudamore. 15/2.Fav.*

DOUBLE SILK
bay gelding by Dubassoff - Yellow Silk.
1994 . . . Fell. (Mr R. C.Wilkins) 10.10-4. Mr.R.Treloggen.6/1.

DAKYNS BOY
chestnut gelding by Deep Run - Mawbeg Holly.
1995 . . . Unseated rider. (Mr A.Parker) 10 10-0. T.Jenks. 50/1.

DESERT LORD
grey gelding by Step Together - Star Mill.
1995 . . . Fell. (Mr P.A.Keogh) 9.10-0 F.Woods. 100/1.

DO BE BRIEF
chestnut gelding by Le Moss - Right Perforrnance.
1995 . . . Fell. (Mr E.Brown) 10.10-0. B.Powell. 66/1.

DEEP BRAMBLE
chestnut gelding by Deep Run - Bardicate.
1996 . . . Pulled-up. (Mr P.K.Barber & Mr M.Coburn) 9.11-5. A.P.McCoy. 12/1.

● Favourite Easter Hero in majestic form in 1929 - but Gregalach was looming.

EXQUISITE, THE
1845 . . . Finished 3rd of 15. (Captain Boyd) L.Byrne. n/q.

EAGLE
1846 . . . Finished 5th of 22. (Mr C. E. Brooke) Capt.W.Peel. 6/1.
1848 . . . Fell. (Mr C.E.Brooke) - 11-4. J.Broome.n/q.

EQUINOX
1849 . . . Fell. (Captain Peyton) - 9-12. Moloney. n/q.

EVERTON
1850 . . . Failed to finish. (Mr D.Lewis) - 10-8. A. Salt. n/q.
1852 . . . Fell (Mr Elmore) - 9-10. Hewitt. n/q.

ESCAPE
1855 . . . Knocked-over. (Mr Buchanan) - 10-4. Knott. 50/1.
1857 . . . Failed to finish. (Mr J.Merry) - 11-2. J.Thrift. 7/1.
1858 . . . Knocked-over. (Mr J.Merry) - 11-0. T.Olliver. 20/1.
1859 . . . Finished 8th of 20. (Mr J.Merry) - 10-5. T.Donaldson. 20/1

EMIGRANT
bay gelding by Melbourne - Pandora. Not in the General Stud Book.
1856 . . . Finished 6th of 21. (Mr G. Hodgman) 10.10-2. C. Boyce.100/6.
1857 . . . WON. (Mr G. Hodgman) 11. 9-10. 28 Ran. C. Boyce.10/1.

EMPEROR, THE
1861 . . . Failed to finish. (Mr D Briggs) - 10-2. Mr.A.Goodman. 100/8.

EMBLEM
chestnut mare by Teddington - Miss Batty. Bred by Mr.R.Swale.
1863 . . . WON. (Lord Coventry) 7.10-10. 16 Ran. G. Stevens. 4/1.
1865 . . . Pulled-up. (Lord Coventry) 9.12-4. W. Walters. 100/8.

EMBLEMATIC
chestnut mare by Teddington - MiSS Batty. Bred by Mr.R.Swale.
1864 . . . WON. (Lord Coventry) 6.10-6. 25 Ran. G. Stevens. 10/1.
1865 . . . Finished 3rd of 23. (Lord Coventry) 7.11-10. G.Stevens. 5/1.Fav. *

EXPRESS
1865 . . . Pulled-up. (Mr D.Collins) - 11-6. Mr.D. Collins. n/q.

EFFENBURG
1866 ...Failed to finish (Count Furstenberg) - 12-8. R.Twiddy. 50/1.

ELK, THE
chestnut gelding by Humming Bird - dam unknown.
1870 . . . Pulled-up. (Mr Rose) aged 10-7. B.Land, jnr. 100/15.

EUROTAS
bay horse by Orphelin - Silistrie. Bred in France.
1874 . . . Failed to finish. (Mr Chaston) 6.11-8. Mr.Thomas. 14/1.

EARL MARSHALL
bay horse by The Earl - Frangipani.
1877 . . . Fell. (Lord Downe) 6.10-10. Mr Rolly. n/q

EMPRESS
chestnut mare by Blood Royal - Jeu des Mots. Bred by Mr.T.Lindesay.
1880 . . . WON. (Mr P. Ducrot) 5/10-7. 14 Ran. Mr. T.Beasley. 8/1.

EAU DE VIE
bay mare by Marsyas - Fairwater.
1882 . . . Ran-out. (Duke of Hamilton) 7.10-8.Mr.D.Thirlwell. 15/1.
1883 . . . Finished 7th of 10.(Duke of Hamilton) 8.11-10. Mr.D.Thirlwell. 9/2.

ET CETERA
bay mare by Town Moor - Fair And Square. Bred in Germany.
1889 . . . Fell. (Count N.Esterhazy) 5.10-13. G.Morris. 8/1.

EMPEROR
chestnut horse by Philammon - Empress.
1890 . . . Finished 6th of 16 (Capt. J. Machell) 5.11-1.Mr.D.Thirlwell. Remounted* 100/6.
1891 . . . Pulled-up (Capt. J. Machell) 6.11-3. W.Nightingall. 25/1.

EMIN
bay horse by Galliard - Venture.
1896 . . . Pulled-up. (Sir S. Scott) 7.10-8. H.Brown. 200/1.

ELECTRIC SPARK
bay mare by Gallant - dam by Pearlfinder.
1898 . . . Pulled-up (Mr R.Wright) 7.9-11. A.Waddington. 100/1
1899 . . . Finished 8th of 19.(Mr R.Wright) 8.9-11. A.Waddington. 20/1.

ELLIMAN
bay horse by Melton - Recovery.
1899 . . . Finished 3rd of 19. (Mr A.Blyth) 8.10-1. E.Piggott. 20/1.
1900 . . . Finished 11th of 16.(Mr A.Blyth) 9.10-1. E.Driscoll. 100/7.

EASTER OGUE
chestnut gelding by Aseetic - Elissa.
1900 . . . Finished 7th of 16. (Lord Wm.Beresford) 6.9-13. C.Hogan. 66/1.

EXPERT II
chestnut gelding by Studley - Weel Done.
1903 . . . Fell. (Mr W.Haven) 6.10-5. S.J.Woodland.40/1.

EREMON
bay gelding by Thurles - Daisy. Bred by Mr.J.Cleary.
1907 . . . WON. (Mr S. Howard) 7.10-1. 23 Ran. A.Newey. 8/1

EXTRAVAGANCE
chestnut gelding by Carlton Grange - Belle Dennoiselle.
1907 . . . Fell. (Mr G.Walmsley) 6.10-11. G. Goswell. 10/1.
1908 . . . Fell. (Mr G.Walmsley) 7.10-12. H.Aylin. 100/7.

EUGENIST
bay gelding by Captain Kettle - Follow Me, Lads
* 1916 . . . Pulled-up. (Mr E.S.Wills) 8.11-10. H.Smyth. 100/6.

EAMON BEAG
bay gelding by Menander - Lady Olton.
1921 . . . Fell. (Mr J. Widger) 8.10-4. M. Connors. 10/1.

EUREKA II
chestnut gelding by Frustrum - Red Damsel.
1923 . . . Fell. (Lord Woolavington) 6.11-0. A.Stubbs. 40/1.
1924 . . . Fell. (Lord Woolavington) 7.11-5. A.Robson. 100/6.

EAGLE'S TAIL
chestnut gelding by White Eagle - Addenda.
1927 . . . Fell. (Mr J. A.Fairhurst) 8.10-9. F. Brookes. 20/1.
1928 . . . Failed to finish. (Mr J.A.Fairhurst) 9.11-0. E.Foster. 50/1.

EASTER HERO
chestnut gelding by My Prince - Easter Week
1928 . . . Fell.(Captain A.Lowenstein) 8.12-5. P. Powell. 100/7.
1929 . . . Finished 2nd of 66. (Mr J.H.Whitney) 9.12-7. J.Moloney. 9/1Fav.*
1931 . . . Fell. (Mr J.H.Whitney) 11. 12-7. F.B.Rees.5/1 Fav.*

EASY VIRTUE
brown gelding by Don Juan - Rusialka.
1931 . . . Fell. (Mr W. P. Tyser) 8.10-12. P. Powell. 100/1.

EGREMONT
chestnut gelding by White Eagle -Queen Mother.
1932 . . . Finished 2nd of 36. (Mrs Ireland) 8.10-7. Mr.E.C.Paget.33/1.
1933 . . . Completed the course. (Mrs Ireland) 9.11-1.Mr.E.C.Paget. 100/7.
1934 . . . Refused. (Mrs Ireland) 10.10-12. Mr.E.C.Paget.66/1.

EVOLUTION
bay gelding by The Vizier - Vab.
1932 ...Fell. (Mr W.C.Langley) aged 10-7. T.B.Cullinan. 50/1

EMANCIPATOR
brown gelding by The Vizier - Emancipation.
1935 . . . Fell. (Mr P. V. F. Cazalet) 7.10-7. Mr.P.V.F.Cazalet. 66/1.
1936 . . . Fell. (Mr P. V. F. Cazalet) 8.10-7. Mr.P.V.F.Cazalet. 20/1.
1937 . . . Pulled-up.(Mr P. V. F. C.azalet) 9.10-5. Mr.P.V.F. Cazalet. 33/1 .
1938 . . . Fell. (Mr P. V. F. Cazalet) 10.10-3. Mr.P.V.F.Cazalet. 100/1

EGO
chestnut gelding by Pomponious - Eggs.
1936 . . . Finished 2nd of 35.(Sir David Llewellyn) 9.10-8.Mr. H.Llewellyn. 50/1.
1937 . . . Finished 4th of 33.(Sir David Llewellyn) 10.10-9.Mr.H.Llewellyn. 10/1.

EVASIO MON
chestnut gelding by Sky-Rocket - Almere.
1936 . . . Fell. (Mr T.Holland-Martin) 10.10-11. Mr T.Holland-Martin. 100/1.

EPIPHANES
bay gelding by Ptolemy - Soda Mint.
1939 . . . Fell. (Mr J B.Roll) 7.10-0. Mr.H.G.Applin.100/1.

E. P.
bay gelding by Cottage - Another Silver.
1946 . . . Pulled-up (Mr J.lsmay) 11.10-2. M.Molony. 50/1.
1947 . . . Fell. (Mr J.Ismay) 12.10-5. M.Molony.100/1.

EARLY MIST
chestnut gelding by Brumeux - Sudden Dawn. Bred by Mr. D.J.Wrinch.
1952 . . . Fell. (Mrs J. V. Rank) 7.10-11. P.Taaffe. 18/1.
1953 . . . WON. (Mr J.H.Griffin) 8.11-2. 31 Ran. B.Marshall.20/1
1955 . . . Finished 9th of 30.(Mr J.Dunlop) 10.12-3. B.Marshall. 9/1.
1956 . . . Fell. (Mr J.Dunlop) 11.12-2. B.Marshall. 25/1.

E. S. B.
bay or brown gelding by Bidar - English Summer. Bred by Miss S.Burke.
1955 . . . Fell. (Mrs L.Carver) 9.11-1. T. Cusack. 66/1.
1956 . . . WON. (Mrs L.Carver) 10.11-3. 29 Ran. D.V. Dick.100/7.
1957 . . . Finished 8th of 35. (Mrs L.Carver) 11.11-13. D.V.Dick. 20/1.
1958 . . . Finished 6th of 31. (Mrs L.Carver) 12.11-12. D.V.Dick. 28/1.

ERNEST
brown gelding by Roi d'Egypte - Calfstown.
1961 . . . Finished 12th of 35. (Mrs L. Brotherton) 9.10-1.H.J East. 33/1.
1962 . . . Finished 9th of 32. (Mrs L.Brotherton) 10.10-0. A.Dufton. 66/1.

EVEN DELIGHT
bay gelding by Even Money - Donard Delight.
1972 . . . Pulled-up. (Mr J.McClorey) 7.10-2. R.Dennard. 40/1.

ENDLESS FOLLY
brown gelding by Immortality - Follette.
1973 . . . Finished 9th of 38. (Mrs V.Vanden Bergh) 11.10-0. J.Guest. 100/1.

ESTOILE
bay mare by Escart III - Gallic Star.
1974 . . . Fell. (Mr H.Burt) 10.10-0. R.Hyett. 66/1.

ESCARI
chestnut gelding by Escart III - Banri.
1974 . . . Finished 15th of 42.. (Mr J.J.McDowell) 8.10-2. P.Black. 66/1.

EVEN DAWN
chestnut gelding by Even Money - Twilight Slave.
1975 . . . Pulled-up. (Mr S.Wainwright) 8.10-4. D.Mould. 50/1.

EVEN UP
brown gelding by Even Money - Safe Harbour
1980 . . . Refused. (Mr N.Whitcomb) 13.10-6. A.Webber. 50/1

ELIOGARTY
chestnut gelding by Lucky Brief - Natanya.
1984 . . . Finished 15th of 40. (Miss C.J.Beasley) 9.11-5. Mr D.Hassett. 16/1.

ESSEX
brown horse by SKy - Efiopea. Bred in Hungary.
1986 . . . Pulled-up. (Mr J Cuba) 8.12-0. V. Chaloupka. 100/1.

ELLIER, THE
bay gelding by Menelek - Betton's Folly.
1987 . . . Finished 7th of 40. (Full Circle Thoroughbred) 11-10-0. F.Berry. 18/1.

EAMONS OWEN
brown gelding by Master Owen - Clerihan.
1987 . . . Unseated rider. (Mr W.G.N.Morgan) 10.10-0. Miss J.Oliver. 200/1.

ETON ROUGE
bay gelding by The Parson- Rouge Shack.
1988 . . . Fell. (Mrs B.P.Jenks) 9.10-5. D.Browne. 80/1.

ENVOPAK TOKEN
chestnut gelding by Proverb - Luck Token.
1991 . . . Pulled-up. (Mr F.Arthur) 10.10-0. M. Perrett. 28/1.

EBONY JANE
brown mare by Roselier - Advantage.
1994 . . . Finished 4th of 36. (Mr J.Lynch) 9.10-1. L.Cusack. 25/1.
1995 . . . Finished 12th of 35.(Mr J.Lynch) 10.10-0. A.Maguire.20/1.

ELFAST
bay gelding by Neltino - Niagara Rhythm
1994 . . . Fell. (Major J.L.Damont & Mr J.Webber) 11.10-4. G.McCourt. 18/1.

ERRANT KNIGHT
chestnut gelding by Deep Run - Dame Lucy.
1995 . . . Unseated rider. (Mrs N.J.Bird & Mrs S.Cartridge) 11. 10-0. M.Perrett 75/1.

ESHA NESS
bay gelding by Crash Course -Beeston.
1995 . . . Fell. (Mr P. Bancroft) 12.10-0. J.White. 50/1.

ENCORE UN PEU
chestnut gelding by Nikos - Creme Caramel. Bred in France.
1996 . . . Finished 2nd of 27. (Mr V.Nally) 9.10-0. D. Bridgwater.14/1.

● Forbra gets home to win the 1932 National after
a tremendous battle with runner-up Egremont.

● Frank Furlong is welcomed by his proud parents
after winning the 1935 race on Reynoldstown.

FIREFLY
1846 . . . Finished 4th of 22. (Lord Waterford) - 12-4. L.Byrne. 7/1.

FALSE HEIR, THE
1847 . . . Failed to finish. (Mr R.Hall) - 11-4. Wilson. n/q.

FREDERICK
1847 . . . Failed to finish. (Mr Preston) - 11-2. T.Abbot. n/q.

FATHER MATTHEW
1848 . . . Fell. (Mr W.S.Crawford) - 11-6. H.Lamplugh. n/q.

FORTUNE-TELLER
1848 . . . Fell. (Mr Kennedy) - 10-10. Stagg. 30/1.

FARNHAM
1850 . . . Finished 5th of 32. (Mr Maugan) 6.11-3. T. Abbot. 15/1.

FISTICUFF
1850 Failed to finish (Mr. J. Nicoll) 10-0 Parr. n/q

FUGITIVE
1851 . . . Fell. (Lord Lurgan) - 10-12. H.Bradley. 15/1.

FUGLEMAN
1851 . . . Failed to finish. (Colonel Shirley) - 10-0. D. Wynne. n/q.

FIELD MARSHALL
1853 . . . Failed to finish. (Mr J.Roberts) - 10-4. Nelson. n/q.

FREETRADER
bay or brown horse by The Sea - Miss Cobden. Bred by Mr.H.B.Powell.
1855 . . . Finished 2nd of 20. (Mr W.Barnett) 6.9-4. D.Meaney. 50/1.
1856 . . . WON. (Mr W.Barnett) 7.9-6. 21 Ran. G.Stevens. 25/1.
1857 . . . Failed to finish. (Mr W.Barnett) 8.10-0. G.Stevens. 25/1.

FRANC PICARD
1856 . . . Failed to finish. (Baron C. de la Motte) - 10-12. Wakefield. n/q.
1861 . . . Failed to finish. (Baron C. de la Motte) -10-0. H.Lmplugh. 14/1 .

FOREST QUEEN, THE
1856 . . . Failed to finish. (Mr Harper) - 10-2. J.Thrift. 15/1.
1857 . . . Finished 8th of 28. (Mr Harper) - 9-8. T. Donaldson. 20/1.

FIRST OF MAY
1857 .. Failed to finish. (Mr Raxworthy) - 9-0. R.Sly,jnr. n/q.

FLATCATCHER
1859 . . . Knocked-over. (Mr Barling) - 9-0. T.Holmes. n/q.

FRESHMAN, THE
1861 . . . FelL (Mr C.Symonds) - 9-7. Mr.Blake. 100/7.
1863 . . . Fell. (Mr W.Meaney) - 11-13. Mr.Edwards. n/q.
1865 . . . Pulled-up. (Mr W.H.Whyte) - 10-10. D. Meaney. 40/1.

FOSCO
1863 . . . Finished 4tH of 16. (Mr G.Holman) - 9-11. Mr.G. Holman. 40/1

FLYFISHER
1865 . . . Finished 6th of 23. (Mr Powell) 6.11-12. Mr.J.R.Riddell. n/q.

FRANK
1866 . . . Failed to finish. (Mr Cockburn) - 11-8. Mr.Lawrence. 50/1.

FAN
bay mare by Volunteer - Miss Harkaway.
1867 . . . Finished 2nd of 23. (Mr Barber) 5.10-3. Thorpe. 9/1.
1868 . . . Refused. (Mr Barber) 6.10-6. Thorpe. 10/1.
1869 . . . Refused. (Mr Barber) 7.10-6. Thorpe. 4/1.
1870 . . . Refused. (Mr Lawrence) 8.10-0. H.Taylor. 100/15.

FORTUNATUS
bay horse by Leamington - Fortuna.
1869 . . . Pulled-up. (Mr E.Brayley) 6.11-4. J.Page. 7/2.Fav.*

FLEURISTE
bay mare by West Australian - Aricie.
1872 . . . Finished 5th of 25. (Duke of Hamilton) 5.10-10. Rickaby. 50/1.
1875 . . . Failed to finish. (Mr Grainger) 8.11-0. R.I'Anson. 100/3

FRANC LURON
bay gelding by Fitz-Gladiator - Miss Diversion.
1872 . . . Fell. (Capt.J. Machell) 6.10-7. J.Cannon. 100/6.

FOOTMAN
brown horse by Tim Whiffler - Whiteleg.
1873 . . . Fell. (Mr Moreton) 6.11-5. R.Marsh. 100/15. Fav.*

FURLEY
chestnut gelding by Honiton - Odine.
1874 . . . Failed to finish. (Mr H.Bruce) 6.11-10. Mr.A.Yates. 12/1.
1875 . . . Refused. (Mr H.Baltazzi) 7.12-2. Mr.J.Goodwin.n/q.

FANTOME
brown horse by Orphelin - Belle de Nuit. Bred in France.
1874 . . . Failed to finish. (Duke of Hamilton) 6.10-10. J.Page 20/1.

FAIR WIND
chestnut gelding by Citadel - Weatherwise.
1881 . . . Fell. (Capt.P.Ducrot) aged 10-13. Mr.H.Beasley. 100/6.

FABIUS
chestnut horse by Loiterer - Cordelia.
1881 . . . Refused (Mr H. F. C. Vyner) 5.10-0. W. Hunt. 25/1

FAY
bay gelding by Pauvre Mignon - Estampe. Bred in France.
1882 . . . Fell. (Capt.J.Machell) - 10-7. Mr.E. P. Wilson. 100/7.

FRIGATE
bay mare by Gunboat - Fair Maid Of Kent. Bred by Mr.M.Maher.
1884 . . . Finished 2nd of 15. (Mr M.A.Maher) 6.11-3.Mr.H.Beasley. 10/1.
1885 . . . Finished 2nd of 19. (Mr M.A.Maher) 7.11-10.Mr.H.Beasley. 7/1
1886 . . . Fell. (Mr Broadwood) 8.11-13. J.Jones. 9/1.
1887 . . . Pulled-up. (Mr F.E.Lawrence) 9.11-5.Mr.F.E.Lawrence. 100/9
1888 . . . Finished 2nd of 20. (Mr M.A.Maher) 10.11-2.Mr.W.Beasley. 100/9
1889 . . . WON. (Mr M.A.Maher) 11.11-4. 20 Ran.Mr.T.Beasley. 8/1
1890 . . . Fell. (Mr M.A.Maher) 12.12-7. Mr.T.Beasley. 100/7.

FONTENOY
bay horse by Victorious - Sweet Galingale
1886 . . . Refused. (Mr Iquique) 9.10-4. J.Page. 200/1.

FAWN, THE
brown mare by Pero Gomez - Gazelle.
1888 . . . Fell. (Lord Cholmondeley) 6.10-6.Mr.E.P.` Wilson.18/1.
1889 . . . Finished 7th of 20.(Lord Cholmondeley) 7.10-10. Mr.W.Beasley. 25/1.

FETICHE
brown horse by Nougat - Fleurines. Bred in France.
1890 . . . Fell. (M.M.E.Phrussi) aged 10-12. V.Baker. 25/1.

FIREBALL
chestnut gelding - pedigree unknown.
1890 . . . Fell. (Mr H.Holmes) aged 10-4. D. Corner. 100/1.
1891 . . . Pulled-up. (Mr H.Holmes) aged 10-0. W.Halsey. 100/1.

FLOWER OF THE FOREST
brown mare by Lord Glenlyon - Forest Maiden.
1891 . . . Fell. (Mr Charter) 6.10-4. R. Clark. 50/1.

FATHER O'FLYNN
bay gelding by Retreat - Kathleen. Not in the General Stud Book.
1892 . . . WON. (Mr G.C.Wilson) 7.10-5. 25 Ran. Capt.E.R.Owen. 20/1.
1893 . . . Finished 6th of 15. (Mr G.C.Wilson) 8.11-11.Mr.G.B.Milne.100/9.
1894 . . . Fell. (Mr C.Grenfell) 9.11-3. Mr. C.Grenfell. 100/7.
1895 . . . Finished 7th of 19.(Mr C.A.Grenfell) 10.11-1. Mr.C.A.Grenfell.100/7.
1896 . . . Finished 2nd of 28 (Mr C.A.Grenfell) 11.10-12. Mr.C.A.Grenfell. 40/1

FLYING COLUMN
bay mare by Chippendale - Manoeuvre.
1892 . . . Finished 5th of 25. (Captain Peel) 7.10-7. Mr.W.Beasley.50/-1.

FAUST
bay or brown gelding by Favo - dam by Lurgan.
1892 . . . Finished 10th of 25. (General Beresford) 7.10-5.Mr.Lushington.100/1.
1893 . . . Finished 8th of 15. (General Beresford) 8.10-6.Captain Yardley. 40/1.

FIELD MARSHAL
bay gelding by Border Minstrel - Rouge Gagne. Formerly narmed Pony Moore.
1893 . Pulled-up. (Mr Eustace Loder) 7.11 -4.Capt. Crawley. 28/1.

FIN-MA-COUL, II
chestnut gelding by Ballinafad dam by Lothario.
1895 . . . Finished 10th of 19. (Mr J.Arnold) 5.10-5. W.Canavan. 40/1.

FLEETWING
brown mare by Studley - Cassoway.
1896 . . . Broke Blood Vessel. (Mr M.J.Corbally) 6.10-6. Mr.Parsons. 100/1.

FILBERT
bay gelding by Regent - dam by Spider.
1897 . . . Finished 2nd of 28. (Mr G.R.Powell) 7.9-7. Mr.C.Beatty. 100/1 .
1898 . . . Finished 4th of 25. (Mr G.R.Powell) 8.9-12. Mr.C.Beatty. 25/1.

FORD OF FYNE
brown gelding by Studley - dam by Memory.
1897 . . . Finished 3rd of 28. (Maj.J.A.Orr-Ewing) 6.10-7. Mr.Withington. 25/1.
1898 . . . Finished 6th of 25. (Maj.J.A.Orr-Ewing) 7.11-0. Mr.F.Withington. 11/2.Fav*
1899 . . . Finished 2nd of 19. (Maj.J.A.Orr-Ewing) 8.10-10. E.Matthews. 40/l.

FAIRY QUEEN
brown mare by Happy Land - Ethelreda.
1897 . . . Finished 7th of 28 (Mr G.S.Davies) 11.9-7. Mr.H.E.Lord. 50/1.
1899 . . . Finished 10th of 19.(Mr S.Davies) 13.9-11. W.Oates. 100/1

FANCIFUL
bay mare by Hackler - Miss Fanny.
1901 . . . Finished 5th of 24. (Mr H.Tunstall-Moore) 6.11-6. Mr. W. P. Cullen. 100/8.
1903 . . . Finished 7th of 23. (Mr H.Tunstall-Moore) 8.11-7. Mr. W.P. Cullen. 100/6.

FAIRLAND
bay mare by Ascetic - Far Away.
1902 . . . Fell. (Mr T. Bater) 9. 9-10. H.Taylor. 25/1
1903 . . . Fell. (Mr T. Bater) 10.10-13. W. Morgan. 20/1.

FOREMAN, THE
bay gelding by Bend Or - Crusado.
1907 . . . Fell. (Mr T.Nolan) 8. 9-7. E. Lawn. n/q.

FLAXMAN
bay gelting by Hackler - Circe.
1908 . . . Finished 4th of 24. (H.M.The King) 8. 9-12. A. Anthony. 33/1.

FETLAR'S PRIDE

bay gelding by Fetlar - Monica 11.
1910 . . . Finished 5th of 25. (Mr A Law) 9.10-11. J.Walsh,jnr. 25/1.
1911 . . . Fell. (Mr C.Pearson) 10.10-7. J.Walsh. 25/1.
1912 . . . Failed to finish. (Mr C.Pearson) 11.10-7. G Lyall. n/q.
1913 . . . Fell. (Mr C.Pearson) 12.11-2. F. Morgan. 33/1.
1914 . . . Refused. (Mr C.Pearson) 13.10-2 D. Dale. n/q

FOOL-HARDY

chestnut gelding by Sainfoin - Retire.
1911 . . . Finished 4th of 26. (Mr W.Macneill) 10. 9-7. Mr.W. Macneill. 50/1. Remounted*
1912 . . . Failed to finish. (Mr W.Macneill) 11.10-3. Mr. W. Macneill.n/q.
1913 . . . Fell (Mr W.Macneill) 12.11-0. Mr.W.Macneill. 200/1.

FLAXEN

bay mare by Hackler - Butterfly.
1911 . . . Fell. (Mr G,.L.Pirie) 9. 9-7. Mr.A.Smith. 50/1.

FEARLESS VII

chestnut- gelding by Red Prince 11 - Fancy Fair.
1913 . . . Fell. (Mr R.Whitehead) l0.11-0. Mr G.Pigot-Moodie. 100/1

FATHER CONFESSOR

chestnut gelding by St Gris - Entrenous.
1915 . . . Finished 3rd of 20. (Lord Suffolk) 6. 9-10. A.Aylin. 10/1.
* 1917 . . . Completed course. (Lord Suffolk) 8.11-7. A.Aylin. n/q.

FLEUR-DE-LYS

chestnut geldding by Oriflamme - Maid Of Honour.
* 1916 . . . Pulled-up. (Sir R.Wilmot) 9.9-7. W.Hives. n/q.

FARGUE

chestnut gelding by Fariman - Kitty Gallerte.
* 1917 . . . Fell. (Mr P.S.Adams) 7. 9-10. Mr.H.A.Brown. 25/1.
1919 . . . Failed to finish. (Mr G.P.Sanday) 9. 9-9. W.Smith. 50/1.

FOREWARNED

bay horse by Foresight - Uneekah.
1921 . . . Fell. (Mr W.A.Bankier) 6. 9-11. R.Burford. 50/1.
1923 . . . Fell. (Mr W.A.Bankier) 8.11-5. J.R.Anthony. 11/2.Fav.*

FLY MASK

bay gelding by Fly Fisher - dam by Bergomask.
1924 . . . Finished 2nd of 30. (Mr T.K.Laidlaw) 10.10-12. J.Moylan. 100/7.
1925 . . . Finished 3rd of 33. (Mr T.K.Laidlaw) 11.11-11. E.Doyle.10/1.

FAIRY HILL II

brown gelding by Bright Bat - Cerg Agile.
1924 . . . Fell. (Major H.A.Wernher) 8.10-0. W.Watkinson. 33/1.

FOXTROT

chestnut gelding by Light Briagde - Flora Dance.
1928 . . . Failed to finish. (Capt.H.Lumsden) 12.10-13. Capt.H.Lumsden. 100/1.

FLEET PRINCE

brown gelding by My Prince - May Fleet.
1929 . . . Fell. (Mr G.S.L.Whitelaw) 11.10-5. Mr.F.R.Thackray. 200/1.

FORBRA

brown gelding by Foresight - Thymbra.
1932 . . . WON. (Mr W.Parsonage) 7.10-7. 36 Ran. J.Hamey. 50/1.
1933 . . . Finished 6th of 34. (Mr W.Parsonage) 8.11-9. J.Hamey. 33/1.
1934 . . . Finished 4th of 30. (Mr W.Parsonage) 9.11-7. G.Hardy.100/8.

FLAMBENT

brown gelding by Foresight - Crusade.
1934 . . . Fell. (Mrs Gilbert Robinson) 9.11-3. T.Duggan. 66/1.

FORTNUM
brown gelding by Fort - Jealousy.
1934 . . . Fell. (Commander A.V.Courage) 9.10-7 .F.Sclater. 33/1.

FOUQUET
brown gelding by Grey Fox II - Toutoune.
1935 . . . Refused. (Mr M.D.Blair) 8.10-7. E. Brown. 100/1.

FLYING MINUTES
bay gelding by Flying Ebony - Chamita.
1937 . . . Fell. (Mrs F.Ambrose Clark) 7.10-2. B. Hobbs. 66/1.

FIELD MASTER
chestnut gelding by Warden of the Marches - Queen of the Hunt.
1937 . . . Fell. (Mr L.Densham) 9.10-3. Mr. Densham. 100/1.

FROBISHER
chestnut gelding by Lemonora - Overround.
1938 . . . Fell. (Miss M.F.Cohen) 7.10-6. Capt. R.Harding. 66/1.

FIRST OF THE DANDIES
brown gelding by Last of the Dandies - Trout Fly.
1947 . . . Fell. (Mr G.Wilson) 10.10-3. J. Moloney. 66/1.
1948 . . . Finished 2nd of 43. (Maj. D.J.Vaughan) 11.10-4. J. Brogan. 25/1.

FLAMING STEEL
bay gelding by Steel Point - Flaming Dawn.
1949 . . . Finished 5th of 43. (Mr A.D.Wimbush) 8.10-9. Mr.J.Spencer. 33/1.

FREEBOOTER
bay gelding by Steel Point - Proud Fury.
1950 . . . WON. (Mrs L.Brotherton) 9.11-11. 49 Ran. J. Power. 10/1. jnt/Fav.*
1951 . . . Brought-down. (Mr L.Brotherton) 10.12-7. J.Power. 10/1.
1952 . . . Fell. (Mrs L Brotherton) 11.12-7. B.Marshall. 10/1.

FIGHTING LINE
brown gelding by His Reverence - B,,¥line.
1950 . . . Refused. (Mrs C.A.Hall-Hall) 11.10-8. Mr.E.Greenway. 50/1.

FINNURE
chestnut gelding by Ca,,≠ador - Hazelly.
1951 . . . Fell. (Lord Bicester) 11.12-0. R.Francis. 22/1.

FOUR TEN
bay gelding by Blunderbuss - Undue Praise.
1957 . . . Fell. (Mr A.Strange) 11.11-11. R.Morrow. 50/1.

FELIAS
brown gelding by Phideas - Feluce.
1957 . . . Brought-down. (Mrs P.Saunders) 9.10-5. W.Rees. 45/1.

FAHRENHEIT
bay gelding by Farrenjorden - Frozen Fruit.
1957 . . . Fell. (Miss P.Edwards) 10.10-0. T.O'Brien. 66/1.

FROZEN CREDIT
chestnut gelding by Within the Law- Eskimo.
1958 . . . Refused. (Mr W.F.Ransom) 12.10-12. Mr.P.Ransom.66/1.

FLOATER
bay or brown gelding by Flocon - Columbia.
1961 . . . Fell. (Mr C.Hambro) 8.10-11. E.P.Harty. 50/1.

FRESH WINDS
brown gelding by Roaring Forties - Loughbeg.
1961 . . . Fell. (Mr A Maiden) 10.10-10. R. Edwards. 66/1.

FREDITH'S SON
bay or brown gelding by Jubilee Day - Tidal Wave.
1962 . . . Finished 5th of 32. (Mr M.P.Keogh) 11.10-11. F.Shortt. 66/1.

FRENCHMAN'S COVE
chestnut gelding by Airborne - Frenchman's Creek.
1962 . . . Brought-down. (Mr S.Joel) 7.11-5. S. Mellor. 7/1.
1963 . . . Finished 20th of 47. (Mr S.Joel) 8.12-0. D.V.Dick. 100/6.

FORTRON
chestnut gelding by Fortina - Castle Saffron.
1962 . . . Finished 15th of 32. (Mr J.D.Pickering) 9.10-0. R.Langley. 100/1.

FRENCH LAWYER
bay gelding by Vulgan - Star Lawyer.
1963 . . . Finished 8th of 47. (Mr R.L.Newton) 9.10-0. T.Ryan. 50/1.

FORTY SECRETS
bay gelding by Fortina - Secret.
1963 . . . Finished 21st of 47. (Mr A.D.Clark) 9.10-7. C.Chapman. 50/1.

FLYING WILD
grey mare by Airborne - Wild Delight.
1964 . . . Fell. (Mr R.R.Guest) 8.11-3. D. Mould 100/7.co/Fav.*
1966 . . . Pulled up. (Mr R.R.Guest) 10.11-0. P.Taaffe. 20/1.

FREDDIE
brown gelding by Steel Chip - dam by Soldado.
1965 . . . Finished 2nd of 47. (Mr R.R.Tweedie) 8.11-10. P.McCarron. 7/2.Fav.*
1966 . . . Finished 2nd of 47. (Mr R.R. Tweedie) 9.11-7. P.McCarron. 11/4.Fav.*
1967 . . . Finished 17th of 44. (Mr R.R.Tweedie.) 10.11-13. P.McCarron. 100/9.

FORGOTTEN DREAMS
bay gelding by Artist's Son - Garrenroe.
1965 . . . Fell. (Mrs P.Meehan) 11.11-0. R.Coonan. 22/1.

FEARLESS CAVALIER
bay gelding by Cavalin - Fearless Queen.
1965 . . . Refused. (Mr J.K.Hooton) 14.10-13. R. West. 100/1.

FRENCH COTTAGE
bay gelding Fortina - Cottage Queen.
1965 . . . Refused. (Mr W.A.Tellwright) 13.10-13. Mr W.Tellwright. 100/1.

THE FOSSA
bay horse by Jena II - Fustian.
1966 . . . Finished 4th of 47. (Mr R.Greatbach) 9.10-8 T.Biddlecombe. 20/1.
1967 . . . Pulled up. (Mr R.Greatbach) 10.10-2. S.Mellor. 100/8.
1968 . . . Finished 5th of 45. (Mr R.Greatbach) 11.10-4. R.Edwards. 28/1.
1969 . . . Finished 11th of 30. (Capt. A.J.Parker-Bowles) 12.10-9. Capt. A.Parker-Bowles. 33/1.
1970 . . . Refused. (Capt. A.J.Parker-Bowles) 13.10-0. G.W.Robinson. 50/1.

FOREST PRINCE
brown gelding by Devon Prince - Forest.
1966 . . . Finished 3rd of 47. (Mrs D. Thompson) 8.10-8. G.Scott. 100/7.

FUJINO-O
chestnut gelding by Bric-A-Brac - Bell Note.
1966 . . . Refused. (Mr K.Fujii) 7.12-0. J.King. 100/1.

FLAMECAP
bay gelding by Flamenco - Another Madcap II.
1966 . . . Fell. (Mr C.Ronaldson) 9.10-0. F.Carroll. 100/1.

FOINAVON
brown gelding by Vulgan - Ecilace.
1967 . . . WON. (Mr C.P.T.Watkins) 9.10-0. J.Buckingham. 100/1.
1968 . . . Brought-down. (Mr M Bennellick) 10.10-5. P.Harvey. 66/1.

FORECASTLE
grey gelding by Fortina - Maiden Castle.
1967 . . . Pulled up. (Mr J.A.Wood) 9.10-10. N.Wilkinson. 50/1.
1968 . . . Pulled up. (Mr J.A.Wood) 10.10-8. Mr. W.McLernon. 50/1.

FRENCH KILT
brown gelding by Trouville - Kilted Angel.
1968 . . . Finished 14th of 45. (Major C.H.Nathan) 8.10-0. S.Mellor. 100/7.

FORT ORD
chestnut gelding by Fortina - Appropriate.
1968 . . . Fell. (Mr P.B.Spanoghe) 8.10-9. T. Norman. 35/1.
1970 . . . Fell. (Dr R.Ehnbom) 10.10-5. A.Turnell. 50/1.

FORT KNIGHT
bay gelding by Fortina - Another Madcap II.
1968 . . . Fell. (Mr W.J.Bebbington) 9.10-0. R.Reid. 40/1.

FORT SUN
chestnut gelding by Fortina - Solar Lady.
1969 . . . Finished 7th of 30. (Mr W.J.Pilsworth) 8.10-4. J.Crowley. 28/1.

FURORE II
chestnut gelding by Falls of Clyde - Sweet Fanny Adams.
1969 . . . Finished 9th of 30. (Mr N.H.Le Mare) 8.10-0. M.C.Gifford. 20/1.

FEARLESS FRED
bay gelding by Pearl Orient - Montreal.
1969 . . . Fell. (Mr B.P.Jenks) 7.11-3. T.W.Biddlecombe. 15/2.

FLOSUEBARB
bay mare by Soldado - Celia.
1969 . . . Fell. (Mrs E.F.Old) 9.10-0. J.Guest. 100/1.
1971 . . . Pulled-up. (Mrs E.F.Old) 11.10-0. J.Guest. 33/1.

FRENCH EXCUSE
bay gelding by Alibi 11 - Ma Poupee.
1970 . . . Fell. (Mr J.Jennings) 8.10-2. K.White. 100/8.

FINAL MOVE
bay gelding by Botticelli - Checkmate.
1971 . . . Finished 11th of 38. (Mr J.Liddle) 11.10-0. T.Stack. 50/1.

FORTINA'S PALACE
chestnut gelding by Fortina - Holy Smoke.
1972 . . . Fell. (Mr J.Nesbitt Davis) 9.10-7. J.King. 16/1.

FAIR VULGAN
bay gelding by Vulgan - Fair Cherry.
1972 . . . Fell. (Mr F.Pullen) 8.10-0. M.Gifford. 14/1.

FORTUNE BAY II
bay gelding by Dumbarnie - Sweet Fanny Adams.
1973 . . . Refused. (Mr G.A.Sloan) 9.10-3. Mr.G.A.Sloan. 66/1.

FRANCOPHILE
bay gelding by French Beige - Desirous.
1974 . . . Refused. (Mr & Mrs S.Powell) 9.10-5. R.Pitman. 16/1.

FEEL FREE
bay gelding by Khalkis - Candy Stall.
1975 . . . Fell. (Mr G.Syvret) 9.10-0. M.Salaman. 66/1.

FOREST KING
bay gelding by Rubor - Workington Wanderer.
1977 . . . Finished 5th of 42. (Mr K.W.Hogg) 8.10-12. R.Crank. 28/1.

FORESAIL
bay or brown gelding by Golden Vision - Sundrum Girl.
1977 . . . Refused. (Mr W.Nolan) 10.10-0. G.Holmes. 100/1.

FLITGROVE
chestnut gelding by Royal Buck - What A Daisy.
1979 . . . Pulled-up. (Lord Vestey) 8.10-0. R.Linley. 50/1.

FLASHY BOY
chestnut gelding by Royal Highway - Sparkling Gold.
1980 . . . Fell. (Mrs A.Bayley & Mr D.Smith) 12.10-8. C.Grant.50/1.

FORT VULGAN
chestnut gelding by Vulgan - Secret Fort.
1977 . . . Brought-down. (Mr A.J.Jacobs & Mr H.K.Zeisel) 9.10-0. N.Tinkler. 50/1.

FORTINA'S EXPRESS
brown gelding by Shackleton - Fortette.
1983 . . . Pulled-up. (Mr P.Piller) 9.10-3. P.Scudamore. 20/1.

FETHARD FRIEND
bay gelding by Megalo - Okeechobee.
1984 . . . Finished 7th of 40. (H.H.Kais Al-Said & Y.Idlibi) 9.10-12. G.Newman. 22/1.
1985 . . . Pulled-up. (H.H.Kais Al-Said & Y.Idlibi) 10.10-7. P.Barton. 16/1.
1986 . . . Pulled-up. (H.H.Kais Al-Said & Y.Idlibi) 11.10-0. P.Barton. 35/1.

FAULOON
brown gelding by Master Buck - Very Very.
1984 . . . Finished 18th of 40. (Mr R.H.Kieckhefer) 9.10-13. W.Smith. 50/1.
1985 . . . Fell. (Mr R.H.Kieckhefer) 10.10-2. K.Mooney. 66/1.

FORTUNE SEEKER
bay gelding by Three Wishes - Gypse Trout.
1984 . . . Fell. (Mrs G.T.McKey) 9.10-0. P.Barton. 100/1.

FRIENDLY HENRY
chestnut gelding by Be Friendly - Henry's Lady.
1988 . . . Finished 6th of 40. (Mr R.V.Wright) 8.10-4. N.Doughty. 100/1.
1989 . . . Fell. (Mr R.V.Wright) 9.10-4. H.Davies. 66/1.

FOYLE FISHERMAN
bay gelding by No Argument - Cute Peach.
1991 . . . Finished 10th of 40. (Mr J.N.Hutchinson) 12.10-0. E.Murphy. 40/1.

FOREST RANGER
bay gelding by The Parson - Nora Grany.
1991 . . . Finished 15th of 40. (K. Al-Said) 9.10-0. D.Tegg. 100/1.
1992 . . . Finished 12th of 40. (K. Al-Said) 10.10-0. D.Tegg. 200/1.

FRAZE
brown mare by Lakmus - Flabela. bred in Czechoslovakia.
1991 . . . Pulled-up. (Statni Statek Benesov) 8.11-10. V. Chaloupka. 100/1.

FIDDLERS PIKE
bay gelding by Turnpike - Fiddlers Bee.
1994 . . . Finished 5th of 36. (Mrs R.G.Henderson) 13.10-0. Mrs.R.Henderson. 100/1.

FELLOW, THE
bay gelding by Italic - L'Oranaise. Bred in France.
1994 . . . Fell. (Marquesa de Moratalla) 9.11-4. A.Kondrat.9/1.

FOURTH OF JULY
bay gelding by Rymer - Wayward Pam.
1994 . . . Fell. (Mrs J.Keeling) 10.10-0. J.P.Banahan. 50/1.

FOR WILLIAM
bay gelding by Whistling Deer - Pampered Sue.
1995 . . . Finished 15th of 35. (Mrs A.M.Daly) 9.10-0. C.O'Dwyer. 100/1. Remounted*

FAR SENIOR
chestnut gelding by Al Sirat - Ross Lady.
1996 . . . Unseated rider. (Mr P.Wegmann) 10.10-0. T.Eley. 150/1

● Gregalach, partnered by Australian Robert Everett, won the National in 1929. It was the second year in succession that the winner had returned 100/1.

GOBLIN
1841 . . . Finished 7th of 11. (Lord Villiers) Mr.Bretherton. n/q.
1843 . . . Finished 5th of 16. (Mr Errington) B.Bretherton. n/q.

GAY LAD
1842 . . . WON. (Mr J.Elmore) 8.12-0. 15 Ran. Tom Olliver. 7/1.

GOLDEN PIPPIN
1846 . . . Ran-out. (Mr Atkinson) Nainby. 12/1.

GRENADE
1847 . . . Failed to finish. (Mr Anderson) - 10-8. Rackley. n/q.

GAYHURST
1847 . . . Failed to finish. (Mr Wesley) - 10-7. Mr. Wesley. n/q.

GIPSY QUEEN, THE
1848 . . . Refused. (Lord Anson) - 10-6. Whitfield. n/q.

GREYSTEEL
1851 . . . Failed to finish. (Mr Onslow) - 9-10. Thrift. n/q.

GENERAL, THE
1853 . . . Finished 6th of 21. (Mr B.Land) - 10-4. T.Ablett. n/q.

GERALDUS
1854 . . . Refused. (Mr Barry) - 9-8. Debean. 50/1. n/q.

GARLAND
1855 . . . Finished 7th of 20. (Mr Minton) - 10-2. R.Sly jnr. 33/1.

GARRY OWEN
1857 . . . Failed to finish. (Col. Dickson) - 9-12. J.Ryan. 30/1.

GLENAMOUR
1858 . . . Fell. (Mr H Maxwell) - 9-0. Knott

GHIKA
1859 . . . Finished 7th of 20. (Mr Moreton) - 9-12. C.Boyce. 20/1.

GIPSY KING
1859 . . . Pulled-up. (Mr.Slaney) - 9-0. Edmunds. n/q.

GIBRALTER
1859 . . . Failed to finish. (Mr Hope) - 9-0. Armstrong. n/q.

GOLDSMITH
1860 . . . Failed to finish. (Capt. G.W.Hunt) - 10-10. B.Land jnr. 100/6.

GLENCAVIN
1866 . . . Failed to finish. (Mr J.Stevenson) - 11-4. J.Jewitt. 50/1.

GAROTTER
1866 . . . Fell. (Mr Oliver) 5.10-7. G.Ryan. 50/1.

GLOBULE
1867 . . . Finished 4th of 23. (Mr T.V.Morgan) - 11-7. G.Holman. 14/1.
1869 . . . Finished 7th of 22. (Mr T.V.Morgan) - 10-12. G.Holman. 25/1.

GENIEVRE
1867 . . . Finished 10th of 23. (Lord Poulett) - 10-5. Mr.Edwards. 20/1.

GARUS
1868 . . . Failed to finish. (Duke of Hamilton) - 10-12. J.Page. 30/1.

GARDENER
1869 . . . Finished 3rd of 22. (Capt. Machell) 7.10-7. Ryan. 1000/15.
1870 . . . Finished 6th of 23. (Capt. Machell) 8.10-12. Ryan. 20/1.

GUY OF WARWICK
1869 . . . Refused. (Mr Dixon) 5.10-0. Mr.Crawshaw. 100/7.
1870 . . . Failed to finish. (Mr E.Weever) 6.10-8. Mr.Edwards. 100/6.

GAMEBIRD
1876 . . . Fell. (Mr Appleton) 7.10-12. Mr.Appleton. 40/1.
1877 . . . Fell. (Mr Moore) 8.10-11. Mr Appleton 25/1.

GAZELLE
1876 . . . Refused. (Mr T.Smyth) 5.10-9. Mr Flutter. 40/1.

GUNLOCK
1880 . . . Refused. (Mr P.Aaron) 6.10-5. H.Davis. 33/1.

GAMECOCK
1885 . . . Fell. (Mr E.Jay) 6.10-0. W.E.Stephens. 50/1.
1886 . . . Finished 3rd of 23. (Mr E.Jay) 7.10-12. W.E.Stephens. 50/1.
1887 . . . WON (Mr E.Jay) 8.10-12. 16 Ran. W.Daniels. 20/1.
1888 . . . Finished 7th of 20. (Mr E.Benzon) 9.12-4. Capt. E.R.Owen. 20/1.
1889 . . . Finished 10th of 20. (Mr W Strong) 10.11-12. W.Dollery. 33/1.
1890 . . . Fell. (Mr Swan) 11.12-6. W.Dollery. 20/1.
1891 . . . Finished 6th of 21. (Mr Swan) 12.12-4. W.Dollery. 66/1.

GLENTHORPE
1889 . . . Fell. (Mr O.H.Jones) 5.10-10. Mr. W.H.Moore. 100/8.

GREAT PAUL
1889 . . . Pulled-up. (Mr B.W.J.Alexander) 7.10-0. W.Ellis. 200/1.

GRAPE VINE
1891 . . . Fell. (Mr G.H.Archer) 6.10-7. J.Hoysted. 9/1.

GOLDEN GATE
1893 . . . Pulled-up. (Capt. E.W.Baird) 6.10-2. G.Mawson. 30/1.

GOLDEN LINK
1893 . . . Refused. (Mr J.Dowling) 6.10-3. N.Behan. 100/1.

GOLDEN CROSS
1897 . . . Fell. (Mr C.O.Pemberton) - 10-2. G.Wilson. 33/1.

GREENHILL
1897 . . . Knocked-over. (Mr C.D.Rose) 6.9-11. E.Matthews. 25/1.
1898 . . . Finished 10th of 25. (Mr C.D.Rose) 7.10-3. C.Hogan. 100/1.

GOLDFISH
1897 . . . Fell. (Mr E.C.Smith) 6.9-7. T.Fitton. 66/1.

GAUNTLET
1897 . . . Fell. (Mr F.D.Leyland) 6.11-3. Capt. W.Hope- Johnstone. 66/1.
1898 . . . Finished 3rd of 25. (Mr F.D.Leyland) 7.10-13. W.Taylor. 100/12.

GRUDON
1898 . . . Finished 7th of 25. (Mr B.Bletsoe) 8.11-5. J.Hickey.25/1.
1900 . . . Finished 6th of 16. (Mr B Bletsoe) 10.10-5. Mr. M.B.Bletsoe. 40/1.
1901 . . . WON (Mr B.Bletsoe) 11.10-0. 24 Ran. A.Nightingall. 9/1.

GENTLE IDA
1899 . . . Fell. (Mr H.Bottomley) 10.11-7. W.Taylor. 4/1.Fav.*

GREYSTONE II
(formerly named GREYSTONE)
1901 . . . Failed to finish. (Mr J.Herdman) 8.10-1. J.H.Stainton. 100/1.

GOSSIP
1901 . . . Failed to finish. (Mr Foxhall Keene) 6.9-7. J.Poletti. 100/1.
1902 . . . Fell. (Mr Foxhall Keene) 7.9-7. H.Hewitt. 100/1.

GILLIE II
bay gelding by Sweetheart - Mountain Queen.
1903 . . . Fell. (Mr C.D.Barrow) 11.9-7. A.Wilkins. 100/1.

GUNNER, THE
chestnut horse by Torpedo - Lady Windermere.
1904 . . . Finished 3rd of 26. (Mr J.Widger) 7.10-4. Mr.J.W.Widger.25/1.

GLADIATOR
bay horse by Fetlar - Arena.
1906 . . . Finished 7th of 23. Remounted. (Mr G.Johnstone) 6.9-9. E.Driscoll.100/6.

GLENREX
bay gelding by Enthusiast or Glenvannon - Royal Naiad.
1906 . . . Fell. (Mr Barclay Walker) 6.9-9. Mr.R.Walker.

GLENSIDE
bay gelding by St. Gris - Kilwinnet.
1910 . . . Fell. (Mr F.Bibby) 8.10-4. G.Goswell. 25/1.
1911 . . . WON. (Mr F.Bibby) 9.10-3. 26 Ran. Mr.J.R.Anthony. 20/1.
1912 . . . Fell. (Mr F.Bibby) 10.11-0. Mr.H.Ussher. 40/1.

GENERAL FOX
(formerly named NO CLASS)
chestnut gelding by Shamrock or Telesinus - Pet Vixen.
1910 . . . Fell. (Lord Suffolk) 6.10-2. T.Willmot. 66/1.

GREAT CROSS
chestnut gelding by Rays Cross - Sedately.
1911 . . . Fell. (Maj. H.M.Cliff) 6.9-13. Mr.C.T.Walwyn.66/1.
1912 . . . Failed to finish. (Maj. H.M.Cliff) 7.10-11. E.Lawn. 40/1.
1914 . . . Failed to finish. (Maj. H.M.Cliff) 9. 11-0. Mr.O.Anthony.n/q

GLENFINDER
bay gelding by Glenvannon - dam by Pathfinder.
1912 . . . Failed to finish. (Capt. H.C.Higgins) 11.10-0. J.Foran. n/q

GOLD SEAL II
black gelding by Gold Reef - Seal Brown.
1912 . . . Failed to finish. (Mrs R.P.Croft) 12.10-0. J.Finn. n/q

GRITHORPE
bay gelding by St.Gris - Lambthorpe.
1917 . . . Fell. (Mr E.S.Wills) 8.9-7. H.Smyth. n/q

GERALD L
bay gelding by Captivation - Lavenne.
1920 . . . Fell. (Maj. F.J.Scott-Murray) 6.9-7. F.Dainty. 10/1.
1924 . . . Pulled-up. (Maj. F.J.Scott-Murray) 10.12-6. I.Morgan.50/1.
1926 . . . Finished 6th of 30. (Mr H.Kershaw) 12.12-2. F.Brookes.40/1.
1927 . . . Failed to finish. (Mr H.Kershaw) 13.12-5. L.B.Rees. 50/1.

GENERAL SAXHAM
bay horse by Saxham - Veldt Girl.
1920 . . . Fell. (Mrs J.Putnam) 7.9-7. Mr.P.Roberts. n/q
1921 . . . Fell. (Mrs J.Putnam) 8.11-4. W.Smith. 66/1.
1922 . . . Fell. (Mrs J.Putnam) 9.10-9. Mr.P.Dennis. 66/1.

GARRYVOE
brown gelding by Fugleman - Lesterlake.
1921 . . . Fell. (Mr C.Bower Ismay) 7.11-2. I.Anthony. 100/9.

GLENCORRIG
brown gelding by Kroonstad - Shinrone.
1921 . . . Refused. (Mr K. Mackay) 7.10-13. H.B.Bletsoe. 50/1.

84

GLENEFFY
brown gelding by The Convert - Katie Bush.
1921 . . . Fell. (Mr S.Stewart) 7.9-7. T.Willmot. n/q

GAY LOCHINVAR
bay gelding by Lochryan - Gaiety.
1922 . . . Fell. (Mr G.F.Godson) 6.10-8. F.Croney. nq
1924 . . . Fell. (Mr G.F.Godson) 8.10-0. S.Duffy. nq

GREY DAWN V
grey gelding by Dandolo - dam's pedigree unknown.
1922 . . . Fell. (Mr G.H.Edwards) 9.10-5. A.Newey. 25/1.

GARDENRATH
bay gelding by Pam - Punnett.
1923 . . . Pulled-up. (Mr P.Layton) 8.10-0. J.Whelehan. 66/1.
1925 . . . Fell. (Mr F.A.Waring) 10.10-0. T.James. 66/1.

GRACIOUS GIFT
bay gelding by Minter- Simon's Lawn.
1925 . . . Fell. (Mr R.H.A.Gresson) 10.10-8. W.Parvin.25/1.

GRECIAN WAVE
bay mare by Prince Hermes - Wavelass.
1926 . . . Fell. (Mr W.Hume) 8.10-8. Major J.P.Wilson.
1927 . . . Ran-out. (Mr W Hume) 9.11-12. J. Meaney. 50/1.

GRAKLE
bay gelding by Jackdaw - Lady Crank.
1927 . . . Fell. (Mr T.K.Laidlaw) 5.10-9. J.Moloney. 9/1.
1928 . . . Refused. (Mr C.R.Taylor) 6.11-5. R.Lyall. 33/1.
1929 . . . Finished 6th of 66. (Mr C.R.Taylor) 7.11-9. J.Hamey.18/1.
1930 . . . Fell. (Mr C.R.Taylor) 8.11-6. K.Piggott. 100/1.Fav.*
1931 . . . WON. (Mr C.R.Taylor) 9.11-7.41 Ran.R.Lyall. 100/6.
1932 . . . Refused. (Mr C.R.Taylor) 10.12-3. Mr.J.Fawcus. 100/12.jnt.Fav.*

GREAT SPAN
brown gelding by Bridge of Earn - Mullion.
1928 . . . Saddle slipped. (Mr W.B.Duckworth) 7.11-9. W.Payne.33/1.
1929 . . . Pulled-up. (Mr W.B.Duckworth) 8.12-0. W.Payne. 100/6.
1931 . . . Finished 9th of 43. (Mr M.D.Blair) 10.11-0. G.Hardy. 50/1.
1932 . . . Fell. (Mr M.D.Blair) 11.10-7. G.Hardy. 20/1.

THE GOSLING
chestnut gelding by St.Petersburg - Vain Chick.
1928 . . . Failed to finish. (Lord Grimthorpe) 8.10-5. Mr.S.H.Dennis. 200/1.
1930 . . . Pulled-up. (Major J.A.Coats) 10.10-0. A.Tannock. 100/1.

GREGALACH
chestnut gelding by My Prince - St.Germanie.
1929 . . . WON. (Mrs M.A.Gemmell) 7.11-4. 66 Ran. R.Everett. 100/1.
1930 . . . Fell. (Mrs M.A.Gemmell) 8.12-0. R.Everett. 100/6.
1931 . . . Finished 2nd of 43. (Mrs M.A.Gemmell) 9.12-0. J.Moloney. 25/1.
1932 . . . Fell. (Mrs M.A.Gemmell) 10.12-7. Mr.F.R.Thackray. 100/9.
1933 . . . Pulled-up. (Mrs M.A.Gemmell) 11.12-7. W.Parvin. 10/1
1934 . . . Broke down/pulled-up. (Mrs M.A.Gemmell) 12.12-7. W.Parvin. 25/1.

GAY DOG II
chestnut gelding by Jovial - Prudence.
1929 . . . Failed to finish. (Sir Lindsay Parkinson) 9.10-3. A.Birch. 200/1.
1930 . . . Pulled-up. (Sir Lindsay Parkinson) 10.10-0. W.Gurney. 66/1.

GLANGESIA
grey gelding by Le Souvenir - Mailline.
1930 . . . Finished 4th of 41. (Mr R.K.Mellon) 10.10-4. J.Browne. 33/1
1931 . . . Finished 7th of 43. (Mr R.K.Mellon) 11.10-10. J.Browne. 40/1.
1932 . . . Fell. (Mr R.K.Mellon) 12.10-9. Mr.J.Ryan. 33/1.

GATE BOOK
grey gelding by Book - Flood Gate.
1930 . . . Fell. (Marquis J.DeSan-Miguel) 9.11-8. T.Morgan. 50/1.

GUIDING LIGHT
brown gelding by Cyllius - Candle Fish.
1930 . . . Fell. (Mrs J.B.D'Ardenne) 9.11-3. Mr.C.W.Langlands. 100/1.
1931 . . . Pulled-up. (Mr O.M.Smith) 10.11-0. Mr.F.E.McKeever. 100/1.
1933 . . . Fell. (Lord Somerton) 12.10-7. Lord Somerton. 100/1.

GIB
bay or brown gelding by The Jabberwock - Bettyville.
1931 . . . Fell. (Mr B.D.Davis) 8.12-5. E.Foster. 33/1.

GEORGINATOWN
bay mare by Kroonstad - Georgina Mac.
1931 . . . Fell. (Mr J.H.Wallace) 10.10-12. F.Maxwell. 20/1.

GYI LOVAM
bay gelding by Oreg lak - Gyerunk csak!.
1931 . . . Fell. (Capt. R.Popler) 9.11-3. Capt. R.Popler.100/1.

GIBUS
chestnut gelding by Llangibby - Pen Dorwyd.
1932 . . . Fell. (Major Keith Menzies) 11.10-7. W.Redmond. 100/1.

GOLDEN MILLER
bay gelding by Goldcourt - Millers Pride.
1933 . . . Fell. (Miss D.Paget) 6.12-2. T.Leader. 9/1.Fav.*
1934 . . . WON (Miss D.Paget) 7.12-2. 30 Ran. G.Wilson. 8/1.
1935 . . . Unseated rider (Miss D.Paget) 8.12-7. G.Wilson. 2/1.Fav.*
1936 . . . Fell, remounted & refused. (Miss D.Paget) 9.12-7. E.Williams. 5/1.
1937 . . . Refused. (Miss D.Paget) 10.12-7. D.Morgan. 8/1.Fav.*

GOLD ARROW
bay gelding by Steel-Point - Lady Patricia.
1940 . . . Finished 3rd of 30. (Mr J.Neill) 8.10-3. P.Lay. 50/1.

● **Golden Miller completed a unique Cheltenham Gold Cup - Grand National double in 1934, beating Delaneige by five lengths at Aintree.**

GYPPO
bay gelding by Haste Away - Zingarella.
1946 . . . Fell. (Mr J.Cousins) 12.10-0. Mr.J.Cousins. 40/1.
1947 . . . Fell. (Mr J.Cousins) 13.10-0. Mr.J.Cousins. 100/1.

GOOD DATE
brown gelding by Young Lover - Hopeful Prospect.
1947 . . . Fell. (Mrs H.H.Jones) 9.10-0. J.Dowdeswell. 100/1.

GRANITZA
bay gelding by Salmon Leap - Orama.
1947 . . . Refused. (Mr C.B.Rendall) 8.10-0. N.Dixon. 100/1.

GORMANSTOWN
bay gelding by Roidore - Proud Maisie.
1947 . . . Pulled-up. (Mr C.Nicholson) 7.10-9. T.Molony. 40/1.
1948 . . . Fell. (Mr C.Nicholson) 8.10-9. M.Hogan. 66/1.

GALLERY
bay gelding by Winalot - Nunnery.
1949 . . . Brought down. (Mr J.Davey) 11.10-8. G.Slack. 40/1.
1950 . . . Fell. (Sir A.Pilkington) 12.10-8. G.Slack. 28/1.
1951 . . . Fell. (Sir A. Pilkington) 13.10-4. A.Mullins. 50/1.

GARDE TOI
chestnut gelding by Le Grand Cyrus - Grey Cloth. (Foaled in France)
1950 . . . Fell. (Marquis de Portago) 9.12-1. Marquis de Portago. 100/1.

GLEN FIRE
bay gelding by Tartan - Fire Alarm.
1951 . . . Fell. (Mr S.Mercer) 8.10-1. F.T.Winter. 33/1.
1952 . . . Refused. (Mr S.Mercer) 10.10-8. M.Lynn. 10/1.

GAY HEATHER
chestnut horse by Gay Morning - Heather Mixture.
1951 . . . Fell. (Mr J.D.Paisley) 10.10-0. R.Curran. 66/1.

GOLDEN SURPRISE
bay horse by Casanova - Recompense.
1952 . . . Fell. (Mr T.Clarke) 7.10-3. Mr.T.Clarke. 100/1.

GRAND TRUCE
bay horse by Flag of Truce - Grandma.
1953 . . . Fell. (Mr J.D.Pickering) 9.10-0. D.Leslie. 66/1.

GAY MONARCH II
chestnut gelding by Gay Morning - dam said to be May Fly.
1954 . . . Fell. (Mr J.R.Roberts) 8.10-4. T.Brookshaw. 50/1.

GENTLE MOYA
black mare by Steel-Point - Laura Gay.
1954 . . . Fell. (Mr J.J.Straker) 8.10-0. Mr.J.Straker. 100/6.
1955 . . . Finished 6th of 30. (Mr J.J.Straker) 9.10-0. Mr J.Straker. 50/1.
1956 . . . Finished 2nd of 29. (Mr J.J.Straker) 10.10-2. G.Milburn.22/1.
1957 . . . Finished 11th of 35. (Mr J.J.Straker) 11.10-6. G.Milburn. 28/1.

GIGOLO
bay gelding by Desmondtoi - Court Ballet.
1955 . . . Finished 4th of 30. (Mrs M.Milne Green) 10.11-3. R.Curran. 100/6.

GLORIOUS TWELFTH
grey gelding by Cadenazzo - Fading Glory.
1957 . . . Finished 4th of 35. (Mr H.J.Joel) 8.11-1. B.Wilkinson. 100/8.
1958 . . . Refused. (Mr H.J.Joel) 9.11-3. B.Wilkinson. 28/1.
1959 . . . Brought down. (Mr H.J.Joel) 10.10-7. G.Slack. 33/1.

OOSANDER
bay gelding by Sandyman - Josie Blink.
1957 . . . Finished 6th of 35. (Mrs Bache Hay) 9.11-7. H.J.East. 5/1.Fav.*
1958 . . . Finished 5th of 31. (Mrs Bache Hay) 10.11-7. T.Molony. 100/7.

GO-WELL
bay gelding by Goldwell - Avondhu Belle.
1957 . . . Fell. (Mr S.C.Wagstaffe) 9.10-0. Capt. P.Bengough. 66/1.

GREEN DRILL
bay gelding by Golden Drill - Verdant.
1958 . . . Finished 3rd of 31. (Lord Cadogan) 8.10-10. G.Milburn.28/1.

GRIFEL
chestnut horse by Grog II - Festina.
1961 . . . Fell. (Mr P.H.Pika) 8.12-0. V.Prakhov. 100/1.

GAY NAVARREE
brown gelding by Roi de Navarre II - Gracious.
1962 . . . Finished 4th of 32. (Mr J.F. Hoey) 10.10-0. Mr.A.Cameron. 100/1.
1963 . . . Fell. (Mr G.Wright) 11.10-1. P.Cowley. 50/1.

GOOD GRACIOUS
brown mare by Harroway - Gracious.
1963 . . . Fell. (Mr J.F.Smith) 9.10-7. P.Connors. 66/1.

GALE FORCE X
chestnut mare by Roaring Forties - dam by Tartan.
1964 . . . Fell. (Mr F.Warrington-Gillet) 7.10-0. R.Coonan. 50/1.
1966 . . . Finished 10th of 47. (Capt. F.Warrington-Gillet) 9.10-0 R.Coonan. 50/1.

GROOMSMAN
bay gelding by Tiverton - Vesington Bride.
1964 . . . Fell. (Mr J.F.Cleary) 9.10-0. F.Shortt. 66/1.
1965 . . . Fell. (Duque de Alburquerque) 10.10-13. Duque de Alburquerque. 100/1.
1966 . . . Refused. (Mr S.Roberts) 11.11-0. Mr.S.Roberts. 100/1.

GAME PURSTON
bay gelding by Prince's Game - Little Purston.
1966 . . . Fell. (Mr J.P.Yeomans) 8.10-0. P.Cowley. 100/1.
1967 . . . Finished 18th of 44. (Mr J.P.Yeomans) 9.10-0. K.B.White. 66/1.
1968 . . . Fell. (Mr J.P.Yeomans) 10.10-0. D.Cartwright. 100/1.
1969 . . . Pulled-up.(Mr John Banks) 11.10-0. S.Mellor. 33/1.
1970 . . . Unseated rider. (Mr M.C.Lloyd) 12.11-5. Mr.M.Lloyd. 100/1.

GREEK SCHOLAR
chestnut gelding by Dionisio - Highbrow.
1967 . . . Finished 4th 44. (Mr J.Thornton,jnr.) 8.10-9. T.Biddlecombe. 20/1.

GREAT LARK
brown mare by Great Captain - Flarke.
1968 . . . Refused. (Mr R.R.Guest) 9.10-6. T.Carberry. 100/6.

GO-PONTINENTAL
bay gelding by Eble - Voliage.
1968 . . . Fell. (Mr F.W.Pontin) 8.10-0. M.Gifford. 25/1.
1973 . . . Finished 16th of 38. (Mrs H.O'Neill) 13.10-4. J.McNaught. 100/1.
1974 . . . Fell. (Mr R.Armstrong) 14.10-0. S.Suthern. 100/1.

GAY TRIP
bay gelding by Vulgan - Turkish Tourist.
1970 . . . WON (Mr A.J.Chambers) 8.11-5. 28 Ran. P.Taaffe.15/1.
1971 . . . Fell. (Mr A.J.Chambers) 9.12-0. T.Biddlecombe. 8/1.
1972 . . . Finished 2nd of 42. (Mr A.J.Chambers) 10.11-9. T.Biddlecombe. 12/1

GINGER NUT
chestnut gelding by Red God - Topnotch.
1970 . . . Finished 5th of 28. (Mr Bryan P.Jenks) 8.10-0. J.Bourke. 28/1.

GAY BUCCANEER
chestnut gelding by Buckhound - Saint Jane.
1971 . . . Finished 10th of 38. (Mr R.W.McKeever) 10.10-0. P.Black. 66/1.
1972 . . . Fell. (Mrs P.G.McCrea) 11.10-0. T.Hyde. 33/1.

GENERAL SYMONS
chestnut gelding by Escart III - Flappy.
1972 . . . Finished jnt 3rd of 42. (Mrs E.N.Newman) 9.10-0. P.Kiely. 40/1.
1973 . . . Pulled-up. (Mrs E.N.Newman) 10.10-0. P.Kiely. 33/1.

GYLEBURN
brown gelding by Solartickle - Bewildered Anne.
1972 . . . Fell. (Mrs Claud Berry) 9.10-4. R.Barry. 20/1.

GREAT NOISE
bay gelding by Pindari - Great Fuss.
1973 . . . Finished 13th of 38. (Mr John W.Rowleys) 9.10-2. D.Cartwright. 50/1.

GREEN PLOVER
chestnut gelding by Democratic - Lapwing.
1973 . . . Finished 14th of 38. (Mr A.M.Darlington) 13.10-0. Mr.M.F.Morris. 100/1.

GREY SOMBRERO
grey gelding by Eudaemon - Easter Bonnet.
1973 . . . Fell. (Mr W.F.Caudwell) 9.10-9. W.Shoemark. 25/1.

GLENKILN
bay gelding by Arctic Slave - Halador.
1973 . . . Fell. (Mr N.H. Le Mare) 10.10-7. J.J.O'Neill. 33/1.
1974 . . . Fell. (Mr N.H. Le Mare) 11.10-2. R.Crank. 50/1.

GLANFORD BRIGG
bay gelding by Naucetra - Fairetra.
1975 . . . Finished 8th of 31. (Mr P.Harper) 9.11-4. M.Blackshaw. 20/1.
1976 . . . Fell. (Mr P.J.Harper) 10.11-3. M.Blackshaw. 28/1.

GLEN OWEN
bay gelding by Master Owen - Glenawina.
1975 . . . Fell. (Lord Cadogan) 8.10-0. D.Atkins. 22/1.

GOLDEN RAPPER
chestnut gelding by Vulgan - Shady Cacador.
1976 . . . Fell. (Mr G.N.Clarke) 10.10-8. J.Francome. 28/1.

GAY VULGAN
bay gelding by Vulgan - Bland Lady.
1977 . . . Pulled-up. (Mrs W.L.Pilkington) 9.10-8. W.Smith. 9/1.

GOLDEN WHIN
chestnut gelding by Charottesvilles Flyer - Margerval.
1978 . . . Finished 11th of 37. (Mrs G.L.Taylor) 8.10-4. S.Holland. 50/1.

GLEAMING RAIN
bay gelding by Raincheck - Sixtina.
1978 . . . Fell. (Mrs J.R.Mullion) 10.10-0. S.Treacy. 25/1.

GODFREY SECUNDUS
bay gelding by Nulli Secundus - Ready Maid.
1979 . . . Brought down. (Mrs G.L.Taylor) 9.10-3. C.Tinkler.200/1.

GRITTAR
bay gelding by Grisaille - Tarama.
1982 . . . WON (Mr F.H.Gilman) 9.11-5. 39 Ran. Mr.C.Saunders. 7/1.Fav.*
1983 . . . Finished 5th of 41. (Mr F.H.Gilman) 10.11-12. P.Barton. 6/1.Fav.*
1984 . . . Finished 10th of 40. (Mr F.H.Gilman) 11.11-10. J.Francome. 12/1.

GANDY VI
chestnut gelding by Athenius - dam's name unregistered.
1982 . . . Fell. (Mrs E.White-Spunner) 13.10-8. N.Madden. 50/1.

GOOD PROSPECT
brown gelding by Orchardist - Cagire's.
1982 . . . Refused. (Mr C.Moorsom) 13.10-10. R.Linley. 50/1.

GREASEPAINT
chestnut gelding by Gala Performance - Wind Swift.
1983 . . . Finished 2nd of 41. (Mrs N.Todd) 8.10-6. Mr.C.Magnier. 14/1.
1984 . . . Finished 2nd of 40. (Mr M.J.Smurfit) 9.11-2. T.Carmody. 9/1.
1985 . . . Finished 4th of 40. (Mr M.J.Smurfit) 10.10.13. T.Carmody. 13/2 jnt.Fav.*
1986 . . . Finished 10th of 40. (Mr M.J.Smurfit) 11.10-9. T. Carmody. 16/1.

GOLDEN TRIX
chestnut gelding by Little Buskins - Over Trix.
1984 . . . Fell. (Mr B.L.Chinn) 9.10-0. K.Mooney. 50/1.

GLENFOX
bay gelding by Proverb - Dark Slave.
1985 . . . Finished 9th of 40. (Mr P.R.Dickson/Mr Russell Bowes) 8.10-0. Mr.D.Gray. 50/1.

GREENHILL HALL
bay gelding by Tarqogan - Pampered Queen.
1985 . . . Pulled-up. (Miss Betty Duxbury) 9.10-0. D.Wilkinson. 200/1.

GAYLE WARNING
chestnut gelding by Perspex - Cathy Gayle.
1986 . . . Finished 17th of 40. (Mr J.G.Dudgeon) 12.10-3. Mr.A.Dudgeon. 50/1.

GLENRUE
chestnut gelding by Carnival Night - Naomi.
1987 . . . Fell. (Coteville Group) 10.10-3. B.Powell. 33/1.

GALA PRINCE
bay gelding by Gala Performance - Zarabanda.
1987 . . . Finished 20th of 40. (Mrs Mary Aston) 10.10-0. T.Jarvis. 500/1.

GEE-A
brown gelding by Arapaho - Artic Daisy.
1988 . . . Pulled-up. (Mr G.A.Hubbard) 9.10-3. Gee Armytage. 33/1.
1990 . . . Finished 18th of 38. (Mr G.A.Hubbard) 11.10-2. D.J.Murphy. 66/1.

GALA'S IMAGE
brown gelding by Gala Performance(USA) - Chilita.
1989 . . . Finished 7th of 40. (Sheikh Ali Abu Khamsin) 9.10-3. N.Doughty. 18/1.
1990 . . . Fell. (Mr Brian Thackray) 10.10-0. J.Shortt. 66/1.

GAINSAY
brown gelding by Tepukei - Swift Response.
1989 . . . Fell. (Mr Errol Brown) 10.10-6. M. Pitman. 25/1.
1990 . . . Fell. (Mr Errol Brown) 11.10-7. M.Pitman. 66/1.

GALLIC PRINCE
bay gelding by Kinglet - Camargue.
1990 . . . Finished 13th of 38. (Iberia Airlines of Spain) 11.10-4. Mr.J.F.Simo. 100/1.

GHOFAR
chestnut gelding by Nicholas Bill - Royale Final.
1990 . . . Finished 14th of 38. (Mr Don Taffner/Sir Hugh Dundas) 7.10-0. B.Powell. 14/1.
1992 . . . Finished 11th of 40. (Sir Hugh Dundas/Mr Don Taffner) 9.10-3. H.Davies. 25/1.

GARRISON SAVANNAH
bay gelding by Random Shot - Merry Coin.
1991 . . . Finished 2nd of 40. (Autofour Engineering) 8.11-1. M.Pitman. 7/1.
1994 . . . Refused. (Autofour Engineering) 11.10-3. J.Osborne. 25/1.
1995 . . . Finished 9th of 35. (Autofour Engineering) 12.10-0. W.Marston. 16/1.

90

GOLDEN MINSTREL
chestnut gelding by Tudor Music - Ethel's Delight.
1991 . . . Finished 7th of 40. (Mr W.E.Gale) 12.10-2. T.Grantham. 50/1.
1992 . . . Finished 15th of 40. (Mr W.E.Gale) 13.10-0. E.Murphy. 150/1.

GOLDEN FREEZE
bay gelding by Golden Love - Freezeaway.
1991 . . . Finished 17th of 40. (Mrs Eliz Hitchens/Mr Rbt. Hitchens) 9.11-0. M.Bowlby. 40/1.

GENERAL CHANDOS
chestnut gelding by Glen Quaich - Kitta.
1991 . . . Pulled-up. (Lady Harris) 10.10-3. Mr.J.Bradburne. 150/1.

GOLDEN FOX
bay gelding by Tyrnavos - Red Spider.
1992 . . . Refused. (Mrs Kate Lyons/Mr Leonard Fuller) 10.10-0. S.Earle. 200/1.

GAY RUFFIAN
bay gelding by Welsh Term - Alcinea.
1994 . . . Fell. (Mr B.McHugh) 8.10-0. R.Farrant. 150/1.

GOLD CAP
chestnut gelding by Noir Et Or - Alkmaar.
1995 . . . Finished 13th of 35. (Mr Geoff Meadows) 10.10-6. G.McCourt. 50/1.

GENERAL PERSHING
brown gelding by Persian - St.Colette.
1995 . . . Fell. (Mr J.E.Potter) 9.10-0. D.Bridgwater. 20/1.

GREENHILL RAFFLES
chestnut gelding by Scallyway - Burlington Belle.
1996 . . . Finished 14th of 27. (Miss Lucinda V. Russell) 10.10-0. M.Foster. 100/1.

HASTY
1840 . . . Fell. (Owner unknown) Rigg. n/q.

HAWK, THE
1841 . . . Finished 5th of 11. (Capt. Nugent) Saunders. 100/6.

HONESTY
1842 . . . Failed to finish. (Lord Clanricarde) Mr.W.McDonough.n/q.

HESLINGTON
1844 . . . Refused. (Mr W.Scott) Mr.W.McDonough. 8/1.

HORNIHIHARRIHO
1846 . . . Fell. (Mr H.L.Carter) Parker. n/q.

HOPE
1850 . . . Fell. (Mr H.Hunter) - 10-1. Mr.Hunter. n/q.
1851 . . . Pulled-up. (Mr S.H.Kemp) - 9-12. Mr.Green. n/q.

HALF-AND-HALF
1851 . . . Finished 4th of 21. (Mr Oakes) - 10-8. R.Sly.jnr. 20/1.
1854 . . . Finished 6th of 20. (Mr Bignell) - 10-8. C.Green. 8/1.
1855 . . . Failed to finish. (Mr Hutchinson) - 10-4. Darby. 50/1.

HOPELESS STAR
1856 . . . Finished 4th of 21. (Mr Tyler) - 10-2. W.White. 25/1.
1857 . . . Pulled-up. (Mr E.Parr) - 10-0. D.Wynne. 9/1.

HARRY LORREQUER
1856 . . . Ran-out. (Mr J.R.Henderson) 5.8-10. W.Fowler. 5/1.
1858 . . . Knocked-over (Mr J.R.Henderson) 7.9-0. W.Fowler. 12/1.

HORNIBLOW
1857 . . . Failed to finish. (Mr T.Day) - 9.10. Dart. n/q.
1860 . . . Failed to finish. (Mr H.Blundell) - 10.10. Enoch. n/q.

HALF CASTE
1859 . . . WON. (Mr Willoughby) 6.9-7. 20 Ran. C.Green. 7/1

HUNTSMAN
1859 . . . Finished 3rd of 20. (Mr B.Land) 6.11-2. B.Land jnr. 100/8.
1860 . . . Finished 2nd of 19. (Capt. G.W.Hunt) 7.11-8. Capt. T.M. Townley. 33/1.
1862 . . . WON. (Viscount de Namur) 9.11-0. H.Lamplugh. 3/1.Fav.*

HARRY
1862 . . . Fell. (Mr W.W.Baker) - 9-5. G.Stevens. n/q.
1864 . . . Fell. (Count Cossett) - 11-10. Cassidy. 50/1.

HALL COURT
1865 . . . Finished 2nd of 23. (Capt. Brown) 6.11-0. Capt. A.C.Tempest. 50/1.
1866 . . . Fell. (Capt. Brown) 7.11-12. W.Reeves. 30/1.
1867 . . . Fell. (Capt. Brown) 8.12-3. Capt. Brown. n/q.
1868 . . . Finished 7th of 21. (Capt. J.M.Brown) 9.11-4. B.Land jnr. 50/1.
1869 . . . Finished 2nd of 22. (Capt. J.M.Brown) 10.10-12. Capt. A.C.Tempest. 100/1.
1870 . . . Failed to finish. (Capt. J.M.Brown) 11.10-12. Mr.Thomas. 40/1.
1872 . . . Failed to finish. (Capt. J.M.Brown) 13.10-0. Mr C.Browne. 66/1.

HAVELOCK
1867 . . . Fell. (Mr J.Wood) 6.10-3. Jarvis. n/q.
1869 . . . Fell. (Mr J. Wood) 8.11-0. Wheeler. 33/1.

HELEN
1868 . . . Finished 6th of 21. (Mr Barber) - 10-1. Mr.A.Goodman. 12/1.

HUNTSMAN'S DAUGHTER
1868 . . . Pulled-up. (Mr T.V.Morgan) - 10-12. G.Holman. 16/1.
1869 . . . Pulled-up. (Mr. T.V.Morgan) - 10-8. J.Holman. 40/1.

HARCOURT
1869 . . . Finished 9th of 22. (Mr Eaton) 8.10-0. Capt. Harford. 25/1.

HARVESTER
1872 . . . Over-reached. (Mr A.Yates) 7.12-0. Mr.A.Yates. 25/1.

HUNTSMAN
1873 . . . Refused. (Mr H.Ellison) 6.10-11. Mr.H.Ellison. n/q.

HERAUT D'ARMES
1874 . . . Fell. (Mr W.Forbes) 7.10-3. Capt. Smith. 25/1.

HIS LORDSHIP
1878 . . . Knocked-over. (Mr G.Brown) 5.10-7. R.I'Anson. 9/2.Fav.*
1879 . . . Refused. (Mr Russell) 6.10-12. Levitt. 20/1.

HARLEQUIN
1885 . . . Refused. (Duke of Hamilton) 10.10-0. D.Sensier. 50/1.

HARRISTOWN
1886 . . . Failed to finish. (Mr J.Purcell) 6.10-7. Mr.J.Purcell. 66/1.

HUNTER, THE
1887 . . . Fell (Lord Cholmondeley) -10-0. Mr.W.Beasley. 100/1.

HETTIE
1889 . . . Fell. (H.R.H. Prince of Wales) 6.10-5. A.Hall. 66/1.
1890 . . . Fell. (H.R.H. Prince of Wales) 7.10-11. Mr.E.P.Wilson. 25/1.

HOLLINGTON
1892 . . . Finished 6th of 25. (Capt. A.E.Whitaker) 6.10-9. G.Williamson. 100/9.

HORIZON
1895 . . . Fell. (Mr F.W.Greswolde-Williams) 6.12-2. G.Mawson. 100/14.

HOBNOB
1898 . . . Fell. (Mr A.Stedall) 6.9-11. H.Box. 40/1.

HALL IN
1898 . . . Fell. (Mr W.Ward) 7.9-8. L.Bland. 100/1.

HIDDEN MYSTERY
1900 . . . Fell. (Col. T.J.Gallwey) 6.12-0. Mr.H.Nugent. 75/20.Fav.*

HORNPOOL
1901 . . . Failed to finish. (Mr B.Wade) - 10-5. E.Acres. 66/1.

HELIUM
1902 . . . Fell. (Mr E.W.Tinsley) 7.10-10. H.Caley. 50/1.

HILL OF BREE
bay gelding by Ascetic - Au Revoir.
1904 . . . Fell. (Mr Hall-Walker) 8.10-4. G.Gowell. 33/1.
1906 . . . Knocked-over. (Mr W.Hall-Walker) 10.10-3. R.Chadwick. 66/1

HERCULES II
chestnut gelding by St Michael - Novice.
1905 . . . Finished 5th of 27. (Mr D.Faber) 9. 9-10. J.Dillon. 33/1.
1909 . . . Finished 5th of 32. (Mr R.Faber) 13. 9-13.Mr.A.Gordon. 33/1.
1910 . . . Fell. (Mr D.Faber) 14. 9-9. ì C.Hawkins. n/q.
1911 . . . Pulled-up. (Mr D.Faber) 15. 9-8. Mr.R.H.Hall. 50/1.

HALLGATE
chestnut gelding by New Barns - Heterodox.
1905 . . . Fell. (Mr Delagarde) 7. 9-7. A.Cole. 100/1.

HARD TO FIND
bay gelding by Rapallo - Souvenir.
1906 . . . Fell. (Prince Hatzfeldt) 6. 9-7. E.R.Morgan. 66/1.

HIGHBRIDGE
bay gelding by Bridgewater - Duress. Bred in U.S.A.
1913 . . . Fell. (Mr J.R.Fell) 7.12-0. F.Williams. 100/9.

HESPERUS MAGNUS
brown gelding by Seaton - Beau Brummel.
1911 . . . Pulled-up. (Mr D.Faber) 9. 9-7. W.Fitzgerald. 66/1.
* 1916 . . . Pulled-up. (Mr D.Faber) 14. 9-10. J.East. n/q.

HACKLER'S BEY
chestnut mare by Kosmos Bey - dam by Hackler.
1915 . . . Failed to finish. (Sir T.R.Dewar) 8.10-2. Mr.H.S.Harrison. 40/1.
* 1916 . . . Completed course. (Sir T.R.Dewar) 9.11-0.Mr.H.S.Harrison. 100/8.
* 1917 . . . Fell. (Sir T.R.Dewar) 10.10-11. Capt.D.Rogers. n/q.

HALSTON
bay or brown gelding by Bealderg - Chimura.
1921 . . . Fell. (Major D.Dixon) 9.10-9. Mr.L.Firth. 50/1.

HILL OF CAMAS
bay gelding by Simontault - dam by Walmsgate.
1921 . . . Fell. (Capt.W.Moloney) 13.10-7. Capt.J.C.Delmege. n/q.

HACKAM
brown horse by Hackenschmidt - Seerdam.
1921 . . . Fell. (Mr A Humphry0 6. 9-7. G.Clancy. 66/1.

HIS LUCK
bay gelding by His Majesty - Madame St George.
1925 . . . Fell. (Capt.A.A.Bankier) 9.10-10. R.Burford. 50/1.

HAWKER
brown gelding by Ardoon - Morganatic.
1927 . . . Ran-out. (Capt. A.E.Grant) 13.11-1. Capt.A.E.Grant.66/1.
1929 . . . Pulled-up. (Capt.A.E.Grant) 15.10-5. Capt.A.E.Grant. 200/1.

HERBERT'S CHOICE
bay gelding by Aldegond - Mount Grace.
1928 . . . Failed to finish. (Miss D.Graeme Thomson) 7.10-8. F.Gurney. 50/1.
1929 . . . Fell. (Miss D.Graeme Thomson) 8.10-8. J.Farrell. 200/1.

HAREWOOD
bay gelding by Southannan - Daisy.
1929 . . . Fell. (Mrs M.L.Meyer) 7.10-0. D.Williams. 40/1.
1930 . . . Fell. (Mrs M.L.Meyer) 8.10-0. J.Hamey. 100/1.
1931 . . . Fell. (Mrs M.L.Meyer) 9.10-7. Mr.K.Goode. 50/1.
1932 . . . Pulled-up. (Mr R.H.Warden) 10.10-7. Mr.R.H.Warden. 66/1.

HEARTBREAK HILL
bay mare by Don Juan - Little Sweetheart.
1932 . . . Finished 6th of 36. (Mrs C.S.Bird,jnr.) 7.11-6. W.O'Grady. 100/12.jnt/Fav.*
1933 . . . Fell. (Mrs C.S.Bird,jnr.) 8.11-9. W.O'Grady.100/8.

HOLMES
brown gelding by Ardoon - dam unknown.
1932 . . . Refused. (Mr E.T.Tyrwhitt-Drake) 12.11-0. Mr.C.C.Beechener.20/1.
1933 . . . Ran-out. (Mr E.T.Tyrwhitt-Drake) 13.10-13. C.C.Beechener.50/1.

HANK
bay gelding by Devolution - Chatalja.
1932 . . . Fell. (Mr H.D.Cherry-Downes) aged. 10-8. Mr.F.E.McKeever.33/1.

HUIC HOLLOA
bay gelding by Sysonby - Marigold.
1933 . . . Slipped-up. (Mr W.Waddington) 8.11-11. Mr.W.Ransom. 50/1.
1935 . . . Fell. (Mr W.Waddington) 10.10-7. Mr.A.Marsh.100/1.

HILLSBROOK
bay gelding by Chevalier - Lady Killeagh.
1936 . . . Fell. (Lord Derby) 10.10-8. W.O'Grady. 40/1.

HOPEFUL HERO
roan or grey horse by Herodote - Golden Hero.
1938 . . . Finished 8th of 36. (Mr H.A.J.Silley) 10.10-9. Mr.W.Dawes. 100/1.

HURDY GURDY MAN
black gelding by Cottage Chase - dam by Ruddygore.
1938 . . . Fell. (Duchess of Norfolk) 10.10-0. Mr.J.Hislop. 100/1.

HOUSEWARMER
bay gelding by Cottage - Madeira.
1946 . . . Finished 4th of 34. (Miss D.Paget) 9.10-2. A.Brabazon. 100/1.
1947 . . . Finished 6th of 57. (Miss D.Paget) 10.10-6. R.J.O'Ryan.25/1.
1948 . . . Fell. (Miss D.Paget) 11.10-6. H.Nicholson. 25/1.

HEIRDOM
brown or black gelding by Birthright - My Friend.
1946 . . . Fell. (Mr H.Quinn) 14.10-10. P.Cahalin. 66/1.

HISTORICAL REVUE
bay gelding by Pharian - Pansoviana.
1946 . . . Fell. (Mr W.R.Porter) 8.10-0. S.Ryan. 66/1.

HANDY LAD
chestnut gelding by Swindon - Great Convenience.
1947 . . . Finished 20th of 57. (Mrs F.Knight) 12.10-0. Capt.W.Williams. 100/1.

HIGHLAND LAD
bay gelding by Tartan - Terpsichore.
1948 . . . Fell. (Mr A.H.Watt) 10.10-0. E.J.Kennedy. 50/1.

HAPPY HOME
bay gelding by Cottage - Golden Emblem.
1948 . . . Finished 4th of 43. (Miss D.Paget) 9.11-10. G.Kelly. 33/1.
1949 . . . Finished 6th of 43. (Miss D.Paget) 10.11-10. B.Marshall.10/1.

HAPPY RIVER
chestnut gelding by River Prince - Glad Tidings.
1950 . . . Pulled-up. (Mrs P.P.Hogan) 7.10-12. D.McCann. 40/1.

HIGHLAND COTTAGE
brown mare by Cottage - Little Minch.
1950 . . . Fell. (Mr C.Nicholson) 10.10-0. M.Hogan. 66/1.

HIERBA
grey gelding by Pampas Grass - Seda.
1952 . . . Finished 7th of 47. (Mrs A.Warman) 7.10-0. A.Mullins. 66/1.
1953 . . . Fell. (Mrs A.Warman) 8.10-0. A.Mullins. 50/1.
1954 . . . Brought down.(Mrs A.Warman) 9.10-0. R.J.Hamey. 66/1.

HAL'S VENTURE
grey gelding by King Hal - Kathleen's Venture.
1952 . . . Fell. (Mr C.Oliff-Lee) 7.10-8. J.Foster. 45/1.

HEAD CREST
bay or brown mare by Headway - Cresserelle.
1953 . . . Fell. (Mr G.H.Dowty) 7.10-0. S.Barnes. 40/1.

HAPPY DAYS
chestnut gelding by Maltravers - Joy For Ever.
1953 . . . Fell. (Mr J.S.Kirkham) 13.10-0. A.Benson. 66/1.

HIGH GUARD
grey gelding by Fishguard - High Places.
1956 . . . Fell. (Mr J.A.Keith) 9.11-1. A.P.Thompson. 22/1.

HART ROYAL
chestnut gelding by Atout Royal - Roe Deer.
1957 . . . Fell. (Mr L.C.Denton) 9.10-10. P.Pickford. 100/7.
1958 . . . Fell. (Mr L.C.Denton) 10.10-11. P.Pickford. 18/1.

HOLLY BANK
bay gelding by Contrevent - dam by Bhuidhaonach.
1958 . . . Finished 7th of 31. (Mr S.H.Brookshaw) 11.10-3. Mr.P.Brookshaw. 50/1.
1960 . . . Fell. (Mr S.H.Brookshaw) 13.10-12. Mr.P.Brookshaw. 50/1.

HENRY PURCELL
bay gelding by Sol Oriens - Spinet.
1959 . . . Fell. (Mrs E.C.Smith) 12.10-0. A.C.Keen. 100/1.

HUNTER'S BREEZE
brown gelding by Cacador - Mountain Breeze.
1961 . . . Fell. (Mrs L.H.Brown) 10.10-13. F.Carroll. 100/7.

HOLM STAR
bay gelding by Again - Lobau Peg.
1963 . . . Pulled-up. (Mr J.F.Smith) 9.10-0. E.F.Kelly. 66/1.

HARRY BLACK
bay gelding by King Hal - Broken Dawn.
1966 . . . Fell. (Mr H.Lane) 9.10-0. R.Court. 100/1.
1967 . . . Pulled-up. (Mr H.Lane) 10.10-0. R.Reid. 100/1.

HIGHLAND WEDDING
brown gelding by Question - Princess. Bred by Mr.J.Caldwell.
1966 . . . Finished 8th of 47. (Mr C.F.W.Burns) 9.10-0. O.McNally. 15/2.
1968 . . . Finished 7th of 45. (Mr C.F.W.Burns) 11.11-0. O.McNally. 18/1.
1969 . . . WON. (Mr T.H.McCoy,jnr.) 12.10-4. 30 Ran. E.P.Harty. 100/9.

HIGHLANDIE
bay or brown gelding by Highland Nectar - Cravenlie.
1968 . . . Finished 15th of 45. (Mr T.Durant) 11.10-12. Mr.T.Durant. 100/1. Remounted*

HOVE
bay gelding by Coxcomb - All Square.
1969 . . . Fell. (Mr F.Parker) 8.10-9. D.Nicholson.100/6.

HIGHWORTH
chestnut gelding by Romany Air - Waitomo.
1971 . . . Pulled-up. (Mr R.H.Woodhouse) 12.10-0. Mr.R.Woodhouse.100/1.

HIGHLAND SEAL
bay gelding by Jock Scot - Sealskin.
1973 . . . Pulled-up. (Mrs J.Dening) 10.10-6. D.Nicholson. 20/1.

HURRICANE ROCK
bay gelding by Rockavon - First Of The Few.
1973 . . . Finished 6th of 38. (Mr D.J.Proctor) 9.10-0. R.Champion. 100/1

HUPERADE
bay gelding by Hugh Lupus - Hyperade.
1974 . . . Fell. (Mr J.Carden) 10.10-9. Mr.J.Carden. 100/1.
1976 . . . Fell. (Mr J.Carden) 12.10-4. Mr.J.Carden. 100/1.
1977 . . . Fell. (Mr J.Carden) 13.10-2. Mr.J.Carden) 200/1.

HIGH KEN
bay gelding by Menelek - High Velocity.
1975 . . . Fell. (Mr R.Hickman) 9.11-1. B.Brogan. 28/1.
1976 . . . Fell. (Mr R.Hickman) 10.10-12. M.Dickinson. 33/1.
1977 . . . Brought down. (Mr R.Hickman) 11.11-3. Mr.J.Edwards. 50/1.

HIGHWAY VIEW
bay gelding by Royal Highway - Rare View.
1976 . . . Finished 12th of 32. (Mr C.Carr) 11.10-10. P.Black. 33/1.

HAPPY RANGER
bay gelding by Counsel - Flirting.
1977 . . . Finished 7th of 42. (Mr N.Devonport) 10.10-5. P.Blacker. 66/1.

HIDDEN VALUE
chestnut gelding by Vulgan - Fenniscourt.
1977 . . . Finished 10th of 42. (Mr S.G.Norton) 9.10-4. J.T.Bourke. 40/1.
1978 . . . Fell. (Mr S.G.Norton) 10.10-0. T.Stack. 25/1.

HARBAN
bay gelding by Harwell - Banitown.
1977 . . . Fell. (Mr J.W.Ashmore) 8.10-0. F.Berry. 66/1.
1978 . . . Unseated rider. (Mr J.W.Ashmore) 9.10-0. J.P.Byrne.66/1.

HENRY HALL
chestnut gelding by Harwell - Allime.
1978 . . . Fell. (Mr St J.G.O'Connell) 9.10-0. F.Berry. 66/1.

HARD OUTLOOK
chestnut gelding by Harwell - Princess Prospect.
1982 . . . Finished 2nd of 39. (Lady Wates) 11.10-1. A.Webber. 50/1.

HOT TOMATO
bay gelding by Giolla Mear - Lickeen.
1983 . . . Fell. (Mr H.A.Insley) 11.10-2. J.Burke. 100/1.

HALLO DANDY
bay gelding by Menelek - Dandy Hall. Bred by Mr.J.P.Frost.
1983 . . . Finshed 4th of 40. (Mr R.Shaw) 9.10-0. N.Doughty. 60/1.
1984 . . . WON. (Mr R.Shaw) 10.10-2. 40 Ran. N.Doughty. 13/1.
1985 . . . Fell. (Mr R.Shaw) 11.10-12. G.Bradley. 14/1.
1986 . . . Finished 12th of 40. (Mr R.Shaw) 12.10-8. N.Doughty. 16/1.

HAZY DAWN
bay mare by Official - Day Fiddle.
1984 . . . Fell. (Mr R.E.Daniels) 9.10-8. Mr.W.P.Mullins.100/1.

HILL OF SLANE
bay gelding by The Parson - Polenka.
1984 . . . Finished 11th of 40. (Mrs M.A.Jarvis & Mrs R.J.Kaplan) 8.10-0. S.Smith Eccles. 33/1.
1985 . . . Fell. (Mrs M.A.Jarvis & Mrs R.J.Kaplan) 9.10-2. S.Smith Eccles. 25/1.

HUPERADE
chestnut gelding by Fidel - Deity.
1987 . . . Refused. (Mrs M.Hefferman) 9.10-0. M.Flynn. 100/1.

HI HARRY
chestnut gelding by Fidel - Deity.
1987 . . . Refused. (Mrs M.Hefferman) 9.10-0. M.Flynn. 100/1.

HARD CASE
bay gelding by Harwell - Legal Argument.
1988 . . . Fell. (Lady Thomson) 10.10-12. K.Morgan. 13/1.

HETTINGER
bay gelding by Maximilian -Fawnamore.
1988 . . . Fell. (Miss L.Quick) 8.10-0. Miss P.Ffitch-Heyes. 200/1.
1989 . . . Fell. (Miss L.Quick) 9.10-0. R.Goldstein. 300/1.

HUNTWORTH
chestnut gelding by Funny Man - Tamorina.
1990 . . . Fell. (Mr W.H.Walter) 10.10-9. Mr.A.Walter. 66/1.
1991 . . . Pulled-up. (Execs. of late Mr W.H.Walter) 11.10-8. Mr.A.Walter. 50/1.
1992 . . . Pulled-up. (Mr A.Walter & Mr M.T.Walter) 12.10-0. M.Richards.66/1.

HUNGARY HUR
chestnut gelding by Prince Hansel - Fortinette.
1990 . . . Pulled-up. (Miss D.Threadwell) 11.11-2. T.Carmody. 50/1.

HOTPLATE
chestnut gelding by Buckskin - Pencil Lady.
1991 . . . Pulled-up. (W.W.Bellamy (Bakers) Ltd.) 8.10-2. P.Niven. 80/1.
1992 . . . Pulled-up. (W.W.Bellamy (Bakers) Ltd.) 9.10-5.G.McCourt. 50/1.

HARLEY
chestnut gelding by Cranley - Harmony Rose.
1991 . . . Finished 12th of 40. (Miss J.Eaton) 11.10-0. G.Lyons.150/1.

HONEYBEER MEAD
chestnut gelding by Le Bavard - Midnight Oil.
1992 . . . Unseated rider. (Mr B.J.M.Ryall) 10.10-0. N.Mann. 100/1.

HENRY MANN
brown gelding by Mandalus - Little Dipper.
1994 . . . Fell. (Mr Lynn Wilson) 11.10-0. C.Swan. 50/1.

HE WHO DARES WINS
bay gelding by Le Bavard - Brave Air.
1994 . . . Pulled-up. (Mr I.D.Cheesbrough & Mr J.A.Stephenson) 11.10-0. C.Grant. 66/1.

● **Hallo Dandy and Neale Doughty going down to post
for the 1984 National — and their date with destiny.**

IRISH BARD, THE
1848 . . . Failed to finish. (Mr Arthur) - 11-0. Freeze. n/q.

IRON DUKE, THE
1849 . . . Failed to finish. (Mr C.Price) 5. 11-0. T.Abbot. n/q.
1850 . . . Failed to finish. (Mr J.Bell) 6. 10-12. J.Hanlon. n/q.

IRISH BOY
1860 . . . Finished 5th of 19. (Mr W.Bevill) - 8-12.Mr.W.Bevill. 12/1.

IRISH EMIGRANT, THE
1861 . . . Fell. (Mr W.Owens) - 9-0. R.Sly, jnr. n/q.

INKERMAN
1863 . . . Fell. (Mr W.E.Dakin) - 9-11. Mr.Smith. n/q.

IRELEY
1864 . . . Knocked-over. (Mr B.J.Angell) - 10-10. Mr.Blake. 40/1.

IBEX
bay gelding by Wild Dayrell - The Hind.
1866 . . . Fell. (Mr Brayley) 6.10-12. C.Boyce. 25/1.

INON
brown horse by Carbineer - Interduca.
1871 . . . Failed to finish. (Captain Pigott) 5.10-4. Capt.Harford.66/1.

ISMAEL
chestnut gelding by Oxford - Egyptian.
1873 . . . Refused. (Mr W.Wilson) 7.10-13. Daniels. n/q.

IGNITION
brown mare by Flash in The Pan - Miss Jephson.
1882 . . . Refused. (Mr H.Rymill) 10.10-5. W.Sensier. 50/1.

IDEA
chestnut horse by Glenelg - Item. Bred in U.S.A.
1884 . . . Failed to finish. (Mr Oeschlaeger) 6.10-2. Mr.W.H.Moore. 100/6.

ILEX
chestnut gelding by Rostrevor - Vatonia. Not in the General Stud Book.
1890 . . . WON. (Mr G.Masterman) 6.10-5. 16 Ran. A.Nightingall. 4/1.Fav.*
1891 . . . Finished 3rd of 21. (Mr G.Masterman) 7.12-3. A.Nightingall. 5/1.
1892 . . . Finished 3rd of 25. (Mr G.Masterman) 8.12-7. A.Nightingall. 20/1.

INQUISITOR
black gelding by Cassock - dam by Umpire.
1902 . . . Fell. (Lord Coventry) 7.10-9. Mr.A.W.Wood. 6/1.jnt/Fav.*
1903 . . . Fell. (Lord Coventry) 8.10-13. E.Matthews. 100/6.
1904 . . . Fell. (Lord Coventry) 9.10-11. E.Acres. 9/1.

IRISH MAIL
brown gelding by King's Messenger - Betty Shannon.
1913 . . . Finished 2nd of 22. (Mr W.T.Drake) 6.11-4. Mr.O.Anthony. 25/1.
1915 . . . Pulled-up. (Mr E.Platt) 8.11-12. Mr.L.Brabazon. 6/1.Fav.*
* 1916 . . . Finished 2nd of 21. (Mr E.Platt) 9.12-5. C.Hawkins. 20/1.
* 1917 . . . Pulled-up. (Mr E.Platt) 10.12-4. E.Piggott. 25/1.

ILSTON
bay horse by Blankney - Lady Rufford.
1914 . . . Fell. (Sir G.Bullough) 6.10-12. I.Anthony. 10/1.
1915 . . . Fell. (Sir G.Bullough) 7.11-8. I.Anthony. 33/1.

IRISH DRAGOON
bay gelding by Charles O'Malley or Orby - Lotus.
1919 . . . Failed to finish. (Mr R.H.Edwards) 5. 9-13. H.B.Bletsoe. 100/1.
1920 . . . Fell. (Mr.R.H.Edwards) 6. 9-8. A.Escott. n/q.

INCA II, THE
chestnut gelding by Indian Runner - dam unknown.
1922 . . . Fell. (Capt.C.W.Brennand) 8.10-0. F.Brookes. n/q.

IRINA
chestnut gelding by Irishman - Nehushta.
1929 . . . Fell. (Mr A.Heathorn) 7.10-0. J.Kelly. 200/1.

IBSTOCK
bay gelding by Fowling-Piece - Marsore.
1930 . . . Pulled-up. (Mr K.Goode) 10.10-13. Mr.K.Goode. 100/1.

INVERSE
brown gelding by St Girons - Inversion.
1932 . . . Fell. (Lady Lindsay) 6.11-7. R.Lyall. 33/1.

IRVINE
chestnut mare by Milton - Estuna.
1937 . . . Fell. (Mr A.P.Parker) 8.10-4. Mr.A.Parker. 40/1.

INVERSIBLE
black gelding by St Girons - Inversion.
1936 . . . Finished 5th of 35. (Lt.Col.W.E.Peel) 8.10-9. S.McGrath. 40/1.
1938 . . . Fell. (Lt.Col.W.E.Peel) 10.10.10. M.Hogan. 33/1.
1939 . . . Fell. (Lt.Col.W.E.Peel) 11.10-7. M.Hogan.22/1.
1940 . . . Finished 9th of 30. (Lt.Col.W.E.Peel) 12.10-6. M.Hogan. 25/1.

IVAN'S CHOICE
bay gelding by Blanding - Dangan Lass.
1950 . . . Fell. (Mr H.J.Jones) 9.10-0. P.J.O'Brien. 100/1.

INVERLOCHY
brown gelding by Lochiel - Hellenize.
1950 . . . Fell. (Mr F.S.Dyson) 11.10-3. P.J.Doyle. 50/1.

INCHMORE
brown gelding by Ballynahinch - Lenamore.
1950 . . . Finished 7th of 49. (Mr H.Falconer) 13.10-0. R.Curran. 100/1.

IRISH LIZARD
bay gelding by Irish Trout - Kiki. Formerly named Dunmacreean.
1951 . . . Brought down. (Lord Sefton) 8.10-1. P.Taaffe. 50/1.
1952 . . . Brought down. (Lord Sefton) 9.10-3. R.J.Hamey.33/1.
1953 . . . Finished 3rd of 31. (Lord Sefton) 10.10-6. R.Turnell. 33/1.
1954 . . . Finished 3rd of 29. (Lord Sefton) 11.10-5. M.Scudamore. 15/2.Fav.*
1955 . . . Finished 11th of 30.(Lord Sefton) 12.10-9. M.Scudamore. 100/8.
1957 . . . Fell. (Lord Sefton) 14.10-2. D.Nicholson. 66/1.

INTER ALIA
bay gelding by Interlace - Snake In The Grass.
1952 . . . Fell. (Mr G.Barry) 9.10-3. C.Sleator. 66/1.

ICY CALM
bay gelding by Dragonnade - Matchless Pride.
1952 . . . Pulled-up. (Marquis de Portago) 9.11-0. Marquis de Portago. 33/1.
1954 . . . Pulled-up. (Mrs O.Martin-Montis) 10.10-5. R.Francis. 40/1.

ICELOUGH
bay gelding by Iceberg 11 - Faunlough.
1957 . . . Brought down. (Mr R.H.Usher) 11.11-3. P.Taaffe. 28/1.

IRISH COFFEE
bay gelding by Reynard Volant - Lady Walewska.
1959 . . . Fell. (Mr J.A.Hale) 9.10-5. C.Finnegan. 33/1.
1960 . . . Pulled-up. (Mr W.St G.Burke) 10.10-11. Mr.W.St G.Burke) 66/1.
1961 . . . Finished 14th of 35. (Mr W.St G.Burke) 11.10-6. J.Magee. 50/1.

IMPOSANT
bay gelding by Vermeil - Nitouche Pas.
1961 . . . Pulled-up. (Mr R.Couetil) 9.10-13. Mr.R.Couetil. 100/1.

IRISH DAY
bay gelding by New Day - Irish Law.
1966 . . . Fell. (Mr A.Pownall) 10.10-0. J.Magee. 40/1.

IN HASTE
bay gelding by J'Accours - Toy Princess.
1966 . . . Pulled-up. (Lord Chelsea) 8.10-3. J.Leech. 100/1.

INVENTOR, THE
chestnut gelding by New Day - Another Port.
1969 . . . Fell. (Mrs R.Sangster) 8.10-0. T.Hyde. 33/1.
1971 . . . Refused. (Mrs R.Sangster) 10.10-7. B.Fletcher. 20/1.
1972 . . . Refused. (Mrs R.Sangster) 11.11.10-2. W.Shoemark.33/1.

INDAMELIA
bay mare by Indian Ruler - Barton's Sister.
1971 . . . Fell. (Mr M.J.Thorne) 8.10-0. Mr.P.Hobbs.100/1.

INDIAN DIVA
chestnut mare by Indian Ruler - Khediva.
1976 . . . Finished 16th of 32. (Miss A.J.Thorne) 9.10-3. Mr.N.Henderson. 100/1.

INYCARRA
bay gelding by Prince Charger - Adalough.
1977 . . . Fell. (Mr C.W.R.Fryer) 10.10-0. S.Jobar. 100/1.

IRISH TONY
bay gelding by Anthony - Princess Of Eire.
1978 . . . Brought down. (Cocked Hat Farm Foods) 10.10-0. D.Atkins. 33/1.

IMPERIAL BLACK
brown gelding by Master Rock - Fort Gloss.
1984 . . . Fell. (Mr T.Webster) 8.10-7. C.Hawkins. 50/1.
1985 . . . Finished 6th of 40. (Mr T.Webster) 9.10-1. C.Hawkins. 66/.1
1986 . . . Finished 14th of 40.(Mr T.Webster) 10.10-0. R.Crank. 66/1.

IMMIGRATE
brown gelding by Tycoon 11 - Elliss Island.
1985 . . . Fell. (Mr W.Stevenson-Taylor) 12.10-0. J.Hansen.100/1.

INSURE
bay gelding by Dusky Boy - Shady Tree.
1987 . . . Finished 22nd of 40. (Mrs E.Turner) 9.10-10. Mr.C.Brooks.45/1.
1988 . . . Unseated rider. (Mrs E.Turner) 10.10-0. B. de Haan. 80/1.

INTO THE RED
chestnut gelding by Over The River- Legal Fortune.
1994 . . . Unseated rider. (Miss E.Saunders & Mr J.Huckle) 10.10-0. J.White. 25/1.
1995 . . . Finished 5th of 35. (Miss E.Saunders & Mr J.Huckle) 11.10-0. R.Guest. 20/1.
1996 . . . Finished 15th of 27. (Miss E.Saunders & Mr J.Huckle) 12.10-0. R.Guest. 33/1.

ITS A CRACKER
bay gelding by Over The River - Bob's Hansel.
1994 . . . Fell. (Mr J.P.Berry) 10.10-0. C.O'Dwyer. 33/1.

ITS A SNIP
chestnut gelding by Monksfield - Snipkin.
1995 . . . Unseated rider. (Icy Fire Partnership) 10.10-0. J.R.Kavanagh. 200/1.

JACK
1839 . . . Fell. (Captain Lamb) Wadlow. n/q.

JERRY
by Catterick - Sister To Jerry. Not in the General Stud Book.
1840 . . . WON. (Mr Elmore / Mr Villebois) Mr.Bretherton. 12/1.

JERRY
1847 . . . Finished 3rd of 26. (Mr Moseley) - 11-6. Bradley. 100/8.
1848 . . . Pulled-up. (Mr Moseley) - 11-7. Sanders. n/q.
1849 . . . Fell. (Mr Moseley) - 10-4. J.S.Walker. n/q.

JOHNNIE BARRY
1850 . . . Failed to finish. (Mr Laing) - 9-0. Maitland. n/q.

JANUS
1855 . . . Finished 4th of 20. (Mr Elmore) - 9-10. H.Lamplugh.33/1.

JEAN DU QUESNE
1856 . . . Failed to finish. (Baron c. de la Motte) - 10-6. H.Lamplugh. 9/2.Fav.*
1857 . . . Finished 6th of 28. (Count de Cunchy) - 10-0. H.Lamplugh. 100/7.
1859 . . . Finished 2nd of 20. (Count de Cunchy) - 9-9. H.Lamplugh. 10/1.

JUMPAWAY
1856 . . . Failed to finish. (Mr Denison) - 9-10. J.Hanlon. 25/1.

JOE GRAHAM
1858 . . . Fell. (Mr Heron Maxwell) - 9-12. Rutherford. 33/1.

JEALOUSY
brown mare by The Cure - dam unknown. Not in the General Stud Book.
1859 . . . Failed to finish. (Mr Bayley) 5. 9-8. J.Kendall. 10/1.
1861 . . . WON. (Mr J.Bennett) 7. 9-12. 24 Ran. J.Kendall. 5/1.
1863 . . . Finished 6th of 16. (Mr Priestley) 9.11-10. J.Kendall. 3/1.Fav.*

JIMURU
bay gelding by Jim Newcombe - Sumuru.
1961 . . . Fell. (Lady Leigh) 10.10-4. Mr J.Leigh. 33/1.

JERUSALEM
1864 . . . Pulled-up. (Mr W.Murray) aged 11-10. Mr.Edwards. 9/2.Fav.*

JOE MALEY
1865 . . . Pulled-up. (Mr Hidson) - 11-10. D.Page. 100/12.

JACKAL
chestnut gelding by Caterer - Maggiore.
1975 . . . Finished 4th of 19. (Mr H.Baltazzi) 7.11-11. R.Marsh. 7/1.
1876 . . . Finished 6th of 19. (Mr H.Baltazzi) 8.11-0. R.Marsh. 100/7.
1878 . . . Finished 4th of 12. (Capt.J.Machell) 10.10-11. Jewitt. 100/8.
1879 . . . Finished 2nd of 18. (Lord Marcus Beresford) 11.11-0. J.Jones. 1000/65.

JUPITER TONANS
bay horse by Thunderbolt - Beatrice Grey.
1880 . . . Finished 4th of 14. (Mr J.F.Lee-Barber) 7.10-5. Mr.J.F.Lee-Barber. 50/1.

JOLLY SIR JOHN
chestnut gelding by Glenelg - Regan. Bred in U.S.A.
1883 . . . Fell. (Mr Dane) 6.10-5. Mr.A.Coventry. 100/12.
1885 . . . Fell. (Mr Dane) 8.10-12. W.Nightingall. 50/1.
1886 . . . Fell. (Mr F.Gebhard) 9.11-6. Mr.C.W.Walker. 40/1.

JOHNNY LONGTAIL
chestnut gelding by Polardine - Debonnaire.
1887 . . . Finished 3rd of 16. (Lord Wolverton) 9.10-6. J.Childs. 40/1.
1888 . . . Failed to finish. (Mr A.Yates) 10.12-0.W.Dollery. 40/1.

JEANIE
bay mare by Jock Of Oran - Ellen.
1888 . . . Finished 6th of 20. (Mr Abington) 5.10-6. A.H.Barker.200/1.
1891 . . . Fell. (Mr Abington) 8.10-4. A.H.Barker. 66/1.

JASON
brown horse by Chippendale - Quick Stream.
1892 . . . Fell. (Mr Abington) - 10-12. G.Mawson. 100/8.

JOAN OF ARC
bay mare by Heart Of Oak - Servant Girl.
1893 . . . Fell. (Capt.H.T.Fenwick) 8.10-4. G.Morris. 50/1.

JOHN M.P.
bay gelding by Britannic - Guiding Star.
1906 . . . Fell. (Mr J.S.Morrison) 7.11-10. W.Taylor. 7/2.Fav.*

JACOBUS
bay gelding by Wavelet's Pride - Kendaline.
1914 . . . Fell. (Mr C.Bower Ismay) 7.11-2. E.Piggott. 100/6.
1915 . . . Finished 2nd of 20. (Mr C.Bower Ismay) 8.11-0. A.Newey. 25/1.
* 1916 . . . finished 4th of 21. (Mr C.Bower Ismay) 9.12-0. A.Newey. 100/6.

JENKINSTOWN
bay gelding by Hackler - Playmate. Bred by Mr.P.Leonard.
1908 . . . Pulled-up. (Mr S.Howard) 7.10-5. F.Morgan. 66/1.
1910 . . . WON. (Mr S.Howard) 9.10-5. 25 Ran. R.Chadwick. 100/8.
1911 . . . Pulled-up. (Mr S.Howard) 10.11-7. P.Woodland. 100/7.
1912 . . . Pulled-up. (Mr W.G.Blundell) 11.11-7. W.Payne. 100/7.

JOHNSTOWN LAD
bay gelding by Red Prince 11 - Golden Holly.
1908 . . . Fell. (Mr J.M.Kerne) 7. 9-12. E.Driscoll. 10/1.

JUDAS
bay gelding by Wild Monk - Little Alice.
1909 . . . Finished 2nd of 32. (Mr B.W.Parr) 8.10-10. R.Chadwick. 33/1.
1910 . . . Fell. (Mr W.W.Bailey) 9.11-5. A.Anthony. 13/2.

JERRY M
bay gelding by Walmsgate - dam by Luminary. Bred by Miss Kate Hartigan.
1910 . . . Finished 2nd of 25. (Mr C.G.Assheton-Smith) 7.12-7. E.Driscoll. 6/1.Fav.*
1912 . . . WON. (Sir C.Assheton-Smith) 9.12-7. E.Piggott. 4/1.jnt/Fav.*

JAMES PIGG
bay gelding by Bealderg - Gweebarra.
1924 . . . Fell. (Mr J.W.Corrigan) 11.10-3. H.Morris. n/q.
1925 . . . Fell. (Mr J.W.Corrigan) 12.10-0. A.Robson. 66/1.

JACKHORNER
chestnut gelding by Cyllius - Melton's Guide. Bred by Mr.J.Musker.
1925 . . . Finished 7th of 33. (Mr K.Mackay) 8.10-0.Mr.M.D.Blair. 40/1.
1926 . . . WON. (Mr A.C.Schwartz) 9.10-5. W.Watkinson. 25/1.

JOLLY GLAD
chestnut gelding by Fariman - Dorfwych.
1926 . . . Fell. (Capt.C.B.Petre) 9.10-0. Mr.P.Dennis. 50/1.

JIMMY JAMES
bay gelding by Rhosmarket - dam by The Christian.
1935 . . . Fell. (Mr B.Mills) 8.10-7. H.Nicholson. 100/1.

JOCK
chestnut gelding by Corbridge - Scotch Bags.
1946 . . . Fell. (Lord Rosebery) 8.10-2. F.Gurney. 50/1.

JACK FINLAY
chestnut gelding by Knight Of The Garter - Miss Finlay.
1946 . . . Finished 2nd of 34. (Mr L.S.Elwell) 7.10-2. W.Kidney.100/1.
1947 . . . Fell. (Mr L.S.Elwell) 8.10-8. W.Kidney. 33/1.

JUBILEE FLIGHT
brown gelding by Grandflight - Very Nice.
1947 . . . Finished 21st of 57. (Mr W.F.Ransom) 12.10-0. E.Hannigan. 100/1.

JOHN JACQUES
bay gelding by Belman - Tiber Win.
1959 . . . Fell. (Mrs D.G.Wares) 10.11-0. H.J.East. 33/1.

JONJO
chestnut gelding by Tartan - Clarion March.
1960 . . . Fell. (Mr J.L.O'Hagen) 10.10-4. P.Taaffe. 50/1.
1961 . . . Finished 7th of 35. (Mr J.L.O'Hagen) 11.10-7. P.Taaffe. 7/1.Fav.*
1963 . . . Fell. (Duque de Alburquerque) 13.10-6. Duque de Alburquerque. 66/1.

JOHN O' GROATS
grey gelding by Jock Scot - Tonsure.
1964 . . . Finished 11th of 33. (Mr F.Clay) 10.10-3. P.Kelleway. 22/1.

JAY TRUMP
bay gelding by Tonga Prince - Be Trump. Bred in the U.S.A. by Mr.Jay Sessenich.
1965 . . . WON. (Mrs M.Stephenson) 8.11-5. 47 Ran. Mr.T.C.Smith. 100/6.

JIM'S TAVERN
brown gelding by Playhouse - Jim's Love.
1966 . . . Finished 5th of 47. (Mrs P.F.J.Colvin) 9.10-0. Mr.N.Gaselee. 100/1.

JUAN
brown gelding by Mazarin - Fond Ann.
1969 . . . Refused. (Mr P.J.H.Wills) 13.10-9. Mr.P.Wills. 100/1.

JUST A GAMBLE
bay gelding by Coronation Year or Combat - Miss Deal.
1972 . . . Fell. (Capt. & Mrs F.Tyrwhitt-Drake) 10.10-1. P.Buckley. 100/1.

JUNIOR PARTNER
brown gelding by Dual - Fauteull.
1975 . . . Fell. (Mrs F.Wheatley) 8.10-0. K.B.White. 18/1.

JOLLY'S CLUMP
bay gelding by Kalydon - Plea.
1976 . . . Finished 13th of 32. (Mr R.Hutchinson) 10.10-3.I.Watkinson. 12/1.

JIMMY MIFF
brown gelding by Nos Royalistes - Lark About.
1980 . . . Fell. (Mr G.Tanner) 8.10-5. A.Brown. 50/1.
1982 . . . Fell. (Mr B.Davies) 10.10-1. Mr.M.Williams. 50/1.

JER
chestnut gelding by Sea Bird II - Macarena II.
1980 . . . Fell. (Mr G.D.Wyse) 9.10-4. P.Tuck. 10/1.

JACKO
bay gelding by Master Buck - Lady Jill.
1984 . . . Finished 22nd of 40. (Mr H.B.Shouler) 12.10-0. S.Morshead. 66/1.

JIVAGO DE NEUVY
bay gelding by Seddouk - Digne du Vernay.
1984 . . . Finished 9th of 40. (Mr R.Grand) 9.11-0. Mr.R.Grand. 60/1.

JUST SO
brown gelding by Sousa - Just Camilla.
1992 . . . Finished 6th of 40. (Mr H.T.Cole) 9.10-2. S.Burrough.50/1.
1994 . . . Finished 2nd of 36. (Mr H.T.Cole) 11.10-3. S.Burrough.20/1.

KHONDOOZ
1848 . . . Pulled-up. (Mr J.Wilson) - 11-0. Rackley. 25/1.
1849 . . . Pulled-up. (Mr Tillbury) - 9-10. Rackley. n/q.

KNIGHT OF GWYNNE, THE
1849 . . . Finished 2nd of 24. (Capt.D'Arcy) - 10-7.Capt.D'Arcy. 8/1.
1850 . . . Finished 2nd of 32. (Mr J.Fort) - 11-8. D.Wynne. 12/1.
1853 . . . Pulled-up. (Mr Drake) - 11-2. Donaldson. n/q.

KILFANE
1849 . . . Fell. (Mr J.H.Holmes) - 11-0. Neale. n/q.

KILKENNY
1850 . . . Failed to finish. (Capt.Fraser) - 9-10. W.Holman. n/q.

KING DAN
1857 . . . Failed to finish. (Mr Jennings) - 9-6. Escott. n/q.

KILCOCK
1860 . . . Failed to finish. (Mr Aylmer) 6.10-0. D.Meaney. n/q.
1861 . . . Failed to finish. (Mr Bowbiggins) 7. 9-10. D.Meaney. 40/1.

KIBWORTH LASS
1861 . . . Refused. (Mr J.L.Manby) - 11-1. Oliver,jnr. n/q.

KING OF HEARTS
bay gelding by Daniel O'Rourke- dam by Sleight -Of-Hand.
1866 . . . Fell. (Mr W.Robinson) - 10-2. A.Sadler. 30/1.

KING ARTHUR
bay horse by The Cure - Miss Agnes.
1867 . . . Pulled-up. (Capt.Brabazon) 5.10-3. Capt.Harford. 5/1.Fav.*

KINGSWOOD
chestnut horse by Chit-chat - Yorkshire Witch.
1868 . . . Fell. (Mr W.Forbes) 6.10-12. Gilroy. n/q.

KNAVE OF TRUMPS
black gelding by King Of Trumps - dam by West Australian.
1869 . . . Fell. (Mr T.Golby) - 10-6. Mr.F.Martin. 20/1.

KEYSTONE
brown gelding by Cornerstone - dam unknown.
1870 . . . Finished 5th of 23. (Mr G.Nelson) - 10-12. Mr.R.Walker. 1000/5.

KARSLAKE
bay gelding by Knight Of Kars - Novelist.
1870 . . . Failed to finish. (Capt.A.C.Tempest) 6.10-0. Capt.A.C.Tempest. 50/1.

KILWORTH
bay gelding by John Davis - dam by Black Prince.
1885 . . . Fell. (Capt.E.R.Owen) - 11-6. Capt.E.R.Owen. 10/1.
1889 . . . Refused. (Lord Dudley) - 10-13. Capt.E.R.Owen. 40/1.

KINFAUNS
bay mare by Wild Oats - Maid Of Perth.
1888 . . . Refused. (Mr T.Brinckman) 7.10-10. J.Page. 100/1.

KESTRAL
brown horse by Spider - dam unknown.
1896 . . . Finished 7th of 28. (Mr W.Lawson) 9. 9-10. H.Smith. 100/1.

KINGSWORTHY
brown horse by Edward The Confessor - The Warren Belle.
1898 . . . Pulled-up. (Mr F.R.Hunt) 7.10-0. E.Acres. 20/1.

KIRKLAND
chestnut gelding by Kirkham - dam by Perizonius.
1903 . . . Finished 4th of 23. (Mr F.Bibby) 7.10-8. F.Mason. 100/8.
1904 . . . Finished 2nd of 26. (Mr F.Bibby) 8.10-10. F.Mason. 100/7.
1905 . . . WON. (Mr F.Bibby) 9.11-5. 27 Ran. F.Mason. 6/1.
1908 . . . Finished 7th of 24. (Mr F.Bibby) 12.11-12. F.Mason. 13/2.Fav.*

KILMALLOG
bay gelding by Torpedo - Ardrea.
1903 . . . Fell. (Mr J.R.Cooper) 6.10-9. T.Moran. 20/1.

KNIGHT OF ST PATRICK
bay or brown gelding by Craig Royston - dam by Ireland Yet.
1904 . . . Pulled-up. (Mr A.Buckley jnr.) 7.10-6. M.Walsh. n/q.

KIORA
brown gelding by Blue Mountain - May.
1904 . . . Fell. (Capt.Scott) 9.10-3. T.McGuire. 40/1.
1905 . . . Fell. (Mr W.H.Pawson) 10.10-5. Mr.W.H.Pawson. 100/1.
1906 . . . Knocked-over. (Mr C.Bewicke) 11.10-4. G.Clancy. 33/1.

KILTS
bay gelding by Kilmarnock - Rockery.
1907 . . . Fell. (Mr T.Arthur) 7.10-3. R.H.Harper. 100/6.

KILKEEL
bay gelding by Wiseman - The Skit.
1912 . . . Failed to finish. (Mr Hunter Moore) 7.10-7. R.Trudgill. n/q.

KENIA
bay mare by Berrill - Diane.
* 1917 . . . Fell. (Mr R.B.Thorburn) 8.10-10. A.Saxby. 33/1.

KEEP COOL
chestnut gelding by Pam - Alexa.
1925 . . . Pulled-up. (Mr W.H.Midwood) 10.10-7. G.Green. 33/1.
1927 . . . Fell. (Mr W.H.Midwood) 12.11-3. J.Goswell. 33/1.
1928 . . . failed to finish. (Mr W.H.Midwood) 13.10-11. J..Goswell.66/1.

KOKO
bay gelding by Santoi - Persister.
1926 . . . Fell. (Mr F.Barbour) 8.11-1. J.Hamey. 100/8.
1928 . . . Fell. (Capt.F.E.Guest) 10.12-2. W.Gurney. 20/1.
1929 . . . Fell. (Capt.F.E.Guest) 11.12-3. S.Duffy. 66/1.

KNIGHT OF THE WILDERNESS
bay or brown gelding by Knight Of Kilcash - Barkaway.
1926 . . . Fell. (Mr G.White) 6.11-0. J.Meaney. 20/1.
1927 . . . Fell. (Mr W.P.Draper) 7.11-9. W.Gurney. 33/1.
1929 . . . Brought down. (Mr F.H.W.Cundell) 9.11-7. M.Keogh. 40/1.

KILBAIRN
brown gelding by Kelso - Cottage Maiden.
1929 . . . Finished 9th of 66. (Mr R.A.Parry) 8.10-0. Mr.L.Parry. 200/1.

K. C. B.
bay gelding by The White Knight -Rill.
1929 . . . Brought down. (Mr V.H.Smith) 7.10-10. J.Hogan,jnr. 50/1.
1930 . . . Knocked-over. (Mr V.H.Smith) 8.10-12. J.Moloney. 22/1.
1932 . . . Fell. (Mr V.H.Smith) 10.10-7. J.Mason. 50/1.

KILBRAIN
bay gelding by Ardoon - Loo Bridge.
1929 . . . Fell. (Mr E.A.Longworth) 9.10-4. V.Piggott. 100/1.

KWANGO
bay gelding by Kwang-Su -Farcical.
1929 . . . Brought down. (Mr C.Goad) 8.10-0. A.Waudby. 200/1.

111

KAKUSHIN
chestnut gelding bu Friar Marcus - Osaka.
1931 . . . Fell. (Mr W.M.G.Singer) 8.11-13. R.Everett. 22/1.

KILBUCK
brown gelding by Great Sport - Tredonna.
1931 . . . Fell. (Mr E.R.Hartley) 11-6. T.Chisman. 50/1.
1934 . . . Fell. (Miss R.M.Harrison) aged. 10-8. T.B.Cullinan. 66/1.

KELLSBORO' JACK
bay gelding by Jackdaw - Kellsboro' Lass. Bred by Mr.J.Hutchinson.
1933 . . . WON. (Mrs F.Ambrose Clark) 7.11-9. 34 Ran. D.Williams. 25/1.

KILTOI
bay gelding by Yutoi - Lass Of Killiecrankie.
1936 . . . Fell. (Mr J.Metcalf) 7.10-8. T.Carey. 66/1.
1937 . . . Fell. (Mr J.Metcalf) 8.10-1. Capt.R.Harding. 100/1.

KEEN BLADE
bay or brown gelding by Declare - Lady Moonshine.
1936 . . . Fell. (Lord Rosebery) 9.10-7. T.Elder. 100/7.
1937 . . . Refused. (Lord Rosebery) 10.10-7. Mr.Paget. 28/1.

K. D. H.
bay mare by Cottage - Golden Land.
1938 . . . Fell. (Mrs Metcalfe) 7.10-0. G.Archibald. 100/1.

KILSTAR
brown gelding by Boris - dam by Munster King.
1939 . . . Finished 3rd of 37. (Miss D.Paget) 8.10-3. G.Archibald. 8/1.Fav.*
1940 . . . Finished 12th of 30.(Miss D.Paget) 9.11-0. G.Archibald. 5/1.

KAMI
bay gelding by Bonny Boy - Kashiwade. Bred in France.
1946 . . . Fell. (Ms.Andre Adele) 9.10-9. H.Bonneau. 33/1.
1947 . . . Finished 3rd of 57. (Sir A.Gordon Smith) 10.10-13. Mr.J.Hislop. 33/1.

KING GESSON
bay or brown gelding by Kindred - Sagesse.
1946 . . . Refused. (Mrs G.Coles) 13.10-0. R.Burford. 100/1.

KNIGHT'S CREST
bay gelding by Wavetop - Eerie.
1946 . . . Fell. (Mr F.E.Renner) 9.10-3. P.J.Murphy. 22/1.

KAMI
bay gelding by Bonny Boy - Kashiwade. Bred in France.
1946 . . . Fell. (Ms.Andre Adele) 9.10-9. H.Bonneau. 33/1.
1947 . . . Finished 3rd of 57. (Sir A.Gordon Smith) 10.10-13. Mr.J.Hislop. 33/1.

KLAXTON
brown gelding by Mr Toots - Orchardstown Lass.
1947 . . . Fell. (Mr T.Radmall) 7.10-5. J.Maguire. 66/1.
1948 . . . Finished 10th of 43. (Mr T.Radmall) 8.11-8. R.Smyth. 40/1.
1950 . . . Fell. (Mr W.D.Gibson) 10.11-13. J.Maguire. 40/1.

KILNAGLORY
grey gelding by Empire Builder - Alvista.
1947 . . . Finished 8th of 57. (Miss D.Paget) 12.11-1. B.Marshall. 40/1.

KNOCKIRR
brown gelding by Walinson - Valiant Woman.
1950 . . . Fell. (Mrs V.Taylor) 10.10-4. T.Cusack. 66/1.

KELEK
chestnut gelding by Canot - Karyatis.
1952 . . . Refused. (Lady Hague) 8.10-13. C.Hook. 40/1.

KNUCKLEDUSTER
bay gelding by Cariff - Flying Rose.
1953 . . . Pulled-up. (Mr P.B.Browne) 9.11-0. Mr.P.B.Browne. 25/1.

KEY ROYAL
bay gelding by Royal Charger - Keyboard.
1956 . . . Finished 5th of 29. (Mr A.H.Birtwhistle) 8.10-8. T.Molony. 28/1.

KERSTIN
brown mare by Honor's Choice - Miss Kilcash.
1959 . . . Brought down. (Mr G.H.Moore) 9.12-0. S.Hayhurst. 25/1.

KILBALLYOWN
bay gelding by Last Of The Dandies - Cringer.
1959 . . . Brought down. (Mrs M.A.Lynch) 12.10-2. E.McKenzie.33/1.

KNOXTOWN
brown gelding by Sir Walter Raleigh - Gallant Princess.
1960 . . . Fell. (Mr M.Cowley) 10.10-5. Mr.E.P.Harty. 45/1.

KINGSTEL
bay gelding by King's Idler - dam unknown.
1961 . . . Fell. (Mr C.Hornby) 9.10-0. G.Slack. 50/1.

KILMORE
bay gelding by Zalophus - Brown Image. Bred by Mr.A.G.C.Webb.
1961 . . . Finished 5th of 35. (Mr N.Cohen) 11.11-0. F.T.Winter. 33/1.
1962 . . . WON. (Mr N.Cohen) 12.10-4. 32 Ran F.T.Winter. 28/1.
1963 . . . Finished 6th of 47. (Mr N.Cohen) 13.11-0. F.T.Winter. 100/8.
1964 . . . Fell. (Mr N.Cohen) 14.10-7. F.T.Winter. 100/6.

KERFORO
bay mare by Foroughi - Kerlogue Steel.
1962 . . . Fell. (Mr F.J.Stafford) 8.10-3. P.Taaffe. 100/9.

KAPENO
brown gelding by No Orchids - Kanjana.
1965 . . . Fell. (Mrs A.T.Hodgson) 8.11-6. D.V.Dick. 100/8.
1966 . . . Fell. (Mr W.H.Whitbread) 9.10-6. D.Mould. 100/7.
1967 . . . Finished 10th of 44. (Mr W.H.Whitbread) 10.11-1. Mr.N.Gaselee. 25/1.

KING PIN
bay gelding by King Hal - Cruagh Bawn.
1966 . . . Pulled-up. (Mrs D.Dye) 10.10-0. Mr.T.Durant. 100/1.

KIRTLE-LAD
chestnut gelding by Exodus - Montlace.
1967 . . . Refused. (Mr R.F.Tinning) 8.10-3. P.Broderick. 28/1.
1968 . . . Fell. (Mr R.F.Tinning) 9.10-0. J.Enright. 50/1.

KILBURN
bay gelding by Battleburn - dam by Steel Point.
1967 . . . Fell. (Mme.Borel de Bitche) 9.11-0. T.Norman. 100/8.
1969 . . . Fell. (Mme.Borel de Bitche) 11.10-9. T.Carberry. 22/1.

KELLSBORO' WOOD
brown gelding by Wood Cot - Kellsboro Jane.
1969 . . . Finished 8th of 30. (Mrs L.M.Prior) 9.10-10. A.Turnell. 66/1.
1971 . . . Fell. (Mrs M.L.Prior) 11.10-0. A.Turnell. 100/1.
1972 . . . Fell. (Mrs L.M.Prior) 12.10-0. A.Turnell. 100/1.

KING VULGAN
bay gelding by Vulgan - Bright Princess.
1971 . . . Finished 8th of 38. (Mr J.P.Costelloe) 10.11-0. J.Crowley. 16/1.

KARACOLA
bay gelding by Pinicola - Chunkara.
1974 . . . Brought down. (Mr D.M.Adams) 9.10-0. C.Astbury. 100/1.

KILMORE BOY
bay gelding by Timobriol - Kilmore Girl.
1975 . . . Fell. (Mr A.Grogan) 9.10-2. P.Blacker. 40/1.

KINTAI
chestnut gelding by King's Leap - Preciptai.
1979 . . . Brought down. (Mr H.Jackson) 10.10-0. B.Smart. 100/1.

KICK ON
bay gelding by Takawalk 11 - Blue Moss.
1979 . . . Brought down. (Mr K.Lewis) 12.10-0. R.Hyett. 50/1.

KININVIE
bay gelding by Raise You Ten - Vacance.
1980 . . . Pulled-up. (Mr S.Sarsfield & Mr A.J.K.Dunn) 11.10-0. J.Williams. 100/1.
1981 . . . Fell. (Lady Dunn) 12.10-0. P.Hobbs. 100/1.

KILKILWELL
brown mare by Harwell - Kilkilane.
1981 . . . Fell. (Mr P.Hamilford) 9.10-6. N.Madden. 33/1.

KYLOGUE LADY
bay mare by London Gazette - Fair Reply.
1981 . . . Fell. (Mr D.English) 9.10-0. T.Quinn. 100/1.

KEENGADDY
bay gelding by Candy Cane - Keenouge.
1983 . . . Fell. (Mr I.Single) 10.10-0. S.Smith Eccles. 15/1.

KING SPRUCE
bay gelding by Harwell - Daemolina.
1983 . . . Fell. (Mr R.N.Carrier) 9.11-4. Mrs.Joy Carrier.28/1.

KUMBI
bay gelding by No Argument - Rusheen Point.
1984 . . . Fell. (Mr D.A.Lunt & Mr T.Webster) 9.10-0. K.Doolan. 100/1.
1985 . . . Fell. (Mr D.A.Lunt & Mr T.Webster) 10.10-0. K.Doolan. 100/1.
1988 . . . Fell. (Mr D.A.Lunt) 13.10-0. C.Llewellyn. 100/1.

KNOCKAWAD
chestnut gelding by Prince Hansel - Lady Settler.
1985 . . . Fell. (Mr M.L.Wilmott) 8.10-0. K.F.O'Brien. 66/1.

KILKILOWEN
bay or brown gelding by Master Owen - Vultang.
1986 . . . Finished 13th of 40. (execs. of the late Mrs W.N.Collen) 10.11-3. K.Morgan. 25/1.

KNOCK HILL
bay gelding by Daybrook Lad - Super Sprite.
1986 . . . Pulled-up. (Mr P.S.Thompson) 10.10-0. M.Dwyer. 18/1.

KERSIL
bay gelding by Keren - Queen's Silk.
1989 . . . Pulled-up. (Mr J.E.Siers) 12. 10-0. A.Orkney. 300/1.

KARAKTER REFERENCE
brown gelding by Reformed Character - Windtown Beauty.
1992 . . . Pulled-up. (Mrs R.J.Doorgachurn) 10.10-1. D.O'Sullivan. 50/1.

KITTINGER
bay gelding by Crash Course - Mandaloch.
1992 . . . Refused. (Mr J.S.Lammiman) 11.10-0. I.Lawrence. 200/1.

LOTTERY
bay gelding by Lottery - Parthenia. Formerly named Chance. Bred by Mr.Jackson.
1839 . . . WON. (Mr J.Elmore) 9.12-0. 17 Ran. J.Mason. 5/1.Fav*
1840 . . . Fell. (Mr J.Elmore) 10.12-0. J.Mason. 4/1.
1841 . . . Pulled-up. (Mr J.Elmore) 11.13-4. J.Mason. 5/2.Fav*
1842 . . . Pulled-up. (Mr J.Elmore) 12.13-4. J.Mason. 5/1.Fav*
1843 . . . Finished 7th of 16. (Mr J.Elmore) 13.12-6. J.Mason. 4/1.

LEGACY
1841 . . . Fell. (Mr Robertson) Mr W.McDonough. 12/1.

LATHER
1844 . . . Finished 5th 0f 15. (Lord E.Russell) Ball. n/q.

LITTLE PETER
1844 . . . Finished 8th of 15. (Mr Hollinshead) Mr.Hollinshead. n/q.

LOUIS PHILIPPE
1844 . . . Finished 9th of 15. (Sir J.Gerrard) Cowell. 20/1.

LANCET
1846 . . . Knocked-over. (Mr Hey) Mr W.McDonough. 10/1.

LAUREL
1850 . . . Failed to finish. (Mr Butler) - 10-8. Mr.Butler. n/q.

LITTLE FANNY
1850 . . . Failed to finish. (Lord Sefton) - 9-0. Fowler. 25/1.

LADY LANGFORD
1842 . . . Fell. (Hon.C.Forester) Abbot. n/q.

LUCKS - ALL
1842 . . . Failed to finish. (Mr R.Ekin) Goddard. 10/1.

LADY GRAY
1846 . . . Fell. (Sir R.Brownrigg) Thomas. n/q.

LATTITAT
1847 . . . Failed to finish. (Mr Bevill) - 11-0. Mr.Bevill. n/q.

LA GAZZA LADRA
1852 . . . Finished 5th of 24. (Mr Goodwin) 6.9-12. J.Neale. 6/1.Fav.*
1854 . . . Refused. (Mr J.Williams) 8.10-0. T.Abbot. 50/1.

LAMIENNE
1852 . . . Failed to finish. (Mr J.G.Murphy) - 9-7. Meaney. n/q.

LADY ARTHUR
1854 . . . Finished 5th of 20. (Mr Delamarre) - 9-10. T.Donaldson. 50/1.
1857 . . . Finished 7th of 28. (Viscomte Lauriston) - 9-4. Weaver. n/q.

LITTLE CHARLEY
bay gelding - Pedigree Unknown. Not in the General Stud Book.
1855 . . . Knocked-over. (Mr C.Capel) 7. 9-4. D.Wynne. 20/1.
1856 . . . Finished 5th of 21.(Mr C.Capel) 8. 9-4. T.Burrows.40/1.
1857 . . . Failed to finish. (Mr C.Capel) 9.10-0. T.Burrows. 100/7.
1858 . . . WON. (Mr C.Capel) 10.10-7. 16 Ran. W.Archer.100/6.
1859 . . . Failed to finish. (Mr W.Barnett) 11.10-11. T.Burrows. 14/1.

LIVERPOOL BOY
1856 . . . Failed to finish. (Mr H.King) 6. 9-0. McClean. n/q.

LOUGH BAWN
1858 . . . Refused. (Mr Buchanan) - 9-8. G.Stevens. 9/2.

LITTLE TOM
1858 . . . Fell. (Capt.Connell) - 9-6. B.Land,jnr. 5/1.

LEFROY
1860 . . . Failed to finish. (Capt.White) - 9-0. C.Green. n/q.

LONGRANGE
1861 . . . Failed to finish. (Mr C.Watts) - 9-10. R.Sherrard. n/q.

LIGHT OF OTHER DAYS
1863 . . . Failed to finish. (Mr W.W.Baker) - 10-4. J.Nightingall. 20/1.

LEONIDAS
1864 . . . Pulled-up. (Capt.J.Machell) - 11-4. C.Boyce. n/q.

LITTLE BAB
1964 . . . Failed to finish. (Mr W.Murray) - 11-0. P.Igon. n/q.

LIGHT HEART
bay gelding by Great Heart - Skylark.
1865 . . . Pulled-up. (Mr A.W.Clayton) aged.10-12. J.Monaghan. 20/1.
1866 . . . Finished 4th of 30. (Mr A.W.Clayton) aged.11-5.E.Jones.50/1.
1867 . . . Finished 5th of 23. (Mr A.W.Clayton) aged.11-1.E.Jones.50/1.

L' AFRICAINE
1866 . . . Pulled-up. (Mr W.R.H.Powell) aged.13-2. G.Holman. 100/7.

LAURA
bay mare by Neville - dam unknown.
1866 . . . Fell. (Mr E.Bourgnet) 5.11-0. H.Lamplugh. 7/1.Fav.*

LITTLE FRANK
bay horse by Gemma di Vergy - Ossifrage.
1867 . . . Knocked-over. (Mr Vallender) aged. 10-13. J.Knott. 30/1.

LITTLE WIDEAWAKE
chestnut gelding by Rataplan - Trochee. Formerly named Whitenap.
1867 . . . Knocked-over. (Mr Schwartz) aged. 10-3. J.Rickaby. 30/1.

LAMB, THE
grey horse by Zouave - dam by Arthur. Bred by Mr.Henchy. Not in the General Stud Book.
1868 . . . WON. (Lord Poulett) 6.10-7. 21 Ran.Mr.Edwards. 9/1.
1871 . . . WON. (Lord Poulett) 9.11-5. 25 Ran. Mr.Thomas. 11/2.
1872 . . . Finished 4th of 25. (Baron Oppenheim) 10.12-7. Mr.Thomas. 100/8.

LORD RAGLAN
brown gelding by Vedette - Helen Ragan.
1871 . . . Broke leg. (destroyed) (Mr O.Perry) 8.10-10. Daniels. 100/1.

LADY GERALDINE
bay mare by The Marquis - Countess Of Westmorland.
1871 . . . Failed to finish. (Capt.Haworth) 5.10-6. C.Cunningham. 100/1.

LINGERER
brown horse by Loiterer - Recluse.
1873 . . . Fell. (Mr W.Burton) 6.10-13. Mumford. 50/1.

LOUSTIC
bay horse by Zouave - Emmy. Bred in France.
1873 . . . Failed to finish. (Colonel Byrne) 6.10-13. Mr.Bambridge. 30/1.

LAST OF THE LAMBS
bay horse by Zouave - out of The Lamb's dam.
1874 . . . Fell. (Mr H.Houldsworth) 5.10-0. Mr.Daglish. 40/1.

LORD COLNEY
chestnut horse by Cathedral - Violet.
1874 . . . Brought-down. (Captain Boynton) 5.10-0. Pickard. n/q.

LA VEINE
chestnut mare by Ventre St Gris - Valeriane. Bred in France.
1875 . . . Finished 3rd of 19. (Baron Finot) 5.11-12. J.Page. 6/1.Fav.*

117

LABURNUM
bay horse by King Tom - Blooming Heather.
1875 . . . Broke-down. (Capt.J.Machell) 6.11-12. Jewitt. 20/1.

LIBERATOR, THE
bay or brown gelding by Dan O'Connell - Mary O'Toole. Bred by Mr. Stokes. Not in the General Stud Book.
1876 . . . Fell. (Mr C.E.Hawkes) 7.10-11. T.Ryan. 50/1.
1877 . . . Finished 3rd of 16. (Mr G.Moore) 8.10-12. Mr.Thomas. 25/1.
1879 . . .WON. (Mr G.Moore) 10.11-4. 18 Ran. Mr.G.Moore. 5/1.
1880 . . . Finished 2nd of 14. (Mr G.Moore) 11.12-7. Mr.G.Moore. 11/2.
1881 . . . Finished 9th of 13. (Mr G.Moore) 12.12-7. Mr.G.Moore. 6/1. Remounted*
1882 . . . Fell. (Mr W.H.Moore) 13.12-7. J.Adams. 20/1.

LANCET
chestnut gelding by Baldwin - dam unknown. Formerly named Blue Pill.
1877 . . . Pulled-up. (Mr J.Johnson) 10.11-0. S.Daniels. 33/1.

LORD MARCUS
bay gelding by Kingsley - Lady Fanny.
1879 . . . Finished 8th of 18. (Mr P.M.Saurin) 7.10-9. Mr.W.Beasley. n/q.

LITTLE PRINCE
bay gelding by Crown Prince - Sympathy.
1881 . . . Refused. (Mr C.G.Way) 6.10-8. D.Canavan. n/q.

LIONESS
bay mare by Uncas - Queen Of The Forest.
1885 . . . Finished 8th of 19. (Mr Hungerford) 7.11-7. Mr.G.Lambton. n/q.

LANG SYNE
brown mare by Cambuslang - Constancy.
1885 . . . Fell. (Mr H. de Windt) 7.10-8. T.Hale. n/q.

LADY TEMPEST
chestnut mare by Ingomar - Sheet Lightning.
1886 . . . Finished 8th of 23. (Mr P.M.V.Saurin) 6.10-5. Mr.W.Beasley. 22/1.

LIBERATOR, THE
bay or brown gelding by Dan O'Connell -Mary O'Toole.
1886 . . . Fell. (Mr E.Woodland) 11.10-10. Mr.S.J.Woodland. 100/1.

LIMEKILN
chestnut horse by Limestone - Leonorah. Bred in the U.S.A.
1886 . . . Fell. (Count Zborowski) 6.10-2. W.Brockwell. n/q.

LORD OF THE GLEN
bay gelding by Lord Gough - The Glen.
1892 . . . Fell. (Mr C.W.Waller) 7.11-0. Mr.C.W.Waller. 33/1.

LORD ARTHUR
chestnut gelding by Duc de Beaufort - dam unknown.
1892 . . . Pulled-up. (Mr H.T.Barclay) 9.10-7. Capt.Lee Barber.25/1.

LADY HELEN
brown mare by Rhidorroch - dam by Lord Roland.
1893 . . . Fell. (Captain Dundas) 7.11-1. R.Nightingall. 50/1.

LADY ELLEN II
bay mare by Prince George - Lady Helen.
1894 . . . Finished 2nd of 14. (Mr J.McKinley) 6. 9-10. T.Kavanagh. 25/1.

LEYBOURNE
chestnut gelding by Galliard - Lottie.
1895 . . . Finished 6th of 19. (Capt.J.M.Gordon) 7.10-3. G.Williamson. 100/8.

LADY PAT
grey mare by Downpatrick - dam unknown.
1895 . . . Finished 8th of 19. (Mr F.D.Leyland) 8.10-13. D.Shanahan. 25/1.

LOTUS LILY
bay mare by Lotus 11 - Skipaway.
1897 . . . Finished 5th of 28. (Capt.R.W.Ethelston) 7. 9-7. Mr.A.W.Wood. 100/1.
1899 . . . Fell. (Capt.R.W.Ethelston) 9. 9-12. J.Latham. 100/8.
1900 . . . Finished 8th of 16. (Capt.R.W.Ethelston) 10. 9-11. Mr.A.W.Wood. 25/1.

LITTLE JOE
chestnut gelding by Blue Grass - Old Fashion.
1897 . . . Fell. (Mr R.T.Bell) 8. 9-10. L.Bland. 100/1.
1898 . . . Fell. (Mr A.Bell) 9.10-0. J.Walsh, jnr. 28/1.

LITTLE NORTON
bay gelding by Chevronal - Belgrade. Formerly named Norton.
1899 . . . Fell. (Mr G.R.Powell) aged. 9-7. C.Clack. 200/1.

LEVANTER
bay gelding by Captivator - Steel All.
1900 . . . Finished 5th of 16. (Captain Scott) aged. 9-8. T.McGuire 50/1.
1901 . . . Finished 4th of 24. (Mr J.E.Edwards) aged. 9-10. F.Mason. 5/1.Fav.*

LURGAN
bay gelding by Arga - Eiver. Formerly named Tiny White.
1902 . . . Finished 5th of 21. (Lord Cadogan) 6.10-12. F.Freemantle. 100/8.

LOCH LOMOND
brown gelding by Blairfinde - Yvette.
1904 . . . Fell. (Mr F.H.Wise) 6. 9-10. F.Freemantle. 66/.1

LONGTHORPE
bay horse by St Serf - Orlet.
1905 . . . Refused. (Lord Sefton) 7.10-7. F.Freemantle. 33/1.

LOOP HEAD
chestnut gelding by Brayhead - Barberry.
1907 . . . Fell. (Mr F.Bibby) 6. 9-12. A.Hogan. n/q.

LAWYER III , THE
chestnut gelding by Broxton - dam by Solon.
1908 . . . Finished 3rd of 24. (Mr P.Whitaker) 11.10-3.Mr.P.Whitaker. 100/7.

LARA
chestnut gelding by Turk's Cap - Galley.
1908 . . . Fell. (Capt.J.Foster) 7.10-8. Mr.W.Bulteel. 25/1.

LUTTEUR III
chestnut gelding by St Damien - Lausanne. Bred in France by M.Gaston-Dreyfus.
1909 . . . WON. (M.James Hennessy) 5.10-11. 32 Ran. G.Parfrement. 100/9.jnt/Fav.*
1911 . . . Fell. (M.James Hennessy) 7.12-3. G.Parfrement. 7/2.Fav.*
1914 . . . Finished 3rd of 20. (M.J.Hennessy) 10.12-0. A.Carter. 10/1.

LEINSTER
bay gelding by Ascetic - Secret.
1909 . . . Finished 6th of 32. (Sir T.Gallwey) 11.11-7. Mr.J.T.Rogers. 100/6.

LOGAN ROCK
bay gelding by Penzance - Sign Post.
1909 . . . Finished 12th of 32. (Mr W.L.Longworth) 9.10-0. H.Jackson. 50/1.
1910 . . . Knocked-over. (Mr W.L.Longworth) 10. 9-7. H.Jackson. 20/1.

LORD RIVERS
bay gelding by Riverstown - dam by Craig Royston.
1909 . . . Finished 14th of 32. (Baron de Forest) 7.10-6. W.Bulteel. 25/1.
1911 . . . Fell. (Baron de Forest) 9.10-9. W.Payne. 33/1.

LORD CHATHAM
bay gelding by Little John - Athela.
1909 . . . Fell. (Mr G.Aston) 6.11-0. J.McKenna. 50/1.
1910 . . . Fell. (Mr G.Aston) 7.10-12. J.Dillon. n/q.

LURCHER, THE
brown gelding by Wildflower - Silver Mine.
1909 . . . Fell. (Mr T.Stacey) 7. 9-9. E.Piggott. 25/1.
1910 . . . Fell. (Mr T.Stacey) 8. 9-9. F.Dainty. 100/6.

LORD MARCUS
brown gelding by Walmsgate or Butterscotch Lady Rivers.
1915 . . . Fell. (Lord Lonsdale) 7.10-3. G.Parfrement. 7/1.
* 1916 . . . Completed course. (Lord Lonsdale) 8.11-13. G.Parfrement. 11/2.

LAMENTABLE
brown mare by Flying Hackle - Lambthorpe.
* 1916 . . . Pulled-up. (Mr F.C.Parker) 9.11-1. S.Walkington. 25/1.

LYNCH PIN
bay gelding by Cherry Stone - dam by Walmsgate.
* 1916 . . . Pulled-up. (Mr W.H.Dixon) 10.10-10. J.Dillon. n/q.

LIMEROCK
bay horse by Rock Sand - Annot Lyle. Bred in the U.S.A.
* 1917 . . . Fell, on flat near finish when leading.(Mr E.W.Paterson) 7.11-5. W.J.Smith. 100/7.

LOCH ALLEN
brown gelding by Lochryan - Kirstie.
1919 . . . Finished 4th of 22. (Mr V.Stewart) 8.10-0. J.Kkelly. 33/1.
1920 . . . Fell. (Mr V.Samuel) 9. 9-12. T.Hulme. 33/1.
1921 . . . Fell. (Mr V.Samuel) 10.11-0. J.Kelly. n/q.

LITTLE ROVER
bay gelding by Highwayman - Bayberry.
1920 . . . Fell. (Mr F.C.Romilly) 14.10-3. Capt.E.C.Doyle.n/q.

LUCY GLITTERS II
chestnut mare by Clarionet - dam by Reduction.
1920 . . . Fell. (Mr H.J.Davis) 8.10-0. L.B.Rees. n/q.

LONG LOUGH
chestnut mare by Lochryan - Pride Of Mabestown.
1921 . . . Fell. (Mr R.Power) 9.10-1. R.Trudgill. n/q.

LIFFEYBANK
chestnut horse by Book - Bonnie Espoir.
1923 . . . Pulled-up. (Mr A.S.Cochrane) 8.10-3. G.Parfrement. 100/8.
1924 . . . Fell. (Sir E.Edgar) 9.10-8. W.O'Neill. n/q.

LEE BRIDGE
chestnut gelding by Sundawn - Lady Lee 11.
1926 . . . Fell. (Mr R.G.Shaw) 9.10-5. W.Stott. 20/1.

LONE HAND
bay gelding by Call O' The Wild - Wine Gal.
1926 . . . Fell. (Mr A.W.Hedges) 8.10-0. T.Morgan. 66/1.

LISSETT III
chestnut gelding by Bachelor's Lodge - dam by Otterton.
1927 . . . Fell. (Lord Grimthorpe) 11.10-5. J.Hamey. 100/1.

LLOYDIE
chestnut gelding by Vedanta - Lizzie Lane.
1929 . . . Fell. (Capt.R.F.H.Norman) 7.11-4. F.B.Rees. 22/1.

LORDI
brown gelding Lormi - Santa Visto.
1929 . . . Fell. (Mr A.M.Jones) 8.11-0. Capt.A.H.Weber. 28/1.
1930 . . . Knocked-over. (Mr A.M.Jones) 9.11-2. W.Stott. 28/1.

LE TOUQUET
bay gelding by Marmouset - La Bourgerie.
1929 . . . Failed to finish. (M.G.Watinne) 7.10-12. J.Teasdale. 200/1.

LONE EAGLE II
bay gelding by Star Hawk - Embassy.
1934 . . . Pulled-up. (Mr J.H.Whitney) 8.10-13. J.Hamey. 50/1.

LAZY BOOTS
chestnut gelding by Frontino - Dorothy Osborne.
1935 . . . Finished 4th of 27. (Sir G.Congreve) 9.10-7. G.R.Owen. 100/1.
1936 . . . Fell. (Sir Geoffrey Congreve) 10.10-7. Capt.R.Moseley. 25/1.
1938 . . . Fell. (Sir Geoffrey Congreve) 12.10-4. Sir G.Congreve. 100/1.
1940 . . . Finished 15th of 30. (Sir G.Congreve) 14.10-10. Sir G.Congreve. 100/1.

LYNTON
chestnut gelding by Blue Ensign - Watersmeet.
1936 . . . Baulked & Refused. (Mr M.D.Blair) 9.10-7. C.Hook. 100/1.

LOUGH COTTAGE
bay gelding by Cottage - Long Lough.
1938 . . . Finished 11th of 36. (Mrs S.H.Creagh) 11.10-7. Mr.R.Black. 40/1.

LUCKY PATCH
chestnut gelding by Spion Kop - Enrichment.
1939 . . . Refused. (Mr N.E.Dixon) 9.10-0. T.Elder. 66/1.

LUCKPENNY
brown gelding by Knight of The Garter - Ballyfare.
1939 . . . Broke-down. (Miss H.M.Hollins) 10.10-12. Maj.Moseley. 100/1.

LUXBOROUGH
bay gelding by Bolingbroke - Lux.
1940 . . . Finished 11th of 30. (Mr J.A. de Rothschild) 6.10-3. E.C.Brown. 100/1.

LITIGANT
bay gelding by Walinson - Moyrath.
1940 . . . Fell. (Major N.Furlong) 9.10-7. Mr.R.Black. 50/1.

LOUGH CONN
bay gelding by Tiger Hill - Mabyn's Pride.
1946 . . . Fell. (Mrs M.Rowe) 10.10-0. D.McCann. 33/1.
1947 . . . Finished 2nd of 57. (Mrs M.Rowe) 11.10-1.D.McCann. 33/1.
1948 . . . Pulled-up. (Mrs M.Rowe) 12.10-5. J.Fitzgerald. 22/1.

LOVELY COTTAGE
bay gelding by Cottage - The Nun III. Bred by Mr.M.J.Hyde.
1946 . . . WON. (Mr J.Morant) 9.10-8. 34 Ran. Capt.R.Petre. 25/1.
1948 . . . Finished 14th of 43. (Mr J.Morant) 10.11-4. C.Hook. 66/1. Remounted*

LIMESTONE EDWARD
brown gelding by Walter Gay - Coup d'Amour.
1946 . . . Finished 6th of 34. (Mr C.Nicholson) 12.10-2. D.Doyle. 13/2.

LARGO
bay gelding by His Reverence - Keen Air.
1946 . . . Fell. (Mrs I.Strong) 7.10-13. J.Cooke. 66/1.

LUAN CASCA
brown gelding by Bayford - Susiewusie.
1947 . . . Fell. (Mr F.More O'Ferrall) 7.10-7. A.Brabazon. 22/1.

LEAP MAN
bay gelding by Salmon Leap - Manna's Folly.
1947 . . . Finished 18th of 57. (Mr A.W.Fletcher) 10.11-0. T.F.Rimell. 50/1.
1949 . . . Fell. (Mr A.W.Fletcher) 12.10-10. E.Vinall. 66/1.

LINTHILL
brown gelding by Corbridge - Varragill.
1947 . . . Fell. (Mr J.M.Sanderson) 11.10-0. P.Taylor. 100/1.

LOYAL ANTRIM
brown gelding by Oojah - Gwendolyn.
1948 . . . Fell. (Mr S.Martin) 11.10-3. E.Newman. 22/1.
1949 . . . Fell. (Mr S.Martin) 12.10-4. Mr.A.Scannell. 50/1.

LE DAIM
bay gelding by Kopi - La Hardiere. Bred in France.
1948 . . . Fell. (Mrs G.I.Osborne) 9.10-1. S.Pinch. 100/1.

LUCKY PURCHASE
bay gelding by Allagash - Shahrinaz.
1949 . . . Finished 8th of 43. (Mrs S.C.Banks) 11.10-2. A.Jack. 50/1.

LIMESTONE COTTAGE
bay gelding by Cottage - Camas.
1950 . . . Fell. (Mr A.Cooper) 10.10-0. J.Dowdeswell. 100/1.

LAND FORT
bay gelding by Landscape Hill - Fort Defiance.
1951 . . . Fell. (Mr H.Oliver) 7.11-3. B.Marshall. 20/1.
1953 . . . Fell. (Mr H.Oliver) 9.10-13. Mr H.Oliver, jnr. 50/1.

LEGAL JOY
bay gelding by Within The Law - Gladiolia.
1952 . . . Finished 2nd of 47. (Miss D.Paget) 9.10-4. M.Scudamore. 100/6.
1954 . . . Fell. (Miss D.Paget) 10.11-3. D.V.Dick. 33/1.

LARRY FINN
bay gelding by Bagman - dam by Johnny Roebuck.
1953 . . . Brought-down. (Mr B.Bealby) 9.10-11. A.P.Thompson.40/1.

LITTLE YID
bay gelding by Farranjordan - Mafia.
1953 . . . Refused. (Mrs E.Truelove) 11.10-1. J.Power. 7/1.Fav.*
1955 . . . Pulled-up. (Mrs E.Truelove) 13.10-10. R.Emery. 50/1.

LUCKY DOME
brown gelding by Domaha - Lucky Pat.
1953 . . . Pulled-up. (Mr J.A.Wood) 7.10-0. P.J.Doyle. 10/1.

LONGMEAD
chestnut gelding by Pactolus - First Seller.
1958 . . . Fell. (Mr F.Rea) 8.11-1. G.W.Robinson. 28/1.

LOTORAY
bay gelding by Lighthouse 11 - Missalot.
1960 . . . Fell. (Mr W.Miller) 10.10-6. M.Batchelor. 6/1.

LOOK HAPPY
bay gelding by Pay Up - Knight's Rapture.
1963 . . . Fell. (Mrs J.C.M.Roberts) 10.10-0. J.Haine. 40/1.

LOVING RECORD
grey gelding by Archive - Admiring.
1963 . . . Pulled-up. (Mr J.L.Young) 9.10-12. T.Taaffe. 100/7.
1965 . . . Finished 8th of 47. (Mr J.J.McDowell) 11.11-0. B.Hannon. 33/1.
1966 . . . Finished 12th of 47. (Mr J.J.McDowell) 12.10-0. B.Hannon. 50/1.

LOYAL TAN
chestnut gelding by Tartan - Clarion March.
1963 . . . Finished 17th of 47. (Mrs G.Kohn) 8.10-5. T.W.Biddleombe. 66/1.

LIZAWAKE
bay gelding by Long Stop - Liza.
1964 . . . Fell. (Mr G.C.Hartigan) 11.10-4. H.R.Beasley. 18/1.
1965 . . . Pulled-up. (Mrs E.M.Marshall) 12.10-13. Mr.G.Hartigan. 100/1.

LAFFY
bay gelding by Rigolo - Vatelinde.
1964 . . . Fell. (H.M.Queen Elizabeth The Queen Mother) 8.10-8. W.Rees. 100/7.co/Fav.*

L'EMPEREUR
chestnut gelding by Foxlight - Nosika.
1964 . . . Pulled-up. (Comte.L de Kerouara) 10.10-5. J.Daumas.40/1.
1965 . . . Finished 6th of 47. (Mr J.Ciechanowski) 11.10-13. Mr.J.Ciechanowski.100/1.
1966 . . . Pulled-up. (Duque de Alberquerque) 12.10-2. Duque de Alberquerque.100/1.

LESLIE
chestnut gelding by Vulgan - Miss Gaiety.
1965 . . . Baulked. (Lord Sherborne) 9.10-13. P.Jones. 33/1.
1966 . . . Brought-down.(Mr J.M.Opperman) 10.10-5. Mr.M.Opperman.100/1.

LEEDSY
bay gelding by Le Sage - Inlet.
1965 . . . Fell. (Mrs C.Levy) 7.10-13. G.W.Robinson. 18/1.
1967 . . . Brought-down. (Mrs C.Levy) 9.10-5. T.S.Murphy.

LUCKY DOMINO
brown gelding by Domaha - Lucky Flirt.
1967 . . . Fell. (Mr G.F.Waring) 10.10-5. J.Kenneally. 66/1.

LIMEKING
chestnut gelding by Limekiln - Scottish Princess.
1967 . . . Brought-down. (Mr A.Chester Beatty) 10.10-13. P.Buckley. 33/1.

LIMETRA
bay gelding by Soletra - Limberette.
1969 . . . Finished 14th of 30. (Mr H.Lane) 11.10-9. P.Broderick.50/1.

LIMEBURNER
chestnut gelding by Limekiln - No Medals.
1969 . . . Finished 12th of 30. (Mrs S.N.J.Embiricos) 8.10-0. J.Buckingham. 66/1.
1971 . . . Finished 11th of 38. (Mrs S.J.N.Embiricos) 10.10-0. J.Buckingham. 100/1. Remounted*
1972 . . . Pulled-up. (Mrs S.J.N.Embiricos) 11.10-0. W.Rees. 100/1.

LAIRD, THE
brown gelding by Border Chief - Pre Fleur.
1971 . . . Fell. (Mr H.J.Joel) 10.11-2. J.King. 12/1.

LORD JIM
brown gelding by Kelling - Jumping Powder.
1971 . . . Fell. (Mr G.Dudley,jnr.) 10.10-9. S.Mellor. 9/1.

LIME STREET
chestnut gelding by Honeyway - Khadidja.
1972 . . . Fell. (Mr P.Buckenham & Mr E.P.Hickling) 8.10-1. R.Pitman. 25/1.

LISNAREE
bay gelding by Dionisio - Kilbelin Belle.
1972 . . . Fell. (Mrs O.Mancinelli) 9.10-0. Mr.F.Turner.100/1.

L'ESCARGOT
chestnut gelding by Escart III - What A Daisy. Bred by Mrs.B.O'Neill.
1972 . . . Knocked-over. (Mr R.R.Guest) 9.12-0. T.Carberry. 17/2.Fav.*
1973 . . . Finished 3rd of 38. (Mr R.R.Guest) 10.12-0. T.Carberry. 11/1.
1974 . . . Finished 2nd of 42.(Mr R.R.Guest) 11.11-13. T.Carberry.17/2.
1975 . . . WON. (Mr R.R.Guest) 12.11-3. 31 Ran.T.Carberry.13/2.

LAND LARK
chestnut gelding by Weensland - Flying Lark.
1975 . . . Fell. (Mr T.Pocock) 10.10-1. G.Thorner. 14/1.

LORD OF THE HILLS
chestnut gelding by Lord Of Verona - Reply.
1977 . . . Pulled-up. (Mrs M.A.Berry) 10.10-1. D.Goulding. 100/1.

LUCIUS
bay gelding by Perhapsburg - Matches. Bred by Dr.Margaret Lloyd.
1978 . . . WON. (Mrs D.A.Whitaker) 9.10-9. 37 Ran. B.R.Davies. 14/1.

LORD BROWNDODD
chestnut gelding by Bargello - Coolnagratten.
1978 . . . Finished 7th of 37. (Mr J.Brazil) 10.10-7. J.Francome.16/1.
1979 . . . Pulled-up. (Mr J.Brazil) 11.10-0. A.Turnell. 25/1.

LEAN FORWARD
bay gelding by Bowsprit - Leney Princess.
1978 . . . Finished 13th of 37. (Sir John Thompson) 12.10-0. H.J.Evans. 33/1.

LEVANKA
bay gelding by Le Levanstell - Kathleen Rua.
1980 . . . Pulled-up. (Mr P.C.Heron) 11.10-4. F.Berry. 100/1.

LORD GULLIVER
brown gelding by Varano - Aran Jacket.
1981 . . . Fell. (Mr P.R.Callender) 8.10-0. C.Brown. 50/1.

LOVING WORDS
grey gelding by Sayfar - Loving And Giving.
1982 . . . Finished 3rd of 39. (Mr A.Netley) 9.10-11. R.Hoare. 16/1. Remounted.*

LADY'S MASTER, THE
bay gelding by Master Owen - Carotene Lady.
1983 . . . Ran-out. (Mr M.C.Duggan) 12.11-2. Mr.W.P.Mullins.200/1.

LUCKY VANE
bay gelding by Lucky Brief - Cronovone.
1984 . . . Finished 4th of 40. (Miss B.Swire) 9.10-13. J.Burke. 12/1.
1985 . . . Pulled-up. (Miss B.Swire) 10.10-13. J.Burke. 10/1.

LENEY DUAL
bay gelding by Dual - Leney Girl.
1985 . . . Fell. (Mr D.F.Pitcher) 10.10-8. Mr.D.Pitcher. 100/1.

LAST SUSPECT
brown gelding by Above Suspicion - Last Link. Bred By The Countess of Mount Charles.
1985 . . . WON. (Anne, Duchess of Westminster) 11.10-5. 40 Ran. H.Davies. 50/1.
1986 . . . Pulled-up. (Anne, Duchess of Westminster) 12.11-2. H.Davies. 14/1.

LANTERN LODGE
bay gelding by Master Buck - Royal Shamrock.
1986 . . . Fell. (Mrs M.E.Farrell) 9.10-7. A.Mullins. 100/1.

LITTLE POLVEIR
bay gelding by Cantab - Blue Speedwell. Bred by Mr.F..G.Harris.
1986 . . . Finished 9th of 40. (Mr M.L.Shone) 9.10-0. C.Brown. 66/1.
1987 . . . Unseated rider. (Mr M.L.Shone) 10.10-2. C.Brown. 33/1.
1988 . . . Unseated rider. (Mr M.L.Shone) 11.10-7. T.Morgan. 33/1.
1989 . . . WON. (Mr E.Harvey) 12.10-3. 40 Ran. J.Frost. 28/1.

LATE NIGHT EXTRA
chestnut gelding by Extra - Lunar Girl.
1986 . . . Pulled-up. (Lt.Col. & Mrs E.C.Phillips) 10.10-0. Mr.T.Thomson Jones. 500/1.

● L'Escargot comes to challenge Red Rum at the last fence in 1975. This time, however, the gallant Red Rum — bidding for the hat-trick — had no answer as Tommy Carberry took the Cheltenham Gold Cup winner on to victory.

LE BAMBINO
bay gelding by Le Prince - Bella Bambino.
1987 . . . Pulled-up. (Mr M.Meade) 10.10-2. C.Warren. 500/1.

LEAN AR AGHAIDH
chestnut gelding by Proverb - Carry On Jackie.
1987 . . . Finished 3rd of 40. (Mrs W.Tulloch) 10.10-0. G.Landau. 14/1.
1988 . . . Finished 9th of 40. (Mrs W.Tulloch) 11.11-0. G.Landau. 10/1.

LUCKY REW
brown gelding by Lucky Brief - Handy Money.
1987 . . . Fell. (Mrs M.S.Teversham) 12.10-0. C.Mann. 500/1.

LUCISIS
chestnut gelding by Lucifer - Thesis.
1988 . . . Brought-down. (Mrs H.McParland) 9.10-6. Mr.J.Queally. 40/1.

LAST OF THE BROWNIES
bay gelding by Giolla Mear - Another Rose.
1988 . . . Fell. (Mr M.J.Smurfit) 8.10-0. T.Carmody. 25/1.
1989 . . . Finished 4th of 40. (Mrs A..Daly) 9.10-0. T.Carmody. 16/1.
1990 . . . Finished 5th of 38. (Mrs A.Daly) 10.10-0. C.F.Swan. 20/1.

125

LANAVOE
bay gelding by Tudor Rocket - Ballincanty.
1990 . . . Fell. (Mr F.J.Lacy) 11.10-0. P.Leech. 100/1.

LEAGAUNE
brown gelding by Over The River - Cora Princess.
1991 . . . Finished 9th of 40. (Mr C.Wright) 9.10-0. M.Richards. 200/1.

THE LANGHOLM DYER
bay or brown gelding by Crash Course - Belle Artiste.
1991 . . . Unseated rider. (Edinburgh Woolen Mill Ltd.) 12.10-6. G.McCourt. 100/1.

LAURA'S BEAU
bay gelding by Beau Charmeur - Laurabeg.
1992 . . . Finished 3rd of 40. (Mr J.P.McManus) 8.10-0. C.O'Dwyer. 12/1.
1994 . . . Fell. (Mr J.P.McManus) 10.10-0. B.Sheridan. 40/1.

LUSTY LIGHT
bay gelding by Strong Gale - Pale Maid.
1995 . . . Fell. (Mr B.R.H.Burrough) 9.10-2. R.Farrant. 12/1.
1996 . . . Finished 16th of 27. (Mr B.R.H.Burrough) 10.10-11. W.Marston.14/1.

LIFE OF A LORD
brown gelding by Strong Gale - Ruby Girl.
1996 . . . Finished 7th of 27. (Mr M.J.Clancy) 10.11-6. C.F.Swan. 10/1.

126

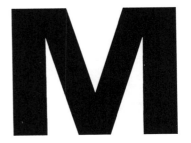

MARENGO
1844 . . . Finished 7th of 15. (Mr Bretherton) Sharkey. 5/1.jnt/Fav.*
1847 . . . Fell. (Captain Barnett) - 11-0. Barker. n/q.

MAJOR A
1846 . . . Failed to finish. (Mr Windham) 6.11-6. Blake. 25/1.

MAMALUKE
1846 . . . Fell. (Captain Barnett) Mr.A.McDonough. 10/1.

MATTHEW
brown gelding by Vestriius - dam unknown. Bred by Mr.J.Westropp.
1847 . . . WON. (Mr Courtenay) 9.10-6. 26 Ran. D.Wynne. 10/1.jnt/Fav.*
1848 . . . Knocked-over. (Mr Courtenay) 1.11-6. D.Wynne. 8/1.

MIDNIGHT
1847 . . . Failed to finish. (Mr H.B.Browne) 5.10-10. Gardner. n/q.

MULLIGAN
1849 . . . Failed to finish. (Mr Westropp) 5.11-2. Ford. n/q.
1850 . . . Failed to finish. (Mr Westropp) 6.10-10. Mr.Westropp. n/q.
1851 . . . Finished 7th of 21. (Mr J.Elmore) 7.10-2. W.Draper. 25/1.

MARIA DAY
1850 . . . Finished 6th 32. (Mr Treadgold) - 10-5. Rackley. 25/1.
1851 . . . Finished 2nd of 21. (Mr C.Higgins) - 10-5. J.Frisby. 100/6.
1852 . . . Fell. (Mr C.Higgins) - 10-6. J.Frisby. n/q.

MEATH
1850 . . . Failed to finish. (Mr Harrison) - 10-10. Neale. n/q.

MAURICE DALE
Formerly named Flycatcher.
1851 . . . Failed to finish. (Mr Cartwright) 9-6. C.Boyce. n/q.
1852 . . . Finished 2nd of 24. (Mr Cartwright) - 9-6. C.Boyce. n/q.
1853 . . . Failed to finish. (Mr Cartwright) - 10-2. C.Boyce. n/q.
1854 . . . Failed to finish. (Mr Cartwright) - 9-10. T.Olliver. 5/1.
1855 . . . Finished 3rd of 20. (Mr Cartwright) - 9-6. R.James. 20/1.
1857 . . . Failed to finish. (Mr Laurence) - 9-2. R.James. 40/1.

MISS MOWBRAY
bay mare by Lancastrian - Norma. Not in the Genral Stud Book.
1852 . . . WON. (Mr T.F.Mason) - 10-4. 24 Ran. Mr.A.Goodman. n/q.
1853 . . . Finished 2nd of 21. (Mr T.F.Mason) - 10-12. Mr.F.Gordon. 5/1.Fav.*
1855 . . . Fell. (Mr T.F.Mason) - 11-6. S.Darling,jnr. 4/1.

MCIAN
1852 . . . Failed to finish. (Mr R.Jones) - 9-10. J.Sadler. 50/1.

MALEY
1852 . . . Fell. (Mr Henderson) - 9-6. Connor. n/q.
1853 . . . Failed to finish. (Mr J.R.Henderson) - 9-8. E.Harrison. n/q.
1854 . . . Finished 4th of 20. (Mr J.R.Henderson) - 9-10. Thrift. 50/1.
1855 . . . Failed to finish. (Mr J.R.Henderson) - 9-6. Fulman. 50/1.

MINERVA
1856 . . . Finished 2nd of 21. (Mr Davenport) 6. 9-10. R.Sly,jnr. 25/1.

MINOS
1856 . . . Finished 3rd of 21. (Mr G.Hobson) - 9-4. R.James. n/q.
1857 . . . Failed to finish. (Mr Mellish) - 10-4. Mr.A.Goodman. 100/15.Fav.*

MIDGE
1857 . . . Failed to finish. (Mr J.Garnett) - 9-6. Mr.Black. n/q.
1859 . . . Finished 4th of 20. (Mr J.Garnett) - 9-4. D.Meaney.33/1.

MORGAN RATTLER
1858 . . . Finished 4th of 16. (Sir E.Hutchinson) - 10-4. T.Burrows. 100/6.

MOIRE ANTIQUE
1858 . . . Fell. (Mr J.R.Henderson) - 9-0. F.Page. 25/1.

MARIA AGNES
1860 . . . Finished 4th of 19. (Mr Golby) 6. 9-8. G.Stevens. 10/1.

MISS HARKAWAY
1860 . . . Refused. (Mr Barber) - 9-8. Mr.F.Lotan. n/q.

MASTER BAGOT
1861 . . . Fell. (Capt.J.F.Little) - 10-0. Mr.Edwards. 8/1.
1863 . . . Failed to finish. (Mr W.G.Craven) - 10-4. Knott. 100/8.

MEDORA
1863 . . . Pulled-up. (Mr F.Rowlands) - 12-0. Mr F.Rowlands. 100/12.

MARTHA
1864 . . . Fell. (Mr T.Wade) - 10-0. J.Land. n//q.

MISS MARIA
1864 . . . Failed to finish. (Mr H.Melville) - 10-0. J.Holman. n/q.

MISTAKE
1865 . . . Finished 4th of 23. (Mr F.Jacobs) 5.10-8. Jarvis. n/q.
1866 . . . Failed to finish. (Baron Von Grootven) 6.10-9. Knott. 25/1.

MERRIMAC
1865 . . . Finished 5th of 23. (Capt.A.C.Tempest) - 11-4. B.Land,jnr. 33/1.
1866 . . . Finished 5th of 30. (Capt.Shaw) -10-7. Capt.A.C.Tempest. 25/1.

MEANWOOD
1865 . . . Pulled-up. (Mr Harvey) 6.11-9. Knott. 50/1.

MARKET GARDENER
1865 . . . Refused. (Lord Sefton) - 10-0. Mr.T.Spence. n/q.

MILLTOWN
1866 . . . Failed to finish. (Mr W.McGrane) 5.10-2. Mr.Thomas. 50/1.

MILLER, THE
1867 . . . Failed to finish. (Mr W.Smith) - 11-4. Mr.Lawrence. n/q.

MARENGO
brown gelding by Greatheart - dam by Philip The First.
1867 . . . Knocked-over. (Mr C.Fermin) - 11-1. Mr.C.Fermin. n/q.

MOOSE
chestnut gelding by Mountain Deer - Constance.
1868 . . . Pulled-up. (Mr E.Brayley) - 10-7. W.White. 8/1.
1870 . . . Failed to finish. (Mr E.Brayley) - 11-7. A.French. n/q.

MENTMORE
bay gelding by Fazzoletto - Calista.
1868 . . . Fell. (Mr W.Forbes) aged. 10-4. Hyland. n/q.

MIDDLETON
bay gelding by Fazzoletto - Hornet.
1870 . . . Failed to finish. (Mr Yardley) - 10-12. Mr.T.Kirk. 1000/5.

MAGNUM BONUM
brown gelding by Ashgill - dam by Pottinger.
1871 . . . Fell. (Capt.J.Machell) aged. 10-10. Mr.J.M.Richardson. 50/1.

MASTER MOWBRAY
bay horse by Mowbray - dam by Footstool.
1872 . . . Finished 6th of 25. (Mr J.Goodliff) aged.10-12. G.Holman. 25/1.
1873 . . . Finished 4th of 28. (Mr J.Goodliff) aged.10-7. G.Holman. 12/1.
1874 . . . Finished 5th of 22. (Mr J.Goodliff) aged.10-5. A.Holman. 50/1.
1876 . . . Finished 7th of 19. (Mr J.Goodliff) aged.11-11.G.Holman. 100/8.

MARIN
brown horse by Sting - Serenade. Bred in France.
1872 . . . Brought-down. (Baron Finot) 6.11-10. Cassidy. 25/1.

MERLIN
brown gelding by Gunboat - The Witch.
1874 . . . Finished 3rd of 22. (Capt.Thorold) - 10-7. J.Adams. 40/1.

MARMORA
chestnut mare by Chattanooga or Stockwell - Ratlagoom.
1875 . . . Finished 5th of 19. (Capt.R.Thorold) 7.11-2. J.Jones. 100/8.

MISS HUNGERFORD
chestnut mare by Wamba - Lady Hungerford.
1875 . . . Fell. (Mr F.Bennett) 8.11-10. Mr.Rolly. 20/1.

MESSAGER
bay horse by Gladiateur - Nuncia. Bred in France.
1875 . . . Fell. (Mr Percival) 7.11-7. Whiteley. 100/3.

MARTHA
bay mare by The Coroner - Martha.
1878 . . . Finished 2nd of 12. (Capt.A.Crofton) 7.10-9. Mr.T.Beasley. 20/1.
1879 . . . Finished 3rd of 18.(Mr Oeschlaeger) 8.10-13. Mr.T.Beasley. 50/1.

MISS LIZZIE
brown mare by Solon - Lizzie.
1878 . . . Finished 5th of 12. (Capt.Davison) 5.10-7. Hunt. 20/1.

MARSHAL NIEL
black horse by Knigh Of The Crescent or Pero - Last Rose Of Summer.
1879 . . . Fell. (Sir J.L.Kaye) 5.10-12. P.Gavin. 100/8.

MONTAUBAN
chestnut gelding by Mandrake - Tau.
1881 . . . Finished 8th of 13. (Mr J.G.Baird-Hay) 7.10-7. Mr.A.Coventry. 100/6.
1882 . . . Pulled-up. (Mr J.G.Baird-Hay) 8.10-7. G.Waddington.100/6.
1883 . . . Finished 6th of 10. (Lord Yarborough) 9.10-9. Mr.E.P.Wilson. 100/12.

MOHICAN
brown horse by Uncas - Castanette.
1882 . . . Fell. (Mr Bunbury) 5.10-7. Mr.H.Beasley. 100/30.Fav.*
1883 . . . Finished 3rd of 10. (Maj.Bunbury) 6.12-1. Mr.H.Beasley. 9/1.

MAGPIE
black gelding by Pell Mell - dam unknown.
1886 . . . Finished 4th of 23. (Mr E.Woodland) 7.10-5. Mr.W.Woodland. 200/1.
1887 . . . Broke-down. (Mr E.Woodland) 8.10-9. Mr.W.Woodland. 10/1.

MAGIC
brown gelding by Berserker - dam unknown.
1888 . . . Finished 8th of 20. (H.R.H.Prince of Wales) aged. 10-12. A.Hall. 20/1.
1889 . . . Finished 5th of 20. (H.R.H.Prince of Wales) aged. 10-9. J.Jones. 25/1.

M. P.
chestnut gelding by Minstrel - dam by Blood Royal.
1889 . . . Finished 3rd of 20. (Mr J.Rutherford) 8.10-9. A.Nightingall. 20/1.
1890 . . . Finished 3rd of 16. (Mr J.Rutherford) 9.11-5. Mr.W.H.Moore. 8/1.

MERRY MAIDEN
bay mare by See Saw - Lizzie Greystock.
1889 . . . Fell. (Captain Childe) 7.10-7. Capt.Lee-Barber. 66/1.

MIDSHIPMITE, THE
bay gelding by Torpedo - dam by New Oswestry.
1892 . . . Fell. (Mr H.L.Powell) 6.11-6. Mr.Atkinson. 25/1.
1893 . . . Finished 5th of 15. (Mr H.L.Powell) 7.12-3. W.T.Sensier.7/1.
1896 . . . Fell. (Mr H.L.Powell) 10.11-4. F.Hewitt. 66/1.

● **Manifesto, the 1899 Grand National winner ridden by George Williamson.**

MELDRUM
bay mare by Lord Gough - Quickstep.
1892 . . . Fell. (Mr B.Goodall) 7.10-12. J.Latham. 100/1.

MUSICIAN
bay gelding by Harmonium - The Kitten.
1894 . . . Finished 6th of 14. (Mr M.Firth) 8. 9-10. F.Hassall. 25/1.

MANIFESTO
bay gelding by Man Of War - Vae Victis. Bred by Mr.H.M.Dyas.
1895 . . . Finished 4th of 19. (Mr H.M.Dyas) 7.11-2. T.Kavanagh. 100/8.
1896 . . . Fell (Mr H.M.Dyas) 8.11-4. J.Gourley.100/7.
1897 . . . WON. (Mr H.M.Dyas) 9.11-3. 28 Ran. T.Kavanagh. 6/1.Fav.*
1899 . . . WON. (Mr J.G.Bulteel) 11.12-7. 19 Ran. G.Williamson. 5/1.
1900 . . . Finished 3rd of 16. (Mr J.G.Bulteel) 12.12-13.G.Williamson. 6/1.
1902 . . . Finished 3rd of 21. (Mr J.G.Bulteel) 14.12-8. E.Piggott. 100/6.
1903 . . . Finished 3rd of 23. (Mr J.G.Bulteel) 15.12-3.G.Williamson. 25/1.
1904 . . . Finished 8th of 26. (Mr J.G.Bulteel) 16.12-1. E.Piggott. 20/1.

MOLLY MAGUIRE
bay mare by Castlereagh - Eserine.
1895 . . . Finished 11th of 19. (Mr J.T.Hartigan) 6.9-9. W.Taylor. 25/1.

MARCH HARE
brown gelding by Baliol - Harebell.
1896 . . . Fell. (Mr F.C.Stanley) 7.11-7. R.Chaloner. 100/6.

MORIARTY
brown gelding by Chippendale - Algoa.
1896 . . . Pulle-up. (Mr J.Hale) 6.11-2. E.Acres. 40/1.

131

MISS BARON
bay or brown mare by Baron Frney - dam unknown.
1896 . . . Fell. (Mr M.Widger) 6.10-0. T.Kavanagh. 66/1.

MEDIATOR
chestnut gelding by Herald - Wrangle.
1897 . . . Fell. (Lord Coventry) 8. 9-8. W.Grosvenor. 100/1.

MUM
bay mare by Hawkeye - Silence.
1899 . . . Finished 9th of 19. (Mr J.G.Mosenthal) 7.10-5. F.Hassall. 100/1.

MODEL
brown gelding by Herald - Hazelwitch.
1900 . . . Finished 10th of 16. (Mr E.Woodland) 7.10-7. P.Woodland. 66/1.
1901 . . . Failed to finish. (Mr W.H.Pawson) 8.11-4.Mr.W.H.Pawson. 40/1.

MAYO'S PRIDE
bay gelding by Portnellan - Primrose.
1901 . . . Failed to finish. (Mr W.W.Lewison) 7.10-5. J.Phillips. 20/1.

MATTHEW
chestnut gelding by Tacitus - Golden Locks.
1902 . . . Finished 2nd of 21. (Mr J.Widger) 6. 9-12. W.Morgan. 50/1.
1903 . . . Fell. (Mr J.Widger) 7.10-7. Mr.J.W.Widger.10/1.
1905 . . . Pulled-up. (Mr W.Bass) 9.10-9. W.Morgan. 66/1.

MISS CLIFDEN II
chestnut mare by Fitz-Clifden - dam unknown.
1902 . . . Finished 10th of 21. (Mr F.W.Polehampton) 6.9-7. Mr.H.M.Ripley. 50/1.
1905 . . . Fell. (Mr D.Faber) 9. 9-13. F.Barter. 100/1.

MARPESSA
brown gelding by Marmiton - Grecian.
1903 . . . Fell. (Maj.Eustace Loder) 6.10-11. Mr.H.A.Persse. 20/1.

MOIFAA
brown gelding by Natator - Denbigh. Bred in New Zealand.
1904 . . . WON. (Mr Spencer Gollan) 8.10-7. 26 Ran. A.Birch.25/1.
1905 . . . Fell. (His Majesty The King) 9.11-12. W.Dollery. 4/1.Fav.*

MAY KING
chestnut gelding by May Boy - Katie Kendal.
1904 . . . Pulled-up. (Mr W.J.Compton) 8.10-5. W.Dollery. 25/1.

MATTIE MACGREGOR
bay mare by Even Macgregor - Ju.
1908 . . . Finished 2nd of 24. (Mr W.C.Cooper) 6.10-6. W.Bissill.25/1.
1909 . . . Refused. (Mr W.C.Cooper) 7.11-4. R.Morgan. 100/6.

MOUNT PROSPECT'S FORTUNE
bay gelding by St Gris - Lady Childers.
1908 . . . Fell. (Mr P.Nelke) 6.11-11. R.Morgan. 100/7.
1911 . . . Fell. (Mr P.Nelke) 9.11-6. E.Driscoll. 66/1.
1912 . . . Finished 5th of 24. (Mr P.Nelke) 10.11-4. J.Kelly. n/q.

MONK V
bay gelding by Lord Percy - Prioress.
1911 . . . Fell. (Mr J.J.Astor) aged. 10-1. Mr.H.W.Tyrwhitt-Drake. 100/1.

MINER, THE
brown gelding by The Explorer - Diadem.
1913 . . . Failed to finish. (Mr W.A.Wallis) 8.11-6. Mr.I.Brabazon. 100/1.

MELAMAR
chestnut gelding by Butterscotch - dam unknown.
1913 . . . Failed to finish. (Mr W.R.Clarke) 7.11-6. W.Payne. 100/8.

MERRY LAND
bay or brown gelding by Chicago - dam by Buckingham.
1913 . . . Fell. (Capt.H.C.Higgins) 9.11-3. R.Trudgill. 100/1.

MINSTER VALE
black mare by Buckminster - Maid Of The Vale.
* 1916 . . . Completed course. (Mr J.Ivall) 6.11-0. G.Calder. 40/1.

MARK BACK
chestnut horse by Marcovil - Oliveback.
* 1918 . . . Completed course. (Mr E.S.Wills) 7.10-5. H.Smyth. 40/1.

MUSIC HALL
bay gelding by Cliftonhall - Molly. Bred by Mrs.F.Blacker.
1922 . . . WON. (Mr H.Kershaw) 9.11-8. 32 Ran. L.B.Rees. 100/9.
1924 . . . Pulled-up. (Mr H.Kershaw) 11.12-7. J.R.Anthony. 25/1.
1925 . . . Refused. (Mr H.Kershaw) 12.12-0. L.B.Rees. 66/1.

MASK ON
bay gedling by Avidity - dam by Bergomask.
1922 . . . Fell. (Mr T.A.O'Gorman) 9.10-2. J.Burns. 50/1.

MASTERFUL
bay gelding by Hastings - Madcap.
1922 . . . Fell. (Mr Foxhall Keene) 9.10-1. Mr.M.D.Blair. 66/1.
1923 . . . Pulled-up.(Mr Foxhall Keene) 10.10-0. Mr.P.Roberts. n/q.

MAX
brown gelding by Zria - Bauble.
1923 . . . Finished 6th of 28. (Mrs R.P.Croft) 7.11-5. J.Hogan,jnr. 25/1.
1925 . . . Finished 8th of 33. (Mrs R.P.Croft) 9.11-5. J.Hogan,jnr. 20/1.

MADRIGAL
brown gelding by Maiden Erlegh - Palm Tree.
1923 . . . Pulled-up. (Mr H.Barry) 6.10-12. D.Colbert. 66/1.

MY RATH
bay gelding by Succouth - Bit Of Thought.
1923 . . . Fell. (Mr P.Ivall) 11.10-8. Mr.C.Chapman. 66/1.

MASTER ROBERT
chestnut horse by Moorside 11 - Dodds. Bred by Mr.McKinlay.
1924 . . . WON. (Lord Airlie) 11.10-5. 30 Ran. R.Trudgill. 25/1.

MAINSAIL
chestnut gelding by Juggernaut - Dutch Pennant.
1924 . . . Refused. (Mr S.C.Wells) 8.10-1. Mr.D.Learmouth. 66/1.
1925 . . . Fell (Mr S.C.Wells) 9.10-5. R.Priolean. 66/1.

MASTER BILLIE
bay gelding by William Rufus - Octocide.
1926 . . . Finished 10th of 30. (Mr W.Parsonage) 7.10-0. E.Foster. 20/1.
1927 . . . Fell. (Mr W.Parsonage) 8.10-13. F.B.Rees. 20/1.
1928 . . . Refused. (Mr W.Parsonage) 9.10-8. F.B.Rees. 5/1.Fav.*
1929 . . . Pulled-up. (Mr W.Parsonage) 10.11-0. M.Rayson. 20/1.

MISCONDUCT
brown gelding by Ardoon - Lady Conway.
1926 . . . Finished 11th of 30. (Maj.D.M.Methven) 7.10-0. W.Parvin. 28/1.
1927 . . . Fell. (Mr H.G.Selfridge) 8.10-12. W.Parvin. 20/1.

MOUNT ETNA
bay gelding by Harry Melton - Last Purchase.
1926 . . . Fell. (Mr S.Sanford) 9.11-2. Mr.S.H.Dennis. 100/6.
1929 . . . Fell. (Mr S.Sanford) 12.11-7. T.E.Leader. 28/1.

MASTER OF ARTS
chestnut gelding by Pam - Juliet 11.
1927 . . . Finished 5th of 37. (Mr M.D.Blair) 10.10-10. Maj.T.F.Cavenagh. 50/1.
1928 . . . Failed to finish. (Mr M.D.Blair) 11.10-6. Maj.T.F.Cavenagh. 50/1.

MARSIN
chestnut gelding by Sunder - St Maria.
1927 . . . Fell. (Mr S.Sanford) 9.11-12. P.Powell. 66/1.

MR JOLLY
bay gelding by Cyllius - Manor Water.
1927 . . . Fell. (Lt.Col.R.W.Tweedie) 12.10-9. J.S.Wight. 66/1.

MISS BALSCADDEN
bay mare by Balscadden - Wilkinstown.
1927 . . . Fell. (Mr D.Thomas) 8.10-5. Mr.D.Thomas. 100/1.
1929 . . . Fell. (Sir David Llewellyn) 10.10-0. G.Bowden. 200/1.

MAGUELONNE
bay mare b y Ecouen - May Day.
1928 . . . Fell. (Comte. P. de Jumilhac) 6.10-13. J.Bedeloup. 20/1.

MAY KING
chestnut gelding by Cherry King - Wigeon's Last.
1928 . . . Failed to finish. (Lord Ednam) 9.10-13. L.B.Rees. 100/1.
1929 . . . Finished 5th of 66. (Mrs H.Mond) 10.11-2. F.Gurney. 66/1.
1930 . . . Fell. (Mrs H.Mond) 11.10-9. G.Goswell. 40/1.
1931 . . . Fell. (Lady Melchett) 12.10-10. Capt.R.G.Fanshawe. 100/1.

MELLERAY'S BELLE
chestnut mare by Melleray - Mountain Lily.
1928 . . . Pulled-up. (Mr W.Wilson) 9.10-5. J.P.Kelly. 200/1.
1929 . . . Finished 4th of 66. (Mr W.Wilson) 10.10-2. J.Mason.200/1.
1930 . . . Finished 2nd of 41. (Mr W.Wilson) 11.10-0. J.Mason. 20/1.
1931 . . . Finished 8th of 43. (Mr W.Wilson) 12.10-10. J.Mason. 8/1.

MABESTOWN'S PRIDE
bay or brown gelding by General Gough - Pride Of Mabestown.
1929 . . . Knocked-over. (Brig.General C.R.P.Winser) 13.10-13. Mr.D.R.Daly. 200/1.

MERRIVALE II
bay gelding by Rising Flour - The Vale.
1929 . . . Fell. (Lord Westmorland) 11.10-3. F.Brookes. 50/1.
1930 . . . Fell. (Lord Westmorland) 12.10-1. F.Brookes. 40/1.

MORE DIN
bay gelding by Morena - Lady Dinneford.
1929 . . . Fell. (Mr H.S.Horne) 9.10-1. A.Harraway. 200/1.

MAY CRESCENT
bay gelding by Marforio - Miller's Pride.
1930 . . . Fell. (Mr D.Faber) 8.10-2. G.Hardy. 25/1.

MONK, THE
bay gelding by Pommern - St Maria.
1930 . . . Pulled-up. (Mr F.J.Honour) 8.10-0. W.Parvin. 100/1.

MOREKEEN
brown gelding by Drinmore - Clonkeen.
1931 . . . Fell. (Miss C.Robinson) 10.10-10. J.Cooke. 100/1.

MALLARD
bay gelding by Fowling Piece - dam by Sheen.
1931 . . . Brought-down. (Mr J.Harrison) 13.10-7. Mr.W.P.Dutton. 100/1.

MERRIMENT IV
bay mare by White Abbey - Cymbal.
1932 . . . Fell. (Lord Haddington) 9.10-10. Lord Haddington. 45/1.
1933 . . . Finished 17th of 34. (Lord Haddington) 10.11-4. Lord Haddington. 20/1. Remounted*

MASTER ORANGE
chestnut gelding by Jus d'Orange -Miss Mousy.
1933 . . . Completed the course. (Mrs D'Oyly-Mann) 8.10-7. Capt.O.Prior-Palmer. 100/1.
1934 . . . Fell. (Mrs D'Oyly-Mann) 9.10-7. Mr.P.Cazalet. 66/1.
1935 . . . Refused. (Mrs D'Oyly-Mann) 10.10-7. Mr.A.Mildmay. 100/1.

MOORLAND VIEW
brown gelding by Moorside 11 - We'll See.
1936 . . . Finished 9th of 35. (Mr A.F.Nicholson) 10.10-7. Mr.E.C.Paget. 66/1.

MISDEMEANOUR II
bay mare by Trespasser - Bridgetina.
1937 . . . Fell. (Sir Peter Grant Lawson) 8.10-4. S.Magee. 20/1.

MILK PUNCH
bay gelding by Dairy Bridge - Sallynoggin.
1937 . . . Fell. (Mr G.S.L.Whitelaw) 13.10-0. G.Wilson. 33/1.

MACMOFFAT
brown gelding by Sir Harry - La Chacra.
1939 . . . Finished 2nd of 37. (Capt.L.Scott Briggs) 7.10-3. I.Alder. 25/1.
1940 . . . Finished 2nd of 30. (Capt.L.Scott Briggs) 8.10-10. I.Alder. 8/1.
1946 . . . Fell. (Capt.L.Scott Briggs) 14.10-8. I.Alder. 50/1.
1947 . . . Fell. (Capt.L.Scott Briggs) 15.10-4. I.Alder. 100/1.

MONTREJEAU II
bay gelding by Le Prodige - Mingarie.
1939 . . . Fell. (Lady Granard) 9.10-5. H.Nicholson. 40/1.

MILANO
chestnut gelding by Apelle - Rhonia.
1939 . . . Fell. (Mrs L.E.Stoddard) 8.10-10. Mr.L.E.Stoddard. 50/1.
1940 . . . Pulled-up. (Mrs L.E.Stoddard) 9.10-9. D.Morgan. 100/9.

MESMERIST
brown gelding by La Brige - Mesmerise.
1939 . . . Fell. (Mr A.E.Berry) 8.10-0. Capt.R.P.Harding.100/1.

MUSICAL LAD
bay gelding by Clarion - Moyle Vale.
1946 . . . Fell. (Mr L.Michaelson) 9.10-0. M.Browne. 100/1.
1947 . . . Fell. (Mr L.Michaelson) 10.10-4. M.J.Prendergast.33/1.
1948 . . . Fell. (Mr L.Michaelson) 11.10-1. M.Browne. 100/1.

MARTIN M
chestnut gelding by Tolgus - Arden Ina.
1947 . . . Finished 12th of 57. (Maj.W.H.Skrine) 7.10-0. Maj.W.H.Skrine.66/1. Remounted*
1949 . . . Fell. (Major W.H.Skrine) 9.10-1. Maj.W.H.Skrine.66/1.

MICHAEL'S PEARL
chestnut gelding by Pearlweed - Old Mona.
1947 . . . Fell. (Mr W.Seward) 8.10-0. E.Reavey. 100/1.

MALTESE WANDERER
brown gelding by Maltravers - Romany Maid.
1948 . . . Finished 8th of 43. (Mr G.J.Wells) 9.10-0. K.Gilsenan. 100/1.

MAGNETIC FIN
brown gelding by Solenoid - Finaghy Belle.
1949 . . . Fell. (Mr N.Willis) 10.10-4. L.Vick. 50/1.

MONAVEEN
bay gelding by Landscape Hill - Great Double.
1949 . . . Fell. (Mr D.Hawkesley) 8.10-3. A.Grantham. 50/1.
1950 . . . Finished 5th of 49. (H.R.H.Princess Elizabeth) 9.10-13. A.Grantham. 20/1.

MORNING STAR II
bay gelding by Visellus - dam by Brown Victor.
1949 . . . Fell. (Maj.J.F.Gresham) 10.10-0. G.Bowden. 66/.1

MERMAID VI
brown mare by Perth - dam by Meteoric.
1950 . . . Fell. (Mr T.B.Palmer) 11.11-0. Mr.T.B.Palmer. 100/1.

MORNING COVER
bay or brown gelding by Apron - Lady Sheelin.
1951 . . . Fell. (Mrs E.G.Williams) 10.10-0. G.Slack. 40/1.

MENZIES
chestnut gelding by Startled - Hatton Maid.
1952 . . . Brought-down. (Mr J.Gilman) 10.10-4. M.O'Dwyer. 33/1.

MONT TREMBLANT
chestnut gelding by Gris Perle - Paltoquette. Bred in France.
1953 . . . Finished 2nd of 31. (Miss D.Paget) 7.12-5. D.V.Dick. 18/1.

MARTINIQUE
bay gelding by Mieuxce - Carouse.
1954 . . . Finished 6th of 29. (Mr A.Greenberg) 8.10-1. Mr.E.Greenway. 66/1.
1956 . . . Finished 6th of 29. (Mr A.Greenberg) 10.10-0. S.Mellor.40/1.

MINIMAX
bay mare by Sandyman - Fire Alarm.
1954 . . . Refused. (Mr A.J.Sellar) 10.10-0. Capt.M.MacEwan. 66/1.

MARINER'S LOG
chestnut gelding by Archive - She Gone.
1955 . . . Fell. (Lord Bicester) 8.11-12. R.Francis. 100/8.
1956 . . . Fell. (The late Lord bicester) 9.11-11. R.Emery. 22/1.

MR LINNETT
bay gelding by Rosewell - Knida.
1955 . . . Pulled-up. (Mr L.Partridge) 7.11-5. Mr.J.R.Cox. 20/1.

M'AS-TU-VU
brown gelding by Pampeiro - Malle Poste. Bred in France.
1955 . . . Fell. (H.M.Queen Elizabeth The Queen Mother) 9.10-7. A.Freeman. 22/1.
1956 . . . Fell. (H.M.Queen Elizabeth The Queen Mother) 10.10-6. A.Freeman. 40/1.

MOOGIE
bay gelding by Wavetop - Star Of the Realm.
1955 . . . Fell. (Mrs M.Westwood) 12.10-0. J.Neely. 66/1.

MUNSTER KING II
brown gelding by Ambassador - Rose Wreath.
1955 . . . Fell. (Mrs A.T.Hodgson) 8.10-0. V.Speck. 66/1.

MUCH OBLIGED
black or brown gelding by Cameron - May Sen.
1956 . . . Fell. (Mr H.Draper) 8.11-0. M.Scudamore. 50/1.
1957 . . . Fell. (Mr H.Draper) 9.11-4. M.Scudamore. 10/1.

MERRY WINDSOR
bay gelding by Foxlight - Courcelle.
1956 . . . Fell. (Mr I.Holliday) 8.10-10. L.McMorrow. 28/1.

MUST
bay gelding by Umidkhan - Cadamstown Lass.
1956 . . . Fell. (Mrs W.L.Pilkington) 8.10-10. R.Morrow. 7/1.Fav.*
1958 . . . Fell. (Mrs W.L.Pilkington) 10.10-1. R.Morrow. 50/1.

MERRY THROW
bay gelding by Overthrow - Sing Song.
1957 . . . Finished 9th of 35. (Maj.A.C.Straker) 9.10-12. T.Brookshaw. 40/1.

MORRCATOR
bay gelding by Headway - San Souvenir.
1957 . . . Fell. (Mr P.M.Jones) 10.10-0. L.McMorrow. 50/1.

MONKEY WRENCH
bay gelding by Eight Thirty - Never Again 11.
1957 . . . Pulled-up. (Mrs J.F.C.Bryce) 12.10-0. R.J.Hamey. 66/1.

MOSTON LANE
bay gelding Gold Drill - Verdant.
1958 . . . Fell. (Mr F.Bramwell) 9.10-0. R.E.Jenkins. 66/1.

MR WHAT
bay gelding by Grand Inquisitor - Duchess Of Pedulas. Bred by Mrs Barbara O'Neill.
1958 . . . WON. (Mr D.J.Coughlan) 8.10-6. 31 Ran. A.Freeman. 18/1.
1959 . . . Finished 3rd of 34. (Mr D.J.Coughlan) 9.11-9. T.Taaffe. 6/1.Fav.*
1960 . . . Fell. (Mr D.J.Coughlan) 10.11-11. A.Freeman. 18/1.
1961 . . . Finished 11th of 35. (Mr D.J.Coughlan) 11.11-9. D.V.Dick. 20/1.
1962 . . . Finished 3rd of 32. (Mr G.V.Keeling) 12.10-9. J.Lehane.22/1.
1963 . . . Brought-down. (Mr G.V.Keeling) 13.10-8. T.Carberry. 66/1.

MAINSTOWN
grey gelding by Owenstown - Ravine.
1959 . . . Fell. (Mrs M.Milne Green) 9.10-10. M.Batchelor. 40/1.

MR GAY
bay gelding by Nosegay - dam by Mr Toots.
1959 . . . Brought-down. (Mr P.Thrale) 12.10-9. D.Ancil. 28/1.

MERRYMAN II
bay galding by Carnival Boy - Maid Marian. Bred by The Marquess of Linlithgow.
1960 . . . WON. (Miss W.H.S.Wallace) 9.10-12. 26 Ran. G.Scott. 13/2.Fav.*
1961 . . . Finished 2nd of 35. (Miss W.H.S.Wallace) 10.11-12. D.Ancil. 8/1.
1962 . . . Finished 13th of 32. (Miss W.H.S.Wallace) 11.11-8D.V.Dick.

MELILLA
brown mare by King Hal - Riff Star.
1962 . . . Pulled-up. (Mr D.H.Ellison) 8.10-0. G.Cramp. 100/1.
1963 . . . Pulled-up. (Mr D.H.Ellison) 9.10-0. G.Cramp. 66/1.

MR JONES
black gelding by Control - Copycat.
1963 . . . Fell. (Major J.G.Lyon) 8.10-10. P.A.Farrell. 28/1.
1965 . . . Finished 3rd of 47. (Mr C.D.Collins) 10.11-5. Mr.C.D.Collins. 50/1.

MERGANSER
chestnut gelding by Vulgan - She Gone.
1963 . . . Fell. (Mrs W.Archdale) 10.10-4. Mr.J.Mansfield.66/1.
1964 . . . Fell. (Mrs W.Archdale) 11.10-0. J.Lehane. 66/1.

MAGIC TRICKS
bay gelding by Happy Monarch - Fitsme.
1963 . . . Fell. (Mr J.H.Boyes) 9.10-0. O.McNally. 66/1.

MOYRATH
bay gelding bu Fortina - Peg's Cottage.
1963 . . . Pulled-up. (Mrs R.L.Johnson) 10.10-2. F.Carroll.33/1.
1965 . . . Finished 14th of 47. (Mrs G.Simpson) 12.10-13. B.Richmond. 100/1.

MR MCTAFFY
chestnut gelding by Jock Scot - Pontypridd.
1965 . . . Pulled-up. (Mrs P.Barnett) 13.10-13. T.Jackson. 100/1.

MONARCH'S THOUGHT
brown gelding by Happy Monarch - Late Thought.
1966 . . . Refused. (Mr D.H.Ellison) 12.10-0. G.Cramp. 100/1.

MAJOR HITCH
bay gelding by Aeolian -Mantilla Vulgan.
1966 . . . Fell. (Mr W.Noddings) 8.10-1. P.Broderick. 50/1.

MAC'S FLARE
chestnut gelding by Fun Fair - dam unknown.
1966 . . . Pulled-up. (Capt J.Wilson) 10.10-0. R.Langley. 100/1.

MY GIFT
by gelding by Hyacinthus - Oh My.
1966 . . . Pulled-up. (Mr P.Rooney) 10.10-0. A.Redmond. 100/1.

MEON VALLEY
bay gelding by Neron - Myrina.
1967 . . . Fell. (Mr A.R.Turnell) 12.10-7. A.Turnell. 66/1.

MOIDORE'S TOKEN
bay gelding by Moidore - Steel Token.
1968 . . . Finished 2nd of 45. (Miss P.Harrower) 11.10-8. B.Brogan. 100/6.
1969 . . . Pulled-up. (Miss P.Harrower) 12.10-9. B.Brogan. 100/6.

MANIFEST
bay gelding by Limekiln - Manzanillo.
1968 . . . Finished 11th of 45. (Mr J.Filmer Wilson) 10.10-0. R.Pitman. 66/1.

MASTER MASCUS
bay gelding by Damascus - Fairylight.
1968 . . . Fell. (Mr J.Bairstow) 9.10-6. Mr.J.Lawrence. 66/1.

MASTER OF ART
bay gelding by Artist's Son - Guapa.
1968 . . . Fell. (Dr.M.L.Slotover) 8.10-2. Mr.B.Hanbury. 100/7.

MIXED FRENCH
chestnut gelding by Coup de Myth - Cloche d'Ecosse.
1968 . . . Fell. (Mrs N.L.Durdy) 9.10-0. G.Holmes. 100/1.

MISS HUNTER
bay mare by Buckhound - Miss Steel.
1969 . . . Finished 10th of 30. (Mrs W.Macauley) 8.10-0. F.Shortt. 50/1.
1970 . . . Finished 3rd of 28. (Mrs W.Macauley) 9.10-0. F.Shortt. 33/1.
1971 . . . Fell. (Mrs W.Macauley) 10. 10-0. Mr.J.Fowler. 33/1.
1972 . . . Pulled-up. (Mrs W.Macauley) 11.10-0. A.L.Moore. 100/1.

MONEY BOAT
bay mare by Halsafari - Hide Out.
1971 . . . Fell. (Mr P.Doyle) 7.10-7. R.Coonan. 16/1.
1972 . . . finished 8th of 42. (Mr P.Doyle) 8.10-3. F.Berry. 16/1.

MILL DOOR
chestnut gelding by Cacador - Lady Sneerwell.
1973 . . . Finished 17th of 38. (Mr E.F.Birchall) 11.10-5. P.Cullis. 100/1.
1974 . . . Fell. (Mr W.E.Lipka) 12.10-2. J.McNaught. 100/1.

MR VIMY
bay gelding by Vimy - Song o'th Mist.
1973 . . . Pulled-up. (Mrs F.Harvey) 10.10-2. J.Haine. 100/1.

MANICOU BAY
brown gelding by Manicou - Girl-In-Bay.
1975 . . . Finished 6th of 31. (Mr D.Bunn) 9.10-7. R.Champion. 40/1.

MONEY MARKET
bay gelding by Even Money - Sell Out.
1975 . . . Finished 4th of 31. (Lord Chelsea) 8.10-13. J.King. 14/1.
1976 . . . Finished 14th of 32. (Lord Chelsea) 9.11-0. R.Champion. 12/1.

MERRY MAKER
chestnut gelding by Hornbeam - Festival.
1976 . . . Fell. (Mr A.Mildmay-White) 11.10-2. Mr.A.Mildmay-White. 50/1.

MERIDIAN II
chestnut gelding by Midlander - Steriolette.
1976 . . . Fell. (Mr B.Aughton) 9.10-0. J.J.O'Neill. 33/1.

MICKLEY SEABRIGHT
bay gelding by Sea Moss - Brightbell.
1978 . . . Finished 6th of 37. (Mr P.T.Brookshaw) 10.10-3. Mr.P.Brookshaw. 33/1.

MASTER H
chestnut gelding by Master Owen - Last Resort.
1978 . . . Unseated rider. (Mr S.P.Marsh) 9.11-2. R.Crank. 10/1.

MASTER UPHAM
chestnut gelding by The Bo'sun - Canal Zone.
1978 . . . Fell. (Mr R.E.Brinkworth) 10.10-0. P.Barton. 25/1.

MR SNOWMAN
bay gelding by Arctic Slave - Foyle Maiden.
1979 . . . Fell. (Lord Leverhulme) 10.10-9. G.Thorner. 10/1.

MANNYBOY
bay gelding by Manicou - Merrydown Girl.
1980 . . . Unseated rider. (Mr F.H.Pullen) 10.10-0. R.Rowe. 33/1.

MARTINSTOWN
chestnut gelding by Spartan General - Last Town.
1981 . . . Fell. (Mrs M.Easton) 9.10-7. Mr.M.Batters. 33/1.
1982 . . . Unseated rider. (Mrs R.Brew) 10.10-3. Miss C.Brew. 100/1.

MIGHT BE
bay gelding by Behistoun - Mighty Grand.
1981 . . . Fell. (Mr H.J.Knott) 10.10-0. A.Webber. 50/1.

MY FRIENDLY COUSIN
bay gelding by Dual - Hardy Lady.
1981 . . . Pulled-up. (Mr R.Scott) 11.10-0. A.Brown. 100/1.

MULLACURRY
brown gelding by Bally Joy - Dale Way.
1982 . . . Fell. (Mr J.Shanon) 10.10-12. Mr.T.J.Taaffe. 16/1.

MAN ALIVE
grey gelding by Falcon - Twinkletoes.
1982 . . . Fell. (Jim Ennis Construction Ltd.) 11.11-0. A.Turnell. 20/1.

MONTY PYTHON
bay gelding by Bargello - Beggar's Birthday.
1982 . . . Refused. (Mr W.Gaff) 10.10-0. B. de Haan. 66/1.
1983 . . . Refused. (Rank Organisation PLC) 11.10-0. P.O'Brien. 150/1.

MID DAY GUN
chestnut gelding by Salvo - Ritournelle.
1983 . . . Fell. (Mr Gibbons) 9.10-8. G.McCourt. 14/1.
1984 . . . Finished 20th of 40. (Mr R.Gibbons) 10.10-2. G.McCourt. 40/1.

MENDER
bay gelding by Cave Of Dracan - Mutch.
1983 . . . Unseated rider. (Miss N.Carroll) 12.10-0. A.Webber. 50/1.

MENFORD
bay gelding by Menelek - Jane Ford.
1983 . . . Refused. (Mr P.Richardson & Shirlstar Container Tpt.Ltd.) 8.10-0. M.Perrett. 100/1.

MIDDAY WELCOME
brown gelding by Crozier - Bore Da.
1983 . . . Fell. (Mr V.Burke) 12.10-0. Mrs.G.Rees. 500/1.

MIDNIGHT LOVE
bay gelding by Golden Love - St Marian.
1984 . . . Fell. (Carpenters Paints Ltd.) 9.11-4. C.Grant. 28/1.

MR SNUGFIT
bay gelding by Jukebox - Sinzinbra.
1985 . . . Finished 2nd of 40. (Mr A.Greenwood) 8.10-0. P.Tuck. 12/1.
1986 . . . Finished 4th of 40. (Mr T.P.Ramsden) 9.10-7. P.Tuck. 13/2.Fav.*

MUSSO
bay gelding by Menelek - Suvonne.
1985 . . . Pulled-up. (R.E.A.Bott(Wigmore St) Ltd.) 9.10-0. Mr.S.Sherwood. 50/1.

MASTER TERCEL
bay gelding by Master Owen - Clonroche Hawk.
1986 . . . Fell. (Mr B.P.Monkhouse) 10.10-0. D.Browne. 150/1.

MOUNT OLIVER
bay gelding by No Argument - Bayview Rambler.
1986 . . . Fell. (Mr D.A.Smith & Mr P.D.Whitehouse) 8.10-0. J.Bryan. 500/1.

MONANORE
chestnut gelding by Prefairy - Mous Kouri.
1986 . . . Finished 8th of 40. (Mr J.Meagher) 9.10-0. T.Morgan.22/1.
1987 . . . Finished 10th of 40.(Mr J.Meagher) 10.10-3. T.Morgan.20/1.
1988 . . . Finished 3rd of 40. (Full Circle Thoroughbreds PLC) 11.10-4. T.J.Taaffe. 33/1.
1989 . . . Finished 6th of 40. (Full Circle Thoroughbreds PLC) 12.10-6. G.McCourt. 20/1.
1990 . . . Carried-out. (Full Circle Thoroughbreds PLC) 13.10-5. T.J.Taaffe. 100/1.

MAORI VENTURE
chestnut gelding by St Columbas - Moon Venture. Bred by Mr.D.U.Morgan.
1987 . . . WON. (Mr H.J.Joel) 11.10-13. 40 Ran. S.C.Knight. 28/1.

MARCOLO
bay gelding by Linacre - Mascarita.
1987 . . . Fell. (Mr D.Ferguson) 10.10-0. P.Leech. 66/1.
1988 . . . Fell. (Mr D.Ferguson) 11.10-0. Miss V.Williams. 200/1.

MIDNIGHT MADNESS
bay gelding by Genuine - Indian Madness.
1988 . . . Pulled-up. (Mr D.Bloomfield) 10.10-5. M.Richards. 25/1.

MEMBERSON
chestnut gelding by New Member - Aileen's Revenge.
1988 . . . Pulled-up. (Mr P.Dufosee) 10.10-3. R.J.Beggan. 33/1.
1989 . . . Pulled-up. (Mr P.Dufosee) 11.10-2. Mr.G.Upton. 33/1.

MITHRAS
bay gelding by Centaurus - Timidora.
1989 . . . Pulled-up. (Mrs H.F.Richards) 11.10-1. R.Stronge. 66/1.

MEARLIN
bay mare by Giolla Mear - Caroline's Money.
1989 . . . Pulled-up. (Mr C.P.House) 10.10-10. S.McNeill. 300/1.

MR CHRIS
chestnut gelding by Lucifer - Dalliance.
1989 . . . Fell. (Mr C.D.Liveras) 10.10-0. B.Storey. 200/1.

MR FRISK
chestnut gelding by Bivouc - Jenny Frisk. Bred by Mr R.Dalton.
1990 . . . WON. (Mrs H.J.Duffey) 11.10-6. 38 Ran. Mr.M.Armytage. 16/1.
1991 . . . Pulled-up. (Mrs H.J.Duffey) 12.11-6. Mr.M.Armytage.25/1.

MICK'S STAR
brown gelding by Orange Bay - Starboard Belle.
1990 . . . Finished 19th of 38. (Mr P.Scammell) 10.10-1. S.J.O'Neill. 66/1.
1991 . . . Finished 13th of 40. (Mrs A.Daly & Mr P.Butler) 11.10-0. C.Swan. 100/1.

MISTER CHRISTIAN
bay gelding by Captain Jason - Grissette. Bred in New Zealand.
1991 . . . Pulled-up. (Mr J.M.T.Gaisford & Mr R.N.Stevens) 10.10-0. S.Earle. 100/1.

MASTER BOB
bay gelding by Pitpan - Good Calx.
1991 . . . Pulled-up. (Mr I.Wills) 11.10-5. J.Osborne. 20/1.

MIGHTY FALCON
bay gelding by Comedy Star - Lettuce.
1992 . . . Finished 18th of 40. (Mr & Mrs R.J.Tory) 7.10-0. P.Holley. 80/1.
1994 . . . Brought-down. (Mr & Mrs R.J.Tory) 8.10-0. P.Holley.250/1.

MISTER ED
chestnut gelding by Monsieure Edouarde - Are You Poaching.
1992 . . . Fell. (The Talking Horse Partnership) 9.10-0. D.Morris. 100/1.
1994 . . . Brought-down. (The Talking Horse Partnership) 11.10-0. D.Morris. 50/1.

MIINNEHOMA
bay or brown gelding by Kambalda - Mrs Cairns. Bred by Mr.P.Day.
1994 . . . WON. (Mr Freddie Starr) 11.10-8. 36 Ran. R.Dunwoody. 16/1.
1995 . . . Pulled-up. (Mr Freddie Starr) 12.11-4. R.Dunwoody. 11/1.

MOORCROFT BOY
chestnut gelding by Roselier - Well Mannered.
1994 . . . Finished 3rd of 36. (Mr K.G.Manley) 9.10-0. A.Maguire. 5/1.Fav.*

MR BOSTON
bay gelding by Halyudh - Edith Rose.
1994 . . . Fell. (Mr M.K.Oldham) 9.10-2. P.Niven. 16/1.

MASTER OATS
chestnut gelding by Oats - Miss Poker Face.
1994 . . . Fell. (Mr P.A.Matthews) 8.10-0. N.Williamson. 9/1.
1995 . . . Finished 7th of 35. (Mr P.A.Matthews) 9.11-10. N.Williamson. 5/1.Fav.*

● Nicolaus Silver (Bobby Beasley) goes a length up over previous year's winner Merryman II at the last fence and goes on to win the 1961 National.

NUN, THE
1839 . . . Finished 5th of 17. (Lord McDonald) Mr.A.McDonough. n/q.
1840 . . . Fell. (Lord McDonald) Mr.Powell. 3/1.Fav*

NIMROD
1843 . . . Finished 2nd of 16. (Mr Mare) Scott. 10/1.
1844 . . . Fell. (Mr Mare) Mr.A.McDonough. 14/1.
1845 . . . Failed to finish. (Mr Mare) French. n/q.

NAWORTH
1848 . . . Failed to finish. (Lord Strathmore) - 9-8. W.Archer. n/q.

NAPOLEON
1849 . . . Pulled-up. (Mr J.Bateman) 6.10-8. W.Archer. 50/1.

NUGGET, THE
1855 . . . Finished 6th of 20. (Mr C.Symonds) - 10-4. W.White. 50/1.

NEEDWOOD
1855 . . . Failed to finish. (Mr B.Land) - 11-2. Fech. 12/1.

NATIONAL PETITION
1864 . . . Failed to finish. (Mr J.Lanigan) - 10-8. J.Monaghan. n/q.

NUN, THE
brown mare by Fly-By-Night - dam unknown.
1868 . . . Fell. (Mr E.Green) - 11-6. Wheeler. 20/1.
1869 . . . Fell. (Mr E.Green) - 11-9. Mr.Thomas. 25/1.

NUAGE
bay horse by Marignan - Nomade. Bred in France.
1872 . . . Broke leg. (Mr Doncaster) 7.11-2. Harding. 100/15.

NEW YORK
chestnut horse by Dollar - Limosina. Bred in France.
1873 . . . Fell. (Lord Stamford) 5.10-6. W.Reeves. n/q.
1875 . . . Fell. (Mr F.Platt) 7.10-13. Mr.Dalglish. n/q.

NORTHFLEET
brown gelding by The Rescue - Compton Lass.
1878 . . . Fell. (Mr T.J.Clifford) 6.10-3. C.Lawrence. 14/1.

NEW GLASGOW
bay gelding by New Oswestry - Corbeille.
1881 . . . Finished 4th of 13. (Mr A.Peel) aged.10-7. Capt.A.J.Smith. 100/8.

NASR-ED-DIN
bay horse by Pellegrino - Nadine.
1891 . . . Fell. (Mr F.Gullane) 5.10-0. H.Brown. 50/1.

NAP
bay gelding by Napsbury - Lady Linton.
1892 . . . Fell. (Mr E.Woodland) 7.10-7. Mr.H.Woodland. 200/1.

NELLY GRAY
bay mare by Ben Battle - Peace.
1894 . . . Bolted. (Mr F.B.Atkinson) 5. 9-12. H.Escott. 5/1.jnt./Fav.*
1897 . . . Finished 9th of 28. (Maj.J.A.Orr-Ewing) 8.11-3. G.Morris. 20/1.

NORTON
chestnut gelding by Ascot - Romp.
1897 . . . Fell. (Mr Spencer Gollan) aged. 10-7. J.Hickey. 10/1.

NEPCOTE
bay gelding by Oedipus - Georgie.
1898 . . . Pulled-up. (Mr Lincoln) 7.10-9. W.Dollery. 25/1.

NOTHING
brown gelding by Hominy - dam unknown.
1900 . . . Bolted. (Mr G.R.Powell) 9. 9-11. W.Hoysted. 100/1.

NAHILLAH
chestnut horse by Baliol - Little Nell.
1904 . . . Finished 7th of 26. (Mr M.Crowther) 8. 9-11. Mr.A.Wood. n/q.

NAPPER TANDY
bay gelding by Ireland - Sweet Ethel.
1905 . . . Finished 2nd of 27. (Capt.McLaren) 8.10-0. P.Woodland. 25/1.
1907 . . . Finished 8th of 23. (Capt.McLaren) 10.10-13. Capt.R.H.Collis. 33/1.

NEREUS
chestnut gelding by Ocean Wave - Storm Witch.
1905 . . . Refused. (Mr C.Bower Ismay) 7. 9-10. G.Goswell. 66/1.

NANOYA
chestnut mare by Winkfield - Elissa.
1908 . . . Fell. (Mr B.W.Parr) 6.10-7. J.Lynn. 66/1.

NEUROTIC
chestnut horse by Marcovil - Hari Kari.
1920 . . . Finished 5th of 24. (Mr T.Miles) 9.9-13. Mr.F.B.Rees. 28/1.

NORTON
bay gelding by Leviathan - Bulmer.
1922 . . . Fell. (Mr V.T.Thompson) 7.11-8. I.Morgan.40/1.

NAVANA
bay mare by Master Magpie - dam by Tredennis.
1923 . . . Pulled-up. (Mr C.F.Kenyon) 9.10-0. F.Mason. 66/1.

NEWLANDS
chestnut gelding by Fugleman - dam by Wildflower.
1924 . . . Pulled-up. (Mr C.Bower Ismay) 10.10-0. R.Burford. 66/1.

NEWSBOY
bay gelding by Drinmore- Chattering Kit.
1930 . . . Fell. (Capt.R.E.Sassoon) 9.11-4. Capt.R.E.Sassoon.50/1.

NEAR EAST
black gelding by Hapsburg - Toi Fair.
1932 . . . Finished 4th of 36. (Mr H.B.Brandt) 7.10-10. T.McCarthy. 50/1.
1933 . . . Completed the course. (Mr H.B.Brandt) 8.10-7. A.Robson. 45/1.

NATIONAL NIGHT
chestnut gelding by Werwolf - Bullet Proof.
1940 . . . Fell. (Mr J.H.Whitney) 8.10-5. H.A.Jones. 100/1.

NEWARK HILL
bay gelding by Kirk-Alloway - Llwyn-yr-Eos.
1946 . . . Brought-down. (Mr T.A.Spiers) 12.10-1. P.Lay. 50/1.

NICKEL COIN
bay mare by Pay Up - Viscum. Bred by Mr.R.Corbett.
1951 . . . WON. (Mr J.Royle) 9.10-1. 36 Ran. J.A.Bullock. 40/1.

NAGARA
chestnut gelding by Astrophel - Nine 11. Foaled in France.
1952 . . . Fell. (Mr J.P.Phillips) 10.11-7. P.Hieronimus. 50/1.

NO RESPONSE
bay mare by Iceberg 11 - Water Gipsy.
1955 . . . Fell. (Sir Thomas Ainsworth) 9.10-2. D.Ancil. 45/1.
1956 . . . Fell. (Sir Thomas Ainsworth) 10.10-1.C.Finnegan.50/1.

145

NEVER SAY WHEN
bay mare by Mustang - Calla Lily.
1958 . . . Fell. (Mr A.H.Wood) 9.10-2. S.Mellor. 50/1.

NIC ATKINS
brown gelding by Nicolaus - Bunty Atkins.
1959 . . . Fell. (Mrs P.M.Lamb) 8.10-1. F.Shortt. 20/1.

NICOLAUS SILVER
grey gelding by Nicolaus - Rays Of Montrose. Bred by Mr.J.Hefferman.
1961 . . . WON. (Mr C.Vaughan) 9.10-1. 35 Ran. H.R.Beasley .28/1.
1962 . . . Finished 7th of 32. (Mr C.Vaughan) 10.10-10. H.R.Beasley. 100/9.
1963 . . . Finished 10th of 47. (Mr B.Sunley) 11.11-0. H.R.Beasley. 28/1.

NEDSMAR
brown gelding by Olein's Grace - Marionette.
1965 . . . Fell. (Mrs E.E.Graham) 11.10-13. J.Hudson. 100/1.

NORTHER
bay gelding by Precipitation - Serenoa.
1966 . . . Finished 7th of 47. (Mr J.G.Jones) 9.10-0. P.Jones. 100/1.
1967 . . . Pulled-up. (Mr J.G.Jones) 10.10-0. Mr.J.Lawrence. 50/1.

NO JUSTICE
black or brown gelding by Doubtless 11 - Conviction.
1970 . . . Refused. (Mr A.S.Neaves) 9.10-0. J.Guest. 50/1.

NEPHIN BEG
chestnut gelding by Phalorain - Toiqueen.
1972 . . . Pulled-up. (Lady Mostyn) 10.10-0. P.Morris. 100/1.

NOM DE GUERRE
bay gelding by Vimy - Fair Rosamond.
1972 . . . Fell. (Mrs T.D.Pilkington) 10.10-0. J.Haine. 100/1.

NEREO
bay gelding by Alfidir - Pajilla. Bred in Spain.
1973 . . . Pulled-up. (Duque de Alburquerque) 7.10-3. Duque de Alburquerque. 66/1.
1974 . . . Finished 8th 42. (Duque de Alburquerque) 8.10-6. Duque de Alburquerque. 100/1.
1976 . . . Fell. (Duque de Alburquerque) 10.10-1. Duque de Alburquerque. 50/1.
1977 . . . Fell. (Duque de Alburquerque) 11.10-0. R.Kington.100/1.
1978 . . . Finished 14th of 37. (Duque de Alburquerque) 12.10-0. M.Floyd. 40/1.

NORWEGIAN FLAG
chestnut gelding by Escart 111 - Battlebridge.
1974 . . . Finished 19th of 42. (Miss Dorothy Squire) 8.10-0. P.Buckley. 50/1.

NEVER ROCK
bay gelding by Never Dwell - Joyful Spirit.
1978 . . . Finished 15th of 37. (Mr G.Barley) 9.10-0. K.Mooney. 50/1.

NO GYPSY
chestnut gelding by Romany Air - Near The Wind.
1979 . . . Brought-down. (Mr C.H.Bennion) 10.10-0. J.Suthern. 66/1.
1981 . . . Fell. (Mr E.Treacy & Mr J.J.Bridger) 12.10-0.J.Suthern. 100/1.

NEVER TAMPER
chestnut gelding by Never Say Die - Plunder.
1983 . . . Refused. (J.J.Saunders Ltd.) 8.10-0. J.Williams. 500/1.
1985 . . . Pulled-up. (J.J.Saunders Ltd.) 10.10-3. C.Brown. 200/1.

NORTHERN BAY
bay gelding by Mon Capitaine - Sand Tack.
1985 . . . Fell. (Twycross Frozen Food Centre Ltd) 9.10-1. P.Hobbs. 66/1.
1986 . . . Finished 11th of 40. (Cheveley Park Stud Ltd.) 10.10-0. P.Hobbs. 33/1.
1987 . . . Finished 9th of 40. (Cheveley Park Stud Ltd.) 11.10-1. R.Crank. 50/1.
1988 . . . Pulled-up. (Mr R.Graham) 12.10-4. H.Davies. 50/1.

146

NEWNHAM
chestnut gelding by Cantab - Ribon Perfume.
1989 . . . Finished 10th of 40. (Mr M.A.Johnson) 12.10-5. Mr.S.Andrews. 50/1.

NUMERATE
bay gelding by Paddy's Stream - Flying Music.
1989 . . . Pulled-up. (Mr P.Davis) 10.10-0. Miss Tarnya Davis 100/1.

NAUTICAL JOKE
bay gelding by Sea Catch - Carnival Jest.
1990 . . . Unseated rider. (Mr P.Piller) 11.10-0. Mr.K.Johnson. 66/1.

NEW HALEN
brown gelding by Dikusa - Miss Pear.
1991 . . . Unseated rider. (Mrs S.Siviter) 10.10-0. S.J.O'Neill. 50/1.
1992 . . . Refused. (Mrs S.Siviter) 11.10-0. R.Bellamy. 66/1.

NEW MILL HOUSE
chestnut gelding by Tobique - Ascess.
1994 . . . Fell. (Mr B.McHugh) 11.10-0. T.Horgan. 150/1.

NUAFFE
bay gelding by Abednego - Miss Magello.
1995 . . . Fell. (Mr J.G.Doyle) 10.10-0. S.O'Donovan. 20/1.

OLIVER TWIST
1841 . . . Fell. (Mr Smith) Mr.Oliver. n/q.

OAKS, THE
1850 . . . Knocked-over. (Mr J.G.Murphy) 5.10-5. S.Canavan. 30/1.

OSCAR
1853 . . . Finished 3rd of 21. (Mr T.F.Mason) - 10-2. Mr.A.Goodman. 6/1.
1854 . . . Knocked-over. (Mr T.F.Mason) - 11-12. S.Darling,jnr. 15/1.

OMAR PASHA
1857 . . . Failed to finish. (Mr W.Williams) - 9-2. J.Kendal. 100/6.

ORKONSTA
1859 . . . Finished 6th of 20. (Viscount A.Talon) - 9-0. G.Stevens. 33/1.

OLD BEN ROE
1861 . . . Finished 3rd of 24.. (Mr W.Briscoe) - 10-7. G.Waddington. 10/1.

O'CONNELL
1862 . . . Fell. (Lord de Freyne) - 9-8. J.Wynne. 33/1.

ORPHAN, THE
1863 . . . Fell. (Mr J.C.Tilbury) 9-11. Mr.W.Bevill. n/q.

OCEAN WITCH
1864 . . . Finished 5th of 25. (Captain Lamb) 5.10-2. W.Reeves. 20/1.

ORNE
bay horse by Feruck Khan - Princess de la Paix.
1869 . . . Knocked-over. (Mr T.Wadlow) 5.11-2. W.White. 50/1.

OURAGAN II
chestnut horse by Monarque - Sunrise.
1872 . . . Finished 7th of 25. (Mr P.Merton) aged.10-10. A.Holman. n/q.
1874 . . . Finished 8th of 22. (Mr J.Pearon) aged.10-5. Mr.G.Mulcaster. 50/1.

OLD JOE
bay gelding by Barefoot - Spot. Bred by Mr.E.H.Banks.
1886 . . . WON. (Mr A.J.Douglas) 7.10-9. 23 Ran. T.Skelton.25/1.
1887 . . . Fell. (Mr A.J.Douglas) 8.11-10. Mr.C.J.Cunningham. 100/8.
1888 . . . Failed to finish. (Mr A.J.Douglas) 9.11-9. W.Daniels. 18/1.

ORANGE PAT
bay gelding by Ascetic - Orange Bitters.
1903 . . . Fell. (Mr B.W.Parr) 7. 9-10. R.Morgan. 40/1.

OLDTOWN
brown gelding by Atheling - dam unknown.
1904 . . . Pulled-up. (Comte de Madre) 13. 9-8. Mr.H.M.Ripley. n/q.

OATLANDS
brown gelding by Waterford - Blanche Nef.
1906 . . . Finished 6th of 23. (Mr C.T.Garland) 6. 9-13. H.Aylin.100/6.

ODOR
chestnut gelding by Chevele D'or - Jessamine.
1910 . . . Finished 3rd of 25. (Mr R.H.Hall) 9. 9-8. Mr.R.H.Hall. n/q.

OLD TAY BRIDGE
chestnut gelding by Bridge Of Earn - Broken Reed.
1921 . . . Fell. (Mr W.H.Dixon) 7.11-8. E.Piggott. 100/8.
1924 . . . Fell. (Mrs W.H.Dixon) 10.11-13. Mr.H.M.Hartigan. 40/1.
1925 . . . Finished 2nd of 33. (Mrs W.H.Dixon) 11.11-12. J.R.Anthony. 9/1.Fav.*
1926 . . . Finished 2nd of 30. (Mrs W.H.Dixon) 12.12-2. J.R.Anthony. 8/1.

OVERDRAFT
bay or brown gelding by St Tudwal - Draft.
1929 . . . Failed to finish. (Mrs R.D.Cohen) 7.10-11. Mr.E.J.R.Bennett. 66/1.

150

ODD CAT
bay gelding by Catmint - Odeon.
1929 . . . Failed to finish. (Mr J.B.D'Ardenne) 8.10-1. J.Sinnott. 200/1.

OXCLOSE
chestnut gelding by Moorside 11 - Hampton Belle.
1931 . . . Fell. (Mr A.Hall Watt) 7.10-10. F.Gurney. 33/1.

OTTAWA
chestnut gelding by Manilardo - Wise Aunt.
1932 . . . Refused. (Mr N.Alvarez) 8.10-8. T.E.Leader. 40/1.

OEIL DE BOUEF
bay gelding by Nouvel An - Beaute de Cour.
1936 . . . Fell. (Marquis de San Miguel) 9.11-0. M.Feakes. 100/1.

OCULTOR
bay gelding by Collaborator - Oculiste. Bred in France.
1947 . . . Finished 9th of 57. (Mr G.R.Owen) 12.10-0. Mr.D.Owen. 100/1.

OH JOE
chestnut gelding by Cri de Guerre - Garconne.
1947 . . . Unseated rider. (Mrs E.P.Moss) 7.10-0. E.Vinall. 100/1.

OFFALY PRINCE
bay gelding by Interlace - Jestaway.
1948 . . . Finished 9th of 43. (Mr G.C.Judd) 9.10-5. Mr.A.Parker. 100/1.
1949 . . . Fell. (Mr G.C.Judd) 10.10-4. Mr.A.Parker. 66/1.

OLE MAN RIVER
chestnut horse by River Prince - Moondyne.
1950 . . . Fell. (Mr A.Dickson) 8.10-0. G.Bonas. 100/1.

OVERSHADOW
grey gelding by Overthrow - Tetrarchia.
1952 . . . Finished 5th of 47. (Mrs J.A.Wood) 12.10-5. E.Newman. 22/1.
1953 . . . Finished 4th of 31. (Mrs J.A.Wood) 13.10-4. P.Taaffe. 33/1.

ORDNANCE
brown gelding by Bakhtawar - Arsenal.
1953 . . . Fell. (Mr W.J.Rimell) 7.10-3. M.Scudamore. 25/1.
1954 . . . Fell. (Sir Ronald Gunter) 8.10-1. J.Dowdeswell. 18/1.

ONTRAY
bay gelding by Legend Of France - Guinea Fowl.
1954 . . . Finished 9th of 29. (Capt.L.Scott Briggs) 6.10-8. Mr.R.Brewis. 66/1.
1955 . . . Finished 5th of 30. (Capt.L.Scott Briggs. 7.10-8. R.Curran. 66/1.
1956 . . . Fell. (Capt.L.Scott Briggs) 8.10-0. R.Curran. 100/6.

ORIENTAL WAY
chestnut gelding by Hyderabad - Fair Terms.
1955 . . . Fell. (Mr L.Abrahamson) 7.10-12. F.T.Winter. 33/1.

OXO
bay gelding by Bobsleigh - Patum. Bred by Mr.A.C.Wyatt.
1959 . . . WON. (Mr J.E.Bigg) 8.10-13. 34 Ran. M.Scudamore. 8/1.
1961 . . . Pulled-up. (Mr J.E.Bigg) 10.11-8. M.Scudamore. 20/1.

OSCAR WILDE
bay gelding by Epigram - Quenington.
1959 . . . Fell. (Mr T.T.Jasper) 9.10-4. R.E.Jenkins. 28/1.
1961 . . . Fell. (Mr T.T.Jasper) 11.10-4. R.E.Jenkins. 45/1.

O'MALLEY POINT
bay gelding by Sea Lover - Ross' Pride.
1961 . . . Finished 3d of 35. (Mr A.Elliott) 10.11-4. P.A.Farrell. 100/6.
1963 . . . Finished 19th of 47. (Maj.L.S.Marler) 12.11-1. M.Scudamore. 33/1.

151

OWEN'S SEDGE
grey gelding by Owenstown- Lady Sedge.
1963 . . . Finished 7th of 47. (Mr Gregory Peck) 10.11-6. P.Taaffe. 20/1.

OUT AND ABOUT
brown gelding by Cabrach - Lovely Out.
1963 . . . Fell. (Mr B.Sunley) 8.10-7. J.Gifford. 25/1.
1964 . . . Finished 14th of 33. (Mr B.Sunley) 9.10-1. B.Gregory. 33/1.

ON THE MOVE
chestnut gelding by Romany Air - Steelakiss.
1970 . . . Fell. (Mr G.Jarvis) 8.10-1. G.Dartnall. 100/1.

OTTER, THE
bay gelding by Border Chief - Sealskin.
1970 . . . Fell. (Mrs J.Denning) 9.10-1. T.M.Jones. 20/1.
1971 . . . Fell. (Mrs J.Denning) 10.10-1. T.M.Jones. 12/1.
1972 . . . Fell. (Mrs J.Denning) 11.10-0. T.M.Jones. 25/1.

ORMONDE TUDOR
bay gelding by Councel - Welsh Rose.
1976 . . . Fell. (Mr W.A.Hickling & Mr J.A.Kelly) 7.10-0. K.Bamfield. 100/1.

OTTER WAY
bay gelding by Salmonway Spirit - Marquita.
1978 . . . Fell. (Mr O.J.Carter) 10.10-0. J.King. 16/1.

OSKARD
bay gelding by Tuny - Olcha.
1979 . . . Fell. (Mr W.W.Smith & Mr C.M.Wilson) 10.10-0. M.Blackshaw. 100/1.

OUR GREENWOOD
bay gelding by Arctic Slave - Knockeen Cross.
1980 . . . Fell. (Mr M.J.Russell) 12.11-6. Mr.A.O'Connell. 100/1.

OLD SOCIETY
bay or brown gelding by Choral Society - Go Day.
1982 . . . Fell. (Mrs D.Fortune) 8.10-8. P.Walsh. 33/1.

O'ER THE BORDER
bay gelding by Border Chief - Hasty Exit.
1983 . . . Refused. (Mr H.F.Harpur-Crewe) 9.10-0. Mr.P.O'Connor. 200/1.

ONAPROMISE
chestnut gelding by Sharp Edge - Halkissimo.
1985 . . . Pulled-up. (Mr J.J.Greenwood & Mr J.E.Ball) 9.10-5. A.Brown. 100/1.

OAKPRIME
bay gelding by Master Owen - Arctic Tack.
1983 . . . Pulled-up. (Mrs D.Nicholson) 8.10-0. R.Linley. 66/1.

OUR CLOUD
bay gelding by Silver Cloud - Clougher Queen.
1985 . . . Refused. (Mr T.D.Strong) 9.10-0. Mr.J.Queally. 150/1.

OYDE HILLS
brown gelding by Night Sky - My Affair.
1988 . . . Refused. (Mrs B.N.Bletsoe & Mr R.C.Parker) 9.10-0. M.Brennan. 100/1.

OVER THE ROAD
chestnut gelding by Over The River - Legal Fortune.
1991 . . . Finished 4th of 40. (Mr J.R.Upson) 10.10-0. R.Supple.50/1.
1992 . . . Finished 8th of 40. (Mr J.R.Upson) 11.10-0. R.supple. 22/1.

OLD APPLEJACK
chestnut gelding by Hot Brandy - Windfall V1.
1991 . . . Finished 8th of 40. (Mr G.Tobitt) 11.10-1. T.Reed. 66/1.
1992 . . . Finished 7th of 40. (Mr G.Tobitt) 12.10-0. A.Orkney.35/1.

OKLAOMA II

bay gelding by Trenal - Koralie 11.
1991 . . . Pulled-up. (Mr R.Mancuso) 11.10-7. R.Kleparski. 66/1.

OMERTA

chestnut gelding by Quayside - Cherry Princess.
1992 . . . Pulled-up. (Mrs E.McMorrow) 12.10-4. L.Wyer. 33/1.

OVER THE DEEL

chestnut gelding by Over The River - Cahernane Girl.
1995 . . . Finished 3rd of 35. (Mr G.Tobitt) 9.10-0. Mr C.Bonner. 100/1.
1996 . . . Finished 9th of 27. (Mr D.Davies) 10.10-0. Mr.T.McCarthy. 33/1.

OVER THE STREAM

bay gelding by Over The River - Bola Stream.
1996 . . . Finished 13 th of 27. (Mesrs.J.D & E.C.Gordon) A.Thornton. 50/1.

● Pelorus Jack (nearside) takes the last in the 1933 race neck-and-neck with Kellsboro' Jack. But disaster is about to strike. Pelorus Jack had clouted the fence and came down heavily, leaving Kellsboro' Jack to run on to victory.

PAULINA
1839 . . . Finished 3rd of 17. (Mr Theobald) Mr.Martin. n/q.

PIONEER
1839 . . . Finished 7th of 17. (Sir D.Baird) Mr.T.Walker. n/q.

PETER SIMPLE
grey horse by Arbutus - dam unknown.
1841 . . . Finished 3rd of 11. (Hon.F.Craven) Walker. 6/1.
1842 . . . Finished 3rd of 15. (Mr Hunter) Mr.Hunter. 7/1. Remounted*
1843 . . . Finished 8th of 16. (Mr W.Ekin) - 13-1. Frisby. 3/1.Fav*
1844 . . . Fell. (Mr W.Ekin) - 12-12. Frisby. n/q.
1845 . . . Finished 2nd of 15. (Mr Thornton) - 11-12. Frisby. 9/1.
1846 . . . Fell. (Mr W.Ekin) - 11-2. Frisby 100/6.

PAGE, THE
1845 . . . Refused. (Mr Holman) - 11-10. Mr.Holman. 7/1.

PETER SWIFT
1845 . . . Failed to finish. (Mr Milbank) - 10-12. Mr.Powell. n/q.

PICKWICK
1846 . . . Failed to finish. (Mr G.Lambden) - 10-10. Dally. n/q.

PIONEER
bay gelding by Advance - dam unknown. Not in the General Stud Book.
1846 . . . WON. (Mr Adams) 6.11-12. 22 Ran. W.Taylor. n/q.
1847 . . . Finished 4th of 26. (Mr O'Higgins) 7.11-12. Capt.Peel. 15/1.
1848 . . . Brought-down. (Mr O'Higgins) 8.11-6. Capt.Peel. 25/1.

PERAMBULATOR
1846 . . . Pulled-up. (Hon.F.Craven) 6.10-8. N.Stagg. 16/1.

PLURALIST, THE
1847 . . . Failed to finish. (Mr Hall) - 11-4. Denby. n/q.

PIONEER
1848 . . . Brought-down. (Mr T.Harrison) - 10-13. Neale. 25/1.

PICTON
1848 . . . Failed to finish. (Mr J.N.Burke) - 10-13. N.Burke. n/q.

PENRITH
Formerly named Charles X11.
1851 . . . Failed to finish. (Mr Johnstone) - 9-4. McClory. n/q.

PETER SIMPLE
bay gelding by Patron - dam unknown. Not in the Genral Stud Book.
1849 . . . WON. (Mr Mason,jnr.) 11.11-0. 24 Ran. T.Cunningham. 20/1.
1850 . . . Failed to finish. (Mr Cunningham) 12.12-12. T.Cunningham. 5/1.Fav.*
1851 . . . Failed to finish. (Mr Cunningham) 13.11-7. D.Tubb. n/q.
1852 . . . Fell. (Mr G.S.Davenport) 14.11-2. Mr.G.S.Davenport.n/q.
1853 . . . WON. (Capt.J.L.Little) 15.10-10. 21 Ran. T.Olliver. 9/1.
1854 . . . Failed to finish. (Mr Bignell) 16.12-0. C.Boyce. 12/1.

PRINCE GEORGE
1849 . . . Finished 3rd of 24. (Mr T.Mason) - 10-10. T.Olliver. 5/1.Fav.*

PROCEED
1849 . . . Refused. (Captain Peel) - 11-11. Capt.Peel. 9/1.

PEGASUS
1850 . . . Failed to finish. (Lord Seaham) - 8-10. Tasker. n/q.

PONY, THE
1850 . . . Failed to finish. (Mr R.Brooke) - 8-7. Maney. n/q.

POLL
1853 . . . Fell. (Mr Hudson) - 9-10. Debean. n/q.

PETER
1854 . . . Failed to finish (Mr Linnell) - 10-12. R.Sly,jnr. 20/1.
1855 . . . Failed to finish. (Mr S.Mansell) - 11-4. T.Ablett. 20/1.

PRIDE OF THE NORTH
1854 . . . Refused. (Mr Olliver) - 9-8. R.James. 50/1.

PIMPERN
1855 . . . Failed to finish. (Mr H.Lewis) - 9-8. Weaver. 50/1.

PASHA, THE
1856 . . . Failed to finish. (Mr Hurley) - 10-4. D.Meaney. 40/1.

POTTER, THE
1856 . . . Failed to finish. (Mr Barber) - 9-8. Kendall. 10/1.

PLAYMAN
1862 . . . Fell. (Mr A.Yates) - 10-8. J.Nightingall. 25/1.

POET, THE
1862 . . . Fell. (Mr J.Henry) - 8-12. Gatt. n/q.

PORTLAND
1864 . . . Fell. (Mr H.Matthews) - 10-12. Mr.A.Goodman. 12/1.

PRINCESS DAGMAR
bay mare by Sir Peter Laurie - dam unknown.
1865 . . . Pulled-up. (Mr H.Melville) - 10-12. G.Holman. 100/8.

PHILOSOPHER
1865 . . . Pulled-up. (Mr Turner) 6.10-8. E.Jones. n/q.
1866 . . . Fell. (Mr W.Murray) 7.10-7. Wheeler. 50/1.
1871 . . . Fell. (Mr Gardner) 11.10-12. H.Ellison. 100/1.
1872 . . . Brought-down. (Mr W.Murray) 12.10-6. T.Gray. n/q.

PLINLIMMON
grey horse by Hampton - dam unknown.
1867 . . . Failed to finish. (Capt.Parkinson) 6.10-13. J.Holman. n/q.

PEARL DIVER
bay gelding by Marsyas - Pearl.
1868 . . . Finished 2nd of 21. (Mr E.Brayley) - 10-12. Tomlinson. 10/1.
1869 . . . Fell. (Mr E.Brayley) - 12-7. W.Reeves. 100/7.
1870 . . . Failed to finish. (Mr E.Brayley) - 12-7. J.Page. 100/6.
1871 . . . Finished 4th of 25. (Mr E.Brayley) - 11-5. J.Page. 4/1.Fav.*

PLOVER, THE
bay gelding by Grey Plover - Alice Grey.
1868 . . . Failed to finish. (Mr R.Walker) - 10-10. Mr.R.Walker.50/1.

PLUM CAKE
chestnut gelding by Plum Pudding - dam unknown.
1869 . . . Fell. (Mr A.Yates) 6.10-0. Mr.G.Spafford. 1000/15.

PRIMROSE
chestnut mare by Bonnyfield - Rosebud.
1870 . . . Finished 3rd of 23. (Mr W.R.Brockton) 6.10-12. Mr.W.R.Brockton. 10/1.
1872 . . . Broke back. (Mr W.R.Brockton) 8.11-9. Mr.W.R.Brockton. 100/6.

PRETENTAINE II
bay mare by Zouave - Sylvia.
1870 . . . Failed to finish. (Mr R.Hennessy) - 10-8. Mumford. n/q.

PURLBROOK
bay horse by Knight Of Kars - dam unknown.
1871 . . . Fell. (Mr W.Bingham) 6.10-10. Marsh. 25/1.

157

PALADIN
brown gelding by Piccador - dam unknown.
1874 . . . Fell (Captain Rising) 5.10-3. J.Rugg. n/q.

PATHFINDER
bay gelding by Mogador - dam unknown. Not in the General Stud Book. Formerly named The Knight.
1875 . . . WON. (Mr H.Bird) 8.10-11. 19 Ran. Mr.Thomas. 100/6.
1876 . . . Faile to finish. (Mr H.Bird) 9.11-0. W.Reeves. 100/6.

PHRYNE
1876 . . . Failed to finish. (Mr C.B.Brookes) 8.11-3. Mr.J.Goodwin. 33/1.

PALM
bay horse by West Australian - Sabine.
1876 . . . Refused. (Mr G.Brown) 8.11-0. Mr.Barnes. 100/8.

PRIDE OF KILDARE
chestnut mare by Plum Pudding or Canary - Hibernia.
1877 . . . Fell. (Capt.Bates) 6.11-4. D.Canavan. 100/8.
1878 . . . Finished 3rd of 12. (Capt Bates) 7.11-7.Mr.G.Moore. 6/1.

PLAYFAIR
black gelding by Ripponden - dam unknown. Not in the General Stud Book.
1888 . . . WON. (Mr E.W.Baird) 7.10-7. 20 Ran. G.Mawson. 40/1.

PAN
bay gelding by Ambergris - Elf.
1890 . . . Finished 2nd of 16. (Mr E.Woodland) 7.10-5. W.Halsey. 100/1.

PARTISAN
black or brown horse by Zeal - Miss May.
1892 . . . Fell. (Captain A'Court) 6.11-1. A.H.Barker. 40/1.

PRIMATE, THE
bay horse by Cardinal York - Myfauwy.
1892 . . . Pulled-up. (Mr F.Bald) 6.10-13. Capt.Bewicke. 100/14.
1893 . . . Fell. (Mr F.Bald) 7.11-3. Capt.Bewicke. 100/7.

PAUL PRY
bay gelding by Play Actor - dam unknown.
1892 . . . Pulled-up. (Mr F.E.Lawrence) 6.10-12. T.Adams. n/q.

PRINCE ALBERT
bay gelding by Althotas - Bessie.
1895 . . . Fell. (Mr W.T.Roden) 7.10-12. Mr W.P.Cullen. 50/1.
1897 . . . Finished 4th of 28. (Mr J.S.Forbes) 9.10-8. Mr.G.S.Davies. 25/1.
1898 . . . Finished 9th of 25. (Mr J.S.Forbes) 10.11-0.Mr.G.S.Davies. 8/1.

PHILACTERY
chestnut gelding by Philammon - Evanthe.
1896 . . . Pulled-up. (Sir S.Scott) 8. 9-11. E.Driscoll. 100/1.

PISTACHE
bay or brown gelding by Zambo - Pomme D'Api.
1899 . . . Fell. (Count de Geloes) 5.10-3. Count de Geloes. 100/1.

PRINCE TUSCAN
brown gelding by Toscano - Bessie.
1901 . . . Finished 8th of 24. (Mr H.Hunt) 8.10-6. Mr.Hunt,jnr. 33/1.

PROSSET
bay gelding by Sweetheart - Fair Edith.
1901 . . . Failed to finish. (Mr H.Barnato) 6. 9-13. Mr.F.Hartigan. 20/1.

PAWNBROKER
chestnut gelding by Westmoreland - Uncertainty.
1901 . . . Failed to finish. (Mr R.C.Dawson) 6. 9-7. J.O'Brien.100/6.
1903 . . . Finished 6th of 23. (Mr R.C.Dawson) 8. 9-9. J.O'Brien.100/1.

PADISHAH
bay gelding by Sheen - Padua.
1901 . . . Failed to finish. (Mr A.Gorham) 8.10-1. A.Birch. 66/1.

PRIDE OF MABESTOWN, THE
bay mare by Ascetic - Witching Hour.
1903 . . . Fell. (Mr O.J.Williams) 7.10-8. W.Dollery. 10/1.
1904 . . . Fell. (Mr O.J.Williams) 8.11-0. Mr.A.Gordon. 66/1.

PATLANDER
bay or brown gelding by Sir Patrick - Theodora 11.
1903 . . . Fell. (Mr W.Nelson) 7.10-7. M.Walsh. 40/1.
1904 . . . Fell. (Mr W.Nelson) 8.10-10. E.Matthews. 7/1.
1907 . . . Finished 3rd of 23. (Mr W.Nelson) 11.10-7. J.Lynn. n/q.

PHIL MAY
chestnut gelding by Milner - Sister May.
1905 . . . Fell. (Col.H.T.Fenwick) 6.11-0. R.Morgan. 20/1.
1906 . . . Finished 9th of 23. (Mr Cotton) 7.11-5. J.Owens. 10/1. Remounted*

PIERRE
bay gelding by Pierrepont - Little Go.
1906 . . . Pulled-up. (Mr W.Paul) 8. 9-7. J.Dillon. 33/1.

PADDY MAHER
bay geldiong by Apollo - Pella.
1908 . . . Fell. (Col.Kirkwood) 8.10-3. Mr.P.O'Brien-Butler. 100/8.
1909 . . . Fell. (Col.Kirkwood) 9.10-9. Mr.P.O'Brien-Butler. 25/1.
1910 . . . Fell. (Col.Kirkwood) 10.10-9. Mr.R.H.Walker. 33/1.

PROPHET III
brown gelding by Horoscope - Royal Nun.
1908 . . . Fell. (Mr Foxhall Keene) aged. 10-0. J.Dillon. 66/1.

PHAETHON
bay gelding by Apollo - Bonheur.
1909 . . . Finished 10th of 32. (Col.Kirkwood) 7.10-5. Mr.H.Ussher.100/1.
1910 . . . Knocked-over. (Col Kirkwood) 8.10-1. F.Morgan. n/q.

PRECENTOR II
chestnut gelding by Chorister - Lady Invercauld. Bred in U.S.A.
1910 . . . Pulled-up. (Mr Foxhall Keene) 11.10-7. W.Rollason. n/q.
1911 . . . Fell. (Mr Foxhall Keene) 12. 9-11. A.Aylin. 100/1.
1912 . . . Failed to finish. (Mr Foxhall Keene) 13.10-0. A.Aylin. n/q.

POETHLYN
bay gelding by Rydal Head - Fine Champagne. Bred by Major H.Peel.
* 1918 . . . WON. (Mrs H.Peel) 8.11-6. 17 Ran. E.Piggott. 5/1.co/Fav.*
1919 . . . WON. (Mrs H.Peel) 9.12-7. 22 Ran. E.Piggott. 11/4.Fav*
1920 . . . Fell. (Mrs H.Peel) 10.12-7. E.Piggott. 3/1.Fav.*

POLLEN
chestnut gelding by Picton - Folle Farine.
1919 . . . Finished 3rd of 22. (Mr J.L.Dugdale) 10.11-4. A.Escott. 100/7.

PAY ONLY
chestnut mare by Walmsgate - Teddie 111.
1919 . . . Finished 7th of 22. (Mr W.P.Hanley) 9.11-4. T.Hulme. 100/7.

PICTURE SAINT
bay gelding by Picton - Wise Saint.
1919 . . . Fell. (Col.R.P.Croft) 7.10-0. F.McCabe. 100/1.
1920 . . . Fell. (Col.R.P.Croft) 8.10-1. Capt.G.H.Bennet. n/q.
1921 . . . Fell. (Col.R.P.Croft) 9.10-5. N.Hhayes. n/q.

PRINCE CLIFTON
bay gelding by Cliftonhall - dam by Red Prince 11.
1921 . . . Fell. (Mr L.Pollock) 8.10-13. L.B.Rees. 66/1.

PROSPERITZ
bay horse by Uncle George - Proserpine.
1921 . . . Fell. (Maj.L.B.Holliday) 7. 9-8. W.Daly. n/q.

PUNT GUN
bay gelding by Fowling Piece - Pernmiller.
1923 . . . Finished 4th of 28. (Mrs J.Putnam) 10.11-1. M.Tighe. 20/1.

PENCOED
brown gelding by Creangate - Peahen.
1923 . . . Pulled-up. (Lt.Col.F.Lort Phillips) 8.10-3. Mr.D.Thomas.n/q.
1924 . . . Pulled-up. (Lt.Col.F.Lort Phillips) 9.10-6. Mr.D.Thomas. 40/1.
1925 . . . Fell. (Lt.Col.F.Lort Phillips) 10.10-3. Mr.D.Thomas. 33/1.
1926 . . . Fell. (Lt.Col.F.Lort Phillips) 11.10-2. Mr.D.Thomas.100/1.

PAM NUT
bay gelding by Pam - Broken Reed.
1923 . . . Pulled-up. (Capt.T.McDougal) 10.10-0. S.Duffy. n/q.

PALM OIL
bay gelding by Coriander - Last Purchase.
1924 . . . Fell. (Mr H.E.Steel) 8.10-0. Mr.P.Roberts. 66/1.

PATSEY V
chestnut gelding by Lord Garvagh - dam by Walmsgate.
1925 . . . Refused. (Mr B.Lemon) aged. 10-12. Mr.B.Lemon. 25/1.
1926 . . . Fell. (Mr B.Lemon) aged. 10-9. Maj.T.F.Cavenagh.66/1.

PETER THE PIPER
bay or brown gelding by The Page or Zria - Gelee.
1925 . . . Fell. (Sir E.Edgar) 13.10-0. G.Turner. 40/1.

POP AHEAD
chestnut gelding by Devolution - Chatalja.
1926 . . . Finished 12th of 30. (Mrs Holroyd Smith) 8.10-0. S.Regan. 66/1.
1927 . . . Fell. (Mr H.Fowler) 9.10-13. Mr.H.Fowler. 40/1.

PEGGIE'S PRIDE
chestnut gelding by Tidal Wave - Magic Maid.
1930 . . . Fell. (Mr H.B.Brandt) 7.10-11. T.McCarthy. 33/1.

PARIS FLIGHT
bay gelding by Rabelais - L'Adorable.
1930 . . . Pulled-up. (Mr W.Harris) 10.10-7. E.Vinall. 100/1.

PIXIE
bay mare by Battle-Axe - Persimma.
1931 . . . Refused. (Mrs D.Fitzgerald) 6.10-7. Capt.R.E.Sassoon. 100/1.

PELORUS JACK
chestnut gelding by Golden Orb - Lady Fairstead.
1932 . . . Fell. (Mr C.P.Brocklehurst) aged.10-7. Mr.R.G.Fanshawe. 22/1.
1933 . . . Fell. (Mrs B.D.Davis) aged.10-7. W.Stott. 100/6.
1934 . . . Fell. (Mrs B.D.Davis) aged.11-2. W.Stott. 25/1.

PRINCE CHERRY
bay gelding by My Prince - Cherry Branch 11.
1932 . . . Refused. (Mr M.D.Blair) 8.10-7. J.Geary. 100/1.
1934 . . . Refused. (Mr M.D.Blair) 10.10-11. J.Goswell. 66/1.

PARSON'S WELL
chestnut gelding by Abbot's Trace - Veradale.
1934 . . . Fell. (Mr G.Bates) 10.11-8. W.Hollick. 66/1.

PRINCESS MIR
chestnut mare by Mirador - Kangaroo Kate.
1935 . . . Fell. (Mr D.A.Jackson) 10.10-7. Mr.D.A.Jackson. 50/1.

PROVOCATIVE
bay gelding by Sun Yat-Sen - Ovoca.
1936 . . . Finished 6th of 35. (Mrs J. de Selincourt) 6.10-9. E.Brown. 33/1.
1938 . . . Finished 12th of 38. (Mrs J. de selincourt) 8.10-7. T.F.Rimell. 22/1.

PERSIAN SUN
brown gelding by Chosroes - Heliope.
1936 . . . Fell. (Mr H.B.Brandt) 10.10-12. E.Vinall. 66/1.

PENCRAIK
bay gelding by Corn Kale - Lady Vain.
1936 . . . Refused. (Mrs I.Strang) 9.10-7. J.Lynn,jnr. 100/1.
1937 . . . Finished 6th of 33. (Mr A.Pilkington) 10.10-3. G.Archibald. 25/1.
1939 . . . Finished 8th of 37. (Mr A.Pilkington) 12.10-0. A.Scratchley. 100/1.

PUCKA BELLE
bay mare by Pucka Sahib - Zriabelle.
1937 . . . Finished 3rd of 33. (Mr E.W.W.Bailey) 11.10-7. Mr.E.W.W.Bailey. 100/6.

PASSING FANCY
brown gelding by Passport - Polly Dear.
1937 . . . Fell. (Lord Berner) 9.10-5. D.Holland. 100/1.

PONTET
brown mare by Ponteland - Farnagh.
1938 . . . Fell. (Mr G.V.Malcolmson) 8.11-7. J.Parkinson. 66/1.

PROMINENT LAD
chestnut gelding by Catalin - Eminent Lady.
1938 . . . Fell. (Mrs E.Tozer) 7.10-2. H.Jones. 100/1.

PERFECT PART
bay gelding by Perfectus - Part Two.
1939 . . . Fell. (Mrs V.Fitzgerald) 9.10-13. J.Ward. 33/1.

PROFESSOR II, THE
bay gelding by Periosteum - Lady Rockville.
1940 . . . Finished 6th of 30. (Mrs I.Strang) 9.11-8. G.R.Owen.100/8.

PRINCE REGENT
bay gelding by My Prince - Nemaea.
1946 . . . Finished 3rd of 34. (Mr J.V.Rank) 11.12-5. T.Hyde. 3/1.Fav*
1947 . . . Finished 4th of 57. (Mr J.V.Rank) 12.12-7. T.Hyde. 8/1.Fav*
1948 . . . Carried-out. (Mr J.V.Rank) 13.12-2. T.Hyde. 25/1.

PARTHENON
bay gelding by Cottage - Greek Girl.
1947 . . . Fell. (Lord Bicester) 8.10-0. P.Murray. 40/1.
1948 . . . Finished 7th of 43. (Lord Bicester) 9.10-0. P.Murray. 100/1.
1949 . . . Fell. (Lord Bicester) 10. 10-5. R.Bates. 66/1.

PRATTLER
brown gelding by Praetor - Lady Jackdaw.
1947 . . . Fell. (Mr E.Manners) 12.10-0. P.Conlon. 50/1.

PATRICKSWELL
bay gelding by Bosworth - Fireship.
1947 . . . Carried-out. (Mr Smurfit) 9.10-0. P.Cahalin. 100/1.

PLATYPUS
chestnut gelding by Trimdon - Bombay Duck.
1948 . . . Finished 5th of 43. (Mr R.I.Sainsbury) 7.10-6. A.Jack. 66/1.

PERFECT NIGHT
brown gelding by Kippet Lee - Perfect Lady.
1949 . . . Finished 11th of 43. (Mr A.F.M.Wright) 11.10-0. Mr.D.Ancil. 66/1.

POSSIBLE
bay gelding by Steel Point - Recollection.
1950 . . . Fell. (Duchess of Norfolk) 10.10-1. P.Conlon. 50/1.
1952 . . . Fell. (Mr E.Weymouth) 12.11-0. Mr.E.Weymouth.100/1.

PASTIME
bay or brown mare by Cottage - Chattanooga.
1950 . . . Fell. (Brigadier R.O.Critchley) 9.10-0. C.Sleator. 66/1.

PRINCE BROWNIE
bay gelding by Brownie - Latonia.
1951 . . . Fell. (Lady Carew-Pole) 9.10-9. A.Grantham. 33/1.

PARTPOINT
brown gelding by Steel Point - Part Two.
1951 . . . Fell. (Major A.C.Straker) 9.10-5. A.P.Thompson. 33/1.

PARSONSHILL
brown gelding by Brown Jester - Pillion Girl.
1951 . . . Fell. (Mr J.Seely) 12.10-2. Mr.J.Seely. 100/1.
1952 . . . Finished 9th of 47. (Mr J.Seely) 13.10-1. Mr.J.Seely. 100/1.

PRINTERS PIE
bay gelding by Epigram - Imprint.
1952 . . . Finished 6th of 47. (Lt.Col.J.Harrison) 8.10-0. G.Slack.100/1.

PEARLY PRINCE
bay gelding by Artist's Prince - dam believed to be Purley.
1952 . . . Fell. (Mr A.Leigh Boulter) 9.10-5. D.Leslie. 25/1.
1953 . . . Fell. (Mr A.Leigh Boulter) 10.10-0. R.E.Jenkins. 66/1.

PARASOL II
brown mare by Soldado - Skilligalee.
1953 . . . Fell. (Mr A.A.Walton) 8.10-4. Mr.A.Oughton. 25/1.

PUNCHESTOWN STAR
brown horse by Bidar - English Summer.
1953 . . . Fell. (Mr J.G.Greenaway) 9.10-0. S.McComb. 66/1.
1954 . . . Refused. (Mr J.G.Greenaway) 10.10-0. S.McComb. 66/1.

PRINCE OF ARRAGON
brown gelding by Foroughi - Coolgaragh.
1954 . . . Fell. (Mr T.A.Connolly) 13.10-2. J.Gorey. 66/1.

PARIS NEW YORK
bay gelding by Victrix - Rosalinde.
1954 . . . Fell. (Mr R.E.Ansell) 7.10-0. M.Roberts. 66/1.

PIPPYKIN
chestnut gelding by Escamillo - Relizane.
1955 . . . Refused. (Mr R.D.Darragh) 8.10-0. J.Power. 100/7.
1958 . . . Fell. (Mr K.R.Redfern) 10.10-5. T.Brookshaw. 22/1.

POLONIUS
chestnut gelding by Epigram - Charmain.
1956 . . . Refused. (Mrs D.Hailstone) 10.10-3. E.F.Kelly. 66/1.

PRINCESS GARTER
bay mare by His Reverence - Dysie's Garter.
1958 . . . Fell. (Mr E.Davies) 11.10-3. Mr.W.Roberts. 66/1.

PINTAIL
chestnut gelding by Torbido - Cornduck.
1959 . . . Pulled-up. (Mr J.P.Bissill) 10.10-4. B.Wilkinson. 100/1.

PENDLE LADY
brown mare by War Lord - Avondhu Belle.
1960 . . . Fell. (Mr A.Watson) 10.10-4. M.Towers. 40/1.

PENNY FEATHER
bay gelding by Mayfair 111 - The Pensioner.
1961 . . . Pulled-up. (Mr N.Hall) 8.10-1. J.Lehane. 66/1.

POLITICS
chestnut gelding by Preciptic - Lonely Polly.
1962 . . . Finished 16th of 32. (Mrs T.M.Stuck) 10.10-0. D.Bassett. 100/1.

PEACETOWN
bay gelding by Phalorain - Maytown.
1963 . . . Fell. (Mrs F.Williams) 9.10-4. R.Langley. 50/1.
1964 . . . Finished 3rd of 33. (Mrs F.Williams) 10.10-1. R.Edwards. 40/1.
1965 . . . Finished 13th of 47. (Mrs F.Williams) 11.11-0. P.Pickford. 25/1.

PURPLE SILK
brown gelding by Flush Royal - Pure Silk.
1964 . . . Finished 2nd of 33. (Mr T.Beattie) 9.104. J.Kenneally. 100/6.

PAS SEUL
bay or brown gelding by Erin's Pride - Pas de Quatre.
1964 . . . Fell. (Mr J.Rogerson) 11.12-0. D.V.Dick. 22/1.

PAPPAGENO'S COTTAGE
chestnut gelding by Pappageno 11 - Dawn Cottage.
1964 . . . Finished 10th of 33. (Mr W.G.King) 9.11-0. P.Taaffe. 100/7.co/Fav.*

PONTIN-GO
brown gelding by Roi de Navarre 11 - Intuition.
Formerly named Gay Navarree.
1964 . . . Finished 5th of 33. (Mr F.W.Pontin) 12.10-0. P.Jones. 66/1.
1965 . . . Fell. (Mr F.W.Pontin) 13.10-13. J.Lehane. 50/1.
1966 . . . Fell. (Mr F.W.Pontin) 14.10-0. T.M.Jones. 100/1.

PHEBU
bay mare by Phebus - Prancing Nancy.
1965 . . . Brought-down. (Mr N.Brereton) 8.10-13. J.Morrissey. 33/1.

PACKED HOME
bay gelding by Cisco Kid - Ballinveney 11.
1966 . . . Fell. (Mr R.R.Guest) 11.10-3. T.Carberry. 33/1.
1967 . . . Finished 5th of 44. (Mr R.R.Guest) 12.10-0. T.Carberry. 100/1.

POPHAM DOWN
bay gelding by Combat - Penelope Ann.
1966 . . . Fell. (Mrs C.Turriff) 9.10-0. G.W.Robinson. 22/1.
1967 . . . Brought-down. (Mrs C.Turriff) 10.10-0. M.Gifford. 66/1.

PRINCEFUL
brown gelding by Devon Prince - Verite.
1967 . . . Brought-down. (Mr R.R.Hitchins) 9.10-2. R.Edwards.100/1.
1968 . . . Finished 9th of 45. (Mr R.R.Hitchins) 10.10-4. J.Leech. 66/1.

PENVULGO
bay gelding by Vulgan - Pengo.
1967 . . . Pulled-up. (Mr J.D.McKechnie) 8.10-0. J.Lehane. 50/1.

PHEMIUS
brown gelding by Melody Maker - Lucy Glitters.
1968 . . . Pulled-up. (Mrs D.Bannister) 10.10-8. G.Scott. 50/1.

PORTATION
grey gelding by Infatuation - Port Beam.
1968 . . . Brought-down. (Mr D.H.Ellison) 10.10-0. G.Cramp. 100/1.

POLARIS MISSILE
chestnut mare by Woodcut - Air Wedding.
1968 . . . Fell. (Mr M.J.Thorne) 9.10-0. Mr.N.Thorne. 66/1.

PECCARD
grey gelding by Hard Ridden - Taipecc.
1969 . . . Fell. (Mr G.Sloan) 8.10-4. Mr.G.Sloan. 50/1.

PRIDE OF KENTUCKY
bay gelding by Primera -Highland Jewel.
1970 . . . Finished 6th of 28. (Mr E.R.Courage) 8.10-0. J.Buckingham. 13/1.
1971 . . . Brought-down. (Mr E.R.Courage) 9.10-0. A.Mawson. 50/1.

PERMIT
chestnut gelding by Rockefella - Persian Mite.
1970 . . . Brought-down. (Mr T.T.Lennon) 7.10-3. P.Buckley. 35/1.
1972 . . . Fell. (Mr J.Pickavance) 9.10-0. R.R.Evans. 100/1.

PERRY HILL
chestnut gelding by Domaha - Miss Victoria.
1970 . . . Fell. (Mr J.U.Baillie) 11.10-0. P.Kelleway. 28/1.

PERSIAN HELEN
bay mare Persian Gulf - Dark Helen.
1970 . . . Refused. (Mr P.E.Smith) 7.10-0. D.T.Hughes. 35/1.

PANTHEON, THE
bay gelding by Domaha - Davon Cawvoge.
1972 . . . Fell. (Mr J.A.Dillon) 9.10-4. K.White. 33/1.

PEARL OF MONTREAL
bay gelding by Pearl Orient - Montreal 11.
1972 . . . Pulled -up. (Mr G.F.F.Fasenfield) 9.10-4. R.Coonan. 55/1.
1974 . . . Pulled-up. (Mr G.F.Fasenfield) 11.10-0. T.Kinane. 50/1.

POOKA, THE
brown horse by Doubtless 11 - Lilac Fairy.
1972 . . . Fell. (Mr C.Ross) 10.10-5. Mr.C.Ross. 50/1.
1973 . . . Finished 12th of 38. (Mrs J.Bowes-Lyon) 11.10-0. A.Moore. 100/1.

PROUD TARQUIN
brown gelding by Black Tarquiin - Leney Princess.
1973 . . . Finished 7th of 38. (Sir John Thompson) 10.10-11. Lord Oaksey. 22/1.

PROPHECY
chestnut gelding by Zarathustra - Parlez-Vous.
1973 . . . Finished 8th of 38. (Mrs C.M.Richards) 10.10-3. B.R.Davies. 20/1.

PRINCESS CAMILLA
bay mare by Prince Barle- Ghana Princess.
1973 . . . Pulled-up. (Mr J.E.Bigg) 8.10-4. R.Barry. 16/1.
1974 . . . Finished 17th of 42. (Miss C.H.Bartholomew) 9.11-4. M.Blackshaw. 28/1.

PROUD PERCY
bay gelding by Guide - Penny Jiffy.
1973 . . . Fell. (Mr R.F.Fisher) 10.10-0. R.R.Evans. 100/1.

PETRUCHIO'S SON
bay gelding by Straight Rule - Bonnie Kate.
1973 . . . Finished 11th of 38. (Mr P.Blackburn) 10.10-5. D.Mould. 50/1.

PERPOL
bay gelding by Perhapsburg - Polenta.
1976 . . . Pulled-up. (Mr O.J.Henley) 10.10-6. K.White. 66/1.

PROLAN
grey gelding by Perhapsburg - Sinic.
1976 . . . Brought-down. (Mr M.Cuddy) 7.10-3. M.F.Morris. 13/1.

PILGARLIC, THE
bay gelding by Royal Buck - What A Daisy.
1977 . . . Finished 4th of 42. (Mr & Mrs A.Poole) 9.10-4. R.R.Evans. 40/1.
1978 . . . Finished 5th of 37. (Mr & Mrs A.Poole) 10.10-1. R.R.Evans.33/1.
1979 . . . Finished 4th of 34. (Mr & Mrs A.Poole) 11.10-1. R.R.Evans. 16/1.
1980 . . . Finished 3rd of 30.(Mr & Mrs A.Poole) 12.10-4.R.Hyett.33/1.

PENGRAIL
bay gelding by Pendragon - Sovereign.
1977 . . . Fell. (Mrs G.T.Morton & Mrs C.E.Thornton) 9.10-8. R.Atkins. 15/1.

PRINCE ROCK
bay gelding by Autre Prince - Roxana 111.
1977 . . . Fell. (Mr M.Buckley) 9.10-6. G.Thorner. 18/1.
1980 . . . Refused. (Mr M.Buckley & Mr F.R.Watts) 12.11-0. T.Carmody. 12/1.

PRIME JUSTICE
chestnut gelding by Primera - Jedburgh Justice.
1979 . . . Finished 7th of 34. (Mr D.A.Malam) 9.10-0. A.K.Taylor. 200/1.

PURDO
chestnut gelding by Lomond - Foveaux Strait.
1979 . . . Fell. (Mr D.W.Samuel) 8.10-11. R.Champion. 25/1.

PACIFY
brown gelding by Rose Knight - Rapossi.
1981 . . . Fell. (Mr C.R.Glyn & Mr B.G.Norman) 11.10-0. S.Jobar. 50/1.

PETER SCOT
bay gelding by Jock Scot - Miss Peter.
1982 . . . Fell. (Mr G.Amey) 11.11-5. P.Barton. 16/1.

PEATY SANDY
bay gelding by Spartan General - Petlow.
1983 . . . Finished 6th of 41. (Exors of the late Mrs I.Hamilton) 9.11-3. T.G.Dun. 12/1.

POLITICAL POP
brown gelding by Politico - Nailing.
1983 . . . Finished 7th of 41. (Mrs A.Starkie) 9.11-3. G.Bradley. 28/1.

PILOT OFFICER
chestnut gelding by Charlottesvilles Flyer - Ellerslie.
1983 . . . Fell. (Mr R.A.Padmore) 8.10-7. S.Morshead. 22/1.
1984 . . . Refused. (Mr R.A.Padmore) 9.10-2.Mr.A.Sharpe. 33/1.

POYNTZ PASS
brown gelding by Gail Star - Limefield Rita.
1984 . . . Finished 21st of 40. (Mr T.F.Harty) 9.10-5. H.Rogers. 100/1.

PLUNDERING
bay gelding by Brave Invader - Ethel's Delight.
1986 . . . Fell. (Mrs Miles Valentine) 9.10-0. S.Sherwood. 25/1.
1987 . . . Finished 16th of 40. (Mrs Miles Valentine) 10.10-11. P.Scudamore. 16/1.

PORT ASKAIG
brown gelding by Quayside - Stargrace.
1986 . . . Fell. (Lord Chelsea) 11.10-0. G.McCourt. 35/1.

PREBEN FUR
bay gelding by Mon Capitaine - Flashing Beauty.
1987 . . . Finished 17th of 40. (Mr J.A.Thole) 10.10-0. A.Stringer.66/1.
1988 . . . Pulled-up. (Mr J.A.Thole) 11.10-0. S.J.O'Neill.100/1.

POLLY'S PAL
bay or brown gelding by Secret Ace - Early Echo.
1988 . . . Jockey knocked out of saddle. (Mr S.G.Payne) 10.10-0. J.K.Kinane.100/1.

PERRIS VALLEY
bay gelding by Le Bavard - Margerval.
1989 . . . Fell. (Mr M.J.Smurfit) 8.10-0. B.Sheridan. 16/1.

POLAR NOMAD
brown gelding by Mandalus - Polar Lady.
1989 . . . Pulled-up. (James Stoddart Ltd.) 8.10-0. A.Merrigan. 80/1.

PUKKA MAJOR
grey gelding by Le Fabuleux - Pakeha. Bred in U.S.A.
1990 . . . Unseated rider. (Mrs S.Thomson Jones) 9.10-4. M.Richards. 100/1.

POLYFEMUS
chestnut gelding by Pollerton - Bardicate.
1990 . . . Pulled-up. (Mr G.Johnson) 8.10-2. R.Rowe. 18/1.

PARTY POLITICS
brown gelding by Politico - Spin Again.
1992 . . . WON. (Mrs D.Thompson) 8.10-7. 40 Ran. C.Llewellyn. 14/1.
1995 . . . Finished 2nd of 35. (Mrs D.Thompson) 11.10-2. M.Dwyer. 16/1.
1996 . . . Fell. (Mrs D.Thompson) 12.10-11. C.Llewellyn. 10/1.

PACO'S BOY
bay gelding by Good Thyne - Jeremique.
1994 . . . Pulled-up. (Mr M.B.Jones) 9.10-0. M.Foster. 200/1.

QUICKSILVER
1847 . . . Failed to finish. (Colonel Taylor) - 10-4. Rawson. n/q.

QUADRUPED
1850 . . . Failed to finish. (Mr Cunningham) - 10-8. G.Arran. n/q.

Q. C.
chestnut gelding by Rataplan - Miss Melbourne.
1869 . . . Finished 5th of 22. (Mr Lynton) 5.10-9. Griffiths. 20/1.
1870 . . . Finished 7th of 23. (Mr H.May) 6.10-10. Mr.A.Yates.100/7.

QUEEN OF KILDARE
chestnut mare by Kidderminster - Hibernia.
1879 . . . Fell. (Mr P.Doucie) 6.11-5. J.Doucie. 40/1.

QUEEN IMAAL
bay mare by Denis Richard - Brown Prince.
* 1917 . . . Completed course. (Col.R.L.Birkin) 9.11-3. A.Newey. 25/1.
* 1918 . . . Completed course. (Mr H.Denison) 10.10-7. A.Newey. 50/1.

QUITE CALM
bay gelding by Loch Lomond - Silver Sea.
1932 . . . Fell. (Mr R.E.Morel) 8.10-7. F.Gurney. 20/1.

QUEEN OF THE DANDIES
bay mare by Last Of The Dandies - Movie Queen.
1951 . . . Fell. (Mrs R.Fowler) 10.10-0. R.Carter. 100/1.

QUITE NATURALLY
chestnut gelding by Tartan or Young Chevalier - Pat's Princess.
1953 . . . Fell. (Mrs G.Kohn) 9.10-8. T.Molony. 18/1.

QUARE TIMES
bay gelding by Artist's Son - Lavenco. Bred by Mr.P.P.Sweeney.
1955 . . . WON. (Mrs W.H.E.Welman) 9.11-0. 30 Ran. P.Taaffe. 100/9.

QUINTIN BAY
bay mare by Copernicus - dam by Oojah.
1965 . . . Pulled-up. (Mr Skeets Martin) 9.10-13. P.Taaffe. 25/1.
1966 . . . Finished 6th of 47. (Mr Skeets Martin) 10.10-0. J.Cullen. 100/1.
1967 . . . Finished 11th of 44. (Mr Skeets Martin) 11.10-0. J.Cullen. 50/1.
1968 . . . Finished 17th of 45. (Mr Skeets Martin) 12.10-0. G.W.Robinson. 66/1.

QUITTE OU DOUBLE L
bay gelding by Le Tyrol - Golden Lily.
1968 . . . Fell. (Mrs A Besnouin) 8.10-8. Mr.J.Ciechanowski. 66/1.

QUEEN'S GUIDE
bay mare by Guide - Regal Coin.
1970 . . . Brought-down. (Mr W.Wade) 9.10-0. Mr.G.Wade. 40/1.

QUINTUS
brown gelding by Quorum - Tiberetta.
1974 . . . Finished 12th of 42. (Mr E.R.Courage) 8.10-0. G.Thorner. 33/1.

QUEENSWAY BOY
chestnut gelding by Kemal - Oscilllation.
1989 . . . Refused. (Queensway Securities Ltd.) 10.10-0. A.Webb. 50/1.

QUIRINUS
bay gelding by Hugben - Quartela. Bred in Slovak Republic.
1994 . . . Unseated rider. (Laksarska Nova Ves) 12.11-10. J.Brecka. 250/1.

RAILROAD
1839 . . . Finished 6th of 17. (Captain Marshall) Mr.Powell. n/q.

RAMBLER
1839 . . . Fell. (Mr H.S.Bowen) Morgan. n/q.

RUST
1839 . . . Pulled-up. (Mr T.Ferguson) Mr.W.McDonough.

REVEALER
1841 . . . Finished 4th of 11. (Mr Villebois) Mr.Barker.

RETURNED, THE
1842 . . . Finished 4th of 15. (Mr W.Hope-Johnstone) Mr.W.HopeJohnstone. 15/1.
1843 . . . Finished 9th of 16. (Mr W.Sterling Crawford) Major Campbell. 4/1.
1844 . . . Finished 2nd of 15. (Mr W.Sterling Crawford) Scott. 15/1.

REDWIING
1843 . . . Fell. (Lord Waterford) Doolan. 8/1.

ROMP, THE
1843 . . . Refused. (Mr Lamplugh) Holingshed. n/q.
1844 . . . Finished 6th of 15. (Lord S.Bentinck) L.Byrne. 25/1.
1845 . . . Failed to finish. (Mr R.H.Jones) Thompson. n/q.

ROBINSON
1844 . . . Refused. (Mr Milbank) Parker. n/q.

REGALIA
1846 . . . Fell. (Lord Waterford) Doolan. n/q.

RED LANCER
1847 . . . Pulled-up. (Lord Strathmore) - 10-8. Lord Strathmore. 20/1.

RAT-TRAP
1850 . . . Failed to finish. (Lord Strathmore) - 11-7. Frisby. 9/1.
1851 . . . Finished 6th of 21. (Mr T.F.Mason) - 10-10. J.Mason. 6/1.Fav.*

ROY-DE-AISEY
1850 . . . Failed to finish. (Lord Lurgan) 5.10-10. Magee. n/q.

REINDEER
formerly named Frank.
1851 . . . Finished 9th of 21. (Mr May) - 9-8. C.Planner. n/q.

RAINBOW
1850 . . . Fell. (Mr J.C.Ranton) - 10-8. Dalby. n/q.

ROYAL BLUE
1852 . . . Fell (Mr Harding) - 9-0. G.Stevens. 100/1.

ROYALTY
1854 . . . Failed to finish. (Captain Rhys) 5. 9-4. Ennis. 50/1.

RED ROSE
1857 . . . Failed to finish. (Mr T.Hughes) - 9-8. J.Hughes. n/q.

ROMEO
1857 . . . Fell. (Mr T.Hughes) - 9-6. D.White. 100/6.
1862 . . . Finished 3rd of 13. (Mr C.Bennett) - 8-12. Mr.C.Bennett. 100/8.
1864 . . . Fell. (Mr de Gray) - 11-0. F.Martin. 33/1.

REDWING
1860 . . . Failed to finish. (Mr Aylmer) - 10-8. Rourke. n/q.
1861 . . . Fell. (Mr E.J.Gannon) - 9-7. J.Murphy. 25/1.

ROVER, THE
1861 . . . Failed to finish. (Mr J.S.Wilson) - 8-8. F.Page. n/q.

REAL JAM

1863 . . . Failed to finish. (Mr T.Hughes) 4. 9-11. D.Hughes. 20/1.
1864 . . . Failed to finish. (Mr T.Hughes) 5.10-8. D.Hughes. 11/1.
1866 . . . Failed to finish. (Mr F.Hughes) 7.10-0. D.Hughes. 12/1.

REPORTER

1864 . . . Fell. (Mr Fiddaman) - 12-2. Mr.Dixon. 40/1.
1866 . . . Failed to finish. (Lord Poulett) - 11-4. R.French. 50/1.

REVOLVER

bay horse by Artillery - Michaelmas Daisy. Formerly named Spring Daisy.
1867 . . . Finished 6th of 23. (Mr T.Jackson) Igoe. n/q.

ROBBER, THE

bay horse by Tadmor - dam by The Saddler.
1869 . . . Finished 8th of 22. (Mr Doncaster) - 11-2. Mr.P.Merton. 100/1.

RUFUS

chestnut gelding by William The Conqueror - dam unknown.
1871 . . . Finished 7th of 25. (Capt.J.F.Montgomery) 7.11-4. Ryan. 100/1.
1872 . . . Failed to finish. (Capt.J.F.Montgomery) 8.11-4. J.Potter. 25/1.

RYSHWORTH

bay horse by Skirmisher - Vertumna.
1872 . . . Fell. (Mr H.Chaplin) 6.10-12. Boxall. n/q.
1873 . . . Finished 2nd of 28. (Mr H.Chaplin) 7.11-8. Boxall. n/q.

ROYAL IRISH FUSILIER

chestnut horse by Royal Oak Day - dam unknown.
1872 . . . Pulled-up. (Baron Oppenheim) 8.10-6. T.Andrews. n/q.

REVIRESCAT

chestnut gelding by Cheerful Horn - dam unknown.
1873 . . . Failed to finish. (Mr J.S.H.Maxwell) 7.11-8. Mr.W.H.Johnstone. n/q.

RED NOB

chestnut gelding by Neville - dam unknown.
1873 . . . Fell. (Mr Sankey) 7.11-3. Mr.J.Goodwin. 40/1.

REUGNY

chestnut horse by Minos - Reine Blanche. Bred in France.
1873 . . . Failed to finish. (Lord Aylesford) 5.10-13. J.Cannon. 40/1.
1874 . . . WON. (Capt.J.Machell) 6.10-12. Mr.J.M.Richardson. 5/1.Fav.*
1877 . . . Pulled-up. (Mr Gomm) 9.11-6. Mr.E.P.Wilson. 8/1.

RICHARD I

chestnut horse by Master Richard - Weatherwise.
1873 . . . Failed to finish. (Capt.McCalmont) 5.10-3. C.Gray. 50/1.

RYE

bay gelding by Brown Bread - Tartlet.
1876 . . . Finished 5th of 19.(Mr W.Weston) 6.10-0. G.Waddington.20/1.

REGAL

black gelding by Saunterer - Regalia. Bred by Mr W.Graham.
1876 . . . WON. (Capt.J.Machell) 5.11-3. 19 Ran.J.Cannon. 25/1.
1877 . . . Fell. (Lord Lonsdale) 6.12-2. Jewitt. 8/1.
1879 . . . Finished 6th of 18. (Capt.J.Machell) 8.11-10. Jewitt. 5/2.Fav* Remounted*.
1880 . . . Fell. (Lord Aylesford) 9.11-11. J.Cannon. 5/1.Fav*
1881 . . . Finished 2nd of 13. (Capt.J.Machell) 10.11-2. J.Jewitt. 11/1.
1884 . . . Pulled-up. (Capt.J.Machell) 13.11-6. W.Hunt. 50/1.

ROSSANMORE

bay horse by Yorkminster - dam unknown.
1879 . . . Finished 7th of 18. (Mr J.Connolly) aged.10-7. Toole. 50/1.

ROQUEFORT
brown gelding by Winslow - Cream Cheese. Bred by Mr.J.Gretton.
1884 . . . Finished 3rd of 15. (Capt.Fisher) 5.10-5. J.Childs. 10/1.
1885 . . . WON. (Mr A.Cooper) 6.11-0. 19 Ran. Mr.E.P.Wilson. 100/30.Fav.*
1886 . . . Fell. (Mr A.Cooper) 7.12-3. Mr.E.P.Wilson. 5/1.
1887 . . . Fell. (Mr J.Lee) 8.12-8. Mr.E.P.Wilson. 7/1.
1889 . . . Fell. (Mr Abington) 10.12-0. Mr.E.P.Wilson. 6/1.Fav.*
1891 . . . Finished 4th of 21. (Mr A.Yates) 12.11-13. F.Guy. 40/1.

REDPATH
chestnut gelding by Uncas - Maggie.
1885 . . . Finished 4th of 19. (Mr Zigomala) 8.10-3. Mr.A.Coventry. 20/1.
1886 . . . Failed to finish. (Mr P.J.Zigomala) 9.11-7. Mr.G.Lambton. 100/6.

RED HUSSAR
chestnut gelding by Lord Ronald - Zouave.
1885 . . . Finished 9th of 19. (Capt.Armitage) 7.10-7. Capt.Armitage. 50/1.

RINGLET
black mare by Highborn - Ladywell.
1888 . . . Finished 4th of 20. (Lord Rodney) 7.11-11. T.Skelton. 100/9.
1889 . . . Finished 8th of 20. (Mr N.Fenwick) 8.11-12. J.Walsh. 66/1.

ROMAN OAK
bay gelding by Ascetic - dam by Whistlebinkie.
1891 . . . Knocked-over. (Mr W.Leetham) 7.12-0. H.Escott. 100/9.
1893 . . . Finished 7th of 15. (Sir H de Trafford) 9.11-9. Mr.W.P.Cullen. 40/1.

RELIANCE
bay or brown gelding by Acetic - Ladywell.
1892 . . . Finished 8th of 25. (Mr W.Whitehead) 10.10-8. Mr.J.C.Cheney. 200/1.

ROLLESBY
chestnut gelding by Troll - Clarissima.
1892 . . . Pulled-up. (Mr O.Vincent-Turner) 7.10-5. H.Brown. 50/1.

ROYAL BUCK
brown gelding by Edward The Confessor - Antelope.
1895 . . . Pulled-up. (Mr F.Greswolde-Williams) 8.10-4. W.Slinn.50/1.

RORY O'MORE
chestnut gelding by Town Moor - Iolanthe.
1896 . . . Finished 6th of 28. (Mr C.Hibbert) 6.10-9. R.Nightingall. 7/1.Fav.*

REDHILL
chestnut gelding by Rotherhill - Whitelegs.
1896 . . . Fell. (Capt.J.E.Aikin) 8.10-12. Mr.G.S.Davies. 100/1.

RED CROSS
bay mare by Ascetic - Ruby.
1897 . . . Fell. (Mr J.E.Rogerson) 6.10-1. H.Taylor. 100/1.

ROBIN HOOD IV
chestnut gelding by Red Prince 11 - dam unknown.
1904 . . . Finished 5th of 26. (Mr E.E.Lennon) 6.10-3. A.Magee. 33/1.
1909 . . . Finished 8th of 32. (Capt.L.H.Jones) 11. 9-9. Mr.R.H.Walker. 33/1.

RAILOFF
bay gelding by Peterhof - Railstown.
1904 . . . Fell. (Mr H.K.Hamilton-Wedderburn) 7. 9-9. E.Sullivan. n/q.

RUNUNCULUS
brown gelding by Quidnunc - Buttercup.
1905 . . . Finished 4th of 27. (Mr T.Nolan) 7. 9-12. C.Hollebone. 7/1.

ROYAL DRAKE
brown gelding by Royal Emperor - Manganese.
1905 . . . Fell. (Sir P.Walker) 7.10-4. A.Waddington. 20/1.

RED LAD
chestnut gelding by Red Prince 11 - Border Lassie.
1906 . . . Finished 2nd of 23. (Mr E.M.Lucas) 6.10-2. C.Kelly. 33/1.
1907 . . . Fell. (Mr C.Hibbert) 7.11-3. J.Dillon. 7/1.jnt/Fav.*

ROMAN LAW
bay gelding by Tacitus - Lady Beatrice.
1906 . . . Knocked-over. (Mr A.Buckley,jnr.) 8.11-5. M.Walsh. 100/7.
1907 . . . Pulled-up. (Mr A.Buckley,jnr.) 9.11-7. A.Anthony. n/q.
1908 . . . Fell. (Mr A.Buckley,jnr.) 10.11-2. A.Newey. 100/7.

RAVENSCLIFFE
bay gelding by Ravensbury - Marie le Ragois.
1907 . . . Finished 4th of 23. (Mr R.J.Hannam) 9.10-9. F.Lyall.100/7.

RATHVALE
chestnut gelding by Northshampton - Ignis-Fatuus.
1907 . . . Fell. (Prince Hatzfeldt) 6.10-13. E.Driscoll. 20/1.
1909 . . . Finished 13th of 32. (Prince Hatzfeldt) 8.11-7. W.Morgan. 100/1.
1910 . . . Fell. (Prince Hatzfeldt) 9.11-1. R.Morgan. 66/1.

RUBIO
chestnut gelding by Star Ruby - La Toquera. Bred by Mr.J.B.Ali Haggin in U.S.A.
1908 . . . WON. (Maj.F.Douglas-Pennant) 10.10-5. 24 Ran. H.B.Bletsoe. 66/1.
1909 . . . Fell. (Maj.F.Douglas-Pennant) 11.11-9. W.Bissill. 20/1.

RED HALL
chestnut gelding by Winkfield - dam by Cairo.
1908 . . . Finished 6th of 24. (Mr H.G.Farrant) 11.10-8. Mr.H.G.Farrant. 66/1.
1909 . . . Finished 15th of 32. (Mr H.G.Farrant) 12.10-12. Remounted* Mr.H.G.Farrant.50/1.

RUSTIC QUEEN
brown mare by Bergomask - Forest Queen.
1909 . . . Fell. (Mr H.Hartland) 7.12-0. Mr.A.W.Wood. 50/1.

RED MONK
chestnut gelding by Timothy - Miss Leap Year.
1909 . . . Pulled-up. (Mr F.W.Greswolde-Williams) 11.10-6. E.Morgan. 100/1.

RATHNALLY
bay gelding by St Pat - Alanna.
1911 . . . Finished 2nd of 26. (Mr O.H.Jones) 6.11-0. R.Chadwick. 8/1. Remounted*
1912 . . . Fell. (Mr O.H.Jones) 7.11-11. R.Chadwick. 7/2.jnt/Fav.*

RORY O'MOORE
chestnut gelding by Royal Meath - Vandala.
1911 . . . Knocked-over. (Mr P.Whitaker) 10.11-6. Mr.P.Whitaker. 100/7.
1912 . . . Failed to finish. (Mr P.Whitaker) 11.11-7. F.Mason. 9/1.
1914 . . . Finished 4th of 20. (Mr P.Whitaker) 13.11-8. Mr.P.Whitaker. 20/1.

ROMAN CANDLE
chestnut gelding by Robertson - Fireworks.
1911 . . . Fell. (Mr W.F.Stratton) 9. 9-7. T.Willmot. 28/1.

REGENT
bay horse by Diamond Jubilee - Western Flower.
1912 . . . Failed to finish. (Sir George Bullough) 7.10-8. F.Morgan.n/q.
1913 . . . Fell. (Sir George Bullough) 8.11-7. Mr.J.R.Anthony.66/1.
1914 . . . Broke-down. (Sir George Bullough) 9.10-12. Mr.H.W.Tyrwhitt-Drake. 33/1.

REJECTED IV, THE
bay gelding by Toussaint - Katie Hermit.
1913 . . . Fell. (Mr E.Platt) 10.11-3. Mr.G.Cotton. 40/1.

RUBINSTEIN
chestnut gelding by Star Ruby - Numeroet. Bred in U.S.A.
1919 . . . Fell. (Lt.Col.F.Douglas-Pennant) 12.11-0. W.Payne. 50/1.

RATHER DARK
bay gelding by Dark Ronald - Jane Shore.
1921 . . . Fell. (Mr W.H.Midwood) 7.10-12. A.Gregson. 33/1.

RUFUS XXI
chestnut gelding by Cherry Tree - dam unknown.
1921 . . . Fell. (Lt.Col.G.Brooke) 10.10-0. Capt.E.C.Doyle. n/q.

REDSTART V
chestnut gelding by Hawfinch - dam by Rugby.
1921 . . . Fell. (Major A.W.H.James) 13. 9-9. Maj.A.W.H.James.n/q.

ROUSHAM
chestnut gelding by Vedanta - Casilda.
1925 . . . Fell. (Mr H.Dyke Dennis) 10.10-0. Mr.P.Dennis. 66/1.

RED BEE
chestnut gelding by Honey Bee - Gate Change.
1926 . . . Finished 8th of 30. (Maj.H.A.Wernher) 8.10-10. D.Behan. 66/1.
1927 . . . Fell. (Maj.H.A.Wernher) 9.11-3. W.Payne. 50/1.

RATHOWEN
black gelding by Drinmore - Avarine.
1928 . . . Failed to finish. (Mr H.Deterding) 8.11-0. Mr.H.Deterding. 33/1.

REDLYNCH
chestnut gelding by Tracery - Gleneree.
1928 . . . Failed to finish. (Mr G.E.Strong) 7.10-5. Mr.W.R.West. 66/1.
1932 . . . Unseated rider. (Mr J.Pendarves) 11.10-7. Mr.K.Goode. 100/1.

RUDDYMAN
bay gelding by Ruddygore - dam by Hermit 11.
1928 . . . Failed to finish. (Mr H.G.Selfridge) 9.10-4. W.Parvin. 66/1.
1929 . . . Fell. (Mr H.G.Selfridge) 10.10-5. W.Parvin. 50/1.
1930 . . . Fell. (Mr H.G.Selfridge) 11.10-2. E.Brown. 100/1.
1931 . . . Refused. (Mr H.G.Selfridge) 12.10-8. E.Brown. 50/1.
1932 . . . Refused. (Mr H.G.Selfridge) 13. 10-7. E.Brown. 100/1.

RATHORY
bay gelding by Poet Laureate - Helen Fenton.
1928 . . . Failed to finish. (Maj.H.E.Lyon) 12.10-2. D.Williams. 100/1.
1929 . . . Fell. (Maj.H.E.Lyon) 13.10-0. R.Burford. 200/1.

RATHMORE
bay gelding by Drinmore - Avarine.
1928 . . . Failed to finish. (Mr Jack Hylton) 11.10-1. Mr.L.Whitfield. 66/1.

ROSSIENY
chestnut gelding by Rossendale - Crimea.
1928 . . . Faild to finish. (Mrs J.Putnam) 9.10-0. Mr.R.Everett. 33/1.

RAMPANT
bay gelding by Don Juan - Red Rambler.
1929 . . . Failed to finish. (Col.W.S.Anthony) 9.10-11. Maj.H.Misa. 100/1.

RICHMOND II
chestnut gelding by Prince Philip - Thyme.
1929 . . . Finished 3rd of 66. (Mr R.McAlpine) 6.10-6. W.Stott. 40/1.

ROYAL ARCH II
brown gelding by Righ Mor - Imaal.
1930 . . . Finished 6th of 41. (Mr V.Emanuel) 9.10-2. Mr.F.Thackray. 50/1.
1931 . . . Brought-down. (Mr V.Emanuel) 10.10-7. J.Bedeloup. 100/1.

RHYTICERE
chestnut gelding by Ramrod - Cosmerops.
1931 . . . Finished 4th of 43. (Mr V.Emanuel) aged.10-12. L.Niaudot. 50/1.

REALLY TRUE
bay gelding by Balscadden - Monica 111.
1933 . . . Finished 2nd of 34. (Maj.N.Furlong) 9.10-12. Mr.F.Furlong. 66/1.
1934 . . . Fell. (Major N.Furlong) 10.11-4. Mr.F.Furlong. 7/1.Fav.*
1935 . . . Fell. (Major N.Furlong) 11.10-13. D.Morgan. 18/1.

REMUS
bay gelding by By George ! - Ilia.
1933 . . . Completed the course. (Mr A.E.Berry) 8.11-12. T.Morgan. 100/6.
1934 . . . Finished 7th of 30. (Mr A.E.Berry) 9.11-9. T.Morgan. 40/1.

RUIN
brown gelding by Kirk-Alloway - Income Tax.
1933 . . . Completed the course. (Mrs R.Fellowes) 8.10-7. Maj.H.Misa. 50/1.

READY CASH
bay gelding by Knight Of Kilcash - Vigora.
1934 . . . Fell. (Capt.C.A.Cartwright) 7.11-9. Mr.F.Walwyn. 20/1.
1937 . . . Refused (Mr V.H.Smith) 10.11-3. T.F.Carey. 22/1.

REYNOLDS TOWN
brown or black gelding by My Prince - Fromage. Bred by Mr.R.Ball.
1935 . . . WON. (Major N.Furlong) 8.11-4. 27 Ran. Mr.F.Furlong. 22/1.
1936 . . . WON. (Major N.Furlong) 9.12-2. 35 Ran. Mr.F.Walwyn. 10/1.

ROYAL RANSOM
chestnut gelding by My Prince - Pay Only.
1935 . . . Fell. (Mr J.H.Whitney) 8.11-8. J.Hamey. 28/1.
1936 . . . Fell. (Mr J.H.Whitney) 9.11-7. H.Jones. 33/1.

RED PARK
bay gelding by Redmond - Lady Alwine.
1935 . . . Pulled-up. (Lady Houston) 9.10-7. P.Fitzgerald. 100/1.

ROD AND GUN
bay gelding by Fly Fisher - Heather Bloom.
1936 . . . Fell. (Mr J.H.Whitney) 9.10-7. Mr.L.Stoddard. 100/1.

ROYAL MAIL
black gelding by My Prince - Flying May. Bred by Mr C.A.Rogers.
1937 . . . WON. (Mr H.Lloyd Thomas) 8.11-13. 33 Ran. E.Williams. 100/6.
1938 . . . Pulled-up. (Mrs C.Evans) 9.12-7. E.Williams. 100/8.
1939 . . . Finished 9th of 37. (Mrs C.Evans) 10.12-7. D.Morgan. 100/8.

ROYAL DANIELI
bay gelding by Roidore - Sweet Honora.
1938 . . . Finished 2nd of 36. (Mr H.C.McNally) 7.11-3. D.Moore. 18/1.
1939 . . . Fell. (Mr H.C.McNally) 8.11-13. D.Moore. 100/8.
1940 . . . Fell. (Mr H.C.McNally) 9.11-13. D.Moore. 4/1.Fav.*

RED KNIGHT II
bay gelding by Lord Hilary - Red Rose.
1938 . . . Finished 6th of 36. (Mr E.T.Hunt) 9.10-0. D.Jones. 28/1.

ROCKQUILLA
chestnut gelding by Romus - Rock Cress.
1938 . . . Fell. (Mr V.H.Smith) 8.10-8. T.F.Carey. 28/1.
1939 . . . Fell. (Lord Bicester) 9.11-7. T.F.Carey. 100/6.
1940 . . . Finished 13th of 30. (Lord Bicester) 10.11-5. T.F.Carey. 20/1.

ROCK LAD
brown gelding by Ladkin - Rock Merry.
1938 . . . Fell. (Mr H.R.Bain) 8.10-4. J.Bissill. 66/1.

RED EAGLE
bay or brown gelding by Marcus Friar - Red Bud.
1940 . . . Finished 16th of 30. (Mr H.B.Brandt) 9.11-2. T.Elder. 50/1.

RED FREEMAN
chestnut gelding by Jackdaw Of Rheims - Red Empress.
1939 . . . Fell. (Mr W.U.Goodbody) 8.10-5. W.Redmond. 50/1.
1940 . . . Fell. (Mr W.U.Goodbody) 9.10-3. W.Redmond. 50/1.

RED HILLMAN
chestnut gelding by Deflation - Galena.
1939 . . . Fell. (Lord Latymer) 11.10-12. E.Foley. 66/1.

RED ROWER
bay gelding by Rameses The Second - Red Maru.
1946 . . . Pulled-up. (Lord Stalbridge) 12.11-7. G.Kelly. 22/1.

REFUGIO
grey gelding by Palatine Bog or Iron Crown - Jo Jean. Bred in U.S.A.
1947 . . . Finished 7th of 57. (Mrs F.Adams) 9.11-0. F.Adams. 100/1.

REARMAMENT
bay gelding by Empire Builder - Vulcania.
1947 . . . Finished 14th of 57. (Mrs C.D.Wilson) 10.11-1. G.Kelly.33/1.
1948 . . . Fell. (Mrs C.D.Wilson) 11.11-2. D.Ruttle. 66/1.

ROWLAND ROY
bay gelding by Monktown - Laurel Lady.
1947 . . . Finished 15th of 57. (Mr A.G.Boley) 8.10-3. Mr.R.Black. 66/1.
1948 . . . Finished 6th of 43. (Mr A.G.Boley) 9.11-8. B.Marshall. 100/9.
1950 . . . Finished 4th of 49. (Mr A.G.Boley) 11.11-7. R.Black. 40/1.
1951 . . . Fell. (Mr A.G.Boley) 12.10-12. D.V.Dick. 50/1.

REVELRY
bay gelding by Rejoice - Amy Gay.
1947 . . . Fell. (Mr J.T.Doyle) 7.10-12. D.L.Moore. 100/6.
1948 . . . Finished 12th of 43. (Mr J.D.Clark) 8.11-6. D.L.Moore. 33/1.

ROIMOND
chestnut gelding by Roidore - Ellamond.
1948 . . . Fell. (Lord Bicester) 7.11-7. R.Black. 22/1.
1949 . . . Finished 2nd of 43. (Lord bicester) 8.11.12.R.Francis. 22/1.
1950 . . . Fell. (Lord Bicester) 9.12-1. R.Francis. 10/1.Fav.*
1951 . . . Fell. (Lord Bicester) 10.12-0. R.Francis. 100/7.
1952 . . . Fell. (Lord Bicester) 11.11-13. T.Molony. 33/1.

RUSSIAN HERO
bay gelding by Peter The Great - Logique. Bred by Mr.W.F.Williamson.
1949 . . . WON. (Mr W.F.Williamson) 9.10-8. 43 Ran. L.McMorrow. 66/1.
1950 . . . Fell. (Mr W.F.Williamson) 10.11-4. L.McMorrow. 22/1.
1951 . . . Fell. (Mr W.F.Williamson) 11.11-1. L.McMorrow. 40/1.
1952 . . . Fell. (Mr W.F.Williamson) 12.10-11. L.McMorrow. 50/1.

ROYAL MOUNT
brown gelding by Knight Of The Garter - Royal Lass.
1949 . . . Finished 3rd of 43. (Mrs M.Harvey) 10.10-12. P.J.Doyle.18/1.
1950 . . . Fell. (Mr T.Goodall) 11.11-0. Mr.A.Corbett. 40/1.

REPLICA
bay gelding by Furrokh Siyar - Alike.
1949 . . . Fell. (Mr R.K.Mellon) 11.10-3. E.Reavey. 66/1.

ROYAL COTTAGE
brown gelding by Cottage - Pretty Helen.
1949 . . . Refused. (Mr H.E.Pretyman) 9.10-12. R.Black. 33/1.

ROYAL TAN
chestnut gelding by Tartan - Princess Of Birds. Bred by Mr.J.Toppin.
1951 . . . Finished 2nd of 36. (Mrs M.H.Keogh) 7.10-13. Mr.A.S.O'Brien. 22/1.
1952 . . . Fell. (Mr J.H.Griffin) 8.11-6. Mr.A.S.O'Brien. 22/1.
1954 . . . WON. (Mr J.H.Griffin) 10.11-7. 29 Ran. B.Marshall. 8/1.
1955 . . . Finished 12th of 30. (Prince Aly Khan) 11.12-4. D.V.Dick. 28/1.
1956 . . . Finished 3rd of 29. (Prince Aly Khan) 12.12-1. T.Taaffe.28/1.
1957 . . . Carried-out. (Prince Aly Khan) 13.11-12. T.Taaffe. 28/1.

REVEALED
bay gelding by Pinxit - Veiled.
1951 . . . Fell. (Mr W.D.Francis) 11.10-0. Mr.W.Benyon-Brown. 100/1.

ROYAL STUART
bay gelding by Tartan - Knight's Lady.
1952 . . . Refused. (Lord Leverhulme) 9.10-3. T.Brookshaw. 50/1.
1954 . . . Refused. (Lord Leverhulme) 11.10-0. J.Power. 66/1.

ROCKET VI
bay gelding by Contrevent - Rumba.
1952 . . . Fell. (Mr C.Robinson) 8.10-1. V.Speck. 100/1.

RED RUBE
bay horse by Pappageno 11 - Rouge Girl.
1955 . . . Finished 10th of 30. (Sir John Carew-Pole) 8.10-3. A.Oughton. 66/1.

ROMAN FIRE
brown gelding by Tiberius - Fiery Light.
1955 . . . Brought-down. (Mrs H.R.Marsh) 12.10-0. J.Dowdeswell. 66/1.

REVEREND PRINCE
bay gelding by His Reverence - Princess Pat.
1956 . . . Fell. (Mr P.Dufosee) 10.10-5. Mr.C.Pocock. 40/1.

ROSE PARK
chestnut gelding by Pactolus - Primulas.
1957 . . . Pulled-up. (Mr G.G.Lawrence) 11.11-13. G.Nicholls. 28/1.

RENDEZVOUS III
chestnut gelding by Samaritain - Raquette.
1957 . . . Brought-down. (Maj.H.S.Cayzer) 9.10-6. A.Freeman. 20/1.
1958 . . . Fell. (Maj.H.S.Cayzer) 10.10-3. J.A.Bullock. 45/1.

RED MENACE
chestnut mare by Flamenco- Pucka Falloch.
1957 . . . Fell. (Mr G.McParland) 8.10-0. L.Wigham. 33/1.

RICHARDSTOWN
bay gelding by Starmond - Magic Bright.
1958 . . . Fell. (Mr J.Neville) 10.10-0. J.Morrisey. 40/1.
1959 . . . Pulled-up. (Mr R.Neville) 11.10-1. F.Carroll 66/1.

ROYAL TOURNAMENT
brown gelding by Combat - Coronet.
1959 . . . Refused. (Lt.Col.M.Gilliat) 9.10-0. R.Morrow. 100/1.

RELJEF
bay horse by Rangir - Fiel. Bred in U.S.S.R.
1961 . . . Unseated rider. (Mr P.H.Pika) 7.12-0. B.Ponomarenko. 100/1.

RED THORN
chestnut gelding by Flamenco - Consuella Rose.
1964 . . . Pulled-up. (Mrs L.H.Brown) 8.10-3. T.W.Biddlecombe. 33/1.

REPRIEVED
pedigree unknown.
1963 . . . Pulled-up. (Mr S.Nossell) 10.10-1. P.Pickford. 50/1.
1964 . . . Fell. (Mr C.S.Gardener) 11.10-0. P.Harvey. 66/1.

177

REPRODUCTION
bay gelding by Last Of The Dandies - Bulgaden Ivy.
1964 . . . Fell. (Mr K.R.Ashton) 11.10-0. R.Langley. 66/1.
1965 . . . Pulled-up. (Mr K.R.Ashton) 12.10-13. R.Langley. 40/1.

RAINBOW BATTLE
bay mare by Raincheck - Duel in The Sun.
1965 . . . Finished 4th of 47. (Mr W.Shand-Kydd) 9.10-13. G.Milburn. 50/1.

RIP, THE
bay gelding by Manicou - Easy Virtue.
1965 . . . Finished 7th of 47. (H.M.Queen Elizabeth The Queen Mother) 10.11-5. W.Rees. 9/1.

RONDETTO
chestnut gelding by Caproetto - Roundandround.
1965 . . . Fell. (Mr A.B.Mitchell) 9.11-6. J.King. 100/8.
1967 . . . Unseated rider. (Mr A.B.Mitchell) 11.11-7. J.Haine. 33/1.
1968 . . . Fell. (Mr A.B.Mitchell) 12.10-12. J.King. 33/1.
1969 . . . Finished 3rd of 30. (Mr A.B.Mitchell) 13.10-6. J.King. 25/1.
1970 . . . Unseated rider. (Mr A.B.Mitchell) 14.10-5. J.King. 22/1.

RED TIDE
chestnut gelding by County Delight - Red Sea.
1965 . . . Fell. (Mr Paul Mellon) 8.10-13. J.Haine. 33/1.

RONALD'S BOY
bay gelding by Ronald - Marlock.
1965 . . . Fell. (Mr G.Kindersley) 8.11-1. Mr.G.Kindersley. 100/1.
1967 . . . Fell. (Mr E.F.Robins) 10.10-13. Mr.P.Irby. 100/1.
1968 . . . Brought-down. (Mr E.F.Robbins) 11.10-0. J.Harty. 100/1.

ROUGH TWEED
bay gelding by Tartan - Rippling Wave.
1966 . . . Fell. (Mr S.L.Green) 12.10-7. P.Buckley. 22/1.

● **Red Rum sails over second Becher's in 1977 on the way to his third win.**

RUBY GLEN
bay gelding by Prince Richard - Frozen Fruit.
1965 . . . Brought-down. (Mrs N.H. Le Mare) 10.10-13. S.Davenport. 33/1.

ROYAL RUSE
bay gelding by Prince Chevalier - Pretexte.
1966 . . . Pulled-up. (Mr R.B.Woodard) 8.10-0. T.Hyde. 100/1.

RED ALLIGATOR
chestnut gelding by Magic Red - Miss Alligator. Bred by Mr.W.Kennedy.
1967 . . . Finished 3rd of 44. (Mr J.Manners) 8.10-0. B.Fletcher. 30/1.
1968 . . . WON. (Mr J.Manners) 9.10-0. 45 Ran. B.Fletcher. 100/7.
1969 . . . Fell. (Mr J.Manners) 10.10-13. B.Fletcher. 13/2.Fav.*
1970 . . . Fell. (Mr J.Manners) 11.10-12. B.Fletcher. 13/1.

ROSS SEA
brown gelding by Arctic Star - Chloris 11.
1967 . . . Finished 15th of 44. (Mrs J.Jones) 11.10-3. J.Cook. 66/1.

RUTHERFORDS
brown gelding by Doubtless 11 - Soldado Maid.
1967 . . . Finished 16th of 44. (Mr R.S.Reynolds,jnr.) 7.10-11. J.Leech. 28/1. Remounted*
1968 . . . Finished 4th of 45. (Mr J.Bonnier) 8.10-6. P.Buckley. 100/9.

REYNARD'S HEIR
chestnut gelding by Reynard Volant - Pride of Skillagalee.
1968 . . . Finished 8th of 45. (Mr R.Buckley) 8.10-4. T.Kinane. 28/1.

REGAL JOHN
bay gelding by John Moore - Regal Chain.
1968 . . . Refused. (Mr H.L.Vickery) 10.10-8. J.Gifford. 100/7.

ROSS FOUR
chestnut gelding by Rabirio - Burrapeg.
1968 . . . Fell. (Mr W.T.Organ) 7.10-0. P.Jones. 100/1.

ROSINVER BAY
bay gelding by Fortina - Candy Kisses.
1969 . . . Refused. (Mr A.W.Riddell Martin) 9.10-5. P.Taaffe. 50/1.

RACOON
bay gelding by The Mongoose - Dubad.
1970 . . . Fell. (Mr R.H.Kieckhefer) 8.10-3. D.Mould. 33/1.

REGIMENTAL
black gelding by March Past - Chanfrin.
1971 . . . Finished 9th of 38. (Maj.D.Wigan) 8.10-6. Mr.J.Lawrence. 66/1.

ROUGH SILK
bay gelding by Black Tarquin - Flossie.
1972 . . . Finished 9th of 42. (Maj.C.H.Nathan) 9.10-6. D.Nicholson. 25/1.
1973 . . . Pulled-up. (Maj.C.H.Nathan) 10.10-0. T.Norman. 66/1.
1974 . . . Finished 5th of 42. (Mrs P.G.McCrea) 11.10-0. M.Morris. 66/1.
1975 . . . Refused. (Brig.Gen.W.Gilbride) 12.10-8. Mr.L.Urbano. 28/1.

RIGTON PRINCE
bay gelding by Straight Deal - Miss Rigton.
1972 . . . Pulled-up. (Maj.E.M.W.Cliff McCullough) 11.10-9. J.Enright. 25/1.

RED RUM
bay gelding by Quorum - Mared. Bred by Mr.M.McEnery.
1973 . . . WON. (Mr N.H. Le Mare) 8.10-5. 38 Ran. B.Fletcher. 9/1.jnt/Fav.*
1974 . . . WON. (Mr N.H. Le Mare) 9.12-0.42 Ran. B.Fletcher. 11/1.
1975 . . . Finished 2nd of 31. (Mr N.H. Le Mare) 10.12-0. B.Fletcher. 7/2.Fav.*
1976 . . . Finished 2nd of 32. (Mr N.H. Le Mare) 11.11-10. T.Stack. 10/1.
1977 . . . WON. (Mr N.H. Le Mare) 12.11-8. T.Stack. 9/1.

ROUGE AUTUMN
bay gelding by Autumn Gold - Rouge Scot.
1973 . . . Finished 5th of 38. (Mr B.P.Jenks) 9.10-0. K.B.White. 40/1.
1974 . . . Finished 7th of 42. (Mr B.P.Jenks) 10.10-0. K.B.White. 28/1.

RICHELEAU
bay gelding by Richard Louis - Pretty Puddy.
1973 . . . Fell. (Mrs E.J.Taplin) 9.10-0. N.Kernick. 50/1.

RAMPSMAN
brown gelding by Live Spirit - Redcross Girl.
1973 . . . Pulled-up. (Mr J.Rose) 9.10-0. D.Munro. 100/1.

ROYAL RELIEF
bay gelding by Flush Royal - French Colleen.
1974 . . . Fell. (Mr E.R.Courage) 10.11-6. Lord Oaksey. 18/1.
1975 . . . Fell. (Mr E.R.Courage) 11.11-1. Lord Oaksey. 22/1.

ROMAN HOLIDAY
bay gelding by Black Tarquin - Last Resort.
1974 . . . Pulled-up. (Lord Chelsea) 10.10-7. J.King. 66/1.

ROUGH HOUSE
brown gelding by Songedor or Ritudyr - Luminous Belle.
1974 . . . Fell. (Mr R.P.Brown) 8.10-6. Mr.J.Burke. 14/1.
1975 . . . Fell. (Mrs W.Brown) 9.10-12. J.Burke. 12/1.

RAG TRADE
chestnut gelding by Menelek - The Rage. Bred by Mr I.Williams.
1975 . . . Finished 10th of 31. (Mr P.B.Raymond) 9.10-0. J.Francome. 18/1.
1976 . . . WON. (Mr P.B.Raymond) 10.10-12. 32 Ran. J.Burke. 14/1.
1978 . . . Pulled-up. (Mr P.B.Raymond) 12.11-3. J.J.O'Neill. 8/1.Fav.*

ROMAN BAR
chetsnut gelding by Bargello - Roman Thistle.
1976 . . . Fell. (Mrs D.I.O'Sullivan) 7.10-10. G.Newman. 33/1.
1977 . . . Fell. (Mrs D.I.O'Sullivan) 8.10-10. P.Kiely. 25/1.
1978 . . . Finished 9th of 37. (Mrs B.O'Sullivan) 9.10-8. P.Kiely. 33/1.

ROYAL THRUST
bay gelding by Light Thrust - Royal Account.
1977 . . . Fell. (Mrs J.Greenhalgh) 8.10-0. C.Tinkler. 100/1.

RUBSTIC
brown gelding by I Say - Leuze. Bred by Mrs.R.Digby.
1979 . . . WON. (Mr J.Douglas) 10.10-0. 34 Ran. M.A.Barnes. 28/1.
1980 . . . Fell. (Mr J.Douglas) 11.10-11. M.A.Barnes. 8/1.Fav*
1981 . . . Finished 7th of 39. (Mr J.Douglas) 12.10-7. M.A.Barnes.11/1.

RED EARL
bay gelding by Sunny Way - Mary Scott.
1979 . . . Pulled-up. (Mr H.Ford) 10.10-0. H.J.Evans. 50/1.

ROUGH AND TUMBLE
bay gelding by Tenterhooks - Domalition.
1979 . . . Finished 3rd of 34. (Mr L.Dormer) 9.10-2. J.Francome. 14/1.
1980 . . . Finished 2nd of 30. (Mr L.Dormer) 10.10-11. J.Francome. 11/1.
1982 . . . Refused. (Mr L.Dormer) 12.10-8. J.Francome. 16/1.

RAMBLING ARTIST
chestnut gelding by Wrekin Wrambler - Belle Artiste.
1979 . . . Brought-down. (Mr E.F.Robbins) 9.10-6. D.Goulding. 16/1.

ROYAL FROLIC
bay gelding by Royal Buck - Forward Miss.
1979 . . . Finished 6th of 34. (Sir John Hanmer) 10.11-10. J.Burke.25/1.
1980 . . . Refused. (Sir J.Hanmer & Mr F.R.Watts) 11.11-4. J.Burke. 16/1.

ROYAL STUART
bay gelding by Bally Royal - Shamayra.
1980 . . . Finished 4th of 30. (Mr & Mrs J.Murray Begg) 9.10-10. P.Blacker. 20/1.
1981 . . . Unseated rider. (Mr & Mrs J.Murray Begg) 10.10-2. H.Davies. 16/1.
1982 . . . Brought-down. (Mr J.Begg) 11.10-4. Mr.D.Gray. 40/1.

RATHLEK
chestnut gelding by Menelek - Rathcoole.
1980 . . . Refused. (Mr D.R.Greig) 10.10-0. P.Barton. 35/1.
1981 . . . Finished 9th of 39. (Mr D.R.Greig) 11.10-0. P.Barton. 50/1.
1982 . . . Brought-down. (Mr J.Carden) 12.10-12. Mr.J.Carden. 100/1.

ROYAL MAIL
chestnut gelding by Bally Royal - Lency.
1981 . . . Finished 3rd of 39. (Mr & Mrs J.Murray Begg) 11.11-7. P.Blacker. 16/1.
1982 . . . Fell. (Mr J.Begg) 12.11-10. B.R.Davies. 17/2.
1983 . . . Fell. (Mr & Mrs J.Murray Begg) 13.11-4. Mr.T.Thomson Jones. 50/1.

ROYAL EXILE
bay gelding by Gun Bow - Boisaralla.
1981 . . . Finished 6th of 39. (Mr W.C.Rigg) 12.10-0. B. de Haan.16/1.

RAMBLING JACK
chestnut gelding by Wrekin Rambler - Gilliana.
1982 . . . Fell. (Mr G.Adam) 11.11-1. T.G.Dun. 16/1.

ROLLS RAMBLER
bay gelding by Wrekin Wrambler - Cross Pearl.
1982 . . . Refused. (Mr B.Brazier) 11.10-12. Mr.A.J.Wilson. 20/1.

ROMAN GENERAL
bay gelding by Spartan General - Romenda.
1984 . . . Unseated rider. (Mr B.Munro-Wilson) 11.10-0. Maj.M.Wallace. 100/1.

RUPERTINO
chestnut gelding by Saucy Kit - Miss Kilmansegg.
1985 . . . Finished 7th of 40. (Lord Kenyon) 10.10-0. R.Stronge.33/1.
1986 . . . Finished 15th of 40. (Lord Kenyon) 11.10-0. G.Charles-Jones. 66/1.

ROYAL APPOINTMENT
bay gelding by Royal Highway - Margaretta.
1985 . . . Fell. (Mrs J.L.White) 10.10-0. T.Carberry. 66/1.

ROMAN BISTRO
bay gelding by Biskrah - Romenda.
1985 . . . Refused. (Mr D.Martin-Betts) 9.10-3. P.Nicholls. 150/1.

RUN TO ME
bay gelding by Clear River - Joyful Tears.
1987 . . . Pulled-up. (Mr N.R.Mitchell) 12.10-2. Mr.N.Mitchell.150/1.

RHYME 'N' REASON
bay gelding by Kemal - Smooth Lady.
1988 . . . WON. (Miss J.E.Reed) 9.11-0. 40 Ran. B.Powell. 10/1.

REPINGTON
brown gelding by Grey Mirage - Heron's Dolly.
1988 . . . Refused. (Mr J.R.Gilman) 10.10-1. C.Hawkins. 16/1.

RAUSAL
bay gelding by Lauso - Aur.
1989 . . . Refused. (Mrs K.Lloyd & Mr T.N.Bailey) 10.10-0. D.Tegg. 50/1.

RINUS
brown gelding by Netherkelly - Pirella.
1990 . . . Finished 3rd of 38. (Mr A.M.Proos) 9.10-4. N.Doughty.13/1.
1991 . . . Fell. (Mr A.M.Proos) 10.10-7. N.Doughty. 7/1.

ROLL-A-JOINT
chestnut gelding by Take-A-Reef - Sark.
1990 . . . Fell. (Mr R.Thomas Williams) 12.10-0. S.McNeill. 28/1.

RUN AND SKIP
bay gelding by Deep Run - Skiporetta.
1991 . . . Fell. (Mr J.L.Chamberlain) 13.10-0. D.Byrne. 66/1.

ROMANY KING
brown gelding by Crash Course - Wiinsome Lady.
1992 . . . Finished 2nd of 40. (Mr L.J.Garrett) 8.10-3. R.Guest. 16/1.
1994 . . . Fell. (Mr Urs E.Schwarzenbach) 10.10-1. R.Guest. 22/1.
1995 . . . Dead-heated 5th of 35. (Mr U.E.Schwarzenbach) 11.10-0. Mr.M.Armytage. 40/1.

RUBIKA
bay gelding by Saumon - Eureka.
1992 . . . Finished 14th of 40. (Mr T.Hemmings) 9.10-2. P.Niven. 28/1.

ROC DE PRINCE
brown gelding by Djarvis - Haute Volta 11.
1992 . . . Finished 17th of 40. (Mrs D.Thompson) 9.10-0. C.Swan.40/1.
1994 . . . Finished 6th of 36. (Mrs D.Thompson) 11.10-0. J.Lower. 100/1.

RADICAL LADY
bay mare by Radical - Peaceful Madrigal.
1992 . . . Finished 19th of 40. (N.B.Mason Farms Ltd.) 8.10-0. J.Callaghan. 80/1.

RAWHIDE
chestnut gelding by Buckskin - Shuil Eile.
1992 . . . Unseated rider. (Mrs H.McCalmont) 8.10-0. K.O'Brien. 50/1.

ROWLANDSONS JEWELS
brown gelding by Avocat - Coolavane.
1992 . . . Unseated rider. (Rowlandsons Jewellers Ltd) 11.10-3. G.Bradley. 60/1.

ROYAL BATTERY
brown gelding by Norfolk Air - All At Sea.
1992 . . . Pulled-up. (Mrs P.M.Cottle & Mr D.H.Barons) 9.10-0. R.Greene. 80/1.

RIVERSIDE BOY
chestnut gelding by Funny Man - Tamorina.
1994 . . . Refused. (Bisgrove Partnership) 11.10-0. M.Richards.33/1.
1995 . . . Finished 8th of 35. (Bisgrove Partnership) 12.10-0. C.Swan. 40/1.
1996 . . . Finished 12th of 27. (Bisgrove Partnership) 13.10-0. D.Walsh. 66/1.

RUST NEVER SLEEPS
bay gelding by Jaazeiro - Alice Kyteler.
1994 . . . Fell. (Mr D.M.Murphy) 10.10-0. P.Carberry. 66/1.
1996 . . . Pulled-up. (Mr D.M.Murphy) 12.10-0. T.Horgan. 20/1.

RUN FOR FREE
bay gelding by Deep Run - Credit Card.
1994 . . . Refused. (Mrs M.R.Freethy) 10.11-7. M.Perrett. 25/1.

ROYAL ATHLETE
chestnut gelding by Roselier- Darjoy.
Bred by Mr.J.Brophy.
1995 . . . WON. (Messrs G & L.Johnson) 12.10-6. 35 Ran. J.F.Titley. 40/1.

ROUGH QUEST
bay gelding by Crash Course - Our Quest. Bred by Mr.M.Healey.
1996 . . . WON. (Mr A.T.A.Wates) 10.10-7. 27 Ran. M.A.Fitzgerald. 7/1.Fav.*

S

SEVENTY FOUR
1939 . . . Finished 2nd of 17. (Sir George Mostyn) T.Olliver. n/q.
1840 . . . Fell. (Sir George Mostyn) T.Olliver. 7/1.
1841 . . . Finished 6th of 11. (Sir George Mostyn) Mr.Whitworth.14/1.
1842 . . . Finished 2nd of 15.(Lord Mostyn) Powell. 6/1.

SEA, THE
1840 . . . Finished 4th of 12. (Marquis of Waterford) Marquis of Waterford. n/q.

SPOLASCO
1840 . . . Fell. (Owner unknown) Rose. n/q.

SELIM
1841 . . . Fell. (Capt.Price) Capt.Price. n/q.

SAM WELLER
1842 . . . Fell. (Mr Jem Mason) Barker. 8/1.

SATIRIST
1842 . . . Failed to finish. (Lord Maidstone) Bretherton. 100/7.

STRANGER, THE
1845 . . . Failed to finish. (Lord Alford) Hill. n/q.

SWITCHER
1846 . . . Finished 3rd of 22. (Lord Howth) 5.12-4. D.Wynne. n/q.
1848 . . . Fell. (Lord Strathmore) 7.11-5. Lord Strathmore. n/q.

SCAVENGER, THE
1846 . . . Refused. (Mr Pearce) 6.10-2. Bradley. n/q.

ST LEGER
1847 . . . Finished 2nd of 26. (Mr Watt) - 12-3. T.Olliver. 15/1.

SAUCEPAN
1847 . . . Failed to finish. (Mr Power) - 12-6.Mr.W.McDonough. n/q.
1848 . . . Refused. (Mr W.Strickland) - 11-11. T.Abbot. n/q.

ST RUTH
1847 . . . Failed to finish. (Mr R.J.Moore) - 11-1. Canavan. n/q.

SAILOR, THE
1848 . . . Fell. (Mr Mason) 6.10-8. Holman. n/q.

STANDARD GUARD
1848 . . . Finished 4th of 29. (Mr Storey) - 10-12. Taylor. 100/6.

SIR ARTHUR
1848 . . . Failed to finish. (Mr Barry) 6.11-1. Murphy. 15/1.

SOPHIA
1848 . . . Failed to finish. (Sir R de Burgh) - 11-0. Ford. n/q.

SPARTA
1848 . . . Fell. (Mr R.Brooke) - 10-0. Turner. n/q.
1849 . . . Fell. (Mr Bathhurst) - 8-12. Wakefield. n/q.

SIR JOHN
1849 . . . Failed to finish. (Mr Sharkie) - 10-10. Mr.Sharkie. n/q.
1850 . . . Finished 3rd of 32. (Lord Waterford) - 11-8. J.Ryan. 7/1.
1851 . . . Finished 3rd of 21. (Lord Waterford) - 11-12. J.Ryan. 7/1.
1852 . . . Finished 7th of 24. (Lord Waterford) - 11-10. J.Ryan. 12/1.

SHINSORE
1850 . . . Failed to finish. (Mr Williamson) 6.10-5. H.Bradley. n/q.
1851 . . . Finished 8th of 21. (Mr King) 7.10-7. Mr.Gaman. n/q.

SOBRIETY
1850 . . . Failed to finish. (Mr Sandford) - 10-4. J.Thompson. n/q.

SIR PETER LAURIE
1851 . . . Failed to finish. (Mr Barnett) - 11-7. W.Scott. 25/1.
1852 . . . Finished 3rd of 24. (Capt.W.Barnett) - 11-7.W.Holman. 30/1.
1853 . . . Finished 4th of 21. (Capt.W.Barnett) - 11-8.W.Holman. 12/1.
1856 . . . Ran-out. (Mr W.Barnett) 10-12. S.Darling,jnr. 12/1.

SILENT FRIEND
1852 . . . Failed to finish. (Mr Courtenay) - 9-12. Parry. n/q.

STAR OF ENGLAND
1854 . . . Failed to finish. (Mr Blood) - 9-10. W.White. 50/1.

SPRING
1854 . . . Finished 2nd of 20. (Mr Barber) 6. 9-10. W.Archer. 20/1.
1859 . . . Fell. (Mr Barber) 11. 8-7. J.Nightingall. 40/1.

SHILLIBEER
1854 . . . Failed to finish. (Lord Sefton) 6. 9-0. E.Southwell. 50/1.

SEAMAN
1856 . . . Failed to finish. (Mr A.McDonough) - 10-2. F.Martin. 7/1.

STAMFORD
1856 . . . Failed to finish. (Mr Hodgman) - 9-2. C.Green. n/q.

STAR OF THE WEST
1857 . . . Failed to finish. (Mr J.Colpitt) - 10-0. E.Jones. n/q.

SQUIRE OF BENSHAM
1857 . . . Failed to finish. (Mr W.P.Wrixon) - 9-8. Mr.Coxon. n/q.

STING
1857 . . . Failed to finish. (Mr J.Cassidy) - 9-6. J.Hanlon. 50/1.

SIR ROBERT
1860 . . . Pulled-up. (Mr J.Courtenay) - 10-2. C.Boyce. 33/1.

SHYLOCK
1860 . . . Failed to finish. (Major Owen) - 9-2. T.Clay. 25/1.

SIR WILLIAM
1864 . . . Failed to finish. (Mr T.Iven) - 11-10. Mr.Davison. n/q.
1866 . . . Refused. (Mr T.Jones) - 10-7. Ellison. 50/1.

SERIOUS CASE
1864 . . . Fell. (Mr T.S.Dawson) - 11-3. G.Waddington. 11/1.

SATANELLA
1864 . . . Fell. (Marquess of Drogheda) - 10-12. D.Meaney. n/q.

SILK AND SATIN
1864 . . . Failed to finish. (Mr Spark) - 10-2. Jarvis. n/q.

STANTON
1865 . . . Pulled-up. (Mr Harvey) - 10-8. G.Waddington. 9/1.
1866 . . . Fell. (Mr J.Coupland) - 10-12. Welsh. 50/1.

SALAMANDER
bay or brown gelding by Fire-eater - Rosalba. Bred by Mr J.Bouchier.
1866 . . . WON. (Mr E.Studd) 7.10-7. 30 Ran. Mr.A.Goodman.40/1.

STELLA
1866 . . . Fell. (Mr Spark) - 10-7. Jarvis. 50/1.

SHANGARRY
brown horse by The Confessor - dam by Greatheart.
1867 . . . Finished 3rd of 23. (Mr E.Studd) 6.10-13. Mr.Thomas. 14/1.

SHAKSPEARE
bay gelding by Gemma di Vergy - Capucine.
1867 . . . Finished 7th of 23. (Mr Carew) 6.11-1. Mr.A.Goodman. 7/1.

SILVER STAR
chestnut mare by Bandy - dam by Magpie. Formerly named Nanette.
1867 . . . Finished 9th of 23. (Mr S.J.Welfitt) - 10-9. G.Waddington. 20/1.

SEA KING
bay horse by Wild Dayrell - Golden Horn.
1867 . . . Failed to finish. (Mr E.Brayley) -10-11. G.Barry. 12/1.

SLIEVE CARNE
bay horse by Fright - The Cook.
1868 . . . Refused. (Mr G.H.Moore) 5.10-0. Mr.Pritchard. 50/1.

SURNEY
bay gelding by Findon - Blackbird.
1870 . . . Finished 4th of 23. (Mr J.Nightingall) - 10-4.R.I'Anson.100/8.

SCARRINGTON
brown gelding by Martext - dam by Mickey Free.
1870 . . . Failed to finish. (Mr T.Wilkinson) 7. 10-12. R.Wheeler. 1000/5.
1871 . . . Finished 3rd of 25. (Mr T.Wilkinson) 8.11-4. Cranshaw. 100/1.
1872 . . . Finished 2nd of 25. (Mr T.Wilkinson) 9.11-2. R.I'Anson. 100/6.

SOUVENANCE
chestnut mare by Fitz Gladiator or Serious - Ne M'oubliez Pas. Formerly named Ada Penelope.
1871 . . . Finished 8th of 25. (Duke of Hamilton) 6.11-2. Rickaby. 25/1.

SNOWSTORM
bay horse by Lord Fauconberg - dam by Professor Anderson.
1871 . . . Fell. (Mr J.N.Leighton) 8.11-7. Mr.R.Walker. 40/1.
1872 . . . Fell. (Mr Chaplin) 9.11-9. Thorpe. 50/1.

SCALTHEEN
brown horse by Gamekeeper - dam by Chit-Chat.
1871 . . . Brought-down. (Lord Eglinton) 6.10-10. G.Gray. 100/1.
1872 . . . Finished 9th of 25. (Lord Eglinton) 7. 10-4. Murphy. n/q.

SCOTS GREY
grey gelding by Claret - dam unknown.
1871 . . . Failed to finish. (Maj.Browne) - 10-5. Welsh. 100/1.
1872 . . . Finished 8th of 25. (Maj.Browne) - 10-11.Mr.G.Moore.50/1.

ST VALENTINE
bay gelding by Ruby - Leda.
1871 . . . Fell. (Lord Anglesey) 6.10-4. J.Adams. 33/1.

SCHIEDAM
bay gelding by Amsterdam - Mrs Fowler.
1872 . . . Brought-down. (Lord Eglinton) 7.11-4. Mr.J.M.Richardson. 10/1.

SAUCEBOX
bay horse by Caractacus - Intimidation. Formerly named Threatener.
1872 . . . Fell. (Mr H.Ellison) 6.10-4. Whiteley. 50/1.

STAR AND GARTER
chestnut gelding by Crater - Medal.
1873 . . . Finished 6th of 28. (Mr Vyner) 6.10-7. Capt.Smith. 66/1.

SOLICITOR
chestnut horse by The Lawyer - Gitanella.
1873 . . . Knocked-over. (Mr Dalglish) 6.10-8. Mr.Dalglish. n/q.

SARCHEDON
bay horse by Cagliostro - Joyeuse. Bred in France.
1873 . . . Failed to finish. (Mr W.R.H.Powell) 5.10-3. Pope. 30/1.

SPARROW, THE
bay gelding by Toxophilite - dam unknown.
1875 . . . Finished 7th of 19. (Mr Percival) 6.11-2. Gregory. 100/7.

ST AUBYN
chestnut horse by St Albans - Crochet.
1875 . . . Fell. (Mr C.A.Egerton) 7.11-7. T.Pickett. 40/1.

SAILOR
bay gelding by Blue Peter - Lena Rivers.
1875 . . . Fell. (Capt.S.Gubbins) 6.11-7. Fleming. 100/8.

SULTANA
grey mare by Thomastown - Arab Maid.
1877 . . . Pulled-up. (Mr A.Crofton) 7.10-11. Mr.T.Beasley. 50/1.

SHIFNAL
brown horse by Saccharometer - Countess Amy. Bred by Mr.J.Eyke.
1876 . . . Finished 3rd of 19. (Mr J.Nightingall) 7.10-13.R.I'Anson.25/1.
1877 . . . Finished 6th of 16. (Sir M.Crofton) 8.11-5. R.I'Anson. 100/15.Fav.*
1878 . . . WON. (Mr J.Nightingall) 9.10-12. 12 Ran. J.Jones. 7/1.
1880 . . . Finished 9th of 14. (Mr J.Nightingall) 11.11-11. Capt.Smith. 20/1.

SPRAY
bay mare by Knight Of St Patrick - Niagara.
1876 . . . Refused. (Capt.Bayley) 6.10-2. T.Cunningham. n/q.

SLEIGHT-OF-HAND
brown gelding by Conjuror - Solferino.
1880 . . . Refused. (Mr C.Howard) 9.10-4. J.Childs. 50/1.

ST GEORGE
bay horse by Speculum - Consequence.
1880 . . . Refused. (Mr Greenall) 8.10-2. G.Levitt. 25/1.

SCOT, THE
chestnut horse by Blair Athol - Columba.
1881 . . . Finished 5th of 13. (Capt.J.Machell) 5.10-0. F.Webb. 25/1.
1882 . . . Fell. (Mr J.B.Leigh) 6.11-8. J.Jewitt. 4/1.
1884 . . . Fell. (H.R.H.Prince of Wales) 8.11-3. J.Jones. 6/1.Fav.*

SEAMAN
bay horse by Xenophon - Lena Rivers.
Bred by Captain Gubbins.
1882 . . . WON. (Lord Manners) 6.11-6. 12 Ran. Lord Manners.10/1.

SATELLITE
chestnut gelding by Siderolite - dam unknown.
1884 . . . Failed to finish. (Mr E.W.Tritton) 5.10-5. Mr.J.Beasley. 100/12.

SINBAD
bay horse by Sir Bevys - Ocyroe.
1886 . . . Fell. (Mr L. de Rothschild) 5.10-3. A.Hall. 25/1.
1887 . . . Brought-down. (Mr J.Percival) 6.10-3. W.Nightingall. 20/1.

SAVOYARD
chestnut gelding by New Oswestry - Solferino.
1886 . . . Fell. (Baron W.Schroder) 8.10-3. G.Kirby. 22/1.
1887 . . . Finished 2nd of 16.(Baron W.Schroder) 9.10-13. T.Skelton. 100/14.
1888 . . . Fell. (Baron W.Schroder) 10.12-4. Mr.G.Lambton. 25/1.
1889 . . . Brought-down. (Baron W.Schroder) 11.11-11. Mr.G.Lambton. 20/1.

SPECTRUM
brown horse by Speculum - Red Leaf.
1887 . . . Fell. (Sir G.Chetwynd) 6.10-10. R.Grimes. 33/1.

SPAHI
chestnut horse by Ben Battle - Minette.
1887 . . . Fell. (Mr J.Gubbins) 6.10-10. Mr.T.Beasley. 9/2.Fav.*
1888 . . . Refused. (Mr J.Gubbins) 7.11-9. T.Kavanagh. 30/1.

SIKH, THE
bay gelding by Lord Gough - Matilda.
1889 . . . Finished 6th of 20. (Lord Dudley) 6.10-4. Mr.D.Thirlwell. 10/1.

SOUTHAM
brown gelding by Soucar - Fantine.
1892 . . . Fell. (Mr F.Swan) 13.10-7. W.Dollery. 50/1.

SCHOONER
brown mare by Favo - Pinnace.
1894 . . . Finished 8th of 14. (Mr M.A.Maher) 6.9-12. W.Taylor. 25/1.

SARAH BERNHARDT
brown mare by Play Actor - Wild Norah 11.
1895 . . . Pulled-up. (Mr C.D.Rose) 9.10-10. E.Matthews. 50/1.

SOARER, THE
bay gelding by Skylark - Idalia. Not in the General Stud Book. Bred by Mr.Doyle.
1896 . . . WON. (Mr W.Hall-Walker) 7. 9-13. 28 Ran. Mr.D.G.M.Campbell. 40/1.
1897 . . . Fell. (Mr W.Hall-Walker) 8.11-4. Mr.D.G.M.Campbell. 100/6.
1898 . . . Fell. (Mr W.Hall-Walker) 9.11-5. A.Nightingall. 100/7.

ST ANTHONY
brown horse by St Gatien - Seacoal.
1896 . . . Fell. (Capt.W.F.Ricardo) 7.10-10. Capt.W.F.Ricardo. 100/1.

SEAPORT II
bay gelding by Ocean Wave - dam unknown.
1897 . . . Finished 8th of 28. (Mr H.M.White) 8.10-7. C.James. 50/1.

SURPLICE
chestnut gelding by Cassock - dam by Don John.
1898 . . . Fell. (Mr Reid Walker) 9.10-1. J.Latham. 100/1.

SHERIFF HUTTON
bay gelding by Petrarch - Stately.
1898 . . . Fell. (Mrs H.B.Singleton) 6.10-0. J.Morrell. 50/1.
1899 . . . Pulled-up. (Mr F.W.Greswolde-Williams) 7. 9-11. C.Hogan. 100/7.

ST GEORGE
brown gelding by St Michael - Mrs Gamp.
1898 . . . Fell. (Mr Jos.Widger) 8. 9-11. Mr.T.J.Widger. 40/1.

SAPPER, THE
bay horse by Hackler - Sunnyside.
1899 . . . Fell. (Maj.J.A.Orr-Ewing) 6.10-11. Mr.G.S.Davies. 10/1.
1901 . . . Failed to finish. (Mr W.H.Pawson) 8.10-5. W.Halsey. 100/8.
1902 . . . Finished 9th of 21. (Mr W.H.Pawson) 9.10-4. H.Brown. 40/1.

SISTER ELIZABETH
bay mare by Toscano - St Faith.
1900 . . . Finished 9th of 16. (Mr A.James) 7.10-0. C.Clack. 40/1.

SUNNY SHOWER
bay gelding by Lasso - Thunder Rain.
1901 . . . Failed to finish. (Mrs J.Widger) aged. 10-8. Mr.J.W.Widger. 100/1.

SHANNON LASS
bay or brown mare by Butterscotch - Mazurka. Not in the General Stud Book. Mr.J.Reidy.
1902 . . . WON. (Mr A.Gorham) 7.10-1. 21 Ran. D.Read. 20/1.

188

STEADY GLASS
chestnut gelding by Shinglass - Irish Belle.
1902 . . . Finished 11th of 21. (Mr R.Hardinge) 10. 9-8. Mr.J.T.Longworth. 100/1.

SAXILBY
bay horse by Carlton - Koza.
1903 . . . Fell. (Mr G.C.Dobell) 6. 9-7. G.Goswell. 50/1.
1905 . . . Pulled-up.(Mr G.C.Dobell) 8. 9-12. P.Heaney. 66/1.

SHAUN ABOO
brown gelding by Chittabob - Thelma.
1904 . . . Finished 4th of 26. (Maj.J.D.Edwards) 6.10-2. A.Waddington. n/q.

SEAHORSE II
chestnut horse by Nelson - Moonga. Bred in New Zealand.
1905 . . . Pulled-up. (Mr Cotton) 7.10-7. J.O'Brien. 20/1.

ST BOSWELLS
bay gelding by Swillington - Belle Brummel.
1906 . . . Fell. (Mr J.Bell-Irving) 8. 9-7. D.Phelan. 66/1.

SEISDON PRINCE
bay gelding by Dog Rose - Fudge.
1907 . . . Fell. (Mr T.Ashton) 8.11-0. M.Phelan. n/q.
1908 . . . Fell. (Mr T.Ashton) 9.11-0. M.Phelan. 100/7.

SPRINGBOK
bay gelding by Springtime - Circe.
1908 . . . Finished 5th of 24. (Col.R.L.Birkin) 7.11-5. J.O'Brien. 8/1.
1910 . . . Pulled-up. (Col.R.L.Birkin) 9.11-5. W.Payne. 25/1.

SHADY GIRL
bay or brown mare by Le Noir - Gertie.
1909 . . . Finished 7th of 32. (Mr P.Nelke) 8.10-9. G.Clancy. 100/9.jnt/Fav.*
1910 . . . Fell. (Mr P.Nelke) 9.10-8. G.Clancy. 33/1.
1911 . . . Finished 3rd of 26. (Mr P.Nelke) 10.10-5. G.Clancy. 33/1. Remounted.*

SUHESCUN
chestnut gelding by Boudoir - Sikhina. Bred in France.
1911 . . . Fell. (Mnsr.Charles de Gheest) aged. 10-1. A.Chapman. 50/1.

SCHWARMER
bay gelding by Enthusiast - Sunburst.
1911 . . . Fell. (Mr J.J.Astor) 8.10-0. F.Dainty. 25/1.

SIR HALBERT
brown gelding by Hackler - Duchess 11.
1912 . . . Finished 6th of 24. (Capt.F.D.Grissell) 9.10-6. Mr.A.Smith. n/q.

SANS PEUR
bay gelding by Pierrepont - Timidity.
1912 . . . Failed to finish. (Mr W.Wilson) 13.10-0. J.Kay. n/q.

SUNLOCH
bay gelding by Sundorne - Gralloch. Bred by Mr H.S.Black.
1914 . . . WON. (Mr T.Tyler) 8. 9-7. 20 Ran. W.J.Smith. 100/6.
1919 . . . Pulled-up. (Mr T.Tyler) 13. 9-10. E.Driscoll. 25/1.

SILVER TOP
grey gelding - Pedigree unknown.
1915 . . . Failed to finish. (Mr A.Browne) 8.10-0. S.Walkington. 9/1.

ST MATHURIN II
chestnut gelding by St Bris - Margot.
1915 . . . Fell. (Mr A.Scott) 10. 9-10. T.H.Dunn. n/q.

SCHOOLMONEY
bay gelding by Silver Streak - Felstead.
* 1916 . . . Finished 3rd of 21. (Mr H.C.Davey) 7.10-2. A.Saxby. 33/1.
1919 . . . Fell. (Mr P.L.R.Savill) 10. 9-10. F.Cullen. 33/1.

STRANGWAYS
bay or brown horse by St Frusquin - Helen Mary.
* 1916 . . . Pulled-up. (Mr F.W.Parnell) 11.10-4. T.Dunn. n/q.

STAG'S HEAD
chestnut gelding by Brayhead - Policy.
* 1916 . . . Fell. (Mr G.P.Sanday) 12. 9-7. W.Smith. 20/1.

SHAUNSPADAH
bay gelding by Easter Prize - Rusialka. Bred by Mr.P.McKenna.
*1918 . . . Completed course. (Mr T.M.McAlpine) 7.10-11. A.Stubbs. 10/1.
1919 . . . Failed to finish. (Mr T.M.McAlpine) 8.11-2. R.Morgan. 33/1.
1921 . . . WON. (Mr T.M.McAlpine) 10.11-7. 35 Ran. F.B.Rees. 100/9.
1922 . . . Fell. (Sir M.McAlpine) 11.12-3. F.B.Rees. 100/8.
1923 . . . Finished 2nd of 28. (Sir M.McAlpine) 12.12-7. F.B.Rees.20/1.
1924 . . . Finished 7th of 30. (Sir M.McAlpine) 13.12-5. F.B.Rees. 100/7.

SERGEANT MURPHY
chestnut gelding by General Symons - Rose Graft. Bred by Mr.G.L.Walker.
*1918 . . . Completed course. (Mr D.Stuart) 8.10-7. S.Walkington. 40/1.
1919 . . . Finished 6th of 22. (Mr D.Stuart) 9.10-7. S.Walkington. 25/1.
1920 . . . Finished 4th of 24. (Mr M.H.Benson) 10.10-1. W.Smith.100/7.
1922 . . . Finished 4th of 32. (Mr S.Sanford) 12.11-0. C.Hawkins. 100/6. Remounted.*
1923 . . . WON. (Mr S.Sanford) 13.11-3. 28 Ran. Capt.G.H.Bennet. 100/6.
1924 . . . Finished 5th of 30. (Mr S.sanford) 14.11-10. J.Hogan,jnr. 100/6.
1925 . . . Finished 10th of 33. (Mr S.Sanford) 15.11-7. A.Escott. 33/1. Remounted.*

SIMON THE LEPPER
bay gelding by Simontault - Antelope.
*1918 . . . Completed course. (Sir G.Bullough) 9.10-0. R.Burford. 50/1.

SVETOI
bay gelding by St Martin - Seisdon Princess.
1919 . . . Fell. (Mr W.E.Wren) 9. 9-8. A.Saxby. 40/1.

SILVER RING
bay gelding by Zria - Queen Silver.
1920 . . . Fell. (Sir J.Buchanan) 8.11-4. G.Duller. 100/7.

SQUARE UP
chestnut horse by Simon Square - Campana.
1920 . . . Fell. (Mr W.Read) 7. 9-8. T.Willmot. n/q.
1922 . . . Felll. (Mr W.Read) 9.10-6. J.Rennison. 20/1.

SHORT KNOCK
bay gelding by Servitor - Prize Cherry.
1921 . . . Fell. (Capt.E.Shirley) 12.10-10. M.Halpin. n/q.

SOUTHAMPTON
brown gelding by Southannan - Pink Lady.
1922 . . . Fell. (Lord Woolavington) 6.11-10. Mr.H.A.Brown. 100/12.Fav*

ST BERNARD
chestnut gelding by St Monans - Lady May 11.
1922 . . . Fell. (Mrs N.Brownlee) 8.11-5. Mr.R.Pulford. 66/1.

SUPER MAN
bay gelding by Manwolf - Lady Superior.
1922 . . . Fell. (Mr W.A.Bankier) 7.10-9. R.Burford. n/q.

SUDAN II
bay gelding by Sundorne - Connie.
1922 . . . Fell. (Sir R.Rankin) 13.10-0. G.Calder. n/q.

190

SUCH A SPORT
chestnut gelding by Just Cause - Playnate IV.
1922 . . . Fell. (Mr R.Hardinge) 11.10-0. Capt.J.C.Delmege. n/q.

SQUARE DANCE
bay horse by Simon Square - Flora Dance.
1923 . . . Fell. (Mr H.M.Curtis) 11.12-0. L.B.Rees. 100/6.

SILVO
bay gelding by Minter - Ever True.
1924 . . . Finished 3rd of 30. (Mr W.H.Midwood) 8.12-2. G.Goswell. 100/7.
1925 . . . Finished 5th of 33. (Sir Edward Edgar) 9.12-7. F.B.Rees. 10/1.
1926 . . . Fell. (Mr W.H.Midwood) 10.12-7. F.B.Rees. 7/1.

SPRIG
chestnut gelding by Marco - Spry. Bred by Capt.R.C.B.Partridge.
1925 . . . Finished 4th of 33. (Mrs M.Partridge) 8.11-2. T.E.Leader. 33/1.
1926 . . . Finished 4th of 30. (Mrs M.Partridge) 9.11-7. T.E.Leader. 5/1.Fav.*
1927 . . . WON. (Mrs M.Partridge) 10.12-4. 37 Ran. T.E.Leader. 8/1.Fav.*
1928 . . . Fell. (Mrs M.Partridge) 11.12-7. T.E.Leader. 100/7.
1929 . . . Fell. (Mrs M.Partridge) 12.12-5. A.Escott. 50/1.

SOLDIER BILL
bay gelding by General Gough - Mollyroe.
1926 . . . Fell. (Mr A.Hood) 10.10-0. Mr.K.Goode. 100/1.

SHAUN OR
chestnut gelding by Radiolus - Turkey Hen.
1927 . . . Fell. (Lord Glanely) 8.11-3. W.Madden. 100/6.

SILVER SOMME
bay mare by Royal Hackle 11 or General Gough - Lady Silver.
1927 . . . Refused. (Mr H.Liddell) 10.11-3. M.Connors. 100/7.

SIR HUON
chestnut gelding by Huon 11 - Lady Daffodil.
1927 . . . Fell. (Mr Geoffrey Gilbey) 13.10-12. M.Rayson.100/1.

SNAPPER
brown gelding by Snap Dragon - Dark Avis.
1927 . . . Fell. (Maj.T.H.Sebag-Montefiore) 9.10-10. Capt.M.E.Dennis. 40/1.

SPEAR O' WAR
chestnut gelding by Spearmint - Ortlinde.
1928 . . . Failed to finish. (Lord Queenborough) 7.10-10. F.Brookes. 50/1.

SCOTCH EAGLE
chestnut gelding by French Eagle - dam by Clanronald.
1928 . . . Failed to finish. (Mr H.Fowler) 12.10-8. Mr.H.Fowler. 100/1.

SETI THE FIRST
brown gelding by Pericles - Blair Anchor.
1928 . . . Failed to finish. (Mr E.Craig Tanner) 13.10-4. Mr.E.Craig Tanner. 40/1.

SCRAPTOFT
bay gelding - Pedigree unknown.
1928 . . . Failed to finish. (Mr W.Ross) 11.10-1. Mr.M.Barry. 200/1.

SOLDIER'S JOY
bay gelding by The Recruiting Officer - The Lady Slavey.
1928 . . . Failed to finish. (Mr S.G.R.Barratt) 10.10-0. D.Quirke. 100/1.
1929 . . . Failed to finish. (Mr S.G.R.Barratt) 11.10-2. Capt.A.F.W.Gossage. 200/1.
1930 . . . Pulled-up. (Mr S.G.R.Barratt) 12.10-0. J.Farrell. 100/1.

STORT
bay gelding by Stortford - Winkie.
1929 . . . Fell. (Mr R.Wright) 10.11-0. T.Chisman. 200/1.

SKRUN PRINCE
bay gelding by The Raft - Daisy.
1929 . . . Fell. (Col.P.D.Stewart) 8.10-12. W.Gurney. 22/1.

SANDY HOOK
bay gelding by Santair - Pin Curl.
1929 . . . Fell. (Mr J.H.Hull) 8.10-9. F.Fish. 100/1.
1930 . . . Knocked-over. (Mr S.Sanford) 9.10-12. T.E.Leader. 25/1.
1931 . . . Fell. (Mr S.Sanford) 10.10-12. F.Fish. 40/1.

SULTAN OF WICKEN
bay gelding by St Martin - Sultanina.
1929 . . . Fell. (Dowager Lady Penrhyn) 10.10-3. T.James. 200/1.

STAGE MANAGEMENT
bay gelding by The Boss - Pauline Chase.
1929 . . . Fell. (Maj.C.W.M.Norrie) 9.10-0. M.Doherty. 100/1.

SHAUN GOILIN
chestnut gelding - sire unknown - Golden Day.
1930 . . . WON. (Mr W.H.Midwood) 10.11-7. 41 Ran. T.Cullinan. 100/8.
1931 . . . Finished 6th of 43. (Mr W.H.Midwood) 11.12-4. M.Keogh. 33/1.
1932 . . . Finished 3rd of 36. (Mr.W.H.Midwood) 12.12-4. D.Williams. 40/1.
1933 . . . Completed the course. (Mr W.H.Midwood) 13.12-1. Mr.P.Cazalet. 40/1.

SIR LINDSAY
brown gelding by Roi Herode - Polynetta.
1930 . . . Finished 3rd of 41. (Mr J.H.Whitney) 9.10-6. D.Williams. 100/7.
1931 . . . Fell. (Mr J.H.Whitney) 10.11-6. Mr.F.R.Thackray. 25/1.

SAVERNAKE
brown gelding by Charles O'Malley - Goura.
1930 . . . Fell. (Mr C.Anson) 10.10-10. R.McCarthy. 100/1.

SWIFT ROWLAND
brown gelding by Sir Rowland - Noble Queen.
1931 . . . Fell. (Mrs Chester Beatty) 10.11-2. T.E.Leader. 28/1.

SOUTH HILL
bay gelding by Southannan - Georgette.
1931 . . . Fell. (Mr H.G.Blagrave) 9.10-12. T.B.Cullinan. 50/1.

STARBOX
bay gelding by African Star - Pratebox.
1931 . . . Fell. (Maj.J.B.Walker) 8.10-10. Mr.K.Urquhart. 100/1.

SOLANUM
bay gelding by Pomme-de-Terre - Speckled Agnes.
1931 . . . Fell. (Miss D.Paget) 6.10-8. J.Hamey. 50/1.

SLIEVE GRIEN
brown gelding by By George! - Broidery.
1931 . . . Brought-down. (Capt.R.B.Moseley) 10.10-7. Capt.R.B.Moseley. 66/1.

SEA SOLDIER
chestnut gelding by Man O' War - Sea Name.
1932 . . . Finished 8th of 36. (Mr A.H.Niblack) aged. 11-7. Mr.A.G.Wilson. 50/1.

SLATER
bay gelding by Southannan - Miss Madcap.
1933 . . . Finished 3rd of 34. (Mr G.S.L.Whitelaw) 8.10-7.Mr.M.Barry. 50/1.
1934 . . . Pulled-up. (Mr G.S.L.Whitelaw) 9.10-12. K.Piggott. 33/1.
1935 . . . Fell. (Mr G.S.L.Whitelaw) 10.10-7. F.Maxwell. 50/1.

SOUTHERN HERO
bay gelding by Bachelor's Jap - Torfrida.
1933 . . . Completed the course. (Mr J.V.Rank) 8.10-12. T.Isaac. 50/1.
1934 . . . Fell. (Mr J.V.Rank) 9.11-5. J.Fawcus. 25/1.
1935 . . . Fell. (Mr J.V.Rank) 10.11-0. J.Fawcus. 20/1.

SOCIETY
chestnut mare by Sonning - Highland Princess.
1933 . . . Fell. (Mr G.P.Shakerley) 7.10-8. Mr.G.P.Shakerley. 20/1.

SORLEY BOY
brown gelding by Cottage - Maura Kishaun.
1934 . . . Fell. (Mrs F.Ambrose Clark) 8.11-1. D.Morgan. 100/7.

SOUTHERN HUE
brown gelding by Southannan - Lady Noggs.
1934 . . . Pulled-up. (Mr A.R.Smith) 10.10-7. T.F.Carey. 66/1.
1935 . . . Fell. (Mr Jos.McGrath) 11.10-7. P.Powell. 100/1.

SUNSPOT II
bay gelding by Sun Charmer - Step Daughter.
1937 . . . Fell. (Mrs M.Burke) 7.10-5. R.Everett. 100/1.

SUGAR LOAF
bay gelding by Sir Berkeley - Sallynoggin.
1937 . . . Fell. (Mrs H.H.Stubbs) 10.10-0. E.Carr. 100/1.

SPIONAUD
bay gelding by Spion Kop - Miss Maud.
1937 . . . Fell. (Mr D.A.Jackson) 9.10-0. E.Brown. 18/1.

STALBRIDGE PARK
chestnut gelding by Finchale - Maybush.
1938 . . . Fell. (Mr C.Hennecart) 7.10-2. G.Wilson. 100/6.

SYMAETHIS
brown mare by Poor Man - Mount Etna's Sister.
1939 . . . Finished 5th of 37. (Mr Arthur Sainsbury) 7.10-0. M.Feakes. 66/1.
1940 . . . Finished 4th of 30. (Mr A.Sainsbury) 8.10-7. M.Feakes.100/6.

SECOND ACT
brown gelding by Achtoi - Think Twice.
1939 . . . Fell. (Mrs A.A.Sidney Villar) 8.10-5. J.Dowdeswell. 100/1.
1940 . . . Broke-down. (Mrs A.A.Sidney Villar) 9.10-3. J.Dowdeswell. 100/1.

SPORTING PIPER
brown gelding by Piper's Son - Clonkea.
1939 . . . Fell. (Mr R.Strutt) 8.10-0. Mr.J.Hislop. 50/1.

SCOTCH WOOD
bay gelding by Hurstwood - Lady Wilavil.
1939 . . . Fell. (Mr A.Gillson) 9.10-0. Capt.P.Herbert. 100/1.

ST GEORGE II
chestnut gelding by St Tudwal - dam unknown
1939 . . . Refused. (Mr A.J.G.Leveson Gower) 8.10-11. Mr.R.Petre. 33/1.

STERLING DUKE
bay gelding by Inverveigh - Tavora.
1940 . . . Pulled-up. (Sir A.Maguire) 9.10-3. T.Hyde. 100/6.

SCHUBERT
bay gelding by Lightening Artist - Wild Music.
1946 . . . Finished 5th of 34. (Mrs K.Cameron) 12.11-0. C.Beechener. 100/7.
1947 . . . Finished 13th of 57. (Mrs K.Cameron) 13.10-11. C.Beechener. 66/1.
1948 . . . Finished 13th of 43. (Mrs K.Cameron) 14.10-2. L.McMorrow. 66/1.

SYMBOLE
bay gelding by Ptolemy -Dolly Varden.
1946 . . . Fell. (Mr M.R.Saint) aged. 11-11. W.Redmond. 33/1.

SUZERAIN II
chestnut gelding by Monarch - Savane.
1946 . . . Fell. (Mr Ben Davis) 8.10-3. G.Archibald. 33/1.

SILVER FAME
chestnut gelding by Werwolf - Silver Fairy.
1946 . . . Fell. (Lord Bicester) 7.10-0. D.Ruttle. 40/1.
1947 . . . Fell. (Lord Bicester) 8.10-12. Capt.R.Petre. 33/1.
1948 . . . Fell. (Lord Bicester) 9.11-6. M.Molony. 9/1.Fav.*

SOME CHICKEN
brown gelding by Scarlet Tiger - Fourfold.
1947 . . . Finished 5th of 57. (Mr J.J.Cleaver) 10.10-2. R.Turnell. 40/1.
1948 . . . Fell. (Mr J.J.Clever) 11.10-0. W.Redmond. 50/1.

SHIELA'S COTTAGE
bay mare by Cottage - Sheila. Bred by Mrs.J.H.Daly.
1947 . . . Fell. (Sir Hervey Bruce) 8.10-1. A.P.Thompson. 40/1.
1948 . . . WON. (Mr J.Proctor) 9.10-7. 43 Ran. A.P.Thompson. 50/1.

SODA II
grey gelding by Biribi - Star. Bred in France.
1947 . . . Fell. (Mr G.Glover) 6.10-2. F.Gurney. 50/1.
1948 . . . Fell. (Mrs V.M.Pulham) 7.10-0. H.Bonneau. 40/1.
1950 . . . Fell. (Mrs V.M.Pulham) 9.10-5. K.Mullins. 33/1.

SHANAKILL
black gelding by Kingcob - Amicitia.
1947 . . . Fell. (Mr R.I.Sainsbury) 9.10-0. W.Denson. 100/1.

SIR JOHN
brown gelding by Knight Of The Garter - Landgirl 1V.
1948 . . . Fell. (Mr F.Dyson) 7.10-3. Maj.C.Blacker. 100/1.

SKOURAS
brown gelding by Phideas - Queen Phyl.
1948 . . . Pulled-up. (Mr R.Collen) 8.10-0. A.Power. 100/1.
1950 . . . Unseated rider. (Mr A.G.Delahooke) 10.10-2. M.Browne. 100/1.
1952 . . . Fell. (Mr R.Keith) 12.10-13. Mr.R.Keith. 66/1.

SERPENTINE
bay gelding by Sea Serpent - Chinese Girl.
1948 . . . Fell. (Mr D.P.O'Brien) 10.10-0. C.Mitchell. 100/1.

SAN MICHELE
brown gelding by Tiberius - Buchaness.
1949 . . . Fell. (Mr H.W.Metcalfe) 9.10-5. Mr.J.Boddy. 66/1.
1950 . . . Fell. (Mr H.W.Metcalfe) 10.10-0. J.Boddy. 100/1.

SOUTHBOROUGH
bay gelding by Gainsborough - Liloan.
1949 . . . Fell. (Contessa di Sant Elia) 11.10-1. P.Murray. 66/1.
1950 . . . Fell. (Contessa di Sant Elia) 12.10-0. E.Reavey. 100/1.

STONE COTTAGE
bay gelding by Cottage - Tavora.
1949 . . . Fell. (Mr C.Nicholson) 8.10-1. M.Hogan. 66/1.

SHIPS BELL
chestnut gelding by Samphire - Tinklebell.
1949 . . . Fell. (Mrs M.Parker) 9.10-0. M.O'Dwyer. 66/1.
1950 . . . Finished 6th of 49. (Mrs M.Parker) 10.10-0. M.O'Dwyer. 66/1.

SAGACITY
chestnut gelding by Nell's Son - Mad Margaret.
1949 . . . Fell on flat after 3rd fence. (Mr J.McCann) 11.10-0. A.Power. 66/1.

SEN TOI
bay gelding by Sun Yat-Sen - Blue Nile.
1949 . . . Brought-down. (Mr J.J.Cleaver) 14.10-5. T.Cusack. 66/1.

SAFETY LOCH
bay gelding by Loch Desmond - Safety Catch.
1950 . . . Pulled-up. (Mrs J.H.Thursby) 9.10-0. Mr.D.Punshon. 100/1.

SAINTFIELD
bay gelding by Match - Edgarette.
1950 . . . Fell. (Lt.Col.N.M.H.Wall) 13.10-0. Mr.M.Gosling. 100/1.

SHAGREEN
bay gelding by Epigram - Cooleen.
1950 . . . Fell. (Mr J.V.Rank) 9.11-8. G.Kelly. 20/1.
1951 . . . Fell. (Mr J.V.Rank) 10.12-2. G.Kelly. 10/1.

SERGEANT KELLY
bay gelding by Roidore - Southern Vale.
1951 . . . Brought-down. (Mr F.C.Brambleby) 10.10-12. R.De'Ath. 40/1.
1952 . . . Finished 10th of 47. (Mr F.C.Brambleby) 11.10-9. R.Cross. 100/1. Remounted.*

STOCKMAN
brown gelding by Cottage - dam said to be Caricato.
1950 . . . Fell. (Mr R.G.Patton) 8.11-1. D.Thomas. 100/1.
1951 . . . Brought-down. (Mrs E.D.Thacker) 9.10-2. G.Vergette.100/1.

STALBRIDGE ROCK
bay gelding by Blunderbuss - Rock Honey.
1951 . . . Fell. (Mr R.Bazell) 8.10-5. Mr.R.McCreery. 66/1.

SKYREHOLME
chestnut gelding by Hastings - Upney Lane.
1952 . . . Fell. (Mr C.Booth) 9.11-3. R.Francis. 40/1.

STARLIT BAY
bay gelding by Noble Star - Decisive Reckoning.
1952 . . . Fell. (Lady Grimthorpe) 8.10-3. Mr.C.Straker. 50/1.

ST KATHLEEN II
black mare by Berwick - Hands Up 11.
1952 . . . Fell. (Mr S.Small) 9.10-2. P.J.Doyle. 50/1.

SENLAC HILL
chestnut gelding by King Hal - Bartilast.
1953 . . . Finished 5th of 31. (Lord Bicester) 8.10-10. R.Francis. 66/1.

STEEL LOCK
brown gelding by Steel Point - Frisky Lass.
1953 . . . Brought-down. (Mr E.Maggs) 9.10-0. Mr.E.Maggs. 66/1.
1955 . . . Knocked-over. (Mrs D.M.Harris) 11.10-0. J.A.Bullock. 66/1.

SANPERION
brown gelding by Perion - Santlet.
1954 . . . Finished 5th of 29. (Mr J.H.Burgess) 9.10-2. D.Leslie. 20/1.

SOUTHERN COUP
bay gelding by Coup de Lyon - Southernmore.
1954 . . . Finished 8th of 29. (Capt.E.A.Gargan) 12.10-10. A.P.Thompson. 40/1.

SWINTON HERO
bay gelding by Gay Morning - Swinton Helga.
1954 . . . Fell. (Mr D.Fowler) 10.10-6. Mr.C.B.Harty. 66/1.

● Sundew races clear of Wyndburgh in 1957, thanks in no small part to the skill of jockey Fred Winter who coolly handled a succession of mistakes.

STATESMAN
bay gelding by Mazarin - Passe.
1954 . . . Fell. (Mrs S.C.Magnier) 8.10-0. E.Newman. 50/1.

SUNDEW
chestnut gelding by Sun King - Parsonstown Gem. Bred by Mr.N.McArdle.
1955 . . . Fell. (Mrs G.Kohn) 9.11-3. P.J.Doyle. 28/1.
1956 . . . Fell. (Mrs G.Kohn) 10.11-4. F.T.Winter. 8/1.
1957 . . . WON (Mrs G.Kohn) 11.11-7. 35 Ran. F.T.Winter. 20/1.

SUN CLASP
bay gelding by Sol Oriens - Buckle.
1955 . . . Fell. (Mr E.O.Boardman) 7.10-0. J.Power. 66/1.

SYDNEY JONES
chestnut gelding by Davy Jones - Prudence 11.
1957 . . . Finished 7th of 35. (Mr P.S.Tory) 10.10-5. Mr.M.Tory. 25/1.
1958 . . . Brought-down. (Mr P.S.Tory) 11.10-12.Mr.M.Tory. 28/1.

SANDY JANE II
bay mare by Sandyman - Mamma 11.
1957 . . . Finished 10th of 35. (Mrs P.M.Lamb) 10.10-2. H.R.Beasley. 40/1.

SENTINA
bay or brown gelding by Fortna - Senria.
1958 . . . Brought-down. (Duchess of Westminster) 8.10-11. P.Taaffe. 18/1.

SPRINGSILVER
chestnut gelding by Fortina - Drumquin.
1958 . . . Fell. (Mrs M.F.Magnier) 8.10-4. F.T.Winter. 18/1.

SOUTHERNTOWN
bay gelding by Rosolio 11 - Southernmore.
1958 . . . Unseated rider. (Mr P.J.M.Place) 12.10-1. P.Cowley. 66/1.
1959 . . . Fell. (Mr P.J.M.Place) 13.10-0. P.Cowley. 100/1.

SLIPPERY SERPENT
chestnut gelding by Water Serpent - Coolcraheen.
1959 . . . Fell. (Mr B.Sunley) 8.10-11. P.Taaffe. 9/1.

SURPRISE PACKET II
chestnut mare by Cacador - Shady Girl 11.
1959 . . . Fell. (Mrs S.Richards) 10.10-5. G.Scott. 100/1.

SOLTOWN
brown gelding by Soldado - Droptown.
1959 . . . Fell. (Mr G.Garratt) 7.10-3. W.Brennan. 25/1.

STOP LIST
bay gelding by Union Jack - dam by Brian Walter.
1959 .. Fell. (Mr A.Watson) 10.10-1. T.Shone. 66/1.

SABARIA
bay gelding by Lighthouse 11 - Pannonia.
1960 . . . Finished 5th of 26. (Mr A.R.Turner) 9.10-3. P.G.Madden. 66/1.
1961 . . . Finished 13th of 35. (Mr A.R.Turnell) 10.10-2. M.Roberts. 100/1.

SKATEALONG
brown gelding by Tom Mix - Roller Skate.
1960 . . . Finished 8th of 26. (Mr H.Thomson Jones) 12.10-0 R.R.Harrison. 66/1.

SKIPPER JACK
bay gelding by Foam Crest - Foroughette.
1960 . . . Fell. (Mr R.A.Keith) 8.10-4. D.O'Donovan. 66/1.

SCOTTISH FLIGHT II
bay gelding by Jai Hind or Scottish Rambler - Gemma.
1961 . . . Finished 4th of 35. (Mrs A.T.Hodgson) 9.10-6. W.Rees. 100/6.

SIRACUSA
chestnut gelding by Patton - Guinea Girl.
1961 . . . Finished 10th of 35. (Mrs E.Truelove) 8.10-1. B.Wilkinson. 100/7.
1962 . . . Fell. (Mrs E.Truelove) 9.10-0. J.Gifford. 33/1.
1963 . . . Finished 14th of 47. (Mrs E.Truelove) 10.10-0. D.Mould. 33/1.

SOLFEN
bay gelding by Soldado - Fenora.
1962 . . . Finished 12th of 32. (Mr B.Naughton) 10.11-2. T.Taaffe. 9/1.

SUPERFINE
bay gelding by Supertello - Cocotte.
1962 . . . Fell. (Miss B.Kerwood) 9.10-6. Sir Wm.Pigott-Brown. 100/6.

SPRINGBOK
bay gelding by April The Fifth - Empire Song.
1962 . . . Fell. (Col.Lord Joicey) 8.10-6. P.Buckley. 100/8.
1963 . . . Finished 5th of 47. (Col.Lord Joicey) 9.10-12. G.Scott. 10/1.Fav.*
1964 . . . Finished 6th of 33. (Col.Lord Joicey) 10.10-11. G.Scott. 100/6.

SEAS END
bay gelding by Mieuxce - Tide Time.
1962 . . . Pulled-up. (Mrs M.D.Kempton) 10.10-5. J.H.Kempton. 100/1.
1963 . . . Pulled-up. (Mrs M.D.Kempton) 11.10-3. J.H.Kempton. 66/1.

SHAM FIGHT
chestnut gelding by Carnival Boy - Strife.
1963 . . . Finished 15th of 47. (Mr R.M.C.Jeffreys) 11.10-1. J.Fitzgerald. 50/1.

SOLONACE
bay gelding by Trimbush - Bright Virginia.
1963 . . . Fell. (Mr S.C.Warner) 12.10-0. K.B.White. 66/1.
1965 . . . Baulked. (Mr W.Clay) 14.10-13. R.W.Jones. 100/1.

SUPERSWEET
chestnut gelding by Supertello - Pegg's Leg.
1964 . . . Finished 12th of 33. (Miss M.Britton) 7.10-1. P.Broderick. 40/1.
1966 . . . Fell. (Miss M.Britton) 9.10-6. Mr.D.Crossley-Cooke. 100/1.

197

SEA KNIGHT
bay gelding by Sea Lover - Knight's Kwan.
1964 . . . Finished 15th of 33. (Mr F.D.Nicholson) 9.11-0. Mr.P.Nicholson. 66/1.

SIZZLE-ON
bay gelding by Aprolon - His Little Sister.
1965 . . . Brought-down. (Mrs I.D.Jordan) 9.10-13. P.Hurley. 100/1.

SWORD FLASH
brown gelding by Fair Copy - Sword Knot.
1965 . . . Pulled-up. (Mr H.T.Smith) 12.10-13. T.Ryan. 100/1.

STIRLING
chestnut gelding by Jock Scot - Clara Barton.
1966 . . . Pulled-up. (Mr W.J.Ingram) 10.10-11. H.R.Beasley. 28/1.

SOLIMYTH
chestnut gelding by Coup de Myth - Solican.
1966 . . . Pulled-up. (Lt.Col.J.R.E.Benson) 10.10-1. Mr.J.Lawrence. 100/1.

SCOTTISH FINAL
chestnut gelding by Jock Scot - Final Line.
1966 . . . Fell. (Mr B.W.Meaden) 9.10-0. J.Gamble. 100/1.
1967 . . . Finished 8th of 44. (Mr B.Howard) 10.10-0. Mr.B.Howard. 100/1.

SOLBINA
brown gelding by Soldado - Baygina.
1967 . . . Finished 6th of 44. (Mrs M.Sobell) 10.11-2. E.P.Harty. 25/1.

STEEL BRIDGE
bay gelding by Straight Deal - Miss Steel.
1967 . . . Finished 13th of 44. (Mrs W.Macauley) 9.10-0. E.Prendergast. 100/1.
1968 . . . Finished 10th of 45. (Mrs W.Macauley) 10.10-4. E.P.Harty. 100/1.
1969 . . . Finished 2nd of 30. (Mr J.Drabble) 11.10-0. R.Pitman. 50/1.

SAN ANGELO
bay gelding by Fortina - Tiberina.
1968 . . . Finished 12th of 45. (Mr E.R.Courage) 8.10-10.W.Rees.25/1.

SOME SLIPPER
chestnut gelding by His Slipper - Some Smasher.
1968 . . . Finished 13th of 45. (Mrs B.S.L.Trafford) 11.10-0. R.Atkins. 66/1.

SPECIFY
brown gelding by Specific - Ora Lamae. Bred by Mr.A.P.Parker.
1970 . . . Brought-down. (Mr F.W.Pontin) 8.10-7. J.Cook. 100/7.
1971 . . . WON. (Mr F.W.Pontin) 9.10-13. 38 Ran. J.Cook. 28/1.
1972 . . . Finished 6th of 42. (Mr F.W.Pontin) 10.10-11. B.Brogan.22/1.

SANDY SPRITE
chestnut mare by Prince Charger - Winged Sprite.
1971 . . . Finished 5th of 38. (Mrs G.M.Sandiford) 7.10-3. R.Barry. 33/1.

SOLDO
bay gelding by Sunny Boy 111 - Donica.
1971 . . . Fell. (Mrs B.Moresby) 10.10-7. D.Mould. 50/1.

SMOOTH DEALER
bay gelding by Straight Deal - Aesculus.
1971 . . . Refused. (Mr R.R.Guest) 9.10-3. A.Moore. 33/1.

SWAN SHOT
bay gelding by Combat - Swan Queen.
1972 . . . Fell. (Mr C.Freestone & Mr J.R.Craig) 9.10-3. P.McCarron. 100/1.
1973 . . . Refused. (Mr C.Freestone & Mr J.R.Craig) 10.10-0. M.Blackshaw. 100/1.

SAGGART'S CHOICE
bay gelding by Black Tarquin - Connivance.
1972 . . . Fell. (Mr V.E.Foy) 9.10-1. T.Stack. 28/1.

SPANISH STEPS
bay gelding by Flush Royal - Tiberetta.
1973 . . . Finished 4th of 38. (Mr E.R.Courage) 10.11-13. P.Blacker. 16/1.
1974 . . . Finished 4th of 42. (Mr E.R.Courage) 11.11-9. W.Smith.15/1.
1975 . . . Finished 3rd of 31. (Mr E.R.Courage) 12.10-3.W.Smith.20/1.
1976 . . . Finished 9th of 32. (Mr E.R.Courage) 13.10-2. J.King. 22/1.

SUNNY LAD
chestnut gelding by Sunny Way - Santa Baby.
1973 . . . Finished 15th of 38. (Mrs R.E.Sangster) 9.10-3. W.Smith. 25/1.
1974 . . . Finished 16th of 42. (Mrs R.E.Sangster) 10.10-4. D.Cartwright. 20/1.

SAN FELIU
bay gelding by Stephanotis - Help Yourself.
1974 . . . Finished 9th of 42. (Lady Hay) 11.10-3. P.Buckley. 22/1.

SCOUT
bay gelding by Vulgan - U . 2 .
1974 . . . Finished 11th of 42. (Mr A.D.W.Allen) 8.10-0. T.Stack. 7/1.Fav.*

STRAIGHT VULGAN
chestnut gelding by Straight Lad - Vulgeeno.
1974 . . . Fell. (Mrs G.M.Sandiford) 8.10-8. R.Barry. 15/1.

SHANEMAN
chestnut gelding by Bowsprit - Vanessa's Pet.
1974 . . . Unseated rider. (Mr T.J.Lawlor) 9.10-2. B.Hannon. 20/1.
1975 . . . Fell. (Mr P.Greenall) 10.10-8. Mr.P.Greenall. 100/1.

STEPHEN'S SOCIETY
chestnut gelding by Choral Society - Stephen's Slave.
1974 . . . Pulled-up. (Mr C.D.Collins) 8.11-5. Mr.C.D.Collins. 40/1.

SIXER
bay gelding by Grit - Queen's Ranger.
1974 . . . Brought-down. (Mr G.Clay) 10.10-0. M.Salaman. 66/1.

SOUTHERN QUEST
brown gelding by Shackleton - Princess Ponder.
1975 . . . Finished 7th of 31. (Mr W.Fletcher) 8.10-6. S.Shields. 33/1.

SPITTIN IMAGE
bay or brown gelding by Paddy's Birthday - Pride And Prejudice.
1975 . . . Fell. (Mrs J.Welch,jnr.) 9.10-0. M.Cummins. 50/1.
1976 . . . Finished 8th of 32. (Exors. of late Mrs M.Welch) 10.10-0. A.Turnell. 66/1.
1977 . . . Fell. (Mr J.Welch,jnr.) 11.10-5. R.Champion. 50/1.

SANDWILAN
brown gelding by Road House 11 - Awaken.
1976 . . . Finished 7th of 32. (Mr M.C.Spedding) 8.10-0. R.Hyett. 100/1.
1977 . . . Refused. (Mr M.C.Spedding) 9.10-0. R.Hyett. 50/1.
1979 . . . Fell. (Mr G.A.Ham) 11.10-0. Mrs.J.Hembrow. 100/1.
1980 . . . Baulked. (Mr G.A.Ham) 12.10-0. Mrs.J.Hembrow) 100/1.

SAUCY BELLE
bay mare by Pendragon - Missy.
1977 . . . Finished 11th of 42. (Mr G.D.Smith) 11.10-0. R.F.Davies. 200/1.

SIR GARNET
bay gelding by Sir Ribot - Troyweight.
1977 . . . Unseated rider. (Mr A.Kay) 8.10-3. J.J.O'Neill. 20/1.

SAGE MERLIN
bay gelding by Border Chief - Gypsy Touch.
1977 . . . Fell. (Mr J.D.Bingham) 9.10-5. I.Watkinson. 20/1.

SEBASTIAN V
chestnut gelding by Game Rights - dam unknown.
1977 . . . Fell. (Mr R.M.C.Jeffreys) 9.10-1. R.Lamb. 22/1.
1978 . . . Finished 2nd of 37. (Mr R.M.C.Jeffreys) 10.10-1. R.Lamb. 25/1.
1981 . . . Finished 11th of 39. (Mr R.M.C.Jeffreys) 13.10-1. R.Lamb. 33/1.

SONGWRITER, THE
brown gelding by Arctic Slave - Cooleen.
1977 . . . Pulled-up. (Mr P.R.Callander) 8.10-0. B.Smart. 200/1.
1978 . . . Finished 8th of 37. (Mr P.R.Callander) 9.10-0. B.Smart. 50/1.

SHIFTING GOLD
bay gelding by Bright As Gold - Short Shrift.
1978 . . . Fell. (Mr R.H.Russell) 9.11-6. R.Champion. 16/1.

SO
chestnut gelding by Little Buskins - Dutch Dish.
1978 . . . Brought down. (Mr R. de Vere Hunt) 9.10-4. Mr.N.Madden. 14/1.
1981 . . . Finished 10th of 39. (Mr R. de Vere Hunt) 12.10-6. J.Francome. 40/1.

SILKSTONE
bay gelding by Hullabaloo - Cullyvor.
1978 . . . Fell. (Mr K.C.Kelsall) 10.10-0. G.Graham. 66/1.

SADALE VI
brown gelding by Dalesa - Miss Otys 11.
1978 . . . Fell. (Mrs J.A.George) 11.10-1. C.Candy. 66/1.

SANDPIT
brown gelding by Le Tricolore - St Mary's Girl.
1979 . . . Fell. (Mrs B.D.Flood) 9.10-7. T.Carmody. 22/1.

SO AND SO
bay gelding by Sobig - Aurora's Pride.
1980 . . . Fell. (Mr D.W.Samuel) 11.10-10. R.Linley. 28/1.

SALKELD
bay gelding by David Jack - Telephonist.
1980 . . . Fell. (Mr E.Bell) 8.10-0. C.Hawkins. 20/1.

SPARTAN MISSILE
chestnut gelding by Spartan General - Polaris Missile.
1981 . . . Finished 2nd of 39. (Mr M.J.Thorne) 9.11-5. Mr.M.J.Thorne. 8/1.Fav.*
1983 . . . Unseated rider. (Mrs M.W.Thorne) 11.11-7. H.Davies. 9/1.
1984 . . . Finished 16th of 40. (Mrs M.W.Thorne) 12.11-4. Mr.J.White. 18/1.

SENATOR MACLACURY
chestnut gelding by Golden Love- Tostal Day.
1981 . . . Finished 5th of 39. (Mr F.D.Cullen) 7.10-0. J.Burke. 20/1.
1982 . . . Fell. (Mr M.Lanigan) 8.10-0. P.Kiely. 20/1.

SON AND HEIR
bay gelding by Le Prince - Killossery Star.
1981 . . . Refused. (Mr R.J.Scandrett) 11.10-0. S.Morshead. 100/1.

SAINT FILLANS
bay gelding by Saintly Song - Cleona.
1982 . . . Fell. (Mr R.Wilson) 8.10-11. P.Tuck. 35/1.

SUN LION
brown gelding by Sunny Way - Winmar's Krocus.
1982 . . . Fell. (Mr R.Waley-Cohen) 12.10-3. S.Smith Eccles. 100/1.

200

SYDNEY QUINN
bay gelding by Mourne - Well Whistled.
1983 . . . Fell. (Mr W.J.Kelly & Mr J.A.Taylor) 11.10-0. P.Double. 300/1.

SILENT VALLEY
bay gelding by Val-de-Loir - Wordless.
1984 . . . Pulled-up. (Mr J.Walby) 11.10-8. T.G.Dun. 33/1.

SCOT LANE
chestnut gelding by Jock Scot - Tandridge Lane.
1985 . . . Finished 8th of 40. (Mr T.H.Isherwood) 12.10-1. C.Smith. 28/1.

SHADY DEAL
bay gelding by Saint Denys - Kitty Shark.
1985 . . . Fell. (Mr G.A.Hubbard) 12.10-3. R.Rowe. 50/1.

SOLIHULL SPORT
bay gelding by Harwell - Vultang.
1985 . . . Fell. (Solihull Sport Services Ltd.) 11.10-0. S.Morshead. 100/1.

SOMMELIER
chestnut gelding by Le Patron - Sweet Coronation.
1986 . . . Finished 5th of 40. (Mr D.Wates) 8.10-0. T.J.Taaffe. 50/1.

ST ALEZAN
chestnut gelding by St Columbus - Alex M.
1986 . . . Brought-down. (Lord Coventry) 9.10-0. C.Smith. 150/1.

SMITHS MAN
grey gelding by Gaberdine - Doone Gate.
1987 . . . Finished 11th of 40. (Smith Mansfield Meat Co.) 9.10-0. M.Perrett. 14/1.
1988 . . . Pulled-up. (Smith Mansfield Meat Co.) 10.10-0. M.Perrett. 50/1.

SMARTSIDE
bay or brown gelding by Shackleton - Ming Tu.
1987 . . . Fell. (Mrs E.Doyle) 12.10-0. P.Gill. 100/1.
1988 . . . Fell. (Mrs V.Hambly) 13.10-4. Mr.A.Hambly. 100/1.
1989 . . . Refused. (Mrs V.Hambly & Mr P.Bartley) 14.10-5. Mr A.Hambly. 300/1.

SPARTAN ORIENT
bay gelding by Spartan General - Laughing Stock.
1987 . . . Knocked-over. (Mr H.B.Geddes & Mr J.S.King) 11.10-0. L.Harvey. 500/1.

STRANDS OF GOLD
bay gelding by Le Coq d'Or - Sweet Fanny.
1988 . . . Fell. (Independent Twine Mnfct.Co.) 9.10-3. P.Scudamore. 20/1.

SACRED PATH
bay gelding by Godswalk - Crepe Walk.
1988 . . . Fell. (Mrs C.Heath) 8.10-0. C.Cox. 17/2.Fav.*

SIR JEST
bay gelding by Sea Catch - Carnival Jest.
1988 . . . Refused. (Mr P.Piller) 10.10-2. K.Jones. 22/1.
1989 . . . Brought-down. (Mr P.Piller) 11.10-1. M.Hammond. 40/1.
1990 . . . Finished 9th of 38. (Mr P.Piller) 12.12-0. B.Storey. 66/1.

SEEANDEM
bay gelding by Frigid Aire - Fanny Fox.
1988 . . . Refused. (Mr B.J.Caffrey) 8.10-0. P.Leech. 100/1.
1989 . . . Fell. (Mr B.J.Caffrey) 9.10-0. L.Cusack. 100/1.

SIDBURY HILL
brown gelding by Cheval - Watermark 11.
1989 . . . Finished 13th of 40. (Mr S.Pike) 13.10-0. K.Mooney. 100/1.

STEARSBY
brown gelding by Politico - Lucky Sprite.
1989 . . . Refused. (Miss C.Burge & Mr P.J.Dugdale) 10.10-9. B.Powell. 14/1.
1992 . . . Pulled-up. (Mr S.Flurry) 13.10-6. S.Mackey. 250/1.

SMART TAR
bay gelding by Seaepic - I'm Smart.
1989 . . . Fell. (Mrs E.R.Courage) 8.10-3. C.Llewellyn. 18/1.

SERGEANT SPRITE
grey gelding by General Ironside - Miss Sprite.
1989 . . . Fell. (Mr D.Worth) 9.10-2. T.J.Taaffe. 50/1.

SOLARES
brown gelding by Free State - Indian Wells.
1990 . . . Finished 17th of 38. (Mr & Mrs J.L.Eyre) 10.10-0. Mr.P.McMahon. 150/1.

STARS DELIGHT
grey gelding by John de Coombe - Vanity Surprise.
1990 . . . Pulled-up. (Mr F.Barr) 8.10-0. J.Lower. 50/1.

SEAGRAM
chestnut gelding by Balak - Llanah. Bred in New Zealand by Mrs.J.A.Broome.
1991 . . . WON. (Sir Eric Parker & Mr D.H.Barons) 11.10-6. 40 Ran. N.Hawke. 12/1.
1992 . . . Pulled-up. (Sir Eric Parker & Mr D.H.Barons) 12.11-4. N.Hawke. 33/1.

SOLIDASAROCK
chestnut gelding by Hardboy - Limefield Rita.
1991 . . . Pulled-up. (Mr L.Randall) 9.10-4. G.Bradley. 50/1.

SOUTHERNAIR
bay gelding by Derryin - Port La Joie.
1991 . . . Fell. (Mr S.Powell) 11.10-1. Mr.J.Simo. 100/1.

STAY ON TRACKS
grey gelding by Roselier - Bee In Bonnet.
1992 . . . Finished 9th of 40. (Mr P.Piller) 10.10-0. C.Grant. 16/1.

SIRRAH JAY
bay or brown gelding by Tug Of War - Dellasville.
1992 . . . Finished 22nd of 40. (Mr J.Gale) 12.10-0. R.J.Beggan. 100/1.

SOUTHERN MINSTREL
chestnut gelding by Black Minstrel
1994 . . . Pulled-up. (Mr B.Hathaway) 11.10-0. M.Dwyer. 50/1.

SUPERIOR FINISH
brown gelding by Oats - Emancipated.
1995 . . . Unseated rider. (Mr G.Henfrey) 9.10-3. P.Niven. 33/1.
1996 . . . Finished 3rd of 27. (Mr P.McGrane) 10.10-3. R.Dunwoody. 9/1.

SIR PETER LELY
bay gelding by Teenoso - Picture.
1996 . . . Finished 4th of 27. (John Doyle Construction Ltd.) 9.10-0. Mr.C.Bonner. 33/1.

SURE METAL
bay gelding by Billion - Sujini.
1996 . . . Finished 17th of 27. (Mr L.A.Morgan) 13.10-1. D.McCain. 200/1.

SON OF WAR
grey gelding by Pragmatic - Run Wardasha.
1996 . . . Unseated rider. (Mrs V.O'Brien) 9.11-0. C.O'Dwyer. 8/1.

TRUE BLUE
1839 . . . Finished 4th of 17. (Mr Stephenson) Mr.Barker. n/q.

TINDERBOX
1843 . . . Fell. (Mr Hunt) G.Moore. n/q.
1846 . . . Fell. (Mr Robertson) P.Daley. n/q.

TEETOTUM
1843 . . . Fell. (Mr Kennedy) Mr.Kennedy. n/q.

TOM TUG
1844 . . . Finished 3rd of 15. (Mr Tilbury) Rackley. n/q.
1845 . . . Finished 4th of 15. (Mr J.T.Blackburn) Mr.Crickmere. 5/1.

TROUBADOR
1846 . . . Fell. (Mr Austin) G.B.Rammell. n/q.

TRAMP
1847 . . . Failed to finish. (Mr W.Hall) - 10-6. W.Archer. n/q.

TROUT
1855 . . . Fell. (Mr W.Moseley) - 10-12. J.Tasker. 3/1.Fav.*

TIPPERARY BOY
1849 . . . Failed to finish. (Mr Terry) 5.10-9. Barley. n/q.
1850 . . . Finished 4th of 32. (Mr Hughes) 6.10-0. S.Darling. n/q.
1851 . . . Failed to finish. (Mr Tollitt) 7.10-3. T.Olliver. 10/1.
1853 . . . Failed to finish. (Mr S.Lucy) 9.10-10. Butler. n/q.

TIMOTHY
1854 . . . Refused. (Mr A.Sait) - 9-6. H.Lamplugh. 40/1.

TREACHERY
1857 . . . Finished 3rd of 28. (Mt T.Hughes) 5. 9-0. Poole. n/q.
1858 . . . Pulled-up. (Mr T.Hughes) 6. 9-8. W.White. 4/1.Fav.*

TEDDESLEY
1857 . . . Failed to finish. (Mr Hylton) - 9-0. R.Ascher. 12/1.

TEASE
1860 . . . Brought-down. (Mr Francis) - 10-2. W.White. 7/1.

TELEGRAM
1860 . . . Failed to finish. (Mr Worthington) - 9-9. Palmer. 100/7.

THOMASTOWN
1862 . . . Refused. (Mr T.Naghten) - 10-4. J.Murphy. 6/1.
1864 . . . Finished 4th of 24. (Mr T.Naghten) - 12-0. J.Murphy. 33/1.
1866 . . . Fell. (Mr T.Naghten) - 11-4. J.Murphy. 50/1.
1867 . . . Pulled-up. (Mr T.Naghten) - 11-3. J.Murphy,jnr. 25/1.

TATTLER, THE
1862 . . . Pulled-up. (Mr W.G.Craven) - 9-8. C.Boyce. 100/8.

TELEGRAPH
1863 . . . Fell. (Mr Campbell) - 9-11. G.Waddington. n/q.

TUMBLER
1865 . . . Refused. (Captain J.White) - 10-6. Mr.Drake. n/q.

TONY LUMPKIN
A gelding by the stallion
1865 . . . Pulled-up. (Colonel Forster) - 10-4. Mr.Thomas. 100/7.

TURNER
1866 . . . Failed to finish. (Mr T.Parr) 6.10-10. Reeves. 50/1.

TENNYSON
brown gelding by Ethelbert - Maud.
1867 . . . Finished 8th of 23. (Lord Coventry) 5.10-10. G.Stevens.50/1.

THALASSIUS
bay horse by Stockwell - Beauty.
1868 . . . Fell. (Lord Stamford) 6.10-0. Mr.Crawshaw.40/1.

TATHWELL
brown gelding by Canute - Imagination.
1870 . . . Failed to finish. (Mr S.J.Welfitt) aged. 10-12. G.Waddington. 20/1.

TRAVELLER
chestnut gelding by Young Birdcatcher - dam by Belzoni.
1870 . . . Fell. (Lord Eglinton) 5.10-4. Napier. n/q.

TUSCULANUM
bay gelding by Stockwell - Frenzy.
1871 . . . Finished 5th of 25. (Capt.W.H.Cooper) 9.11-0. Capt.Smith. 40/1.

TRUE BLUE
bay gelding by Romulus - Attack.
1873 . . . Fell. (Lord Queensberry) 7.10-13.Lord Queensberry. n/q.

THYRA
brown mare by Tim Whiffler - Jollyboat.
1876 . . . Refused. (Mr J.Robinson) 6.10-6. W.Daniels. 20/1.

TATTOO
brown horse by Belladrum - Breaffy.
1878 . . . Fell. (Mr J.G.Blake) 6.10-3. W.Canavan.

TURCO
black horse by Selim - Breda.
1879 . . . Finished 9th of 18. (Mr R.Stackpoole) 7.10-9. Mr.H.Beasley.100/7.

THORNFIELD
bay gelding by Favonius - Juliana.
1881 . . . Finished 3rd of 13. (Mr L. de Rothschild) 5.10-9. R.Marsh. 11/2.jnt/Fav.*

TOM JONES
bay gelding by Paul Jones - Lady Gertrude.
1884 . . . Fell. (Sir W.Eden) 7.10-4. Capt.Lee Barber. 25/1.

TERRIER
chestnut gelding by Barbillon or Wild Tommy - Hopbine.
1884 . . . Fell. (Duke of Hamilton) 4.10-0. Mr.D.Thirlwell.25/1.

TOO GOOD
brown gelding by Ingomar or Uncas - Mary Hyland.
1886 . . . Finished 2nd of 23. (Count Erdody) 7.11-12. Mr.H.Beasley.7/1.
1887 . . . Finished 6th of 16. (Count Erdody) 8.11-10. Mr.H.Beasley.100/7.

TRAP
bay horse by Macgregor - Ambuscade.
1888 . . . Fell. (Mr Churton) 8.10-6. G.Lowe. 20/1.

TENBY
brown gelding by The Brigand - dam unknown.
1892 . . . Fell. (Mr A.M.Singer) 9.11-2. C.Gregor. 100/7.

TIT FOR TAT
brown gelding by Quits - Evelyn.
1893 . . . Finished 4th of 15. (Col.A.G.Lucas) 9.10-0. G.Williamson. 25/1.

TROUVILLE
chestnut mare by Beaurepaire - Woinika. Bred in France.
1894 . . . Finished 4th of 14. (Duke of Hamilton) 6.10-6. Mr.J.C.Cheney. 25/1.

TIMON
bay horse by Timothy - Mabel Emma.
1897 . . . Finished 6th of 28. (Mr R.W.Brown) 6. 9-10. J.Tervit. 20/1.

TRADE MARK
bay gelding by Prism - Hall Mark.
1899 . . . Pulled-up. (Mr A.Alexander) 6.10-2. J.Knox. 25/1.

TRUE BLUE
brown or roan gelding - - pedigree unknown.
1901 . . . Broke leg. (Mr V.A.Parnell) 10. 9-13. P.Woodland. 66/1.

TIPPERARY BOY
bay or brown horse by Royal Meath - The Tart.
1902 . . . Finished 6th of 21. (Mr T.B.Holmes) 8.11-6. T.Moran. 100.8.

TIMOTHY TITUS
chestnut gelding by Timothy - Precipice.
1905 . . . Fell. (Mr W.B.Partridge) 7.10-5. E.Morgan. 100/6.
1906 . . . Fell. (Mr W.B.Partrdige) 8.10-12. E.Morgan. 10/1.
1907 . . . Fell. (Mr W.B.Partridge) 9.11-10. C.Kelly. 100/8.

TOM WEST
bay gelding by Old Buck - Mother Shipton.
1907 . . . Finished 2nd of 23. (Mr H.Hardy) 8. 9-12. H.Murphy.100/6.
1908 . . . Fell. (Mr H.Hardy) 9.10-7. H.Murphy. 8/1.
1909 . . . Finished 4th of 32. (Mr H.Hardy) 10.10-9. H.Murphy. 100/6.

TEDDIE III
bay mare by Warsprite - Bayberry.
1907 . . . Fell. (Mr W.P.Hanly) 9. 9-13. Mr.P.O'Brien-Butler. n/q.

TRIANON III
grey gelding by Champaubert - Marie Antoinette.
1911 . . . Fell. (Mnsr.H de Mumm) 6.11-8. R.Sauval. 33/1.
1913 . . . Fell. (Mnsr.H de Mumm) 8.12-3. W.O'Connor. 33/1.
1914 . . . Finished 2nd of 20. (Mnsr.H. de Mumm) 9.11-9. C.Hawkins.100/8.

THOWL PIN
bay gelding by Pilot - Hairpin.
1913 . . . Fell. (Mr F.Bibby) 8.11-9. I.Morgan. 20/1.
1914 . . . Fell. (Mr F.Bibby) 9.10-10. I.Morgan. 33/1.
1915 . . . failed to finish. (Mr F.Bibby) 10.10-8. W.J.Smith. 33/1.
*1916 . . . Completed course. (Mr F.Bibby) 11.10-12. C.Kelly. 8/1.
*1917 . . . Pulled-up. (Mr F.Bibby) 12.10-7. C.Kelly. n/q.

● **Tipperary Tim and Bill Dutton came home alone in 1928 to probably the quietest reception ever accorded a National winner. The price? 100/1**

206

TOKAY
black or brown gelding by Santoi - Sweet Muscat.
1913 . . . Fell. (Mr J.Langley) 7.11-0. M.Hopper. 50/1.

TEMPLEDOWNEY
bay gelding by Bushey Park - Galway Girl.
* 1917 . . . Fell. (Major D.Dixon) 8.12-7. T.Hulme. 25/1.

TOP HOLE
chestnut gelding by Caedmon - Childish.
* 1918 . . . Completed course. (Mr F.W.Parnell) 8.11-2. C.Hawkins.50/1.

TURK II, THE
brown gelding by Turk's Cap - Ethel's Darling.
1919 . . . Fell. (Mr C.L.Willcox) 9. 9-7. Mr.P.Roberts.100/1.
1920 . . . Finished 2nd of 24. (Mr C.L.Willcox) 10. 9-8. R.Burford.n/q.
1922 . . . Fell. (Mr T.A.Skelton) 12.10-11. I.Anthony. 33/1.
1923 . . . Fell. (Mr T.A.Arthur) 13.10-2. C.Donnelly. n/q.

TROYTOWN
brown gelding by Zria - Diane.Bred by Major T.G.Collins.
1920 . . . WON. (Major T.G.C.Gerrard) 7.11-9. 24 Ran.Mr.J.R.Anthony. 6/1.

TURKEY BUZZARD
bay horse by White Eagle - Therapia.
1920 . . . Fell. (Mrs H.M.Hollins) 7.10-7. W.Payne. 100/7.
1921 . . . Finished 4th of 35. (Mrs H.M.Hollins) 8.12-2.Remounted.* Capt.G.H.Bennet. 100/9.
1923 . . . Fell. (Mrs H.M.Hollins) 10.12-6. F.Brookes. 33/1.

TAFFYTUS
bay gelding by Eaves Dropper - Faithful Lassie.
1922 . . . Finished 3rd of 32. (Mr J.C.Bulteel) 9.11-0. T.E.Leader.66/1.
1923 . . . Fell. (Mr J.C.Bulteel) 10.11-7. T.E.Leader. 100/8.
1924 . . . Fell. (Mr J.C.Bulteel) 11.10-6. T.E.Leader. 100/12.
1925 . . . Refused. (Mr J.C.Bulteel) 12.10-9. R.Lyall. 40/1.

TRENTINO
brown gelding by Frontino - Enchanted Queen.
1923 . . . Fell. (Major W.N.Hillas) 9.11-7. Maj.J.Wilson. 66/1.

THROWN IN
chestnut horse by Beau Bill - Va Largo.
1925 . . . Fell. (Mr D.Faber) 9.10-8. J.Goswell. 28/1.
1926 . . . Finished 7th of 30. (Lord Stalbridge) 10.10-11.Mr.H.Grosvenor. 33/1.
1927 . . . Fell. (Lord Stalbridge) 11.11-10. Mr.H.Grosvenor. 100/8.

TEST MATCH
brown gelding by Captivation - The Test.
1926 . . . Fell. (Mr H.Mosenthal) 8.10-5. P.L'Estrange. 66/1.
1927 . . . Fell. (Mr G.L.Redmond) 9.11-1. R.Lyall. 50/1.
1928 . . . Refused. (Mr G.L.Redmond) 10.10-9. J.M.Maloney.66/1.

TRUMP CARD
brown gelding by Clarionet - Peggy Symons.
1927 . . . Fell. (Mr G.Newall Nairn) 9.11-1. Mr.S.H.Dennis. 33/1.
1928 . . . Fell. (Mr G.Newall Nairn) 10.11-10. K.Piggott. 11/2.
1929 . . . Fell. (Mr G.Newall Nairn) 11.11-12. T.Morgan. 33/1.
1931 . . . Refused. (Lord Stalbridge) 13.11-5. W.Gurney. 66/1.

TIPPERARY TIM
brown gelding by Cipango - Last Lot.Bred by Mr.J.J.Ryan.
1928 . . . WON. (Mr H.S.Kenyon) 10.10-0. 42 Ran. Mr.W.P.Dutton.100/1.
1929 . . . Fell. (Mr H.S.Kenyon) 11.10-10. Mr.W.P.Dutton. 100/1.

THEOREM
black or brown gelding by Bushido - Theobald's Park.
1929 . . . Fell. (Mr H.M.Llewellyn) 12.10-0. T.Costello. 200/1.
1930 . . . Fell. (Sir David Llewellyn) 13.10-0. Mr.G.Owen,jnr. 100/1.

TOY BELL
brown gelding by Santoi - Clarebell.
1929 . . . Fell. (Mrs R.D.Cohen) 7.10-0. D.Morgan. 100/1.
1930 . . . Fell. (Mrs R.D.Cohen) 8.10-5. D.Morgan. 66/1.
1931 . . . Brought-down.(Mrs R.D.Cohen) 9.10-7. D.Morgan. n/q.

TOOTENHILL
bay gelding by Poet Laureate - Think Of Me.
1930 . . . Fell. (Mrs D.H.Boswall- Preston) 8.10-7.C.Wenham. 33/1.
1932 . . . Refused. (Mrs D.H.Boswall-Preston) 10.10-7. R.McCarthy.66/1.

THERAS
chestnut gelding by Lomond - Thera H.
1931 . . . Fell. (Mr Holford Harrison) 6.11-2. J.Walsh. 100/1.
1932 . . . Baulked. (Mr J.Metcalf) 7.10-12. Mr.G.Owen,jnr.66/1.
1933 . . . Fell. (Mr J.Metcalf) 8.10-10. G.Owen. 40/1.
1935 . . . Refused. (Mr J.Metcalf) 10.10-7. T.F.Carey. 100/1.

TAMASHA
black or brown gelding by Santoi - Reception.
1931 . . . Fell. (Mr G.Elliott) 10.10-7. Mr.G.Elliott. 40/1.

TROUBLE MAKER
bay gelding by Berrilldon - The Busybody.
1933 . . . Comppleted the course. (Mrs T.H.Somerville) aged. 11-6. Mr.N.Laing. 100/1.

TROCADERO
bay horse by Jaeger - Nivoletta.
1933 . . . Completed the course. (Vicomte Max de Rivaud) aged.11-2.M.Thery. 100/1.
1934 . . . Fell. (Vicomte Max de Rivaud) aged.10-13. M.Thery. 100/7.
1935 . . . Fell. (Mr G.F.Perry) aged. 10-8. T.B.Cullinan. 50/1.

THOMOND II
chestnut gelding by Drinmore - dam by St Luke.
1934 . . . Finished 3rd of 30. (Mr J H.Whitney) 8.12-4. W.Speck. 18/1.
1935 . . . Finished 3rd of 27. (Mr J.H.Whitney) 9.11-13. W.Speck. 9/2.

TAPINOIS
bay gelding by Tapin - Pepita.
1935 . . . Fell. (Mr F.E.Peek) 7.10-7. F.Gurney. 8/1.
1937 . . . Fell. (Mr W.Hutchinson) 9.10-10. F.Maxwell. 40/1.
1938 . . . Pulled-up. (Mr W.Hutchinson) 10.10-1. A.Scratchley. 100/1.

TRUE BLUE
bay gelding by Obliterate - True.
1937 . . . Fell. (Mr P.Eliot-Cohen) 9.10-0. Mr.P.Eliot-Cohen. 100/1.

TAKVOR PACHA
chestnut gelding by Mazeppa 11 - Have-A-Care.
1938 . . . Unseated rider. (Marquis de San Miquel) 6.10-9. A.Kalley.100/7.
1940 . . . Finished 7th of 30. (Maj.H.P.Rushton) 8.10-4. Maj.O.Prior-Palmer. 33/1.

TEME WILLOW
brown gelding by Border Minstrel - Sirvente.
1939 . . . Fell. (Sir E.Hanmer) 8.10-13. T.F.Rimell. 100/9.

TUCKMILL
bay gelding by Jackdaw-Of-Rheims - Brightlingsea.
1939 . . . Carried-out. (Mr G.Roll) 9.10-0. G.Kelly. 100/1.
1940 . . . Finished 17th of 30. (Mr G.Roll) 10.10-3. G.Kelly. 100/1.

TULYRA
bay gelding by Mascot - Jobstown Lady.
1946 . . . Fell. (Mr D.A.Jackson) 10.10-0. Mr.D.Jackson. 100/1.
1947 . . . Refused. (Mr D.A.Jackson) 11.10-0. Mr.D.Jackson. 100/1.

TOYETTE
bay gelding by Yutoi - Movie Queen.
1947 . . . Finished 16th of 57. (Maj.R.Waugh-Harris) 10.10-6.Maj.R.Waugh-Harris. 100/1.

TRIBUNE
bay or brown gelding by Bhuidhaonach - Trefoil.
1947 . . . Pulled-up. (Mrs G.Jansen) 13.10-0. K.Gilsenan. 100/1.

TUDOR CLOSE
bay gelding by Wavetop - Eerie.
1948 . . . Fell. (Mr P.D.Turner) 11.10-3. T.Maher. 100/1.

TOMMY TRADDLES
brown gelding by Felstead - Gleesome.
1948 . . . Unseated rider. (Mr J.S.Schillizi) 7.10-0. C.Harrison. 100/1.
1950 . . . Fell. (Mr J.S.Schillizi) 9.10-1. F.O'Connor. 66/1.

TONDERMAN
brown gelding by Tonton - St Mary Cray.
1949 . . . Finished 7th of 43. (Mr J.Bloom) 12.10-4. Mr.J.Bloom. 66/1.

TEXAS DAN
bay gelding by Jesmond Dene - Mrs Witch.
1951 . . . Brought-down. (Mr H.Riddell) 9.10-1. P.Fitzgerald. 66/1.

TASMAN
bay gelding by Invershin - Middy's Gal.
1951 . . . Fell. (Mr G.Varnavas) 11.10-0. C.Hook. 100/1.

TEAL
bay gelding by Bimco - Miltown Queen. Bred by Mr.G.Carroll.
1952 . . . WON. (Mr H.Lane) 10.10-12. 47 Ran. A.P.Thompson.100/7.

TANTIVY
bay gelding by Foxhunter - Tivoli 11.
1952 . . . Fell. (Mr C.Burns) 11.11-1. Mr.M.Westwick. 50/1.

TAVOY
chestnut horse by Airway - Nem Tavol.
1952 . . . Pulled-up. (Mr T.Johnson) 9.10-0. D.McCann. 100/1.

TRAVELLER'S PRIDE
brown mare by Bagman - Mrldoon's Pride.
1952 . . . Fell. (Mr S.Pickles) 9.10-1. L.Stephens. 100/1.

TUDOR LINE
chetsnut gelding by King Hal - Miss Lucy Glitters.
1954 . . . Finished 2nd of 29. (Mrs E.Truelove) 9.10-7. G.Slack. 10/1.
1955 . . . Finished 2nd of 30. (Mrs E.Truelove) 10.11-3. G.Slack. 10/1.

TRIPLE TORCH
chestnut gelding by Victory Torch - Triskeles.
1954 . . . Unseated rider. (Maj.J.I.Medlicott) 8.10-0. D.Ancil. 66/1.

TIBERETTA
bay mare by Tiberius - Drumrora.
1957 . . . Finished 3rd of 35. (Mr E.R.Courage) 9.10-0. A.Oughton.66/1.
1958 . . . Finished 2nd of 31. (Mr E.R.Courage) 10.10-6. G.Slack. 28/1.
1959 . . . Finished 4th of 34. (Mr E.R.Courage) 11.10-9. A.Oughton.20/1.

TUTTO
chestnut gelding by Totaig - Tut Tartan.
1957 . . . Fell. (Miss E.R.Armitage) 10.10-6. J.Lehane. 100/6.

TURMOIL
bay gelding by Lighthouse 11 - Capitation.
1959 . . . Pulled-up. (Mrs G.Kohn) 9.10-1. J.Hudson. 20/1.

TEA FIEND
bay gelding by Colombo - Maureen's Lass.
1960 . . . Finished 4th of 26. (Mr J.D.Pickering) 11.10-0. P.G.Madden.33/1.

TEAM SPIRIT
bay gelding by Vulgan - Lady Walewska. Bred by Mr.P.J.Coonan.
1960 . . . Fell. (Mrs D.R.Brand) 8.10-12. G.W.Robinson. 9/1.
1961 . . . Finished 9th of 35. (Mrs D.R.Brand) 9.10-13.G.W.Robinson.20/1.
1962 . . . Fell. (Mr R.B.Woodard) 10.10-6. G.W.Robinson. 22/1.
1963 . . . Finished 4th of 47. (Mr R.B.Woodard) 11.10-3.G.W.Robinson. 13/1.
1964 . . . WON. (Mr J.K.Goodman) 12.10-3. 33 Ran.G.W.Robinson. 18/1.

TAXIDERMIST
bay gelding by Ujiji - Rage Bleue.
1961 . . . Fell. (Mrs P.Hastings) 9.11-4. Mr.J.Lawrence. 40/1.
1962 . . . Pulled-up. (Mrs P.Hastings) 10.10-10. Mr.J.Lawrence. 20/1.

TIME
bay gelding by Colonist 11 - Cash Column.
1964 . . . Fell. (Mr J.Cheatle) 9.10-4. M.Scudamore.100/7.co/Fav.*
1965 . . . Fell. (Capt.M.H.Scott) 10.10-13. Mr.B.Scott. 40/1.

TANT PIS
grey gelding by Tantieme - Rosy Dawn.
1965 . . . Finished 9th of 47. (Mr J.Alder) 10.10-13. Mr.J.Alder. 40/1.

TOWER ROAD
chestnut gelding by Jock Scot - Penelope Ann.
1967 . . . Fell. (Mrs D.Dallimore) 9.10-0. R.Williams. 40/1.

TEROSSIAN
chestnut gelding by Ossian 11 - Interrogated.
1969 . . . Refused. (Mr H.W.Hooker) 9.11-3. Mr.P.Sloan. 50/1.

TAM KISS
grey gelding by Tambourin - Princess Casamassima.
1969 . . . Brought-down. (Mr J.R.Hindley) 10.10-13.Mr.J.Hindley.50/1.

TUDOR FORT
bay gelding by Fortina - Bramble Tudor.
1969 . . . Fell. (Lord Joicey) 9.10-4. J.Haldane. 50/1.

TWO SPRINGS
brown gelding by Balck Tarquin - Some Gain.
1970 . . . Fell. (Mr D.H.Barnes) 8.10-7. R.Edwards. 13/2.Fav.*
1971 . . . Finished 6th of 38. (Mr D.H.Barnes) 9.11-4. R.Edwards.13/1.

TWIGAIRY
bay gelding by Prefairy - Twigina.
1971 . . . Brought-down. (Mr V.C.Matthews) 8.10-6. E.P.Harty. 25/1.
1972 . . . Pulled-up. (Mr V.C.Matthews) 9.10-9. T.G.Davies. 28/1.

TARQUIN BID
brown gelding by Black Tarquin - Olein's Nut.
1973 . . . Fell. (Mrs J.H.Weekes) 9.10-0. J.Bracken. 100/1.

TUBS VI
bay gelding by Renwood - Arabian 11.
1974 . . . Finished 14th of 42. (Mr T.V.O'Brien) 11.10-6. V.O'Brien.22/1.

THE TUNKU
chestnut gelding by Richard Louis - Charming White Rose.
1974 . . . Pulled-up. (Mr D.W.Rimmer) 8.10-1. R.R.Evans. 100/1.

TUDOR VIEW
bay gelding by Will Somers - Flaming View.
1975 . . . Brought-down. (Mr P.Upton) 9.10-0. G.McNally. 100/1.
1976 . . . Fell. (Mr P.Upton) 10.10-0. C.Read. 100/1.

TREGARRON
bay gelding by Never Say Die - Impudent.
1976 . . . Fell. (Mr H.W.Blyth) 9.10-1. C.Tinkler. 12/1.

THOMOND
bay gelding by Menelek - Shuleen.
1976 . . . Brought-down. (Miss T.Pearson) 11.10-3. Mr.A.J.Wilson.100/1.

TAMALIN
brown gelding by Linacre - Tamasine.
1978 . . . Finished 12th of 37. (Mr T.A.Metcalfe) 11.11-2. G.Thorner.25/1.

TIED COTTAGE
bay gelding by Honour Bound - Cottage Ray.
1978 . . . Fell. (Mr A.Stanley Robinson) 10.11-4. T.Carberry. 9/1.

TEDDY BEAR II
chestnut gelding by Rubor - Admiral's Rose.
1978 . . . Fell. (Mr G.D.Smith) 11.10-4. P.Blacker. 50/1.

THREE TO ONE
chestnut gelding by Even Money - Yukon Girl.
1980 . . . Fell. (Mr J.C.Manners & Mrs J.K.M.Oliver) 9.10-0. Mr.T.G.Dun. 25/1.
1981 . . . Finished 4th of 39. (Mr J.C.Manners & Mrs J.K.M.Oliver) 10.10-3. Mr.T.G.Dun. 33/1.
1982 . . . Fell. (Mr J.C.Manners) 11.10-3. R.Lamb. 12/1.
1983 . . . Fell. (Mr D.H.Cavendish-Pell) 12.10-2. P.Tuck. 25/1.
1984 . . . Fell. (Mr D.H.Cavendish-Pell) 13.10-0. P.Tuck. 66/1.

TENECOON
bay gelding by Tycoon 11 - Tenelee.
1981 . . . Fell. (Mr F.A.Smith) 12.10-0. C.Mann. 100/1.

THREE OF DIAMONDS
chestnut gelding by Three Wishes - Love Of Diamonds.
1981 . . . Fell. (Mr Chester Barnes) 9.10-0. P.Leach. 100/1.
1982 . . . Finished 7th of 39. (Mr H.Harpur-Crewe) 10.10-7.Mr.P.O'Connor. 100/1.

TRAGUS
bay gelding by Tanerko - Nectanda.
1982 . . . Finished 6th of 39. (Lord Hartington) 10.11-4. P.Scudamore.14/1.

TIEPOLINO
bay gelding by Timmy My Boy - Tiepolina.
1982 . . . Refused. (Mrs B.House) 10.10-4. H.Davies. 50/1.

THIS WAY
bay gelding by Grey Love - Harroanna.
1982 . . . Fell. (Mrs J.George) 11.10-2. C.Candy. 100/1.

TACROY
bay gelding by Royal Buck - Tactina.
1983 . . . Pulled-up. (Mr A.J.Duffield) 9.11-9. F.Berry. 33/1.
1984 . . . Finished 12th of 40. (Mr A.J.Duffield) 10.10-7. F.Berry.28/1.
1985 . . . Fell. (Mr A.J.Duffield) 11.10-3. A.Stringer. 33/1.
1986 . . . Fell. (Mr A.J.Duffield) 12.10-0. A.Stringer.200/1.

THAT'S IT
brown mare by Adropejo - That's-That.
1983 . . . Fell. (Mr L.A.White) 9.10-0. G.Holmes.200/1.

TOWER MOSS
grey gelding by Tower Walk - Katie Moss.
1983 . . . Fell. (Mr A.S.Neaves) 10.10-0. R.Rowe. 300/1.

TWO SWALLOWS
grey gelding by My Swallow - Two Blues.
1984 . . . Finished 6th of 40. (Mr & Mrs G.Steinberg) 11.10-0. A.Webber. 22/1.

TALON
chestnut gelding by George Spelvine - Battling Bessie.
1985 . . . Fell. (Mr Brod. Munro-Wilson) 10.10-0. A.Webber. 33/1.

TUBBERTELLY
chestnut gelding by Stubs Gazette - What-A-Bird.
1985 . . . Refused. (Mr F.T.McCann) 8.10-1. T.J.Taaffe. 50/1.

TSAREVICH, THE
bay gelding by Mummy's Pet - Madam Russe.
1986 . . . Finished 7th of 40. (Maj.I.C.Straker) 10.10-7. J.White. 16/1.
1987 . . . Finished 2nd of 40.(Maj.I.C.Straker) 11.10-5. J.White. 20/1.
1988 . . . Finished 7th of 40. (Maj.I.C.Straker) 12.10-10. J.White. 18/1.

TRACYS SPECIAL
bay gelding by High Top - Devastating.
1986 . . . Fell. (Mr L.A.H.Ames) 9.10-6. S.C.Knight. 150/1.
1987 . . . Finished 6th of 40. (Mr L.A.H.Ames) 10.10-0. S.McNeill.50/1.
1988 . . . Pulled-up. (Mr L.A.H.Ames) 11.10-0. S.C.Knight. 33/1.

TEN CHERRIES
bay gelding by Raise You Ten - Cherry Tart.
1986 . . . Fell. (Mr M.Bell & Capt.B.W.Bell) 11.10-0. A.Sharpe. 66/1.

TULLAMARINE
chestnut gelding by Dep Run - Clonmoney.
1988 . . . Fell. (Mr P.Burfield) 11.10-0. M.Bowlby. 200/1.

THINKER, THE
chestnut gedling by Cantab - Maine Pet.
1989 . . . Finished 3rd of 40. (T.P.M.McDonagh Ltd.) 11.11-10.S.Sherwood. 10/1.

TEAM CHALLENGE
chestnut gelding by Laurence O - Maid O'The Wood.
1989 . . . Finished 9th of 40. (Mrs E.Hitchins) 7.10-0. M.Bowlby. 30/1.
1990 . . . Finished 11th of 38. (Mr & Mrs Hitchins) 8.10-0. B.de Haan. 50/1.
1991 . . . Refused. (Mr Mrs Hitchins) 9.10-0. B.de Haan. 50/1.
1992 . . . Finished 21st of 40. (Mr & Mrs Hitchins) 10.10-0. B.de Haan. 100/1.

THIRSTY FARMER, THE
bay gelding by Grisaille - Hooks-And-Eyes.
1989 . . . Finished 11th of 40. (Mrs H.M.Read) 10.10-2. L.Kelp. 100/1.

TORSIDE
chestnut gelding by Funny Man - Annaghmore.
1990 . . . Pulled-up. (Mr G.C.Bisgrove) 11.10-3. J.Frost. 66/1.

THINKING CAP
chestnut gelding by Bargello - Grangeclare Lady.
1990 . . . Fell. (Mr M.O'Connor) 9.10-0. P.Malone. 100/1.

TEN OF SPADES
bay gelding by Raise You Ten - Hansel Money.
1991 . . . Finished 14th of 40. (Mr W.H.Whitbread) 11.11-1. J.White.15/1.

TOPSHAM BAY
bay gelding by Proverb - Biowen.
1994 . . . Unseated rider. (Sir Eric Parker & Mr D.H.Barons) 11.10-11. J.Frost. 25/1.
1995 . . . Finished 10th of 35. (Sir Eric Parker) 12.10-0. P.Hide. 20/1.

TINRYLAND
bay gelding by Prince Regent - Tonduff Star.
1995 . . . Fell. (Mr M.Buckley) 11.10-2. M.A.Fitzgerald. 50/1.

THREE BROWNIES
bay gelding by Strong Gale - Sommerville Rose.
1996 . . . Finished 6th of 27. (Mrs A.M.Daly) 9.10-0. P.Carberry.100/1.

UNKNOWN, THE
1861 . . . Failed to finish. (Mr Spencer Lucy) - 8-12. G.Eatwell. n/q.

USNA
chestnut gelding by Umpire or Alpenstock - The Doe.
1888 . . . Ran-out. (Mr J.Gubbins) 7.12-7. Mr.H.Beasley.15/1. jnt/Fav.*

ULYSSES
bay gelding by Ascetic - Penelope.
1892 . . . Finished 9th of 25. (Lord E.Talbot) 8.10-10. Mr.G.B.Milne. 50/1.

UPTON LAD
bay gelding by Benvenuto - Twang.
1926 . . . Fell. (Mr J.C.Paterson) 11.10-8. Mr.W.P.Dutton. 50/1.
1927 . . . Fell. (Mr J.C.Paterson) 12.10-10. Mr.W.P.Dutton. 66/1.

UNCLE JACK
bay or brown gelding by Juggernaut - Tzigane.
1927 . . . Fell. (Captain A.Gollans) 8.11-1. T.O'Sullivan. 50/1.

UNCLE BEN
bay gelding by Ben Alder - Frankfield.
1929 . . . Fell. (Mr H.B.Brandt) 8.10-8. P.Powell. 40/1.

UNCLE BATT
grey gelding by Saxham Boy - Rosa Mulholland.
1935 . . . Finished 5th of 27. (Mr H.B.Benadt) 9.10-7. T.Isaac. 40/1.
1936 . . . Fell. (Mr H.B.Brandt) 10.10-7. T.McNeill. 66/1.
1937 . . . Brought-down. (Mr H.B.Brandt) 11.10-0. D.McCarthy. 100/1.

UNDER BID
bay or brown gelding by La Brige - Accepted.
1938 . . . Finished 9th of 36. (Lord Derby) 6.10-2. M.Pringle. 40/1.
1939 . . . Finished 11th of 37. (Lord Derby) 7.10-0. G.Wilson. 22/1.Remounted.*
1940 . . . Fell. (Lord Derby) 8.10-3. H.Nicholson. 33/1.

ULSTER MONARCH
chestnut gelding by Mahoonagh - Nydia.
1948 . . . Fell. (Mr N.P.Donaldson) 9.10-1. Capt.J.E.Smith. 100/1.
1949 . . . Fell. (Mr N.P.Donaldson) 10.1-1. R.Curran. 28/1.

ULTRA BENE
brown gelding by Motley - Neque Ultra.Bred in France.
1948 . . . Fell. (Lord Mildmay) 9.10-1. A.Grantham. 100/1.

UNCLE BARNEY
bay gelding by Resenda - Dublin City.
1952 . . . Finished 4th of 47. (Mr L.Michaelson) 9.10-4. J.Boddy. 100/1.
1953 . . . Fell. (Mr H.Bannister) 10.10-4. J.Boddy. 40/1.
1954 . . . Finished 7th of 29. (Mr H.Bannister) 11.10-0. L.McMorrow. 50/1.
1955 . . . Finished 13th of 30. (Mr H.Bannister) 12.10-0.L.McMorrow. 50/1.

UNCLE WHISKERS
bay gelding by Uncle Willie - Miranda's Lace.
1960 . . . Fell. (Mr W. St George Burke) 8.10-1. C.Finnegan. 50/1.

UNCLE MERLIN
bay gelding by Easy Gallop - Aunt Sheila.Bred in U.S.A.
1990 . . . Unseated rider. (Mrs R.V.Chapman) 9.10-3. H.Davies. 16/1.

USHERS ISLAND
brown gelding by Sandalay - Star Luck.
1994 . . . Unseated rider. (Mr R.L.W.Bowden) 8.10-0. A.Dobbin.66/1.

VALENTINE
1840 . . . Finished 3rd of 12. (Mr A.Power) Mr.A.Power. n/q.

VANGUARD
bay gelding by Old Advance or Belzoni - dam unknown. Not in the General Stud Book.
1843 . . . WON. (Lord Chesterfield) - 11-10. 16 Ran. T.Olliver. 12/1.
1845 . . . Pulled-up. (Mr Tom Olliver) - 12-10. T.Olliver. 4/1.Fav.*

VICTORIA
1843 . . . Fell. (Mr T.Taylor) - 11-10. Mr.T.Taylor. n/q.

VELUTI
1846 . . . Broke-down. (Mr W.Sterling Crawford) 6.10-8. J.Mason.11/2.Fav.*

VALERIA
1847 . . . Failed to finish. (Mr Oakley) 5.10-3. Dally. n/q.

VARIETY
1848 . . . Failed to finish. (Mr C.Towneley) - 10-8. Powell. n/q.

VICTIM, THE
1849 . . . Failed to finish. (Lord Chesterfield) - 10-11. W.Taylor. n/q.
1850 . . . Failed to finish. (Mr Hassall) - 11-2. W.Taylor. 12/1.
1851 . . . Failed to finish. (Mr Palmer) - 10-13. W.Taylor. n/q.
1852 . . . Fell. (Mr Gooch) - 9-7. H.Bradley. n/q.
1853 . . . Pulled-up. (Capt.Scott) - 10-6. J.Tasker. 12/1.

VENGEANCE
1850 . . . Finished 7th of 32. (Mr W.Vevers) - 9-10. W.Archer. 15/1.

VAIN HOPE
1851 . . . Finished 5th of 21 (Mr W.Vevers) - 11-8. S.Darling. 8/1.

VOLATILE
1851 . . . Fell. (Mr W.Vevers) - 9-10. W.Fowler. n/q.

VIEW HALLOO
1853 . . . Failed to finish. (Mr Megson) - 9-10. W.Archer. 100/6.

VICTOR EMMANUEL
1856 . . . Fell. (Mr Pickering) 6. 9-4. Seffert. n/q.

VINTNER
brown gelding by Claret - Alma.
1874 . . . Fell. (Sir R.B.Harvey) 7.10-3. Mr.Crawshaw. n/q.

VICTOIRE
bay mare by Monarque - Nuncia. Bred in France.
1875 . . . Finished 6th of 19. (Mr G.Bracher) 6.10-13. Mr.Barnes. n/q.

VERITY
chestnut mare by Filbert - Little Jane.
1878 . . . Fell. (Mr J.Hefford) 7.10-10. Gregory. 20/1.

VICTOR II
brown horse by Victor - Maid of Honour.
1879 . . . Pulled-up. (Mr Denny) 5.10-12. Mr.J.Beasley. n/q.
1880 . . . Finished 7th of 14. (Mr E.Wills) 6.10-7. Mr.W.B.Morris.50/1.

VICTORIA
bay mare by Victor - Maid of Honour.
1880 . . . Finished 8th of 14. (Mr J.Schawel) 7.10-7. Mr.J.Beasley.12/1.

VOLUPTUARY
brown gelding by Cremorne - Miss Evelyn. Bred by Her Majesty Queen Victoria.
1884 . . . WON. (Mr H.F.Boyd) 6.10-5. 15 Ran. Mr.E.P.Wilson. 10/1.
1889 . . . Fell (Mr H.F.Boyd) 11.11-3. T.Skelton. 100/6.
1890 . . . Fell. (Mr H.F.Boyd) 12.11-7. T.Skelton. 10/1.
1891 . . . Pulled-up. (Mr H.F.Boyd) 13.11-3. T.Wilson. 66/1.

VEIL
brown horse by Tattoo - dam by Lothario.
1891 . . . Fell. (Sir James Miller) 6.10-13. Mr.W.H.Moore. 25/1.

VARTEG HILL
bay gelding by Masaniello - Lady Teazle.
Finished 9th of 14. (Mr Lort Phillips) 8. 9-10. D.Davies. 50/1.

VAN DER BERG
bay gelding by Dutch Skater - Yurata.
1895 . . . Finished 3rd of 19. (Maj.A.Crawley) 9. 9-13. W.A.Dollery.25/1.
1896 . . . Finished 9th of 28. (Mr W.Pritchard Gordon) 10.10-9.G.Mawson. 20/1.

VIZ
bay gelding by Vitez - Mabel 11.
1911 . . . Fell. (Mr G.D'Arcy Edwardes) 7.10-5. H.Bletsoe. 50/1.

VERMOUTH
bay gelding by Barcaldaile - dam by Bushey Park.Bred Mr.P.J.Hartigan.
*1916 . . . WON. (Mr P.F.Heybourne) 6.11-10. 21 Ran. J.Reardon.100/8.
*1917 . . . Finished 4th of 19. (Mr P.F.Heybourne) 7.12-3. J.Reardon.100/12.
*1918 . . . Completed course. (Mr P.F.Heybourne) 8.11-13.Mr.J.R.Anthony. 100/8.
1919 . . . Failed to finish. (Mr P.F.Heybourne) 9.10-12. G.Parfrement.20/1.

VAULX
brown gelding by Benvenuto - Bairgen Breac.
1922 . . . Fell. (Mr E.S.Patterson) 8.10-0. A.Escott. 25/1.

VINICOLE
bay gelding by The Adler - Tintara.
1932 . . . Fell. (Capt.J.W.Bridges) 8.11-3. D.Morgan. 33/1.

VENTURESOME KNIGHT
bay gelding by Nothing Venture - Bridal Wreath.
1940 . . . Finished 5th of 30. (Lt.Col.H.E.Joicey) 10.10-8. Mr.R.Tweedie. 28/1.

VAIN KNIGHT
bay gelding by Lone Knight - Lady Vain.
1946 . . . Fell. (Mr H.C.Falconer) 13.10-2. R.Curran. 100/1.

VIRGINIUS
chestnut gelding by Vezzano - War Strategy.
1957 . . . Brought-down. (Mr R.R.Guest) 8.10-12. Mr.A.Lillingston. 50/1.

VALIANT SPARK
bay gelding by Pylon 11 - Valiant Nymph.
1958 . . . Fell. (Mr O.H.Gilbey) 9.10-7. M.Scudamore. 20/1.
1959 . . . Fell. (Mr O.H.Gilbey) 10.10-3. J.Lehane. 40/1.

VIGOR
bay gelding by Victrix - Chateau Nell Gow.
1959 . . . Refused. (Mrs A.R.B.Owen) 11.10-5. W.Rees. 66/1.

VIVANT
brown gelding by Trois Moulins - La Rosay.
1961 . . . Fell. (Mrs T.W.Parker) 8.10-6. D.Nicholson. 50/1.
1962 . . . Pulled-up. (Mrs T.W.Parker) 9.10-0. R.J.Hamey. 100/6.
1963 . . . Brought-down. (Mrs T.W.Parker) 10.10-0. R.J.Hamey. 40/1.

VULTRIX
bay gelding by Vulgan -Little Trix.
1965 . . . Finished 5th of 47. (Mr H.Dare) 7.11-1.D.Nicholson. 100/6.
1966 . . . Pulled-up. (Mr H.Dare) 8.10-7. S.Mellor. 100/7.
1968 . . . Fell. (Mr H.Dare) 10.10-8. T.W.Biddlecombe. 28/1.

VULCANO
chestnut gelding by Vulgan - Sanolien.
1965 . . . Pulled-up. (Miss Enid Chanelle) 7.10-13. T.Carberry. 50/1.
1966 . . . Finished 9th of 47. (Miss E.Chanelle) 8.10-1. J.Gifford.25/1.
1967 .. Brought-down. (Miss E.Chanelle) 9.10-0. J.Speid-Soote. 40/1.

VALOUIS
bay gelding by Richard Louis - Valeo.
1966 . . . Brought-down. (Mr J.Prendergast) 7.10-0. E.Prendergast.50/1.
1968 . . . Fell. (Mr J.Prendergast) 9.10-1. E.Prendergast. 40/1.

VILLAY
bay gelding by Vuldon - Elusive Day.
1969 . . . Pulled-up. (Mr D.D.Scott) 11.10-3. Mr.D.Scott. 100/1.
1970 . . . Fell. (Mr D.D.Scott) 12.10-0. Mr.D.Scott. 100/1.

VULTURE
bay gelding by Vulgan - Cherry Bud.
1970 . . . Finished 2nd of 28. (General R.K.Mellon) 8.10-0. S.Barker.15/1.
1971 . . . Fell. (Mrs R.K.Mellon) 9.10-0. S.Barker. 16/1.
1972 . . . Refused. (Sir Hugh Fraser) 10.10-2. P.Brogan. 100/1.

VALBUS
brown gelding by Phebus - Valerita.
1968 . . . Finished 6th of 45. (Mr T.H.Shepherd) 10.10-0. R.Langley. 100/1.

VICHYSOISE
bay gelding by Vulgan - But Why.
1971 . . . Finished 7th of 38. (Lord Chelsea) 9.10-0. P.Blacker. 100/1.
1972 . . . Refused. (Lord Chelsea) 10.10-3. P.Blacker. 100/1.

VULGAN TOWN
bay gelding by Vulgan - Bannitown.
1974 . . . Finished 6th of 42. (Brig.Gen.W.P.Gilbride) 8.10-8. J.Haine.35/1.

VINDICATE
bay gelding by Vulgan - Indicate.
1979 . . . Fell. (Mr P.J.Doyle) 12.10-0. Mr.A.O'Connell. 200/1.

VINTNER, THE
bey gelding by Little Buskins - First Page.
1980 . . . Pulled-up. (Westwood Garages Ltd.) 9.10-8. B.R.Davies.16/1.
1983 . . . Refused. (Mr D.O.Williams) 12.10-0. C.Grant. 66/1.

VENTURE TO COGNAC
bay gelding by Hot Brandy - Venture More.
1983 . . . Finished 8th of 41. (Mr N.E.C.Sherwood) 10.11-12. Mr.O.Sherwood. 28/1.

VALENCIO
brown gelding by Seal - Vasilka. Bred in Czechoslovakia.
1987 . . . Fell. (Mrs P.Seabrook & Miss S.Meyer) 10.12-0. R.Rowell. 500/1.

VICOMPT DE VALMONT
bay gelding by Beau Charmeur - Wish Again.
1996 . . . Finished 10th of 27. (Mr J.C.Blackwell) 11.10-1. P.Hide.22/1.

WEATHERCOCK
1840 . . . Fell (Owner unknown) Barker. n/q.

WIVERTON
1844 . . . Fell. (Lord Maidstone) T.Olliver. 8/1.

WOLVERHAMPTON
1848 . . . Failed to finish. (Mr R.H.Jones) - 11-12. Mr.B.Bretherton. n/q.
1849 . . . Fell. (Mr B.Bretherton) - 11-5. Mr.B.Bretherton. 12/1.

WARNER
1852 . . . Finished 6th of 24. (Lord Waterford) - 10-8. W.Archer. n/q.

WANDERER
bay horse by Verulam - Mrs Stapley. Not in the General Stud Book.
1855 . . . WON. (Mr Dennis) - 9-8. 20 Ran. J.Hanlon. 25/1.

WEATHERCOCK
1857 . . . Finished 2nd of 28. (Mr B.Land) 6. 8-12. C.Green. 25/1.
1858 . . . Finished 2nd of 16. (Viscount Talon) 7. 11-7. Mr.Edwards. 25/1.
1859 . . . Brought-down. (Viscount Talon) 8.10-13. Enoch. 33/1.

WEE NELL
1861 . . . Failed to finish. (Mr Mackey) - 9-11. Knott. n/q.
1864 . . . Pulled-up. (Mr T.Hunt) - 11-6. Knott. 12/1.

WILLOUGHBY
1862 . . . Pulled-up. (Mr H.Lington) - 10-0. Mr.Lington. 20/1.

WEST END
1866 . . . Failed to fiinish. (Colonel Forester) - 10-5. W.White. 50/1.

WHITEHALL
bay gelding by Sir Tatton Sykes - dam unknown.
1867 . . . Knocked-over. (Mr P.Herbert) - 10-13. Mr.Milward. n/q.

WILD FOX
chestnut gelding by Cardinal - Wild Daisy.
1871 . . . Fell. (Colonel Ainslie) 6.10-12. Murphy. 40/1.

WILD MONARCH
bay gelding by Wild Oats - Gentille Dame.
1879 . . . Finished 4th of 18. (Marquis sw St Sauveur) 8.11-7. H.Andrews. 20/1.
1880 . . . Finished 6th of 14. (Count de St Sauveur) 9.11-11. R.I'Anson. 11/2.
1882 . . . Fell. (Mr C.Cunningham) 11.10-12. H.Andrews. 100/6.

WOODBROOK
chestnut gelding by The Lawyer - The Doe. Bred by Captain Kirkwood.
1880 . . . Finished 5th of 14. (Capt.T.Y.L.Kirkwood) 6.11-7. Mr.H.Beasley. 25/1.
1881 . . . WON. (Capt.T.Y.L.Kirkwood) 7.11-3. 13 Ran. Mr.T.Beasley. 11/2.jnt/Fav.*

WHY NOT
bay gelding by Castlereagh - Twitter. Bred by Miss Nugent.
1889 . . . Finished 2nd of 20. (Mr D.Jardine) 8.11-5. Mr.C.J.Cunningham. 11/1.
1890 . . . Finished 5th of 16. (Mr D.Jardine) 9.12-5. Mr.C.J.Cunningham.100/9. Remounted*
1891 . . . Fell. (Mr C.Perkins) 10.12-4. Mr.C.J.Cunningham.100/9.
1893 . . . Finished 3rd of 15. (Mr C.H.Fenwick) 12.11-12. A.Nightingall. 5/1.
1894 . . . WON. (Capt.C.H.Fenwick) 13.11-13. 14 Ran. A.Nightingall. 5/1.jnt/Fav.*
1895 . . . Finished 5th of 19. (Capt.C.H.Fenwick) 14.12-0. Mr.E.G.Fenwick. 50/1.
1896 . . . Finished 5th of 28. (Mr E.G.Fenwick) 15.11-5. A.Nightingall. 100/7.

WILD MAN FROM BORNEO
chestnut gelding by Decider - Wild Duck. Bred by Mr.G.Keays.
1894 . . . Finished 3rd of 14. (Mr J.Widger) 6.10-9. Mr.Jos.Widger. 40/1.
1895 . . . WON. (Mr John Widger) 7.10-11. 19 Ran. Mr.Jos.Widger. 10/1.
1896 . . . Fell. (Mr John Widger) 8.12-0. Mr.T.J.Widger. 40/1.
1897 . . . Pulled-up. (Miss F.E.Norris) 9.11-5. Mr.Jos.Widger. 9/1.

220

WATERFORD
bay horse by York - Lady Violet.
1896 . . . Fell. (Mr F.E.Irving) 8.10-13. Mr.Jos.Widger) 100/12.

WESTMEATH
bay gelding by Ascetic - Deodar.
1896 . . . Fell. (Mr F.D.Leyland) 7. 9-8. G.Morris. 100/1.
1897 . . . Fell. (Mr F.D.Leyland) 8.11-4. W.Taylor. 100/1.

WHITEBOY II
chestnut gelding by Mayboy - Granuaile.
1899 . . . Finished 6th of 19. (Mr R.Bourke) 10. 9-10. A.Banner.200/1.

WHITEHAVEN
chestnut gelding by Favo - Fair Haven.
1902 . . . Pulled-up. (Lord Denman) 10. 9-13. P.Woodland. 20/1.

WHAT NEXT
black or brown Horse by Dictator or Quidnunc - Veda.
1905 . . . Refused. (Mr H.B.Black) 7.10-2. Capt.Rasbotham. 50/1.

WOLF'S FOLLY
bay gelding by Wolf's Crag - Valentine.
1906 . . . Finished 5th of 23. (Mr A.Gorham) 8.10-6. T.Fitton. 100/6.

WEE BUSBIE
bay gelding by Lord Fitzwilliam - Claret.
1908 . . . Fell. (Mr J.E.Rogerson) 11. 9-11. D.Phelan. 66/1.
1909 . . . Finished 11th of 32. (Mr J.E.Rogerson) 12. 9-13. D.Phelan. 100/1.

WILD FOX II
brown gelding by Spook - Wild Vixen.
1908 . . . Fell. (Capt.W.A.Pallin) 6. 9-9. Capt.W.A.Palin. 66/1.
1909 . . . Refused. (Capt.W.A.Pallin) 7. 9 -9. Capt.W.A.Pallin. 100/1.

WICKHAM
chestnut gelding by Childwick - Powderham.
1909 . . . Fell. (Mr F.Bibby) 8.10-10. Capt.R.H.Collis. 50/1.
1910 . . . Fell. (Mr F.Bibby) 9.10-11. W.Bulteel. 66/1.

WHITE LEGS II
chestnut gelding — Pedigree unknown.
1912 . . . Finished 7th of 24. (Mr E.Brandon) aged. 10-2. J.Farrell.n/q.

WAVELET
bay gelding by Wavelet's Pride - Mrs Bowser.
1913 . . . Fell. (Mr A.H.Straker) 6.11-0. A.Newey. 100/9.

WAVERTREE
brown gelding by Wavelet's Pride - Kendal Lily.
* 1918 . . . Fell. (Capt.B.Bibby) 7.10-12. E.Driscoll. 5/1.co/Fav.*
1920 . . . Fell. (Mr.F.Bibby) 9.10-13. C.Kelly. 40/1.
1922 . . . Fell. (Mr.F.Bibby) 11.11-10. H.B.Bletsoe. 25/1.

WAVEBEAM
bay gelding by Wavelet's Pride - Princess Thera.
1920 . . . Fell. (Mr H.Kershaw) 9 9-7. A.Aylin. n/q.
1921 . . . Fell. (Mr H.Kershaw) 10.10-7. Mr.S.C.E.Lloyd. n/q.

WHITE SURREY
grey gelding by Nabot - Dejeuner.
1921 . . . Fell. (Admiral Sir Hedworth Meux) 9.10-12. A.Escott. 33/1.
1925 . . . Fell. (Admiral Sir Hedworth Meux) 13.11-4. M.Tighe. 66/1.
1926 . . . Fell. (Admiral Sir Hedworth Meux) 14.10-7. M.Farragher. 66/1.

WHITE COCKADE
grey horse by Uncle George - Proserpine.
1921 . . . Fell. (Mr T.D.Longworth) 8. 9-10. H.Wicks. n/q.

WAVETOWN
brown gelding by Kroonstad - Waveoff.
1924 . . . Finished 6th of 30. (Mr A.Hood) 9.10-12. R.Lyal. n/q.

WINNALL
bay gelding by Fowling-Piece - Clayton.
1924 . . . Fell. (Mr H.Liddell) 7.10-11. C.Donnelly. 40/1.
1925 . . . Refused. (Mr H.Liddell) 8.11-0. F.Gurney. 28/1.

WINTER VOYAGE
chestnut gelding by Torpint - Mince Pie.
1924 . . . Fell. (Mr T.D.Oakshott) 7.10-2. J.H.Goswell. 66/1.

WALLSEND
bay gelding by Adam Bede - Broderie.
1926 . . . Fell. (Mrs E.A.Cameron) 6.10-7. Capt.H.Lumsden) 100/1.

WHITE PARK
chestnut gelding by Redmond - Lady Alwine.
1927 . . . Finished 6th of 37. (Maj.J.T.North) 8.12-5. E.Foster. 20/1. Remounted.*

WILD EDGAR
grey gelding by Edgar's Pet - D'Arenberg.
1929 . . . Fell. (Mrs E.A.Ryan) 9.10-0. S.Regan. 200/1.

WHAT HAVE YOU
chestnut gelding by Tryster - Prodigy.
1937 . . . Fell. (Mr F.M.Gould) 9.11-5. Mr.W.Streett. 40/1.
1938 . . . Fell. (Mr F.M.Gould) 10.10-7. S.Magee. 100/1.

WORKMAN
brown gelding by Cottage - Cariella. Bred by Mr.P.J.O'Leary.
1938 . . . Finished 3rd of 36. (Sir Alexander Maguire) 8.10-2. J.Brogan. 28/1.
1939 . . . WON. (Sir Alexander Maguire) 9.10-6. 37 Ran. T.Hyde. 100/8.

WEST POINT
bay gelding by Steel Point - Lady Patricia.
1939 . . . Finished 7th of 37. (Mr P.Dunne Cullinan) 6.10-2. J.Brogan. 66/1.

WAR VESSEL
chestnut gelding by Man O' War - On Her Toes.
1939 . . . Fell. (Mrs M.Scott) 6.10-7. W.Parvin. 50/1.

WICKLOW WOLF
black or brown gelding by Werwolf - Cloneylogan.
1947 . . . Pulled-up. (Mr H.Lane) 7.10-0. M.J.Hogan. 100/1.

WAR RISK
grey gelding by Cri de Guerre - Riskanhope.
1948 . . . Finished 11th of 43. (Mrs J.Rogerson) 9.11-1. R.Turnell. 33/1.

WEEVIL
chestnut gelding by Werwolf - Manna 11.
1948 . . . Fell. (Mr D.Morris) 9.10-11. V.Mooney. 33/1.

WOT NO SUN
bay gelding by Sun Yat-Sen - Hopeful Lass.
1949 . . . Fell. (Maj.T.D.Wilson) 7.10-3. G.Kelly. 40/1.
1950 . . . Finished 2nd of 49. (Maj.T.D.Wilson) 8.11-8.A.P.Thompson. 100/7.
1952 . . . Finished 3rd of 47. (Maj.T.D.Wilson) 10.11-7. D.V.Dick. 33/1.

WHISPERING STEEL
bay gelding by Steel Point - Boltown. Formerly named Adieu Steele.
1952 . . . Fell. (Mr F.Dyson) 7.10-11. R.Morrow. 40/1.
1953 . . . Brought-down. (Mr F.H.Curnick) 8.10-13. R.Morrow. 9/1.
1954 . . . Fell. (Mr F.H.Curnick) 9.10-12. R.Morrow. 40/1.

WOLFSCHMIDT
chestnut gelding by Werwolf - Calumny. Formerly named Calumny's Last.
1952 . . . Fell. (Mr G.Clark) 12.10-3. F.O'Connor. 100/1.

WITTY
bay gelding by Foroughi - Brown Wings. Formerly named Ruthin Scar.
1953 . . . Unseated rider. (Mr C.Nicholson) 8.10-5. G.Slack. 22/1.
1956 . . . Fell. (Mr C.Nicholson. 11.10-4. P.A.Farrell. 66/1.

WAIT AND SEE
bay gelding by Overthrow - Lady Standfast.
1953 . . . Brought-down. (Mrs E.Taylor) 8.10-5. A.Freeman. 50/1.

WILD WISDOM
brown gelding by Perion - Miss Fix-it.
1955 . . . Finished 8th of 30. (Mr G.R.Marsh) 10.10-0. Lt.Col.W.Holman. 66/1.
1956 . . . Finished 9th of 29. (Mr E.Foster) 11.10-1. Mr.L.Bridge. 66/1.
1957 . . . Pulled-up. (Mr L.Bridge) 12.10-0. Mr.L.Bridge. 66/1.

WYNDBURGH
brown gelding by Maquis - Swinnie.
1957 . . . Finished 2nd of 35. (Miss R.M.P.Wilkinson) 7.10-7. M.Batchelor. 25/1.
1958 . . . Finished 4th of 31. (Miss R.M.P.Wilkinson) 8.11-3. M.Batchelor. 6/1.Fav.*
1959 . . . Finished 2nd of 34.(Mrs J.K.M.Oliver) 9.10-12. T.Brookshaw. 10/1.
1960 . . . Fell. (Mrs J.K.M.Oliver) 10.11-7. M.Scudamore. 8/1.
1961 . . . Finished 6th of 35. (Mrs J.K.M.Oliver) 11.11-5.T.Brookshaw. 33/1.
1962 . . . Finished 2nd of 32. (Mrs J.K.M.Oliver) 12.10-9. T.A.Barnes. 45/1.

WAKING
brown gelding by Snow King - Kirkway.
1957 . . . Fell. (Capt.A.W.C.Pearn) 13.10-0. Capt.A.W.C.Pearn. 66/1.

WISE CHILD
bay gelding by Almaska - Miss Hopkins.
1958 . . . Pulled-up. (Wing Commander R.E.Stephenson) 10.11-6. S.Hayhurst. 45/1.

WILY ORIENTAL
chestnut gelding by Bidar - Twist.
1961 . . . Fell. (Mr E.H.Mount) 9.10-6. P.G.Madden. 40/1.

WOODBROWN
bay gelding by Hindostan - Take No Chances.
1963 . . . Finished 18th of 47. (Mr P.Brown) 9.10-0. J.Kenneally. 66/1.

WINGLESS
grey gelding by Doubtless 11 - Mentores.
1963 . . . Fell. (Mr O.H.Gilbey) 8.10-3. A.Biddlecombe. 66/1.

WARTOWN
bay gelding by Bakhtawar - Maytown.
1963 . . . Fell. (Colonel R.L.Crouch) 12.10-1. J.Gamble. 66/1.

WILLOW KING
chestnut gelding by Snow King - Glenwillow.
1966 . . . Pulled-up.(Capt.C.A.G.Perry) 11.10-0. L.McGoughlin.100/1.

WHAT A MYTH
chestnut gelding by Coup de Myth - What A Din.
1966 . . . Fell. (Lady Weir) 9.11-4. P.Kelleway. 11/2.
1967 . . . Finished 9th of 44. (Lady Weir) 10.12-0. P.Kelleway. 20/1.
1968 . . . Fell. (Lady Weir) 11.12-0. P.Kelleway. 28/1.

WILLING SLAVE
brown gelding by Arctic Slave - Jari Pataka.
1968 . . . Pulled-up. (Mr A.Maiden) 8.10-2. M.B.James. 100/1.

WELL TO DO
chestnut gelding by Phebus - Princess Puzzlement. Bred by Mrs.H.Lloyd Thomas.
1972 . . . WON. (Captain T.Forster) 9.10-1. 42 Ran. G.Thorner.14/1.

WOLVERHAMPTON
chestnut gelding by Royal Buck - What A Honey.
1974 . . . Pulled-up. (Mr Bill Davies) 7.10-0. R.Quinn. 25/1.

WHAT A BUCK
bay gelding by Royal Buck - What A Daisy.
1977 . . . Finished 6th of 42. (Lord Vestey) 10.11-4. J.King. 20/1.

WAR BONNET
bay gelding by Cantab - Topping News.
1977 . . . Fell. (Mr R.K.Agnew) 9.10-6. T.Carberry. 16/1.
1978 . . . Fell. (Mr S.Flynn) 10.10-8. D.T.Hughes. 50/1.

WINTER RAIN
bay gelding by Raincheck - Shean Lass.
1977 . . . Fell. (Mr F.Tyldesley) 9.10-6. M.Dickinson. 16/1.

WILLY WHAT
grey gelding by No Argument - What Ever.
1977 . . . Fell. (Mr M.D.R.Williams) 8.10-0. J.Glover. 50/1.

WAGNER
brown gelding by Choral Society - Pride Of Kilnockin.
1979 . . . Finished 5th of 34. (Mr P.Piller) 9.10-0. R.Lamb. 50/1.

WAYWARD SCOT
brown gelding by Jock Scot - Wayward Damsel.
1979 . . . Fell. (Mr Emlyn Hughes & Mr D.McCain) 10.10-7. R.F.Davies. 100/1.

WILLIAMSON
chestnut gelding by Straight Lad - Ecurie.
1983 . . . Brought-down. (Hillfield Farming Co.) 9.10-0. C.Mann.100/1.

WEST TIP
bay gelding by Gala Performance - Astryl. Bred by Mr.T.J.Hayes.
1985 . . . Fell. (Mr P.Luff) 8.10-1. R.Dunwoody. 13/2.jnt/Fav.*
1986 . . . WON. (Mr P.Luff) 9.10-11. 40 Ran. R.Dunwoody. 15/2.
1987 . . . Finished 4th of 40. (Mr P.Luff) 10.11-7. R.Dunwoody. 5/1.Fav.*
1988 . . . Finished 4th of 40. (Mr P.Luff) 11.11-7. R.Dunwoody. 11/1.
1989 . . . Finished 2nd of 40.(Mr P.Luff) 12.10-11.R.Dunwoody. 12/1.
1990 . . . Finished 10th of 38. (Mr P.Luff) 13.10-11. P.Hobbs. 20/1.

WHY FORGET
brown gelding by Deep Run - Shuil Dubh.
1986 . . . Finished 16th of 40. (Mr P.Piller & Mr W.A.Stephenson) 10.10-3. R.Lamb. 35/1.
1987 . . . Finished 19th of 40. (Mr P.Piller & Mr W.A.Stephenson) 11.10-0. C.Grant. 40/1.

WHATS THE CRACK
bay gelding by The Parson - Mighty Crack.
1992 . . . Finished 13th of 40. (Mr J.Wright & Mr J.S.Rigby) 9.10-0. J.Osborne. 20/1.

WILLSFORD
bay gelding by Beau Charmeur - Wish Again.
1992 . . . Finished 20th of 40. (Mr A.Kaplan & Mr R.Johnson) 9.10-0. M.Bowlby. 16/1.

WYLDE HIDE
bay gelding by Strong Gale - Joint Master.
1996 . . . Unseated rider. (Mr J.P.McManus) 9.10-0. F.Woods. 12/1.

XANTHUS
1858 . . . Finished 3rd of 16. (Mr Craven) - 11-0. F.Balchin. 33/1.
1859 . . . Fell. (Mr Craven) - 10-7. F.Balchin. n/q.
1860 . . . Finished 3rd of 19. (Mr Craven) - 10-0. F.Balchin. 10/1.
1861 . . . Finished 5th of 24. (Mr Craven) - 9-8. C.Boyce. 50/1.
1862 . . . Finished 4th of 13. (Lord Sefton) - 9-6. R.Sherrard. 25/1.

XEBEE
bay gelding by Torpedo - Georgina.
1899 . . . Fell. (Mr R.C.B.Cave) 7.11-4. Mr.A.W.Wood. 33/1.

YALLER GAL
1863 . . . Finished 3rd of 16. (Mr W.Briscoe) aged.10-13. Mr.Dixon. 20/1.

YOUNG GLASGOW
brown gelding by New Oswestry - Corbeille.
1891 . . . Fell. (Mr W.Gordon-Canning) 10.10-3. R.Mitchell. 40/1.

YORK II
chestnut gelding by Tostig - Conclusion.
1907 . . . Fell. (Mr L.Robinson) 8.10-6. T.Moran. n/q.
1908 . . . Fell. (Mr G.Walmsley) 9.10-4. W.Rollason. n/q.

YOUNG BUCK
bay gelding by Old Buck - Rupee.
1909 . . . Fell. (Mr F.M.Freake) aged. 9-12. H.B.Bletsoe. n/q.

YELLOW CHAT
chestnut gelding by Chatsworth - Yella.
*1917 . . . Completed course. (Lord Lonsdale) 6.11-0. G.Parfrement. 100/12.

YOUTELL
chestnut gelding by Mountaineer - Pointel.
1933 . . . Fell. (Mr P.V.F.Cazalet) 8.10-7. Mr.A.Mildmay. 100/1.

YUNG-YAT
brown gelding by Sun Yat-Sen - Little Hope.
1946 . . . Fell. (Mr F.W.S.Gradwell) 10.10-0. T.Cullen,jnr. 100/1.
1947 . . . Pulled-up.(Mr F.W.S.Gradwell) 11.10-1. J.Brogan. 100/1.

YER MAN
chestnut gelding by Lucifer - Ballyfin.
1983 . . . Finished 3rd of 41. (Mr N.Keane) 8.10-0. T.V.O'Connell. 80/1.
1984 . . . Finished 17th of 40. (Mr N.Keane) 9.10-2. T.V.O'Connell. 25/1.

YOUNG DRIVER
bay gelding by Linacre - Pepe.
1986 . . . Finished 2nd of 40. (Mr J.B.Russell) 9.10-0. C.Grant. 66/1.
1990 . . . Pulled-up. (Mr M.Harker) 13.10-4. J.Duggan. 150/1.

YOU'RE WELCOME
chestnut gelding by Deep Run - Our Dream.
1987 . . . Finished 5th of 40. (Mr & Mrs Embiricos) 11.10-2. P.Hobbs. 50/1.
1988 . . . Pulled-up. (Mr & Mrs Embiricos) 12.10-1. P.Hobbs. 33/1.

YAHOO
bay gelding by Trombone - Coolroe Aga.
1991 . . . Finished 16th of 40. (Mr A.Parker & Mr H.Parker) 10.11-1. N.Williamson. 33/1.

YOUNG HUSTLER
chestnut gelding by Import - Davett.
1994 . . . Brought-down. (Mr G.MacEchern) 7.10-12. D.Bridgwater. 16/1.
1995 . . . Unseated rider. (Mrs M.McKever) 8.11-2. C.Llewellyn. 10/1.
1996 . . . Finished 5th of 27. (Mr G.MacEchern) 9.11-7. C.Maude. 8/1.

ZERO
bay gelding by Asteroid - N Minus.
1876 . . . Fell. (Mr J.M.Richardson) 6.10-10. Mr.Rolly. 20/1.
1877 . . . Refused. (Lord C.Beresford) 7.11-2. Sherrington. 50/1.

ZOEDONE
chestnut mare by New Oswestry - Miss Honiton. Not in the General Stud Book.
1882 . . . Finished 3rd of 12. (Mr Clayton) 5.10-0. Capt.A.J.Smith.25/1.
1883 . . . WON. (Count C.Kinsky) 6.11-0. 10 Ran. Count C.Kinsky. 100/7.
1884 . . . Finished 5th of 15. (Count C.Kinsky) 7.12-2.Count C.Kinsky. 100/7.
1885 . . . Fell. (Count C.Kinsky) 8.11-11. Count C.Kinsky. 5/1.

ZITELLA
bay mare by Xenophon - Vanessa.
1883 . . . Finished 5th of 10. (Mr J.Gubbins) 5.11-2. Mr.T.Beasley. 3/1.Fav.*
1884 . . . Failed to finish. (Mr J.Gubbins) 6.12-0. Mr.T.Beasley. 20/1.

ZODIAC
chestnut gelding by Astrologer - Far And Wide.
1901 . . . Failed to finish. (Mr F.Bibby) 6. 9-7. A.Banner. 100/1.
1902 . . . Pulled-up. (Mr F.Bibby) 7. 9-7. A.Banner. 100/1.

ZAG
bay gelding by Irish Battle - Zagger.
1936 . . . Fell. (Capt.C.L.Prior-Palmer) 11-10-11. Capt.C.L.Prior-Palmer.100/1.

ZAHIA
bay mare by Cottage - Greek Girl.
1948 . . . Ran-out. (Mr F.N.Gee) 8.10-2. E.Reavey. 100/1.

ZARTER
bay gelding Knight Of The Garter - Zarile.
1950 . . . Fell. (Capt.L.A.Henderson) 10.10-0. Mr.J.Straker. 66/1.

ZARA'S GROVE
black gelding by Zarathustra - Persian Grove.
1971 . . . Fell. (Mr N.H.Le Mare) 8.10-0. G.Holmes. 50/1.

ZIMULATOR
bay horse by Narrator - Zimarra.
1975 . . . Fell. (Mrs N.Swan) 8.10-0. Capt.D.Swan. 100/1.

ZETA'S SON
brown gelding by Orchadist - Southern Zeta.
1977 . . . Fell. (Mr M.Buckley) 8.11-4. M.Morris. 18/1.

ZONGALERO
bay gelding by David Jack - Lendy.
1979 . . . Finished 2nd of 34. (Mr D.Montagu & Sir James Goldsmith) 9.10-5. B.R.Davies. 20/1.
1980 . . . Refused. (Mr D.Montague & Sir James Goldsmith) 10.10-13. S.Smith Eccles. 11/1.
1981 . . . Fell. (The Honourable D.Montagu & Sir James Goldmsith) 11.10-11. S.Smith Eccles. 14/1.

ZETA'S LAD
chestnut gelding by Over The River - Zeta'Daughter.
1994 . . . Fell. (Mr A.L.Cohen) 11.10-13. R.Supple. 16/1.
1995 . . . Unseated rider. (Uplands Bloodstock) 12.10-3. G.Bradley. 50/1.

ROLL OF HONOUR

ABD-EL-KADER

As the first horse to win the Grand National twice, Abd-El-Kader holds a special place in racing history. His dam was English Lass, whose early life included a spell as a coach-horse. Employed as a member of the team which pulled the Shrewsbury to Holyhead mailcoach, she became a decent steeplechaser in Ireland. Less successful when sent to stud, the mare's only decent offspring was Abd-El-Kader, a small but strong horse who, despite winning over fences many times in Ireland, was completely ignored in the betting for the 1850 Grand National. Jumping the Aintree fences brilliantly, 'Little Ab', as he affectionately became known, was an instant hit with the crowds for the manner in which he won that 1850 'National. The following year, starting joint second favourite at 7/1, Abd-El-Kader won again after a hard fought struggle in the closing stages with the runner-up Maria Day. In all Abd-El-Kader ran five times in the Grand National, finishing fifth in 1853 and failiing to get round on the other two occasions, but it was his first two appearances in the race which earned him his fame.

ALCIBIADE

This French-bred chestnut began his racing on the flat in this country but was of little account and was, in fact, bought out of a selling race at Epsom for £400 by Mr 'Cherry' Angell. Incredibly his first ever appearance in a steeplechase was in the 1865 Grand National, which he won in a very close finish by a head from Hall Court. Despite competing in the race a further five time and finishing third, fourth and eighth in the process, Alcibiade never appeared in the winner's enclosure again.

ALDANITI

Trained by former jockey, Josh Gifford, Aldaniti suffered a series of fitness set-backs before making his first attempt in the Grand National of 1981. Bob Champion, his jockey, was also under the gravest of clouds, having only recently completed a course of chemotherapy for the cancer he had been suffering. Together, Champion and Aldaniti triumphed against the worst possible forms of adversity, to produce possibly the most emotion-filled Grand National victory ever in that 1981 event.Attempting to win the race for a second time in 1982, Aldaniti fell at the very first fence and was then retired from racing. Since then, Champion and Aldaniti have been regularly reunited on countless charity walks throughout the country, through which huge amounts of money have been raised for the Bob Champion Cancer Research Trust.

ALLY SLOPER

A real 'Liverpool' horse, who also won Aintree's Stanley and Valentine 'Chases, Ally Sloper won the 1915 Grand National for Lady Nelson, thus making her the first woman to own a 'National winner. Only a six-year-old at the time of his victory, the gelding was ridden by that outstanding amateur Jack Anthony and as the 1915 race was the last to be held at Aintree until after the Great War, Ally Sloper did not get another chance to repeat his success until 1919, when he failed to finish. In the interim period he ran in the three substitute races at Gatwick, running third in the second of these in 1917.

AMBUSH II

After running seventh in the 1899 'National when still only five years of age, Ambush II won the race 12 months later by five lengths, in the colours of HRH The Prince of Wales. He remains the only horse to provide a member of the Royal Family with a Grand National winner. In 1903 Ambush II became the first horse to represent a reigning British Monarch in the Aintree race, for by that time his owner had become King Edward VII. Tragically, Ambush II dropped dead on the gallops in Ireland when being prepared for the 1905 'National.

ANATIS

The mare Anatis won the 1860 Grand National as the 7/2 favourite, a position in the market she occupied as a result of finishing fifth in the race 12months before. What few people knew was that she had not jumped a fence since that first 'National effort in 1859, because her forelegs were so weak that trainer William Holman was afraid she would break down completely. On her only two other appearances int the race Anatis failed to complete the course.

ANGLO
Winner of the 1966 Grand National, Anglo was a half-brother to the 1968 Aintree hero Red Alligator and formerly ran on the flat under the name of Flag Of Convenience. The winner of five hurdle races and eight steeplechases before victory in his first 'National, Anglo provided Fred Winter with his second successive training success in the race. His jockey, Tim Norman, was involved in a car crash near the racecourse the evening before the big race, which resulted in his having many stitches inserted in his face. Anglo only ran in one other Grand National, when in 1967 he was pulled up by his jockey Bobby Beasley when well to the rear.

ASCETIC'S SILVER
After falling at the third fence in the 1905 Grand National, Ascetic's Silver continued riderless, actually passing the winning post first in front the winner Kirkland. Purchased for 800 guineas before the next 'National by Aubrey Hastings, who trained the horse for his patron Prince Hatzfeldt, Ascetic's Silver was ridden by the trainer and won comfortably by ten lengths at 20/1.Two years earlier the horse had won the Irish National but after his Aintree success he failed to win another race and was eventually retired in 1908.

AUSTERLITZ
A complete failure when running on the flat, Austerlitz won two hurdle races and a steeplechase at Sandown Park before making his only appearance in the Grand National of 1877, when still but a five-year-old. Ridden by his owner, Mr Fred Hobson, Austerlitz made most of the running and jumped perfectly throughout the race, to win unchallenged by ten lengths at 15/1. After only one subsequent race, in which he finished unplaced, Austerlitz was retired.

AYALA
Owned by the society hairdresser, Mr P.B.(Teazy-Weasy) Raymond, Ayala was another who proved useless as a flat racehorse. Showing a greater ability over fences, the gelding won four steeplechases before making his Grand National debut in 1963 as an unconsidered 66/1 outsider. Trained by Keith Piggott, father of the legendary Lester Piggott, Ayala jumped well throughout the 'National, although it was only in the final 100 yards that he overtook the better fancied Carrickbeg, to win by three quarters of a length. In two further attempts at 'National glory Ayala fell and his subsequent career was extremely disappointing.

BATTLESHIP
Owned by Mrs Marion du Pont Scott, the wife of film star Randolph Scott, Battleship was a most successful jumper in his native America where he won the American Grand National. Upon being sent to Britain to be trained by Bruce Hobbs for the real thing at Aintree, Battleship lost his form and consequently was allowed to start for the race at 40/1. Ridden by the trainer's son, 17 year old Bruce Hobbs, Battleship jumped well in the race although being such a small horse, he had difficulty with the big drops on the landing sides of some of the fences. In one of the closes finishes ever witnessed in the Grand National, Battleship produced a spirited run close home, to get up in the final strides of the race and win by a head from the Irish challenger Royal Danieli. The last stallion to be successful in the 'National, Battleship returned to America where he became the leading sire of jumpers and died in 1958.

BEN NEVIS
American owned but English bred, Ben Nevis won the Grand National at his second attempt in 1980 at 40/1. Ridden by his owner's son-in law, the Baltimore banker Mr Charlie Fenwick, Ben Nevis had been strongly fancied for the race in 1979 but was caught up in a melee at the Chair, where he was brought down. On very heavy going in the 1980, Ben Nevis was left in front a long way from home and, out-staying his tired rivals, won easily by 20lengths from the only three others to complete the trip.

BOGSKAR
Owned and trained by Lord Stalbridge, the seven-year-old Bogskar won the 1940 Grand National from 29 others, some six months after the start of the Second World War. It was the last 'National to be held until 1946. A most disappointing performer in his first three seasons 'over the sticks', Bogskar won three races besides the 'National in the 1939-1940 season, although he was still allowed to start at 25/1 at Aintree. His jockey, Mervyn Jones, was a flight-sergeant in the Royal Air Force at the time of his victory, but sadly failed to return from a bombing mission over enemy territory two years later. Bogskar continued to race until well after the war, though his 1940 Aintree success was the last of his career.

● Caughoo leads at the water in 1947.

BOURTON

Formerly named Upton, the gelding Bourton won the 1854 Grand National at the third attempt after twice falling in the race. Ridden by the little known jockey J.Tasker, Bourton was 4/1 favourite on the day of his victory and he won by 15 lengths after producing a surprising burst of finishing speed in the closing stages of the contest. The following year Bourton met his end when involved in a fatal fall at the Water Jump at Warwick. Barely six weeks later at the same racecourse, his Grand National partner J.Tasker also lost his life in a fall.

CASSE TETE

Another reject from flat-racing, the mare Casse Tete found her forte when put to jumping. Most unattractive in appearance, she ran in the 'National five times, winning it at her third attempt in 1872 which was the only occasion in which she completed the course. The winner of three steeplechases in her career, Casse Tete never won another race after her day of glory at Aintree.

CAUGHOO

Purchased as a two-year-old for just £50 by Mr John McDowell, a Dublin jeweller, Caughoo was trained by the owner's brother Hector near Dublin. The winner of the Ulster National in 1945 and 1946, Caughoo was a totally unconsidered outsider at 100/1 among the 57 runners at Aintree in 1947 when making his Grand National debut. Through that long hard winter, racing had been so badly interrupted that only a handful of those competing in the race were anywhere near fully fit and Caughoo had benefitted by being trained on the beach near Dublin. Apart from a late mistake at the final fence, the little Irish gelding jumped well throughout the 'National and came home a clear winner by 20 lengths from his fellow countrymenn Lough Conn and the favourite Prince Regent. Some time afterwards his jockey was accused of only going round Aintree once, by waiting in the fog besides the 12th fence until the second circuit was almost completed. The newsreel films of the race, however, prove that Caughoo did, in fact, cover every yard of the distance, showing clearly that he was well placed at the water jump and in a commanding position at Becher's Brook second time round.

CHANDLER

Given the name because he once pulled a chandler's cart around Sutton Coldfield, the gelding won the Grand National in 1848 on extremely heavy going, when ridden by his owner Captain 'Josie' Little. A genuine and very game jumper, Chandler also won the Worcester Great Handicap 'Chase and the Leamington Hunt 'Chase, the latter being one of the most important events of that time. A 12-year-old at the time of his Liverpool victory, Chandler ran fifth in the race in 1849 and on his final attempt in the 'National the following year failed to complete the course.

CHARITY

The first mare to win the Grand National, Charity was from the stone wall jumping county of Gloucestershire and was strongly fancied to win the first running of the race in 1839. On that occasion she ironically refused at Aintree's stone wall. A 14/1 shot when winning the 1841 'National, Charity arrived late on the scene to win by one length and half a length from the two greys, Cigar and Peter Simple. Her third and final effort in the the great Liverpool race came in 1844 when she fell at the Water Jump.

CLOISTER

After twice finishing second in the 'National, Cloister won at the third attempt in 1893, carrying top weight of 12st 7lbs and as the 9/2 favourite. He was the first of only four horses to carry this maximum burden to victory in the big race and the mark of greatness was further emphasised by the fact that Cloister won in the most convincing manner by 40 lengths. Hailed as a superhorse, Cloister was a short-priced ante-post favourite for the race in 1894 but under the most mysterious of circumstances he was withdrawn from the National shortly before the race. Again in 1895, the same thing happened, with Cloister unable to compete at the last minute. Itt was widely rumoured that some unscrupulous bookmakers were responsible. Eventually he was retired to his owner's country estate in Caernarvonshire.

THE COLONEL

A beautiful looking, almost black entire, The Colonel won eight times in the colours of his owner-breeder Mr John Weyman, two of these victories being in the Grand National's of 1869 and 1870. The second of his big Aintree wins provided his regular jockey George Stevens with his fifth success in the Grand National. Subsequently sold Baron Oppenheim, The Colonel was taken to Germany where he was unsuccessful, although he returned to Aintree for the 1871 'National, in which he finished in sixth place under top weight of 12st 4lbs. Retired to stud in Germany, The Colonel proved to be a valuable stallion and in between his breeding duties acted as ceremonial charger for the Kaiser.

COME AWAY

A truly splendid steeplechaser, Come Away ran in only ten races throughout his jumping career, yet won eight of them including the Conyngham Cup, the Valentine 'Chase at Liverpool and the 1891 Grand National. Trained by the man who partnered him to his Aintree victory, Mr Harry Beasley, Come Away won the 'National in superb style by half a length from the future winner Cloister, with the former winner Ilex a distance behind in third place.After the race it was discovered that Come Away had pulled up lame and despite intensive treatment, the gelding never ran again.

CORBIERE

The eight-year-old Corbiere won the Grand National at his first attempt in 1983, giving his trainer, Mrs Jenny Pitman, the unique distinction of being the first woman to saddle the winner of the great race. Prior to his Aintree victory Corbiere won the Welsh 'National at Chepstow and when younger had been a first class hurdler. The gelding's owner, 23 year old Bryan Burrough, became the youngest person to own the winner of the big Liverpool Steeplechase. Proving himself something of an Aintree specialist, Corbiere competed in another four Grand Nationals after his day of glory, only once failing to complete the course. He finished third in both 1984 and 1985 and, on his last appearance in the race, finished 12th in 1987.

CORTOLVIN

After finishing second in the 1866 'National, Cortolvin was bought by the Duke of Hamilton, whose colours he carried to victory in the race in 1867. Considered by many so-called experts as ungenuine and a non-stayer, the eight-year-old gelding started at 16/1, jumped splendidly all the way and won comfortably by five lengths. His owner, who had been in financial difficulties for some time, collected over £16,000 from the bookmakers which restored His Lordship to a healthier position of solvency. Cortolvin never ran again in England after winning the 'National.

CURE-ALL

The Yorkshire-bred Cure-All lamed himself jumping some rails and it was only the devoted attention of his female groom, Kitty Crisp, which restored the gelding to fitness. After finishing a good second in an obscure steeplechase, the decision was taken to run him in Aintree's famous steeplechase and Kitty Crisp walked Cure-All every inch of the way from Grimsby to Liverpool. So little was known of him that Cure-All remained unquoted in the betting but, well ridden by the amateur Mr Loft, he ran on strongly at the end of the race to win the 1845 race by two lengths. Cure-All and his faithful groom walked all the way back to Grimsby after their victory, to be welcomed by the local church bells chiming in their honour.

DISCOUNT

Originally named Magnum Bonum when running on the flat, this chestnut entire became Discount when put to jumping. The reason for was that his new owner, Mr Quartermaine, had been offered the animal on a number of occasions and each time he offered less money for the horse. In winning the 'National in 1844, Discount became the first horse to succeed in the race who was actually entered in the General Stud Book. A well-backed joint favourite at 5/1, Discount was a very easy 20 length winner on a day when the rain never ceased to fall. Discount never ran in the race again.

DISTURBANCE

The winner of several races on the flat, Disturbance became equally useful when competing in hurdle races and steeplechases. Still only a six-year-old when making his Grand National debut in 1873, Disturbance was nonetheless top weight of the 28 runners with 11st 11lbs but in a very fast run race, he ran on tremendously well from the final obstacle to win by six lengths from Ryshworth. Top weight again in 1874, this time with 12st 9lbs, Disturbance once more ran a fine race to finish seventh in the field of 22. As an entire, he then retired to stud duties and, now the property of Lord Hastings, stood at the Melton Constable stud where sadly his produce proved to be of little account on the turf. Disturbance died at the age of 29.

DOUBLE CHANCE

As the winner of just two moderate races on the flat, the owner of Double Chance, Captain Anthony de Rothschild gave the gelding to a former trooper in his regiment, the trainer Fred Archer. A nephew of the legendary jockey Fred Archer, Double Chance's new owner trained at Newmarket and was obviously delighted with his 'gift horse', the more so when Double Chance won five small 'chases. Shortly before the 1925 Grand National, Archer sold a half-share in the gelding to the Liverpool cotton broker David Goold and it was this man's colours the horse carried at Aintree. Ridden by Major Jack Wilson, Double Chance was always at the forefront of the race but it was the favourite Old Tay Bridge who looked set for victory with a little over 200 yards to run. Timing his challenge perfectly, Major Wilson brought Double Chance with a fine run and, staying on well,, won by four lengths. Double Chance never ran in the 'National again.

DROGHEDA

A very plain looking horse, Drogheda was named after the town close to where he was born in Ireland and bore the distinction of having as his dam, the winner of the 1887 Irish Grand National, Eglantine. After winning four steeplechases in his native land, Drogheda was bought by Richard Marsh and brought to England, where he subsequently became the property of Richard Dawson and Mr G.C.M.Adam. Starting at 25/1 for the 1898 Grand National, Drogheda bravely jumped his way to the front approaching the Water Jump in conditions which were absolutely appalling due to a continuous snowstorm. Holding on strongly, Drogheda won by three lengths from the second favourite Cathal, with Gauntlet four lengths further back in third place. It was the only time Drogheda ran in the 'National.

DRUMCREE

Bred in Ireland by Mr C.Hope, Drumcree was bought by the English trainer Sir Charles Nugent on behalf of his patron Mr Owen Williams and it was in the latter's colours that the gelding finished second in the 1902 Grand National. In 1902 he ran seventh in the race, when the property of a new owner, Mr J.S.Morrison and for the same owner won the 1903 Grand National as 13/2 favourite. Drumcree also ran the race in 1906, when finishing eighth and again in 1907 when he fell.

EARLY MIST

Formerly owned by Mr J.V.rank, the chestnut Early Mist was sold after theowner's death in 1952 to the Dublin businessman Mr Joe Griffin. Having fallen at the first fence in the 1952 Grand National, Early Mist won the race in 1953 in Mr Griffin's colours by 20 lengths, when still just eight years old. The gelding was trained by Vincent O'Brien and ridden by Bryan Marshall. Missing the 1954 race, Early Mist finished ninth in the 1955 'National and fell in 1956 and on both these occasions he was owned by Mr John Dunlop.

EMBLEM

A chestnut mare, Emblem won seven races on the flat before being put over fences and at first she proved most difficult to train, with little idea of how to jump. One day with the North Cotswold Hounds, however, did the trick and from the on Emblem became a perfect steeplechaser. In 1863 she won the Grand National for her owner Lord Coventry and in the same year was also successful in the Cheltenham Steeplechase. She only made one other appearance in the great Aintree event — in 1865 when she was pulled-up. At stud she produced four foals, of which only Deerhurst was of any consequence, winning over hurdles. Emblem died in 1871.

EMBLEMATIC
A full sister to Emblem, Emblematic was also a mare and had the same owner as her sister, Lord Coventry. A very weedy-looking individual, she was far from anyone's idea of a conventional type of 'chaser. Competing in her first 'National in 1864, when only a six-year-old, Emblematic won in most emphatic style by three lengths in the hands of jockey George Stevens who had also ridden Emblem the year before. In 1865 Emblematic finished third in the race and never ran in the 'National again. When sent to stud, Emblematic bred three fillies for Lord Coventry, after which she was sent to Prussia for breeding purposes.

EREMON
Irish-bred Eremon was bought for only £400 because he was said to be thick-winded. His new owner Mr Stanley Howard sent the gelding to be trained by Tom Coulthwaite at Hednesford and it was not until Eremon was six years old that he had his first race. Adapting well to jumping fences, he won the first ever steeplechase to be run at Newbury in the autumn of 1906 and before lining up for the 1907 Grand National, had won another two 'chases at Warwick and Haydock Park under big weights. With only 10st 1lb to carry at Aintree he was considered to have a good chance but early in the race his jockey, Alfred Newey, ran into serious trouble when one of his stirrup leathers broke. Further problems also arose when a riderless horse continually attempted to savage Eremon for the best part of the journey. Holding off a number of late challengers, Eremon stayed on to win by six lengths. Ten days later he won the valuable Lancashire Steeplechase but shortly afterwards he got loose on the gallops, injuring himself so badly that he had to be put down.

EMIGRANT
Winning the 'National at the second attempt in 1857, after finishing seventh in the race the year before, Emigrant survived seven false starts and very heavy going in the course of his victory. Fortunately his jockey, Charlie Boyce, spotted some firmer ground on the edge of the Canal after the Canal Turn which saved Emigrant much wasted effort on both circuits and this undoubtedly helped them to win by three lengths. After the race it was discovered that the winning jockey had ridden with one arm strapped to his side as the result of injury received earlier. After this race the racecourse management erected flags at the outer extremes of all fences to avoid Charlie Boyce's ploy ever being repeated.

EMPRESS
This chestnut mare was named after Elizabeth, the Empress of Austria and won the Grand National on her first and only attempt in the race in 1880 when still just a five-year-old. Ridden by the outstanding Irish amateur Tommy Beasley and trained by Henry Eyre Kinde at the Curragh, Empress was strongly challenged by two others in the closing stages of the race but settled the issue with a spectacular leap at the last obstacle which was estimated to measure thirty feet. At the post she was two lengths clear of two better-fancied runners, The Liberator and Downpatrick. Empress never ran in another race and was sent to stud, where she produced some fine offsprings, included an exceptionally good 'chaser called Red Prince II.

E. S. B.
A very tough gelding, E.S.B. was a very good all-round steeplechaser out of the old mould who, in a long career 'over the sticks', won 22 steeplechases including the 1956 Grand National. Owned by Mrs Carver and trained at Kinnersley by Fred Rimell, E.S.B. fell at Becher's Brook first time round in his first 'National in 1955, and although one of the better fancied runners in 1956, he appeared a well-beaten second with less than 100 yards to run. It was that year though, when Her Majesty The Queen Mother's Devon Loch inexplicably fell within sight of the winning post, leaving E.S.B. to win and be described as the 'luckiest winner of the race ever'. In the 1957 'National E.S.B. finished eighth and the following year got round in sixth place.

FATHER O'FLYNN
Ridden by the Welsh amateur Captain Roddy Owen, Father O'Flynn won the 1892 Grand National by 20 lengths at 20/1, beating the mighty Cloister into second place. Bred in Shropshire, the gelding was seven years old at the time of his success which was his first appearance in the race. He ran in a further four 'Nationals, finishing sixth in 1893, seventh in 1895 and second in 1896. In the 1894 race he fell. Strange to relate, this consistant Aintree performer was ridden in all his Grand Nationals by amateurs.

FOINAVON

The Irish-bred Foinavon was originally owned by the Duchess of Westminster and trained by Tom Dreaper, but after winning two novice 'chases for these connections he became very disappointing, was sold and found his way to the yard of John Kempton at Compton in Berkshire. Considered a complete no-hoper in the Grand National of 1967, Foinavon started at 100/1 and so forlorn appeared his chances that neither the owner nor the trainer bothered attending Liverpool to see him run. Some way behind the leaders at the second Becher's, his jockey John Buckingham had a clear view of the chaos in front of him, when at the fence after the brook, the riderless Popham Down cut right across the leaders and brought the whole field to a standstill - all except Foinavon and his diligent jockey. They raced past and stayed in front to win by 15 lengths from the favourite Honey End. In the 1968 'National Foinavon was brought down and he never ran in the race again. On the day of his victory the Tote paid out a colossal 444/1 against Foinavon.

FORBRA

One of the safest jumpers of his day, Forbra was owned by Ludlow bookmaker Mr William Parsonage and trained by Tom Rimell at Kinnersley in Worcestershire. A 50/1 shot, Forbra won the Grand National at his first attempt in 1932, when a seven-year-old, ridden by Licolnshire born Tim Hamey. In 1933 the gelding finished sixth behind Kellsboro' Jack and in 1934 fourth behind the brilliant Golden Miller. In January 1935 Forbra broke a leg when contesting a steeplechase at Newbury and had to be put down.

FREEBOOTER

A real Liverpool type of 'chaser, Freebooter was owned by Mrs Lurline Brotherton and trained by Bobby Renton at Ripon in Yorkshire. Bred in Waterford by Mr W.F.Phelan, his jockey when he won the 1950 Grand National was Jimmy Power, also a product of Waterford. The winner of 17 steeplechases in all, his victories at Aintree became legend over a few short years, for as well as winning the 1950 'National at his first attempt, he also won the Becher 'Chase, the Champion 'Chase and the Grand Sefton 'Chase twice, all over Aintree's notorious fences. He was brought down at the second fence in the chaotic 1951 'National and fell at the second Canal Turn the following year when leading.

FREETRADER

A reasonably decent horse on the flat, Freetrader actually ran at Royal Ascot as a youngster but really found his mark when put over obstacles. After running second behind Wanderer in the 1855 Grand National, Freetrader won the race the following year, providing his jockey George Stevens with his first success in the race. In his only other appearance in the 'National - in 1857 - Freetrader failed to finish.

FRIGATE

A small though wiry and brave mare, Frigate ran in the Grand National seven times between 1884 and 1890, winning the race in 1889 and finishing second three times. Owned by her breeder Mr M.Maher and trained by him at Ballinkeele, County Wexford in Southern Ireland, Frigate was ridden to victory by fellow countryman, the amateur Tommy Beasley. Apart from her consistantly brave efforts in the 'National, Frigate won the Conyngham Cup when only five years old and twice won steeplechases over one circuit of the Aintree course.

GAMECOCK

The winner of 28 steeplechase in a seven-season period, Gamecock continually lived up to his name, for he was a very game and consistent performer, especially around Aintree. Winning the Grand National at his third attempt in 1887, Gamecock competed in the race a total of seven times. As well as his victory, the gelding finished third , sixth, seventh and tenth and failed to complete the course only twice. Owned by Mr Jay, Gamecock was trained by James Gordon near Tarporley in Cheshire.

GAY LAD

Owned by Mr John Elmore and ridden by Tom Olliver, Gay Lad won the big Liverpool Steeplechase in 1842 on the only occasion he appeared in the race. Six days after his Aintree victory, Gay Lad won a valuable race at Oxford carrying 13st 1lb and before that season ended chalked up another two wins at Nottingham and Chelmsford.

GAY TRIP

A small but very versatile steeplechaser, Gay Trip was formerly trained by Dan Moore in Ireland and upon being bought by Mr A.J.Chambers, was sent to be trained by Fred Rimell at Kinnersley. The winner of eight steeplechases in all, including the Heinz 'Chase at Ascot and Cheltenham's Mackeson Gold Cup twice, the gelding had not travelled further than two and a half miles before setting out in the 1970 Grand National. Beautifully ridden by Pat Taaffe, Gay Trip won the race by 20 lengths from Vulture and Miss Hunter. Falling at the first fence when favourite the next year, he put up a splendid performance in 1972, on going which was completely against him, finishing a two-length second behind Well To Do to whom he was conceding 22lbs.

GLENSIDE

A one-eyed gelding with respiratory problems was hardly the ideal recipe for a 'National winner, yet Gleside as such, achieved his place in racing history by being the only horse to complete the Grand National course without falling in 1911. Owned by Mr Frank Bibby and trained by Captain R.H.Collis at Kinlet in Worcestershire, Glenside was ridden by that outstanding amateur Jack Anthony on a day of foul weather in a race packed with incident. Only three other runners followed the winner homethat year after being remounted. But all the honours quite rightly went to Glenside and Jack Anthony. The horse also competed in the race in 1910 and 1912, but fell on both occasions.

GOLDEN MILLER

As the winner of five Cheltenham Gold Cups and the only horse to win both the most important Cheltenham event and the Grand National in the same year, Golden Miller was dubbed 'the horse of the century'. Owned by Miss Dorothy Paget and trained at the time of his Aintree victory by Basil Briscoe at Exning in Suffolk, 'The Miller' carried everything before him over Park courses. After falling in his first Grand National in 1933, Golden Miller set the racing world alight in 1934 when winning Aintree's supreme prize in record time and, by now considered unbeatble, he started the shortest-priced favouite in the history of the 'National at 2/1 in 1935. Unseating his rider just beyond Valentine's Brook first time round, Golden Miller was thought by some to have been the subject of some devious bookmakers' plot. Subsequent performances showed, however, that Golden Miller had taken an obvious dislike to Aintree's unique obstacles. In his remaining three attempts in the race Golden Miller failed to complete the course. Golden Miller lived in happy retirement until 1957, when he was put down at the age of 30

GRAKLE

The winner of a total of 12 steeplechases, Grakle made his first appearance in the Grand National in 1927, when only a five-year-old he was, in fact, the last of that age to take part in the race. Beetween 1927 and 1932 Grakle ran in the 'National six times, eventually winning the event in 1931 when ridden by Bob Lyall. A very game horse, if somwhat temperamental, Grakle was inclined to hang when under pressure and as a result a special crossed bridle was devised in an attempt to correct the inclination. Known today as a 'Grakle noseband' , it is often used for controlling unruly horses.

GREGALACH

Making his first appearance in the Grand National of 1929, the seven-year-old Gregalach won at 100/1 from 65 opponents, the largest number of runners ever to contest the race. Owned by Mrs M.A.Gemmell, trained by Tom Leader at Newmarket and ridden by Australian-born Bobby Everett, Gregalach jumped perfectly throughout the race to win by six lengths from the 9/1 favourite Easter Hero. Something of a late developer, Gregalach did not set foot on a racecourse until he was five years old but then immediately prove his worth by winning four steeplechases including Aintree's Stanley 'Chase. A period of frustrating second placings followed and, just eight days before the 1929 'National, Gregalach fell in his warm-up race. He won a further five races after his Aintree success and competed in the 'National on another five occasions but only managed to get round once. That was in 1931, when he ran a terrific race to finish second, just a length and a half behind the winner Grakle.

GRITTAR

Bred, owned and trained by Mr Frank Gilman of Morcott in Leicestershire, Grittar won the 1982 Grand National at his first attempt in the race. An exceptional hunter-chaser, the gelding had previously won the Liverpool Foxhunters' 'Chase over one circuit of the 'National course and as the 7/1 favourite on the day of his Grand National victory, became the first favourite to win the race for 22 years. His partner in victory, the amateur Dick Saunders was also making his first appearance in the race and after weighing-in after his victory, Mr Saunders immediately announced his retirement from the saddle.Grittar subsequently finished fifth in the race in 1983 and tenth in 1984.

238

● Grittar and veteran Dick Saunders on their way to victory in 1982.

HALF CASTE

A brown horse not tergistered in the General Stud Book, Half Caste won the 1859 Grand National at his first and only attempt in the race. Second favourite at 7/1, he was ridden by Chris Green who had won the race nine years earlier aboard Abd-El-Kader and although always well up with the leaders, both Half Caste and his jockey had to pull out all the stops in a very close finish. Half Caste won by a short neck and one length from the French challenger Jean Du Quesne and a future winner Huntsman.

HALLO DANDY

Trained by Gordon W.Richards at Greystoke in Cumbria, Hallo Dandy won the 1984 Grand National, ridden by Welshman Neale Doughty after finishing fourth in the race on his first appearance in 1983. A fine jumper with plenty of stamina, Hallo Dandy was always well up with pace and after jumping clear at the last fence, held of the strong challenge of the Irish invader Greasepaint to win by four lengths, with the 1983 hero Corbiere one and a half lengths back in third place. This 1984 'National was the first to be sponsored by Seagram U.K.Limited. Featuring in two further 'Nationals, Hallo Dandy fell at the first fence in 1985 and finished 12th of 40 in 1986.

HIGHLAND WEDDING

Bred by Mr John Caldwell at Prestwick in Ayrshire, Highland Wedding was jointly owned by the American Thomas McKoy and Canadian Charles Burns and was trained by Toby Balding when he won the 1969 Grand National. It was the gelding's third appearance in the race after finishing eighth in 1966 and seventh in 1968. Third in the betting at 100/9, Highland Wedding went to front at the second Canal Turn and from there on was never headed, staying on well at the end to win by 12 lengths from Steel Bridge and Rondetto. He never ran in the 'National again and in the spring of 1970 was taken to a well-earned retirement in Canada.

HUNTSMAN

A most consistent performer around Aintree, Huntsman won the Grand National in 1862, at the third time of asking. Third in 1859, second in 1860, the nine-year-old entire was 3/1 favourite in 1862 when he won by four lengths from 12 opponents. Bought shortly before his victory by the French nobleman, Vicomte de Namur, Huntsman was ridden by the Yorkshire-born but French-based jockey Harry Lamplugh. Huntsman never ran in the race again after his triumph.

ILEX

Considered by his jockey Arthur Nightingall to be the best horse he ever rode, Ilex won the 1890 Grand National as 4/1 favourite in a field of 16 runners. It was his first attempt in the race, for which was trained by his jockey's father, John Nightingall at Epsom. Taking up the running at the Second Valentine's Brook, Ilex romped home to a rather easy 12-length victory. Later in the season he enjoyed further success by winning the Lancashire 'Chase at Manchester. In his two other Grand National appearances, Ilex finished third in both 1891 and 1892 when carrying 12s 3lbs and 12st 7lbs respectively.

JACK HORNER

Bred by Mr John Musker at the Melton Stud, Jack Horner won the 1926 Grand National National when owned by the wealthy American Charles Schwartz and trained by Harvey Leader at Exning in Suffolk. Worked with two year olds by his trainer in an attempt to improve the gelding's speed, Jack Horner had finished seventh in the race in 1925 but in 1926 he was always well placed in the race and came with a fine run close home to capture the prize by three lengths. The grateful owner made a very generous present of £1,000 a year for four years to the winning jockey, Tasmanian born William Watkinson but only three weeks after his victory in the 'National, the rider was tragically killed in a fall at Bogside. While being prepared for a return to Aintree in 1927, Jack Horner broke down so badly that he was at once retired and taken to spend the rest of his days at his owner's home in America.

JAY TRUMP

Bred by Mr Jay Sessenich at Lancaster, Pennsylvania, in the United States, Jay Trump showed little ability when racing on the flat, but improved tremendously when sent jumping, winning nine steeplechases including the famous Maryland Hunt Cup twice. Sent to England to be trained for the 1965 Grand National, he was accompanied by his trainer and rider, Mr Tommy Compton Smith, although his preparation was conducted by Fred Winter who had just begun training at Lambourn in Berkshire. Involved in a fierce dual with the favourite Freddie from the second Canal Turn in the race, Jay Trump held on well to a narrow advantage after the final fence to win by three-quarters of a length from Freddie at odds of 100/6. Returning to the United States a hero, Jay Trump spent his retirement being ridden by his owner Mrs Stephenson with the Camango Hounds in Ohio.

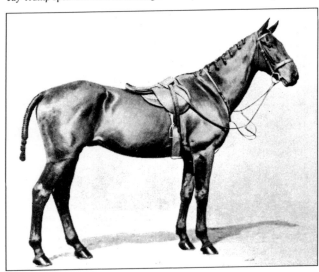

● Jerry M became only the third horse in the history of the National to carry 12st 7lbs to victory with his 1912 success. Cloister and Manifesto had achieved the feat.

● **Kellsboro' Jack leads at the water in 1933 – and was still there at the post.**

JEALOUSY

A brown mare, Jealousy was second favourite at 5/1 when winning the 1861 Grand National on her second appearance in the race. Having failed to complete the course two years before, Jealousy won a hard fought contest to win by two lengths from The Dane, with Old Ben Roe third of the 24 runners. In 1863 Jealousy made her final appearance in the race, finishing sixth in a field of 16.

JENKINSTOWN

Bred in Ireland by Mr P.Leonard, the gelding Jenkinstown was the winner of two small 'chases in his native land before being purchased by Mr Stanley Howard for £600 and arriving in England to be trained by Tom Coulthwaite at Hednesford. Apparently taking a good deal of time to acclimatise to his new surroundings, Jenkinstown was pulled-up in his first Grand National in 1908 and by the time he turned out for the 1910 race had won only one mediocre race since arriving in this country. Ridden by 30 year old Yorkshireman Bob Chadwick, Jenkinstown battled on bravely in the final mile of the race in an exciting dual with the favourite, the brilliant Jerry M. At the post Jenkinstown was three to the good over Jerry M, with only three others managing to stay the course.Pulled-up in his two subsequent 'National appearances in 1911 and 1912, Jenkinstown never won another race and died in 1912.

JERRY

Winner of Aintree's major steeplechase in 1840, Jerry was an out-and-out stayer, who was said to be able to run all day at his own pace. Having won the 1837 Leamington Grand Steeplechase and two good races at Northampton and Daventry, Jerry was a 12/1 outsider in a field of 12 for the big race at Aintree in 1840, but out-stayed his rivals to win by four lengths from the remounted Arthur. He never ran in the race again.

JERRY M

Unquestionably the outstanding steeplechaser of the early part of this century, Jerry M rose above leg, wind and back problems to thrill racegoers for four exciting seasons. Even before he was six years old, the gelding had won four of his first five races in his native Ireland. When purchased by Sir Charles Assheton-Smith for £1,200, Jerry M was sent to be trained by Bob Gore at Findon in Sussex and on his Grand National debut in 1910, gave a perfect display of jumping under top weight of 12st 7lbs to finish second, three lengths behind Jenkinstown. At his second attempt in 1912, again at the top of the handicap, Jerry M trounced his 23 opponents emphatically to win by six lengths. He was ridden that day by Ernest Piggott, whose grandson Lester became a living turf legend two generations later. To the despair of countless thousands, Jerry M never ran anywhere again and very tragically had to be put down in 1914.

241

KELLSBORO' JACK

Despite his obvious brilliance as a steeplechaser, American owned Kellsboro' Jack only ever ran in the Grand National once, but his performance that day in 1933 was a tribute to the horse and all connected with him. Owned by Mrs F.Ambrose Clark, who purchased the gelding from her husband for just £1 some time before his 'National triumph, Kellsboro' Jack was trained by Ivor Anthony at Wroughton in Wiltshire and ridden by Dudley Williams. Mrs Clark decided after the 1933 Grand National that Kellsboro' Jack would never be subjected to rigours of that race again, although he did win over Aintree's huge obstacles a number of times. The Stanley 'Chase and two Champion Chase's were captured by this brilliant jumper and he also added the Scottish Grand National to his tally of victories. Upon retiring, Kellsboro' Jack was taken by his owner back to the United States and is buried there, in the foothills of the Adirondack Mountains.

KILMORE

A great favourite among regular visitors to Aintree, Kilmore finished fifth on his initial attempt at the National in 1961, before winning the race as a 12 year old in 1962. Trained by Ryan Price at Findon in Sussex, the gelding was ridden by Fred Winter, who was recording his second success in the race. On the day of Kilmore's victory in 1962, the going was very heavy, making the race a more severe test of stamina than ever, but Kilmore ran a great race to win by 12 lengths from Wyndburgh and the former winner Mr What. He never won another race, although he finished sixth of 47 in the 1963 'National and made his final appearance in the race in 1964 when he fell.

KIRKLAND

Bred in Ireland by the Reverend E.Clifford, Kirkland was bought by the Liverpool businessman Mr Frank Bibby and quickly repaid a large portion of his purchase price by winning ten steeplechases before he was even six years old. Most encouraging was the fact that one of these victories was gained over one circuit of the 'National course in the 1902 Grand Sefton 'Chase. After such a whirlwind start to his career, Kirkland's form dropped off during the next two seasons, although he ran a good race in the 1903 Grand National to finish fourth. At his second attempt in the 'National of 1904, Kirkland came second behind the New Zealand bred Moifaa and as a result of this performance became one of the leading fancies for the 1905 race. Starting second favourite at 6/1 and again ridden by the Liverpool born jockey Frank Mason, Kirkland was settled in mid-division for most of the journey and only moved smoothly into the lead as they crossed the Melling Road for the final time. Resisting the determined challenge of Napper Tandy on the run-in, Kirkland won unextended by three lengths, with only the riderless Ascetic's Silver in front of him. Three years after his Grand National victory, Kirkland paid a return visit to Aintree as 13/2 favourite for the 1908 'National, finishing seventh of 24 runners after being remounted.

THE LAMB

Bred in County Limerick by a Mr Henchy, the grey entire The Lamb was a very small and frail youngster but he could jump brilliantly and when just five years of age won the Kildare Hunt Plate at Punchestown. Then leased to Lord Poulett, the little grey came to England where he won the 1868 Grand National, after which he suffered from a wasting disease which at one time threatened his life. Off the racecourse for two years, The Lamb returned to Aintree in 1871 to repeat his earlier victory in the 'National. Some weeks before the race, his owner had had a dream in which he claimed he clearly saw his tiny grey champion romping triumphantly past the Aintree winning post . In his last appearnce in the Grand National in 1872, The Lamb finished fourth of 25 and in due course was sold to Baron Oppenheim who took him to Germany. In the most tragic of circumstances, the little grey dual Grand National winner, was put down after breaking a leg in a steeplechase at Baden-Baden.

LAST SUSPECT

The winner of the 1985 Grand National at his first attempt, Last Suspect was within days of actually being withdrawn from the race. Trained by Captain Tim Forster at Letcombe Bassett in Oxfordshire, the gelding had developed a moody temperament which too frequently had led to Last Suspect deciding he had done enough in races and pulling himself up. It was the realisation of this willful tendancy which led to owner, the Duchess of Westminster and trainer Forster deciding that they would withdrawn Last Suspect at the next declaration stage for the 1985 Grand National. Fortunately the stable jockey, Welshman Hywel Davies, convinced the Duchess at the very last moment that the horse was worth another chance and so it was that sporting history was made. Last Suspect justified his jockey's faith by coming from a long way back to get up in the final 100 yards to snatch victory by a length and half from Mr Snugfit. Running in the race again in 1986, it was a different story, with Last Suspect resorting to his old ways and eventually being pulled-up after completing just one circuit of the race.

L'ESCARGOT

The American owned L'Escargot had twice won the Cheltenham Gold Cup before first running in the 1982 Grand National, in which he was knocked over by another horse at the third fence. Obviously a very class horse, the chestnut had with increasing age lost some of his speed but could still jump fences with the best of them. Always at the top of the handicap for the 'National, L'Escargot finished third in the 1973 race behind Red Rum and Crisp and improved that placing by coming second in the 1974 Aintree spectacular, again behind Red Rum. In 1975 L'Escargot at last won the Grand National, this time turning the tables on the people's favourite Red Rum. Despite a bad mistake at the seventh fence, which his jockey Tommy Carberry brilliantly corrected, L'Escargot gave owner Raymond Guest the Aintree winner of which he had for so long dreamed. Mr Guest generously gave L'Escargot to the wife of his trainer Dan Moore, assured that his champion would enjoy a happy and contented retirement.

THE LIBERATOR

Irish-bred, The Liberator was a giant of a horse, with powerful shoulders and what many described as donkey-like feet, but he made a name for himself by winning the Grand National at his third attempt in 1879. In all the gelding competed in the race six times and besides winning the race, also finished third in 1877, second in 1880 and ninth in 1881. Shortly before the 1879 'National, an attempt was made by a former owner of The Liberator to prevent the horse competing at Aintree but a ruling was given in the Dublin court that his entry was perfectly legal. It is not recorded if the wise judge who made that decision backed The Liberator.

LITTLE CHARLEY

Another without registration in the General Stud Book, Little Charley won the Grand National at his fourth attempt in 1858, after the race had been postponed for three days due to the appalling weather. The result brought great celebrations in Cheltenham, for owner Christopher Capel, trainer William Holman and jockey William Archer were all from that city. William Archer was the father of the great Fred Archer, whose flat race exploits became famous throughout the world.

LITTLE POLVEIR

After finishing ninth in his first Grand National in 1986, Little Polveir unseated his rider in the race in 1987 and 1988 and shortly before the 1989 event was bought by Mr Harvey and sent to be trained by Toby Balding. Ridden by Jimmy Frost, the gelding jumped superbly all the way and stayed the trip out well to beat former winner West Tip by seven lengths, with the former Cheltenham Gold Cup The Thinker back in third. Prior to his Aintree triumph, Little Polveir had finished fourth in Sandown's Grand Military Gold Cup when ridden by his owner's son. Little Polveir also won the 1987 Scottish Grand National on very heavy going.

LOTTERY

Formerly named Chance, Lottery eventually assumed the name of his sire and even before that memorable day in 1839, had become famous throughout the land as the most spectacular steeplechaser of the age. Owned by John Elmore, trained by George Dockeray at Epsom and always ridden by Jem Mason, the bay gelding had one peculiar trait which could well have changed the course of racing history. Lottery could not bear the sight of his jockey Jem Mason. The only way the rider was able to mount the horse was by disguising himself in long coats, yet once in the saddle, the pair were almost unbeatable. In February 1839 Lottery started favourite at 5/1 for the first running of the Grand Liverpool Steeplechase at Aintree and, always well to the fore, settled the issue with an incredible leap at the final obstacle which was reputed be over 33 ft in length. Such was Lottery's fame that many racecourse executives took the unusual step of forbidding him to run at their meetings, because it was feared that he would frighten away most opposition. He nonetheless continued winning steeplechases all over the country, although despite running in the great Aintree 'chase a further four times, he only completed the course once when finishing seventh in 1843. By far the saddest aspect concerning this brightest star of the early days of English steeplechasing, was the fact that he ended his days pulling a cart around the back streets of Neasden.

LOVELY COTTAGE

Bred in County Cork, Ireland by Mr M.J.Hyde, Lovely Cottage learned the art of jumping in the hurly-burly world of hunter-chasing, quickly graduating to steeplechasing proper to such effect that during the 1943-44 season he won three 'chases including the important Conyngham Cup. Sold to Mr John Morant at end of 1945, the gelding came to England to be trained by Tommy Rayson at Headbourne Worthy in Hampshire. A 25/1 shot for the 1946 Grand National, the first to be held since the end of the war, Lovely Cottage was ridden Captain Bobby Petre, an officer in the Scots Guards who was awaiting demob. With the focus of attention directed on the red-hot 3/1 favourite Prince Regent, little was seen of Lovely Cottage during the first circuit and the excitement grew as Prince Regent led over the last fence. Then steadily Lovely Cottage gained ground and ran out a clear winner by four lengths from Jack Finlay, with Prince Regent third. Missing the race the following year through injury, Lovely Cottage ran just once more in the 1948 'National, when, merely a shadow of his former self, he finished 14th of 43 after being remounted.

LUCIUS

This bay gelding, bred by Doctor Magaret Lloyd, came to Aintree for the Grand National but once, yet made his visit a winning one in 1978. The late withdrawal of Red Rum cast a shadow over the 1978 'National and left the race more wide open than for many years, but the thrilling close finish of the event brought all those present to their feet. Lucius stayed on gallantly in the closing stages to hold on and win by half a length from Sebastian V, with Drumroan just a neck behind in third place. Trained by Gordon W.Richards in Cumbria and ridden by Bob Davies, Lucius started at 14/1.

LUTTEUR III

The last five-year-old and the last French-bred horse to win the Grand National, Lutteur III was trained by Harry Escott at Lewes and gained his victory in 1909 by two lengths from Judas in a field of 32. Proving somewhat difficult to train after his 'National success, Lutteur III fell in the 1911 'National when again ridden by Frenchman Georges Parfrement and got round to finish third in the 1914 race.

MANIFESTO

One of the greatest - probably the greatest - of horses ever to set foot on Aintree's turf, Manifesto was bred in County Meath, Ireland by Mr H.M.Dyas and. apparently possessing the constitution of a lion, competed in races for 13 successive seasons. Twice a winner of the Grand National, in 1897 and 1899, on the latter occasion and thereafter never carried less than 12st in the race. By the time Manifesto competed in his last Grand National in 1904 at the age of 16, he had taken part in no fewer than eight 'Nationals. His Aintree record speaks for itself ; twice a winner of the race, three times third, fourth once and at the age of 16 in his last 'National a brave and very gallant eighth. Only once did he fail to complete the course and that was when he was barged into by another horse in 1896. No words can ever do justice to the truly mighty; suffice to say that Manifesto was a great and very remarkable horse. His skeleton is housed in the veterinary department of the Liverpool University.

MAORI VENTURE

Considered by many as too much of a chancy jumper to succeed at Aintree, Maori Venture won the 1987 Grand National without putting a foot wrong through the entire journey. Owned by the very elderly Mr Jim Joel, trained by Andrew Turnell and ridden by Steve Knight, the gelding won the 'National on his first and only attempt at odds of 28/1. Delighted by winning the great Aintree race after so many years of trying, Mr Joel left Maori Venture to the horse's partner in victory, Steve Knight, in his will.

MASTER ROBERT

Bred in County Donegal by Mr McKinlay, Master Robert suffered constantly from navicular and thisk-windedness and at one time, in an effort to restore his fitness, Master Robert was used as a plough horse. With his fitness still in question, Master Robert lined up for the 1924 Grand National, his first ever attempt at the big race and, although trailing the field for a long way, the gelding gradually wore down the opposition to win by four lengths. Winning jockey Bob Trudgill, who been injured the day before in a fall, almost collapsed on dismounting but, always the professional, weighed-in before getting the racecourse doctor to re-stitch his damaged leg. Master Robert never raced again.

MATTHEW

The first Irish-trained winner of the race in 1847, the year when the event finally became officially named the Grand National Steeplechase, Matthew was ridden by Dennis Wynne and started joint favourite at 10/1. Attempting to win the race for a second time in 1848, Matthew was knocked over in very heavy going. He only ran in the race twice.

MERRYMAN II
The former hunter-chaser Merryman II won the Liverpool Foxhunters 'Chase in 1959 before starting favourite at 13/2 for his first Grand National in 1960. It was in this year that the BBC first televised the race and nothing could have been more appropriate than that the best-backed horse should win. Owned by Miss Winifred Wallace and trained by Neville Crump at Middleham in Yorkshire, Merryman II was ridden Gerry Scott, who had his arm strapped up as a result of breaking his collar bone shortly before the race. Foot perfect at every fence and beautifully ridden, Merryman II stayed the distance better than any of his rivals to win by 15 lengths from Badanloch and Clear Profit. He was the first clear favourite to win the race since Sprig in 1927 and also the first winner to be owned by an unmarried lady. He ran a splendid race in the 1961 'National to finish second behind Nicolaus Silver and in 1962 bade farewell to Aintree when finishing 13th behind Kilmore. After retiring, Merryman II spent leisurely days in the hunting field and died suddenly in 1966 while attending a meet of the North Northumberland Hounds.

MIINNEHOMA
Owned by the Liverpool-born comedian Freddie Starr and trained by Martin Pipe at Wellington, Miinnehoma won the 1994 Grand National at his first attempt in the race. On very heavy going, Miinnehoma - at 16/1 - made one bad mistake at Becher's Brook, but jockey Richard Dunwoody sat firm, gathered his mount and after being led into the final fence by the favourite Moorcroft Boy, took up the running early in the straight to win well.Attempting to win the race a second time in 1995, Miinnehoma was never going well and was pulled up when tailed off nearing Becher's second time round.

MISS MOWBRAY
A very good staying mare, Miss Mowbray won the 1852 'National completely ignored in the betting and on the basis of that victory went off favourite for the 1853 race. On heavy going which didn't suit her at all, she did very well to finish second - just three lengths behind the winner. When strongly fancied to win the race in 1854, the mare was 'got-at' shortly before the start and had to be withdrawn. Tragically, in her last attempt to repeat her victory, Miss Mowbray was so badly injured in the 1855 Grand National that she had to be put down.

MOIFAA
The New Zealand bred Moifaa was a very large, ungainly looking individual, who, went sent over to contest the 1904 Grand National, was shipwrecked off the south coast of Ireland. Having swum onto a sand-spit, he was rescued some little time later by fishermen and duly won the Aintree race by eight lengths at 25/1. Representing His Majesty King Edward VII in the 'National of 1905, Moifaa was the 4/1 favourite but fell and was retired to the hunting field.

MR FRISK
Trained by Kim Bailey at Upper Lambourn in Berkshire and owned by American, Mrs H.J.Duffy, Mr Frisk won the 1990 race when ridden by the very talented amateur Marcus Armytage.He been been strongly fancied for the race the previous year, but when the going became heavy the gelding was withdrawn shortly before the race. Encountering fitness problems, Mr Frisk was pulled up in the 1991 'National and never competed in the race again.

MR WHAT
Bred by Mrs Barbara O'Neill in County Westmeath, Ireland, Mr What was considered little more than a novice when making his Grand National debut in 1958. Trained by Tom Taaffe and ridden by Arhtur Freeman the gelding beat a field of good seasoned 'chasers by all of 30 lengths. He ran in a further five 'Nationals, finishing third in both 1959 and 1962 and was 11th of 35 in 1961. Mr What never won another race after that 1958 Grand National success, despite taking part in 33 other races.

MUSIC HALL
Winning the 'National in 1922 at the first attempt, Music Hall had won the Scottish 'National two years before and was, at his best, a very good all-round performer. Having been bred by Mrs F.Blacker in County Kildare, the gelding developed leg trouble after winning a race at Nottingham which kept him off the racecourse for some time. Music Hall ran in the 'National twice more after his victory, being pulled-up in 1924 and refusing the following year.

NICKEL COIN

The third mare to win the race this century and the last one to date, Nickel Coin was bred by Mr R.Corbett and purchased for just 50 guineas by Mr Jeffrey Royle, achieving some success in the show-jumping ring before being trained for 'chasing by Jack O'Donaghue at Reigate in Surrey. Proving herself a resolute stayer, she won the 1951 Grand National on her only appearance in the race when ridden by Johnny Bullock and at the somewhat generous odds of 40/1.After a dreadful start, the 1951 'National turned into chaos, with a third of the runners coming to grief at the the very first fence and only Nickel Coin and the runner-up Royal Tan completing the course without falling. The only other to actually get round was the remounted Derrinstown. When sent to stud Nickel Coin bred three foals, of which only King's Nickle proved himself on the racecourse.

NICOLAUS SILVER

Only the second grey to win the 'National, Nicolaus Silver was bought at Goffs Sales for £2,000 by Mr Charles Vaughan and sent to be trained by Fred Rimell at Kinnersley. He won the 1961 Grand National at his first attempt, jumping brilliantly all the way and rallying well in the closing stages to beat the previous year's winner Merryman II by five lengths. In the 1962 race he finished seventh and in 1963 tenth.

OLD JOE

Bred by Mr E.H.Banks, Old Joe won a total of 13 races including the 1886 Grand National, when trained by George Mulcaster at Burgh-by-Sands, Carlisle, and ridden by Tommy Skelton. Producing a rare turn of speed in the run to the winning post, Old Joe won the 'National at the first time of asking by six lengths from Too Good and the future winner Gamecock. Old Joe fell in both the 1887 and 1888 events.

OXO

Bred by Mr A.C.Wyatt in Dorset, OXO was an eight-year-old when winning the 1959 Grand National on his first appearance in the race. A very good point-to-pointer before being trained for steeplechasing by Willie Stephenson at Royston in Hertfordshire, the gelding won four other steeplechases besides the 'National, in which he was ridden Michael Scudamore. He missed the 1960 Aintree race as a result of breaking down in training, but ran in the 1961 event and was pulled-up. Although continuing to race for a further three seasons, OXO never won again.

PARTY POLITICS

A very big horse, standing over 17 hands high, Party Politics won the 1992 Grand National on his introduction to the race, jumping well all the way and out-staying the runner-up Romany King on the run to the line. Bred by Buckinghamshire farmer David Stoddart, Party Politics quickly made his mark in 'chasing, becoming one of the leading novices of his generation. Trained by Nick Gaselee at Upper Lambourn in Berkshire, the big horse was turned out perfectly for his Aintree victory. In the 1995 Grand National, Party Politics again gave an impressive display of jumping when finishing a good second to the winner Royal Athlete, but in the 1996 race was clearly not himself when falling at the third fence.

PATHFINDER

Formerly named The Knight, Pathfinder won the 1875 Grand National at his first attempt, getting up in the closing stages to beat Dainty half a length. His rider, the amateur Tommy Pickernell, afterwards disclosed that he had almost pulled Pathfinder up at Becher's Brook second time round because he felt the gelding had reached the end of his tether. On his only other run in the race the following year, Pathfinder failed to complete the course.

PETER SIMPLE

This gelding, who was not registered in the General Stud Book, ran in the 'National six times, winning it at his first attempt in 1849 and repeating the victory four years later in 1853. On his four other appearances in the race he failed to complete the course. Apart from being a dual Grand National winner, Peter Simple is remembered for being the oldest horse to succeed in the race, being 15 years old at the time of his second win in 1853..

PIONEER

Described before his first Grand National in 1846, as 'a rough looking fellow in poor condition', Pioneer defied that criticism by winning the race by three lengths. His victory was even more meritorious for the fact that, due an error in marking the course, the distance was wrongly extended to five miles. In the 1847 Grand National Pioneer ran another splendid race to finish a decent fourth to the Irish trained Matthew, but in his final effort in the race of 1848 he was brought down when going well.

PLAYFAIR

A black gelding who was not registered in the General Stud Book, Playfair ran only once in the 'National, but sprang a surprise when winning the 1888 race by ten lengths from the very good Aintree horse Frigate and at the long odds of 40/1. His career began in the humblest of circumstances - in Farmers' Hunt Races - but Playfair developed into a very game Hunter-Chaser and there can no question that he won his Grand National on merit. His only other race after winning the 'National was the Grand International 'Chase at Sandown Park in which he ran out.

POETHLYN

Bred by Major Hugh Peel at Bryn y Pas on Deeside, Poethlyn was very weak and sickly when a foal and was sold to a hotelier in Shrewsbury for just £7. Fortunately his breeders regreted the transaction, bought him back for £50 and allowing him time to mature, proceeding to win 15 races with him. Running in the name of his breeder's wife, Mrs Peel, Poethlyn won the 1919 Grand National as 11/4 favourite, the shortest priced horse ever to win the race and an example of his excellence was the fact that he carried off the victory under top weight of 12st 7lbs.Favourite again for the 1920 'National, this time at 3/1, Poethlyn fell at the first fence and was immediately retired to his breeder's estate in Shropshire. Poethlyn was trained by Harry Escott at Lewes and ridden by Ernie Piggott.

QUARE TIMES

Bred in Ireland by Mr P.P.Sweeney, Quare Times remained unraced until he was six years old and for a couple of seasons showed little ability. His first victory came at Gowran Park, after which he came on by leaps and bounds. Trained by Vincent O'Brien, Quare Times won the National Hunt 'Chase at Cheltenham in 1954 and in 1955 made his only appearance in the Grand National a winning one. Ridden by the incomparable Pat Taaffe, Quare Times won the 'National by 12 lengths, providing his trainer with the unique distinction of saddling three successive Grand National winners. After his Aintree success Quare Times won only two other races.

RAG TRADE

The winner of eight races in all, including the Welsh Grand National at Chepstow and the real thing at Aintree in 1976, Rag Trade was bred by Mr I.Williams in Ireland and trained by Fred Rimell at Kinnersley. His success in the 1976 Grand National was at the expense of the great Red Rum, who ran his usual terrific race, only to be caught close home by Rag Trade's late spurt. It was Rag Trade's second attempt at the 'National, having finished tenth and last in 1975. On his final run in the race in 1978, Rag Trade started 8/1 favourite but broke down so badly that he had to be put down.

RED RUM

Definitely the most famous Grand National winner of all time and certainly the best-loved horse ever to face the perils of Aintree, Red Rum is the only steeplechaser ever to win the race three times. Bred by Mr Martin McEnery in Ireland and trained for each of his five Grand Nationals by Donald McCain at Birkdale near Southport, he won the Grand National at the first attempt in 1973. Getting up in the final strides to win from the Australian champion Crisp, Red Rum - receiving 23 pounds - was criticised rather unfairly by some members of the press as a rather lucky winner. In 1974 however, Red Rum proved beyond all doubt that his ability and courage were unquestionable by winning the Grand National again, this time under the top weight burden of 12 stone. Second the following year behind L'Escargot and again in 1976, when Rag Trade pipped him close home, Red Rum had, by now, become not only a household name but a living symbol of the finest traditions of sport. His final appearance in the race he had restored to greatness, came in 1977 when, again top weight, he won the Grand National for the third time in devastating style by 25 lengths. Red Rum was retired in 1978, although he led the parade of Grand National runners before the start for many years and in 1995 Aintree Racecourse Company celebrated his 30th birthday in a unique manner by putting on an evening race meeting in his honour. In October 1995 Red Rum suffered a heart attack at Donald McCain's training establishment and the gallant gelding was put down to save him furthering suffering.Most appropriately, and with great dignity, Red Rum was buried alongside the winning post at Aintree Racecourse, truly his spiritual home.

RED ALLIGATOR

Bred by Mr William Kennedy in Northern Ireland, Red Alligator was trained by Denys Smith at Bishop Auckland in County Durham and after finishing third in the chaotic 1967 'National on his first appearance, won the 1968 race by 20 lengths ridden by Brian Fletcher. Altogether Red Alligator won 11 steeplechases and was a most reliable and resolute stayer. Red Alligator fell in both the 1969 and 1970 'Nationals.

247

● **Royal Athlete brushes through the last fence in 1995 on his way to recording a second National success for trainer Jenny Pitman.**

REGAL

Bred by Mr W.Graham, Regal was of little account when running on the flat, but developed into a very good staying 'chaser, winning the 1876 Grand National on his debut in the race. The gelding ran a further five times in the event, finishing sixth in 1879 and second in 1881 and failing to complete the course on the other three occasions.Owned by the famous Captain Machell, Regal was just five years old at the time of his Aintree success.

REYNOLDSTOWN

Dual Grand National winner in successive years, 1935 and 1936, Reynoldstown was owned and trained by Major Noel Furlong at Skeffington in Leicestershire. He was ridden to victory in 1935 by the Major's amateur rider son Frank and in 1936 he was piloted home by another fine amateur, Fulke Walwyn. Almost black in colour, Reynoldstown won four hurdle races and eight steeplechases during the 1930's when there existed an abundance of fine jumping talent in this country.

REUGNY

A French-bred chestnut entire, Reugny - the property of Lord Aylesford - began his jumping career very early, winning a hurdle race and three 'chases when just four years old. Under the same ownership he ran in his first Grand National in 1873 but failed to complete the course. Starting favourite at 5/1 for the 1874 race and now owned by Captain Machell, Reugny won by six lengths from Chimney Sweep and Merlin and was ridden to victory by that very talented amateur John Maunsell Richardson. In 1877 he competed for the final time in the 'National but was never going well and was pulled-up. Reugny never won another race.

RHYME 'N' REASON

Bred by Mrs J.F.C.Maxwell at Downpatrick in County Down, Rhyme 'N' Reason was an out-and-out stayer who, in only his second season, won the Irish Grand National. In 1988 he made his only appearance in the Grand National, when trained by David Elsworth at Whitsbury in Hampshire and ridden by Irishman Brendan Powell. Making a dreadful mistake at the first Becher's, Rhyme 'N' Reason slithered along the ground on his belly, dropped back to last place and looked to be completely out of the race. Patiently ridden, the gelding gradually fought his way back into contention and although some three lengths in arrears at the final fence, bravely ran on to win by four lengths from that very good Aintree horse Durham Edition. He never ran in the race again.

ROQUEFORT

After finishing third in the 1884 Grand National, Roquefort won the race the following year when six years old and ridden by the amateur Edward P.Wilson. By all accounts a very difficult horse to ride, Roquefort was a very good jumper with a fine burst of finishing speed but unfortunately he had something of a wayward streak to his character and could be most cunning. After winning the 'National, Roquefort ran a further four times in the race, falling in 1886, 1887 and 1889 and then, on one of his less moody days, finishing fourth on his final appearance in 1891.

ROUGH QUEST

After finishing a good second to Imperial Call in the 1996 Cheltenham Gold Cup, Rough Quest was soon back in action as the 7/1 favourite for the Grand National. Bred by Mr Michael Healy, owned by Mr Andrew Wates and trained by Terry Casey at Dorking, Rough Quest was held up in the 'National by his jockey Mick Fitzgerald, who only began making a forward move on the approach to the 20th fence.Lying second over the final obstacle, some five lengths behind the leader Encore Un Peu, Rough Quest took the lead some 200 yards from home to win by a length and a quarter in a most impressive manner.

ROYAL ATHLETE

Bred by Mr John Brophy in Ireland, Royal Athlete was bought by Mrs Jenny Pitman for 10,000 Irish guineas at Ballsbridge Sales and under her care developed into a very good staying 'chaser. Although often troubled with a variety of injuries, Royal Athlete finished a good third in the 1993 Cheltenham Gold Cup but shortly afterwards badly damaged a leg when running in the Hennessy Gold Cup. The gelding was off the racecourse for a long period and was a 40/1 shot for the 1995 Grand National, in which he was ridden by the 24 year old Irish jockey Jason Titley. Given a splendid ride by his jockey, Royal Athlete was always in a handy position and won by seven lengths from the 1992 winner party Politics. Royal Athlete never ran in the 'National again.

ROYAL MAIL

The winner of the Grand National in 1937 at his first attempt, Royal Mail was bred by Mr Charles Rogers, trained by Ivor Anthony at Wroughton in Wiltshire and ridden by Welshman Evan Williams. Often ridden in races by his owner, Mr H.Lloyd Thomas, Royal Mail jumped perfectly in the 'National and, leading over the last fence, produced a good turn of foot on the run-in to beat the mare Cooleen by three lengths. In the race the following year Royal Mail carried top weight of 12st 7lbs and was pulled-up. In 1938 the gelding finished ninth of 37.

ROYAL TAN

Bred by Mr J.Topin in County Tipperary, Royal Tan ran in the Grand National for the first time in 1951 when finishing second behind Nickel Coin. The following year he fell at the last fence when certain to be placed and after that race Royal Tan was on the sidelines for over a year. In 1954, ridden by Bryan Marshall, Royal Tan won the 'National, after a hard fought tussle on the run-in, by a neck from Tudor Line. In 1955, under the new ownership of Prince Aly Khan, the gelding finished 12th of 30 and the following year ran third behind E.S.B. The last occasion in which Royal Tan competed in the race was in 1957 and he was carried out by a loose horse.

RUBIO

The first American-bred winner of the Grand National, Rubio caused a shock in 1908 when coming home ten lengths clear of his stable-mate, the mare Mattie Macgregor at 66/1. Having broken down earlier in his career, Rubio was used for some time to pull a hotel bus in Towcester, a course of action intended to strengthen him and restore him to fitness. That the exercise was worthwhile was amply proved by his brilliant display of jumping when succesful in the 'National. On his second and final appearance in the race, in 1909, Rubio fell and was immediately retired from racing.

RUBSTIC

Bred by Mrs R.Digby, the ten-year-old Rubstic became the first Scottish trained winner of the Grand National when winning the race at his first attempt in 1979. Owned by Mr John Douglas, trained by John Leadbetter at Denholm in Roxburghshire and ridden by Maurice Barnes, Rubstic won at 25/1 by a length and a half from Zongalero. Favourite at 8/1 in 1980, the gelding fell at the Chair when up with the leaders and in his last 'National run the following year finished seventh of 39.

SALAMANDER

Born with a deformity of a foreleg which left it crooked, the gelding was, as a result, bought very cheaply by Mr Edward Studd, taken back to the owner's home in Rutland and in time put into training as a steeplechaser. Some time before taking part in the 1866 Grand National, Salamander was beaten over 40 lengths in a race at Warwick by the brilliant L'Africaine and when the pair met up again at Aintree in the Grand National, Salamander was almost ignored in the betting at 40/1.Ridden by the amateur Mr Alec Goodman, Salamander was kept to the rear for best part of the race, only being brought to challenge the leaders as they approached the second last. Running on strongly on the flat, Salamander won by ten lengths from Cortolvin, with Creole a further four lengths away in third place. A week later the crooked-legged hero was also successful in the Warwick Grand Annual Steeplechase, but sadly was later killed in a 'chase at Crewkerne.

SEAGRAM

Bred in New Zealand by Mrs J.A.Broome, Seagram was purchased as a three year old by the wife of Kingsbridge trainer David Barons and in the colours of the Liverpool van-hire company Maincrest Limited, developed into a most useful hurdler. In his first season the gelding finished second in the Liverpool Hurdle and the following year won the White Satin Hurdle at the same venue. Continuing to improve, the gelding finally broke down badly after winning a steeplechase at Hereford, which resulted in him being off the racecourse for more than a year. During this time Seagram had carbon-fibre implants inserted into both forelegs and when restored to fitness he won twice over fences and subsequently becoming the joint property of Sir Eric Parker and his trainer David Barons, it was in the former's colours that he lined up for the 1991 Grand National. Landing in second place over the final fence when still some eight lengths behind Garrison Savannah, Seagram produced a good burst of speed on the run-in to win five lengths.

SEAMAN

A somewhat small individual, Seaman was constantly unsound as a youngster and it was found necessary to fire him when he was still only a two year old in training under Henry Eyre Linde at the Curragh. When still only five years of age, Seaman won the both the Conyngham Cup and the principal French hurdle race, the Grande Course des Haies but at the end of that season became unfit once more. Sold to Lord Manners, the gelding was sent to be trained by Captain James Machell and, partnered by his owner, took his place at the start for the 1882 Grand National. A 10/1 shot at the Off, his trainer freely admitted that he had only been able to get Seaman three parts fit for Aintree. The race was run in a blizzard and at the final fence the result lay between Cyrus and Seaman, who touched down together, Early in the straight Seaman broke down. but, running on instinct, guts and virtually just three legs, the courageous horse somehow battled on to draw level with Cyrus and then stick out his neck far enough to win by a head. The very brave Seaman never ran in another race and spent the remainder of his days in contented retirement at his owner's estate.

SERGEANT MURPHY

Irish-bred by Mr G.L.Walker, Sergeant Murphy won ten steeplechases in all, including the 1922 Scottish Grand National and the real thing at Aintree the following year. The gelding became the first American-owned winner of the 'National in 1923, when carrying the colours of Mr Stephen Sanford, a Cambridge undergraduate whose wealthy father had bought the horse for his son. Ridden by that fine amateur Captain G.H. 'Tuppy' Bennet, Sergeant Murphy won the 'National by three lengths from the former winner Shaun Spadah at 100/6 and was 13 years old at the time.Captain Bennet was killed as the result of a fall at Wolverhampton some nine months after his Aintree victory and his partner in glory, Sergeant Murphy, tragically had to be put down three years later after breaking a leg at Bogside.

SHANNON LASS

Bred by Mr James Reidy at County Clare in Ireland, Shannon Lass became the first mare to win the Grand National since 1889 when coming home three lengths clear of Matthew in 1902, with the great Manifesto a further three lengths back in third place. Trained by James Hackett at Telscombe in Sussex, the mare was owned by the English bookmaker Ambrose Gorham for whom she won seven other steeplechases besides the National. Gorham donated all his winnings to the restoration of the church at Telscombe. Shannon Lass never won another race.

SHAUN GOILIN

It was not until the gelding Shaun Goilin was seven years of age that he won his first race but from then on he quickly developed into a very reliable jumper. The winner of five steeplechases, including the Grand Sefton at Aintree in 1929, before making his first attempt at the the Grand National of 1930, Shaun Goilin was owned by Liverpool cotton broker Mr W.H.Midwood and started second favourite at 100/8. In a very close finish, three horses jumped the last fence almost in line and after a desperate battle up the straight, Shaun Goilin prevailed by a neck from Melleray's Belle, with Sir Lindsay a length and a half back in third place. Trained by Frank Hartigan at Weyhill in Hampshire, Shaun Goilin finished sixth in the race the following year and third in 1932.

SHAUN SPADAH

Bred in Ireland by Mr P.McKenna, Shaun Spadah won a total of 19 races including the Coventry 'Chase at Kempton and the Becher 'Chase at Aintree and of course an incident packed Grand National in 1921. Owned by Mr T.M.McAlpine, trained by George Poole at Lewes in Sussex and ridden by the brilliant Welsh jockey Fred Rees, Shaun Goilin was the only competitor from 35 runners to complete the course without falling. The gelding won by a distance from The Bore, All White and Turkey Buzzard, all of whom were remounted after falling. In 1923 Shaun Spadah finished second behind Sergeant Murphy and in 1924, seventh.

SHIELA'S COTTAGE

Described by her trainer, Neville Crump of Middleham in Yorkshire, as 'an ornery old cow' the mare Sheila's Cottage was bred by Mrs P.Daly in County Limerick and had inherited her dam's fiery temper. First purchased by Sir Hervey Bruce, who at the time was adjutant of Catterick Camp, the mare was placed in the care of trainer Crump and failed to finish the course in her first Grand National venture in 1947. Changing ownership for the next big Antree race, Sheila's Cottage became the property of Mr John Proctor, a Grimsby fishing-trawler owner and again partnered by the only jockey able to control her, Arthur Thompson, got up close home to win the 1948 Grand National by a length from First Of the Dandies. When sent to stud, Sheila's Cottage bred six foals, 'though not before she had bitten the top off one of Arthur Thompson's fingers two days after their Aintree victory. Upon her death, the mare was buried at bottom of jockey Thompson's garden in Wexford.

SHIFNAL

After finishing unplaced in a selling plate at Alexandra Park, Shifnal was bought by the Epsom trainer John Nightingall, who trained him to win nine steeplechases during his career, which included the Grand National of 1878. Owned by the trainer and ridden John Jones, Shifnal was a nine-year-old at the time of his Aintree victory and won by two lengths at 7/1. He had previously finished third in the 1876 'National.

THE SOARER

Irish-bred The Soarer was bought as a four-year-old by Mr David Campbell, a subaltern in the 9th Lancers then stationed in Ireland. Riding the gelding himself, Campbell enjoyed immediate success by winning seven races with him. The Soarer subsequently becamevery difficult to train and shortly before the 1896 Grand National was sold to the Liverpool businessman Mr William Hall Walker for £500 with a condition that Mr David Campbell be allowed to partner the horse at Aintree. At the generous odds of 40/1, The Soarer won by one and a half lengths from previous winner Father O'Flynn. In both his following attempts to win the National, The Soarer fell and he never won another race.

SPECIFY

Owned by Mr Fred Pontin, the holiday camp king, trained by John Sutcliffe at Epsom and ridden by John Cook, the nine-year-old Specify won the 1971 Grand National in a very close finish. The gelding's first effort at Aintree had been in the 1970 'National, when strongly fancied, he ran a good race only to be brought-down at Becher's second time round. Starting at 28/1, Specify was one of five horses who jumped the final fence in the 1971 Grand National almost in line abreast. Making his move at the elbow, jockey John Cook brought his mount with a great run on the inside rail, found a way through and ran on to win by a neck from the Irish horse Black Secret, with Astbury two and a half lengths away third. The following year, Specify put up another good performance in the 'National, finishing sixth behind Well To Do, but he, like many before and since, never won another race.

SPRIG

Bred by Captain Richard Partridge when that gentleman was home on leave during the Great War, Sprig became the object of the officer's deepest wish: to ride the little chestnut in the Grand National once peace was restored. Sadly Captain Partridge was killed in action shortly before the Armistice and as a memorial to her lost son, Mrs Partridge, his mother, put the horse into training with Tom Leader at Newmarket. Although something of a problem horse, Sprig won five hurdle races before facing the major obstacles. In all, the gelding won 11 steeplechases, including Aintree's Stanley 'Chase in 1924 and a most emotional Grand National in 1927, when ridden by the trainer's son Ted Leader. Having finished second in the two previous 'Nationals, Sprig was the 8/1 favourite at the time of his victory.

SUNDEW

A very big horse, Sundew was owned by Mrs Geoffrey Kohn, trained by Frank Hudson at Henley-in-Arden and ridden by the leading jockey of his era, Fred Winter. The geldinmg was bought by Mrs Kohn shortly before his first 'National in 1955 for £3,000. On that occasion he fell, as he did also the following year after making much of the early running. In 1957, however, at odds of 20/1, Sundew made almost all the running and, despite making a number of errors, his strength and size served him well and he ran out an easy eight-length winner from the newcomer Wyndburgh. Sundew won seven steeplechases in an all too brief career. Some eight months after his Aintree victory, Sundew met his end at Haydock Park when breaking his shoulder in a fall at the water jump. Sundew is buried at Haydock Park racecourse and a steeplechase there is named after him.

SUNLOCH

Bred by Mr H.S.Blair, Sunloch could well be said to be 'bred in the purple', for his grand-sire George Frederick, had won the Epsom Derby in 1874 and before being trained for steeplechasing Sunloch won many prizes at horse shows in and around Leicestershire. After some modest success as a 'chaser, Mr Tom Tyler, from Loughborough in Leicestershire, bought the gelding for £300 and prepared him himself for the 1914 Grand National. Ridden by the Cheltenham-based jockey, William Smith, Sunloch made all the running straight from the Off in the 'National and, surviving a last fence blunder, came home the winner by eight lengths from the French horse Trianon III, at 100/6.

TEAL

Bred by Mr Gerald Carroll near Clonmel in Ireland, Teal was first bought for the meagre sum of £35 in his home land and again for the same amount when arriving in England.Eventually becoming the property of Mr Ridley Lamb, the renowned Northumbrian sportsman, it was this gentleman who developed the latent talent in the gelding, winning two point-to-points and a hunter-chase before selling him for £2,000 to a construction magnate from South Shields. In Mr Harry Lane's colours, trained by Neville Crump and ridden by Arthur Thompson, Teal won the 1952 Grand National in good style by five lengths from Legal Joy, with trainer Crump's second runner Wot No Sun in third place. Sadly Teal injured himself so badly in the Cheltenham Gold Cup the following year, that he had to be put down, before being given a chance at a second 'National.

TEAM SPIRIT

An absolute model of persistence, Team Sprit won the 1964 Grand National at the fifth attempt when trained by Fulke Walwyn, at Lambourn in Berkshire and ridden by Irishman Willie Robinson. In all, Team Spirit won four hurdle races and seven steeplechases, the early part of his racing life being conducted in Ireland, where he was trained by Dan Moore and it Moore who saddled him for the 'Nationals of 1960, 1961 and 1962. At 18/1 for the 1964 big Aintree race, Team Spirit came from behind on the run-in, with a very spirited run which gained him victory by half a length, from Purple Silk and and the long-time leader Peacetown.

TIPPERARY TIM

Totally useless as a two-year-old on the flat, Tipperary Tim was gelded and allowed time to mature before being put 'over the sticks'. An out and out stayer, who was considered to be usually sure-footed, Tipperary Tim caused a major shock in 1928 by winning the Grand National, not only as a 100/1 'no hoper', but as the only one of the 42 runners to get round the course without falling. The American challenger, Billy Barton, fell at the final fence when jumping alongside Tipperary Tim and although he was remounted to finish second, he was a long way behind Tipperary Tim and the only other survivor in a race memorable for absolute chaos at the Canal Turn on the first circuit. Ridden by the amateur Mr Bill Dutton, who later became a sucessful trainer, Tipperary Tim was trained by Joseph Dodd at Whitchurch, Shropshire.

TROYTOWN

A thoroughly magnificent horse, Troytown was bred by Major T.G.C.Gerrard in Ireland, in whose colours the gelding ran and, when still only a six-year-old, won the 1919 Champion 'Chase at Aintree by six lengths. Shortly afterwards, Troytown went to France and, making all the running, won the Grande Steeplechase de Paris in very easy fashion. Second favourite at 6/1, behind the previous year's winner Poethlyn, Troytown once more proceeded to make a procession of the 1920 Grand National and despite making a dreadful mistake at the fence after the second Valentine's, came home 12 lengths ahead of the The Turk II, with The Bore six lengths back in third place. After again competing in the big Paris race later that year, in which he finished third, Troytown came out a few days later to contest the Prix des Drags also at Auteuil, crashed at a post and rails and was so badly injured that was put down. Troytown was buried at the racecourse where he met his end.

VANGUARD

Starting at 12/1, Vanguard won the 1843 big Liverpool steeplechase in the year the race first became a handicap. Providing his rider Tom Olliver with a second success in the race, Vanguard won by three lengths from Ninrod, with Dragsman half a length behind in third place. In 1845 Vanguard ran again the 'National, this time owned by his jockey Tom Olliver, who also partnered him but sadly, on very heavy ground the former winner was pulled up on the second circuit.

VOLUPTUARY

Bred by Her Majesty Queen Victoria, Voluptuary ran on the flat in the colours of Lord Rosebery, winning three times for His Lordship and actually leading around Tattenham Corner in the Epsom Derby of 1881. Passing into the ownership of Mr H.F.Boyd, the gelding was trained for jumping by the brothers, William and Ted Wilson and it was Ted, who rode Voluptuary in his races. Having won a hurdle race at Doncaster in December 1883 and without ever having jumped a steeplechase fence in public, he lined up with 14 others for the 1884 Grand National. Making a forward move as the leaders approached the second last fence, Voluptuary drew level over the final obstacle and, producing a fine burst of finishing speed, ran on to win by four lengths from Frigate, with Roquefort six lengths further back in third place. For a number of years Voluptuary appeared on the stage at the Drury Lane Theatre, having become the property of the actor Mr Leonard Boyne. A 'National winner's appearance in the play, 'The Prodigal Daughter', was a great attraction to London theatre-goers.

WANDERER

A racing journal of the time somewhat cruelly referred to the Irish-bred Wanderer as a 'rough, undersized, common-looking hunter', the same critic expressing the view that the field for the 1855 Grand National was the worst ever seen at Aintree. Due to severe frost, the race was postponed from the Wednesday and when at last the starters were despatched, the ground had become extremely muddy as a result of a sudden thaw. At odds of 25/1 and ridden by J.Hanlon, Wanderer challenged the leaders at the final obstacle and ran out a good winner by two lengths from Freetrader, with Maurice Daley four lengths away in third place.

WELL TO DO

Bred by Mrs H.Lloyd Thomas, the widow of the man who had owned Royal Mail when he won the 1937 Grand National, Well To Do was bought when a three-year-old by Mrs Heather Sumner. Rather slow to mature, the gelding eventually showed sufficient promise to win one hurdle race and five steeplechases in Mrs Sumner's colours but tragically in June 1971, Mrs Sumner died. In her will she left Well To Do to the man who trained him, Captain Tim Forster and it was only at the very last moment that he decided to run the horse in the 1972 Grand National. Ridden by Graham Thorner, Well To Do jumped brilliantly throughout the race and after landing on the flat ran on strongly to win by two lengths from former winner Gay Trip, with General Symons and Black Secret dead-heating for third place three lengths in arrears.

WEST TIP

After becoming the property of Mr Peter Luff as an unbroken three-year-old, West Tip was put into the care of Michael Oliver at his Droitwich yard in Worcestershire and despite being badly injured when in collision with a lorry, quickly developed into a very useful jumper. Together with his jockey Richard Dunwoody, they made their Grand National debut in 1985. The 13/2 joint favourite - with the Irish-trained Greasepaint - was going well at the head of affairs at Becher's Brook second time, but lost some concentration and paid the penalty by falling. Foot perfect the following year, West Tip was given a copy-book ride by Dunwoody, Lying second at the final fence West Tip struck the front at the elbow, holding off the outsider Young Driver by two lengths for a good victory. In all, West Tip ran in six 'Nationals, finishing fourth in both 1987 and 1988, second in 1989 and tenth in his final Aintree appearance in 1990.

WHY NOT

The Irish-bred Why Not won the 1894 Grand National on his fifth attempt in the race, having previously finished second, fifth and third. Trained by W.H.Moore and ridden by Arthur Nightingall, the gelding started 5/1 joint favourite in 1894 and won by a length and a half from Lady Ellen II, with a future winner, Wild Man From Borneo, a head back in third. Why Not was 13 years old at the time of his victory and carried 11st 13 lbs. He also ran in the 1895 and 1896 'Nationals, finishing fifth on both occasions.

WILD MAN FROM BORNEO

Having finished third on his first appearance in the race in 1894, Wild Man From Borneo won the 1895 Grand National in splendid style, ridden by the amateur Joe Widger from Waterford in Ireland. Trained by James Gatland at Alfriston, Wild Man From Borneo was owned by the Widger family. Attempting a repeat victory in

1896, the gelding fell. In 1897 he carried the colours of a Miss Norris, was again ridden by young Joe Widger and was pulled. With this run Miss Norris became the first lady to have a runner in the race and a few years later she became Mrs Joseph Widger.

WOODBROOK

Trained by Henry Eyre Linde at the Curragh and always carrying the colours of his breeder, Captain Kirkwood, Woodbrook was a brilliant young gelding who finished fifth in his first Grand National in 1880. As the 11/2 joint favourite for the race in 1881 and ridden by the exceptional Irish amateur Tommy Beasley, Woodbrook defied the heavy going to jump superbly and win by four lengths from Regal. Shortly after his victory, Woodbrook was bought for £1,300 by Mr Oeschlaeger but sadly died after an illness the following year at Newmarket.

WORKMAN

Bred in Ireland by Mr P.J.O'Leary, Workman won an important hunter-chase at Punchestown when still only six years of age and in 1937 was bought by the Liverpool industrialist Sir Alexander Maguire. Trained by Jack Ruttle at Celbridge, County Dublin, the gelding made his first appearance in the Grand National of 1938. Ridden by Jimmy Brogan, he ran a terrific race to finish third behind Battleship and Royal Danieli. Starting at 100/8 for the 1939 'National, Workman was this time partnered by Tim Hyde and again gave a perfect display of jumping to win by three lengths from the Scottish trained MacMoffat, with the favourite Kilstar a further 15 lengths back in third place. He never ran in the race again; his form went totally to pieces and he never won another race.

ZOEDONE

A very game and lovely mare, Zoedone won two steeplechases in 1882 before finishing third in the Grand National in the colours of Mr Clayton. Subsequently bought by Count Charles Kinsky, a diplomat at the Austro-Hungarian Embassy in London, she was sent to be trained by Mr W.H.P.Jenkins at Upton and while still only six years of age made her seccond attempt in the 'National in 1883. Ridden by her owner, Count Kinsky, Zoedone won by ten lengths from Black Prince and Mohican at 100/7. The manner of her victory and the tremendous nature of the mare made her a great favourite with Liverpool racegoers and her popularity increased when she ran another brave race in the 1884 'National to finish fifth. A heavily-backed second favourite for the Grand National of 1885, Zoedone was poisoned by some villain shortly before the race and although Count Kinsky insisted on riding her in the race because so many people had backed her, Zoedone was never herself and fell at Becher's Brook second time round. Zoedone never ran again, nor did her owner ride in another race.

● How many horses can you spot in this picture of the first fence in 1929? There were actually 66 of them at this stage. Easter Hero was a warm favourite but he could only finish second to 100/1 winner Gregalach.